# Brian Jones Straight From The Heart

First Edition published by High Seas Publishing
P.O. Box 266, Johnstown, CO 80534

Cover Design: Oswaldo Rosales

Front Cover Photo: Gered Mankowitz

No portion of this book may be used or reproduced, or stored in a retrieval system, or transmitted in any form or by any means, without express,
written permission of High Seas Publishing.

Library of Congress Cataloging-In-Publication Data

Shepherd, Gloria
Brian Jones Straight from the Heart—The Rolling Stones Murder

1. Jones, Brian. 2. Rock musicians—England—Biography.
3. Murder—Investigation—Cold Case Studies.
4. Murders—Psychology.

A portion of all proceeds from this book will benefit various animal charities.

This book is for entertainment purposes and not to be taken as fact or meant for the accuracy or authenticity of the subject matter.

Copyright © 2007 Gloria Shepherd
All rights reserved.
ISBN: 0-9742093-6-8
ISBN-13: 978-0974209364

Visit www.booksurge.com to order additional copies.

GLORIA SHEPHERD

# BRIAN JONES STRAIGHT FROM THE HEART

## THE ROLLING STONES MURDER

2007

Brian Jones Straight From The Heart

# TABLE OF CONTENTS

| | | |
|---|---|---|
| FOREWORD I | | xvii |
| FOREWORD II | | xxi |
| INTRODUCTION | The World's Best Kept Secret | xxv |
| CHAPTER ONE | The Awakening | 1 |
| CHAPTER TWO | The Murder, Part I | 5 |
| CHAPTER THREE | A House Is Not A Home | 7 |
| CHAPTER FOUR | The One-Eyed Cat | 23 |
| CHAPTER FIVE | The Dawn Of A Dream | 39 |
| CHAPTER SIX | The Birth Of A Musical Legend | 53 |
| CHAPTER SEVEN | The Band Without A Name | 57 |
| CHAPTER EIGHT | A Love Affair Gone Wrong | 63 |
| CHAPTER NINE | A Dirty Business | 71 |
| CHAPTER TEN | Roommates & Other Strangers | 79 |
| CHAPTER ELEVEN | Pas De Deux | 101 |
| CHAPTER TWELVE | The Leader Of The Band | 109 |
| CHAPTER THIRTEEN | Between A Rock & A Hard Place | 115 |
| CHAPTER FOURTEEN | A House Divided | 125 |
| CHAPTER FIFTEEN | On Top Of The World! | 137 |
| CHAPTER SIXTEEN | Fans, Fatherhood & Friends With Privileges | 151 |
| CHAPTER SEVENTEEN | The Music Makers | 161 |
| CHAPTER EIGHTEEN | From Bad Boys To Glamour Girls | 181 |
| CHAPTER NINETEEN | The Dark Side | 195 |
| CHAPTER TWENTY | International Brahim | 209 |
| CHAPTER TWENTY-ONE | The Land Of Oz | 245 |
| CHAPTER TWENTY-TWO | I'm So Lonesome I Could Cry | 279 |
| CHAPTER TWENTY-THREE | The Right-Hand Man | 303 |
| CHAPTER TWENTY-FOUR | The Murder, Part II— The Death Of An Angel | 311 |
| EPILOGUE | | 321 |
| CONCLUSION | | 325 |
| BRIAN'S FINAL THOUGHTS | | 329 |
| APPENDIX | | 333 |

# DEDICATION

*For Brian, Who Freely Bared His Heart And Soul, Despite The Fact He Knew Doing So Would Perhaps Open His Life To Even More Unwarranted Questions And Criticism.*
*He Also Knew That By Discussing These Sensitive Areas, He'd Be Forced To Relive Them—The Areas Of His Life He Thought Were Well In His Past And He'd Never Have To Revisit.*

# ACKNOWLEDGMENTS

To Bill Wyman for the generous use of Brian's childhood photo and other support.

To author Jeremy Reed for his kind, supportive words, when he discovered I was preparing my book on Brian Jones, "The living need to help the dead in this way. Kind wishes, Jeremy"

To Mark Riddle for the reproduction of certain of Brian's handwritten letters, www.memorabilia-uk.co.uk

To all friends, acquaintances, and supporters worldwide who have given me the encouragement and inner strength to continue with this most difficult project—especially during those times when I so much wanted to give up due to second-guessing myself, skepticism, and fear of retaliation from those who may misunderstand the book's true purpose. The intention is to tell Brian Jones' story, from his point of view as he saw it at the time, and as he wanted it told.

To researcher Trevor M. Hobley, of Warwickshire, England, who—together with his personal advisor of over three years, who has guided Trevor's investigation into the death of Brian Jones—insisted I take on the awesome responsibility of writing Brian's life, as the story unfolded. Very kindly, Mr. Hobley, in an email to me of December 8, 2005, stated, "Nice talking this evening, as always; and I'm so confidant that we're on the right track. I'm glad that you're part of the team, especially cos I know that Brian *'ordained it'*."

# LIST OF ILLUSTRATIONS AND CREDITS

| Illustration # | Courtesy Of: |
|---|---|
| Cover Photo | Gered Mankowitz |
| 801 | Bill Wyman |
| 802 | Author's private collection |
| 803 | Nils Jorgensen/Rex Features |
| 804 | Bill Orchard/Rex Features |
| 805 | Michael Ward/Rex Features |
| 806 | Jak Kilby |
| 807 | Mark Hayward |
| 808 | Dezo Hoffmann/Rex Features |
| 809 | Gered Mankowitz |
| 810 | Gered Mankowitz |
| 811 | Mark Riddle |
| 812 | Mark Riddle |
| 813 | Mark Riddle |
| 814 | Mark Riddle |
| 815 | Author's private collection |
| 816 | Author's private collection |
| 817 | Mark Riddle |
| 818 | Mark Riddle |
| 819 | Mark Riddle |
| 820 | Mark Riddle |
| 821 | Jan Olofsson |
| 822 | Jan Olofsson |
| 823 | Jan Olofsson |
| 824 | Gered Mankowitz |
| 825 | Gered Mankowitz |
| 826 | Author's private collection |
| 827 | Author's private collection |
| 828 | Author's private collection |
| 829 | Author's private collection |
| 830 | Author's private collection |
| 831 | Author's private collection |
| 832 | Author's private collection |
| 833 | Author's private collection |
| 834 | Gered Mankowitz |

| | |
|---|---|
| 835 | David Magnus/Rex Features |
| 836 | Mark Hayward |
| 837 | Mark Hayward |
| 838 | Mark Hayward |
| 839 | Mark Hayward |
| 840 | Mark Hayward |
| 841 | Mark Hayward |
| 842 | Rex Features |
| 843 | David Graves/Rex Features |
| 844 | Author's private collection |
| 845 | Mark Hayward |
| 846 | Mark Hayward |
| 847 | Author's private collection |
| 848 | Author's private collection |
| 849 | David Magnus/Rex Features |
| 850 | Mark Hayward |
| 851 | Mark Hayward |
| 852 | Mark Hayward |
| 853 | Dezo Hoffmann/Rex Features |
| 854 | David Magnus/Rex Features |
| 855 | David Magnus/Rex Features |
| 856 | David Magnus/Rex Features |
| 857 | Author's private collection |
| 858 | Artist interpretation/Oswaldo Rosales |
| 859 | Author's private collection |

# FOREWORD I

Author Roger Harrison, in the Foreword to his novel *The Wanted and the Unwanted*, states: "The events which truly change the world are usually ones that take place over a short period of time. They burn with a mystical intensity that transforms us forever, and they pass into history as quickly as they come. Something happens—a concatenation of circumstances, a karmic storm of sorts, a drawing together of events and personalities previously unassociated—and from it spring changes that suggest an importance far greater than the sum of its parts…. The Sixties, a time which everyone associates with free love, the Vietnam war and its opponents, and the onset of widespread drug use, is often simply a term unknowingly used to describe the summer of 1967, a four-month period with the intersection of San Francisco's Haight and Ashbury at its epicentre."

As the founder and leader of the Rolling Stones, Brian Jones was that lightning-quick moment in history that transformed the world of music. To ignore the enormity of his position as "founder and leader of the Rolling Stones" would be to completely miss the staggering implications of the man and his legacy. For a moment, let us imagine there never was a rock group named the Rolling Stones. Now let us take that concept back to the early 60's and remember the music of the day with their predominant competition, the Beatles. John, Paul, George, and Ringo were initially portrayed as the good guys, the fresh faced group whose greatest offense was long hair—or more accurately—clean, fluffy hair that fell over the brow line.

Enter twenty-year old Brian Jones to the music scene, handpicking his group: Ian, Mick, Keith, Bill, and Charlie, painstakingly teaching band members his unique moves and sounds. Brian was determined to forage an entrance on to the world stage through the back alleys of poverty and Blues. Through Brian's extreme ingenuity the bad boys of rock were born. He, alone, was the motivating force that orchestrated the tidal wave of musical change through critical mass.

With the face of an angel and the knowing of a concubine, the bad boy extraordinaire unleashed his unbridled sexuality and creativity as he strutted, grimaced, and gyrated an androgynous come-on to his energized and captivated audiences. Brian was akin to a universal beam of sound and light rushing down to earth, where joyous anticipation met and clashed with angry bewilderment at so much promise and so much pain. Exciting a generation of youth and musical expression into the depths of self-expression and experimentation, Brian Jones stood alone as the unofficial King of the Monterey Pop Festival—even though he stood in exile from the band he dreamed, created, tutored, and propelled into rock stardom.

Brian Jones' Rolling Stones were depravity at their worst, and complete freedom of expression at their best; here to set the world on fire and burn it—from the top of its crew cuts, down to its puritanical white socks. The "decade of love" was an era in which television dictated a world where "father knows best", and mums wore white gloves and pearls, while vacuuming in their high-heeled shoes. It was an era in which America bore the assassinations of its leaders—President Kennedy, Martin Luther King, and brother Bobby—its dreams, and the loss of its cultural innocence. Within the crushing revolt of a mindset that had been in puritanical recovery from World War II, the stage was being set for the mainstream fascination with "sex, drugs, and rock and roll". And—Brian Jones was there to usher them in.

If there had been no Brian Jones' Rolling Stones…would there have been a generation in crisis facing the Age of Aquarius, Hair, and LSD? Probably. But, who would have come forward and inspired such an in-your-face, anti-establishment, cultural compilation as the Stones if there were no Brian Jones? With an explosive rebellion and willingness to explore the realms of consciousness, gender bending, and sexual identity, Brian ensured his band made an aggressive move to tell the story in song and anthem, shadow side up, with music imitating life and life imitating art. One can only speculate at the world at large without the influence of Brian's Stones. He was the force that changed the perception for those musicians who followed, what boundaries existed both musically and in life, and which would take on a new definition.

Since Brian's mysterious "death by misadventure" at age twenty-seven on July 2, 1969, the inconsistencies of the stories told both on and off the record about Brian, personally, his life, and his death, have led to a series of circumstances that have intrigued many fans and detractors alike. We can only speculate into the deeper truth of the man, and in reading these seamless stories and quotations in Ms. Shepherd's book, there is a stark tone of realism. She has created a masterpiece of harmony by interweaving her narrative with Brian's quotes, and it is for you to decide whether this story is one possibility of what happened to Brian, or if his life is finally being revealed in *Straight from the Heart*.

The time has come for Brian's place in Music History to be understood, to show what his musical genius ultimately meant to his life; and what a similar gift might mean to others who are yet to walk the path that Brian so determinedly forged. He changed the course of music history, pure and simple, as evidenced by the continuing presence and dominance of his creation, The Rolling Stones. However, even in those formative years, the music industry played swift and deadly to promote a "money as God" philosophy that continues to this day.

We must ask—what is the soul price of fame and fortune? In looking at Brian Jones' life, there is a great dichotomy between the desire for freedom and liberation through musical expression, and the trading off of one's soul to that end. Brian was the heart and soul of the band. Being told what to record, what would bring fans and money, rather than being able to showcase his evolving creativity, is death to the artist's soul. Had he lived, his musical legacy would no doubt have seen his 20's merely as his foundational years, leading to a greater breadth and maturity while he blended the music of the world. But again, we can only speculate as we consider the synthetic music of today and the lack of need for real talent (as long as the sound/mixer is up to speed with the latest software configurations), with the man who could pick up anything and make it into an instrumental expression of music.

Gloria Shepherd has painstakingly researched and reviewed many accounts of Brian's life and death for accuracy in what she has written. She is to be commended for her tireless efforts in seeking to get to the bottom of the mystery surrounding his death in using every resource available. If through this book enough questions are asked, perhaps Scotland Yard will find sufficient reason to reopen the case of Brian Jones mysterious death. Next to understanding the JFK assassination, this would be one of the biggest Cold Cases from that era to be solved.

Brian Jones was one of the first, great Rock Stars. He was friends with Bob Dylan, John Lennon, and Jimi Hendrix. This was their time. His human frailty and musical genius showcased a life of intensity and brevity that left his mark on the entire world through his creation of the most famous rock group of all time, the Rolling Stones. Here's to following the dream, the magic, and the passion at the root of all creation!

This book is a must-read for Brian Jones fans!

*Nancy Lee*, D.D., B.A., CEO
Visionary Communications
Author, Speaker
Radio Host and Producer
Holistic Psychotherapist
www.NancyLee.net

# FOREWORD II

One afternoon early last year Gloria Shepherd and I spoke for the first time by phone, and we shared a most interesting conversation. She explained to me that she had been asked to write a book on the life and times of Rolling Stones founder, Brian Jones. She was troubled by what she had learned and wanted my impression of the man.

I had never heard of Brian Jones before in my life, let alone knowing that he was the founder of the Rolling Stones rock band. I was most certainly not oblivious to the Rolling Stones; however, I also was not an overly-huge fan of theirs, either. Of course, I knew some of their songs from hearing them on radio or seeing the odd video clips from old music shows, but I just never knew who held what position of authority, or who held that position as starting the band.

I had been under the impression the very skinny fellow known as Mick Jagger was the principal behind this band, for he was the lead singer—at least that was my way of thinking at the time. This new-found knowledge got me thinking as well and then realizing that the reason why I was never really attracted to the Stones' type of music was because of the hidden darkness that now surrounds them. This feeling was similar to the darkness that surrounds certain people, which one can feel outright. Now I know there is more behind the current Rolling Stones staged act than meets the eye.

Gloria and I began to share the most wonderful conversations as we discussed what she came to know of what made Brian Jones—Brian Jones. We discussed the purpose of this beautiful human being's life and questioned what led to his untimely death. Behind his demise lay a cast of shoddy characters who were involved with an ensemble of wretched thieves.

The fact that Gloria acquired Brian's well-hidden thoughts without ever having to search them out only lends credence to the following story of his life. The truth that lays within the pages of this book couldn't have come better if Brian had personally written them, to let the world know what is proper, what is true, and who is now at the judgment table.

The truth is out there, waiting, craving the attention of those who will pay attention and recognize the painted portrait of evil that men do—all for the price of fame! I ask each of you who reads this to take the time to really look within and realize there is much more to life as we live it. There is much more watching us. We are the very essence of life here as well as life on the other side.

Now go forward and be touched by what you are about to read, which leaves no question unanswered. I can honestly say that by the time you are done reading this book, the total picture is going to be laid before you, giving the insight as to what truly took place during Brian's lifetime. Be the judge for this, sit in waiting to see what comes forth from the darkness that you will be exposed to, see the things people do to actually become more than they were meant to handle, and the greed of which they are capable.

The truth will always come back to haunt you, as you will see!

*\*\*\**

Going back to the earliest of days in Brian's life, he suffered horrendous abuse and mistreatment from family members. All he ever wanted was to be loved and understood; however, his mother only had eyes of caring for his sister. Brian learned to settle into the background of life as a child—the invisible boy. He believed his mother wasn't really his biological mother and that she was the evil stepmother, as he'd read about in Cinderella.

As far as the man of the family, Brian's father—where was he while all this was going on? He had no time for his only son. "Out of sight, out of mind," was Lewis Senior's philosophy. Brian never knew what it was like to have parents who cared. He kept wondering, "Why am I alive? Who needs this loathing to be thrown at me from those who should love me and care for me?" He wanted to scream out for help, but there was no one to hear.

Life growing up was very difficult for him, having a father who pushed him away each time he tried to get close, and a mother who only had love for her daughter—that is, until she needed Brian for her own depraved uses. He sat alone in despair, keeping to himself the hidden family secrets.

In his relationship with the Rolling Stones, feelings of jealousy and envy ran thick towards him, from those who were his bandmates. Brian wanted to take his band to a different level musically, opposite of what the others wanted and not part of their plans. The fact he wanted to take the band's direction into a different area of the Blues came to a head, and this caused controversy and strife among the band.

Those with all the power discovered Brian at times sat in with other bands and contributed to their records. He did this only to help and never for the money; however some now wanted him disposed of. Additionally, those with all the power discovered Brian was conducting his own investigation into the fact he believed the Rolling Stones money was being diverted away from the band. A confrontation of things to come began to surface.

Someone who Brian initially brought into the band's circle now acted as a Judas, and that person's jealousy ran deep and completed the mutiny that led to the last moments of Brian's life. The ones to whom Brian gave a chance to have a good life eventually took his.

The people he trusted most plotted to make him think he was going crazy and that, if they pushed him far enough mentally, he would end his own life. When they realized they weren't winning the battle quickly enough, they had to act. These people were fearful that Brian would start a new band with a new heightened stardom.

Additionally, there is much to be told in the way many songs were written by Brian, but those who are now singing them never gave him credit for any of those. These men are confused in that they began to believe they actually owned his songs. There was a conspiracy of sorts to steal his music. One must realize Brian, who taught his band to perform, wrote the arrangements to most, if not all, of the Stones' music and re-directed a majority of the lyrics to make them fit with their music. He was the backbone of this group, the creator, and the founder of the famous name, *Rolling Stones*.

As a result of this book many will be fearful that those who want to solve the mystery of Brian's death may now take another look at this case. Ms. Shepherd's writing is the intricate conduit that makes this story such a special collage of answers that began and then continued to flow with heightened awareness. Each who reads this book will realize there is more than meets the eye, and each will begin to look deeper into the aspects of the truth, eventually uncovering what is real. What you will witness here is only the beginning to the truth that is going to come out, which will shake the world and make everyone awaken to something not yet known. The truth that comes forward makes secrets kept no longer secret.

There is a dark, brooding face that looks over his shoulder with each step he takes. He listens closely; he fears for the truth that he cannot hide from any longer. He listens for the calling out from those who seek justice for the insane acts he has committed, upon which his thumbprint is raised. The forgiveness he seeks can only come at his own hands, for he who has created this dilemma so long ago—wanting fame and fortune—has opened a door that will soon close in upon him.

Picture a coward in waiting, a hooded man who waits in the dark knowing his life is slipping away. The ill will he created long ago has become infested, and he now realizes that time will tell…time will tell!

*Robbie Thomas*
Author, Spiritual Advisor
Television & Film Personality, Radio Host
Columnist, Seminar Speaker

# INTRODUCTION
## The World's Best Kept Secret

*"As I created my music, I reached for even higher frontiers of never before heard sounds and wanted to share them with the world."*

Brian Jones

The world may be aware of who the current Rolling Stones are, however, few are aware of how they came into existence and to whom they owe their gratitude. Ever so often, perhaps once in a generation, a brilliant beam of creative genius enters the Earth's atmosphere in the form of a child. Too often, that brilliant beam burns itself out before reaching full maturity. Many believe such a phenomenon occurred during Brian Jones' fleeting life—a life filled with contradictions, unanswered questions, and wondrous music that personified and transformed the decade of the Sixties.

In 1959, a homeless, seventeen-year old, petite, platinum haired, blue-eyed British teen decided upon his life's mission. He decided that his purpose in life was to educate the world in the majesty and ethereal pleasure that could be derived from learning about and listening to the Black roots music that had come out of America's Deep South.

Brian Jones had always imagined, since he first learned to walk and talk, that great music was life's one saving grace, and the one constant beauty in a world filled with pain and rage. While living on the streets of France a couple of months earlier, he barely survived an all-too-real visit from the Grim Reaper. As a result, he believed the reason he didn't succumb to the nothingness was so he could realize his goal to entertain the masses, through the wondrous music he would create for them.

During the several months he had spent traveling as a vulnerable, homeless teen, he had witnessed countless instances of man-on-man cruelty or man-on-animal cruelty, and couldn't understand why any human being would find the urge to hurt, injure, maim, or double-cross another, pleasurable. He had even witnessed men and women reach orgasms from such premeditated, calculated acts of depravity and vindictiveness.

Additionally, in 1959-60, most of Europe was still reeling from the effects of two world wars that had been fought on its soil. Countless towns and cities were still in the process of rebuilding, and innumerable families were barely getting by. Too many citizens led desolate lives, with little to cheer them.

Brian believed he had overcome the horrific situations in which he had been forced to live during the past several months in order to grow internally and then be able to reach out to the masses with his newfound knowledge. The knowledge he had acquired was that music could sustain the human spirit through any hardship or adversity. While he, personally, had survived starvation and countless assaults on the streets, music had been his friend…his only friend. His ability to strum a guitar, play harmonica, and beat out a sound or rhythm on his leg—or anything else from which he could get a sound—helped to ease the pain of the reality he had to face day after day.

However, at this time, the average European still wasn't open to listening to the gospel of the Delta Blues, and many weren't even aware of their existence. The only exceptions were the few referred to as the beat generation who hung out in coffee shops and jazz clubs.

Before having become homeless, Brian visited some of these clubs in his hometown and was fascinated by what he saw. He could feel the pain and anguish represented in the rich heritage that was contained in the original Blues. He honestly believed that he, too, had personally felt the same anguish contained in these legendary songs and felt just as misunderstood, ridiculed, and looked down upon as any Blues performer had been in his or her lifetime. He felt a real kinship with the Black soul expression and longed to achieve that same depth of expression through his own music.

Brian believed he had the ability to help heal much of the inner pain that everyday people experienced and to make them feel that they were not alone in their misery and suffering. He would do so by giving them the opportunity to see, hear, and understand the feelings of relief and bliss that could be derived through his idyllic style of music.

Nevertheless, in the back of his mind there remained a lingering doubt as to whether he could actually make it in the fast-paced world of a professional musician. There was no question he had the raw talent and creative genius to perform the music he heard being played over and over in his head. However, he worried that all the chronic physical, mental, and emotional pains—from which he suffered—would gather together and mount an offensive against his frail body, which he would not be able to overcome.

From the 1940's, and well into the 1960's and mid '70's, hardly anything was known, understood, or diagnosed within the medical community about what are now considered everyday ailments among today's children. Brian suffered from attention deficit disorder, hyperactivity, clinical depression, and to make everything worse, bi-polar disorder, which was and still is common among extremely creative, ultra-intelligent individuals, and those in the entertainment world.

Sadly, as he grew into young adulthood and later became leader of the Rolling Stones, his bi-polarism (or manic depression) remained undiagnosed and untreated. In many ways all these disorders permanently crippled him, in that they altered and extinguished his ability to cope with the many stresses connected to his duties as leader of the band. The disorders also hindered his ability to interact with his band-mates or anyone with whom he might begin a loving, personal relationship.

Additionally, with what we now know of modern-day medicine and diagnosis, and by putting together the constant, assorted aches and pains Brian complained about on a regular basis, we can safely say that he suffered from arthritis at an early age and a certain amount of narcolepsy, together with the most elusive ailment we now know exists—fibromyalgia. Sadly for him, the medical community would not recognize this crippling condition for another forty-plus years.

Regardless, Brian followed through with his dream and succeeded in bringing his band, the Rolling Stones, to the fore of the world of rock music. Not only was he the band's creator and leader, but he was also the originator and leader of what has become known as the youthful revolution of the sixties. The decade's social revolution was embodied in the radical changes that were occurring worldwide in attitudes toward sex, drugs, and the style of clothing men and women wore.

Brian had the soul of a true poet, and he harkened back to the days of the Renaissance. That period of time was marked by a significant change in dress, especially for the male gender. Men wore their hair long and curled or wore wigs that gave that appearance. Their clothing was made from silks, brocades, furs, and other exotic materials—many of which were adorned with fanciful jewels. The clothing was worn loose and comfortable. Brian had his band adopt a similar style, wherein the band wore whatever felt right and comfortable to them, and they enjoyed the freedom to wear as colorful attire as they desired. The look they achieved was on the feminine side, or to be more accurate, unisex.

Soon, other bands adopted the premise of appearing feminine on stage and in person, and they also felt free to perform wearing full-face makeup, wigs, and girlie dress.

As a whole, the Stones openly encouraged the use of LSD and heroin among their peers and insisted on being at the forefront of the drug movement. They wanted the reputation of being the biggest, baddest, and the most over-the-edge of any outrageous experimentation.

When it came to radical concepts of sexual expression, Brian had his band lead the way. They espoused bi-sexuality and free love, and taught by example to not be ashamed or fearful of doing what felt good or right, at the time. His natural instinct was to free people from needless inhibitions, and he was recognized as the first to take the initiative in leading the way for the sexual revolution of the days' youth.

However, despite the fact he promoted freedom of expression and behaving as one saw fit, Brian, the man, continued to speak in a respectful, eloquent tone whenever addressing his fans or the media.

He explained his philosophy honestly: "We were everything that we ever were all of the time, we were complex, and we were spontaneous. I thought that was the point of what we were doing—being free and uninhibited—living big and living large. We were to be an example for all those things, instead of exemplifying the historical repression of the Brits and—as God only knows—the repression of the entire human race.

"We were experimenting with new ways of being, thinking, expressing, and playing. Some of it went well, and much of it did not."

He was the leader of the revolution to feel free to experiment—the sexual experimentation, the fashion experimentation, and the drug experimentation—but especially—the musical experimentation. His premature death was a loss to everyone. He was the beautiful golden boy, and he was the beautiful wilted flower. His life was as much an exposé of the times, as much as he was the individual at the head of the Sixties' parade.

Any revolutionary leader has always been misunderstood, and for us to think that because Brian did drugs—to think that fact should take away from everything else that he did—would be an extreme injustice. In his mind, Brian was the experiment. He agreed to it, and that ultimately cost him his life.

***

Brian was heard to have said, "Originally my vision was for the Rolling Stones to be free and not the institution that would close the doors down on creative freedom, soul, and life—as they have become. My music was about heart, soul, and ethereal sounding—and no one but me can do it. I hope to be back again, and my music will be back again…all in time."

# AUTHOR'S NOTES

For purposes of clarity and ease of reading, the majority of Brian Jones' original quotes are rewritten in the past tense. Some, however, switch between the present and past tenses because, as he told his story, he spoke freely and without regard to correct grammar—the same as we all do in our everyday conversations. Similarly, scenes, thoughts, and dialogue depicting Brian's last day are also intentionally written in the past tense to assure continuity.

The author has made every attempt not to take away from or embellish upon Brian's spoken word, or to diminish the context of what he meant to convey at the time.

Additionally, for purposes of clarity and ease of reading, the author has substituted current terms for medical ailments that were not used or known during his lifetime. One example is the use of the terms "manic depression" or "bi-polarism" in place of the only phrases Brian knew to explain his emotional upheavals, such as "my roller-coaster rides," or "my up and down mood swings."

In deference to Brian Jones' offspring, most abrasive language and sexually explicit scenes or terminology have been eliminated from the text. Scenes depicting incest and extreme violence have also been reduced to a minimum.

# CHAPTER ONE
# The Awakening

*"Is all that we see and hear but a dream within a dream?"*
Edgar Allen Poe

The slight-built, platinum-haired youngster, with vivid crystal clear blue-green eyes, sat under his favorite tree in front of the family home listening to his music. Seven-year old Brian Jones had done this forever, he thought to himself, sat under the tree listening to the music, especially when things at home had taken another downward spiral. He heard music in everything, from leaves rustling in treetops to the wind as it swept across his fair face. Music was the only thing that brought him solace any longer, along with the camaraderie he felt towards his gray tabby cat that he lovingly named Rollader.

Once again, his mother had thrown herself into a tirade of verbal and physical abuse, which she gleefully hurled in his direction. And, once again Brian had been Louisa Jones' personal punching bag and whipping boy. This particular morning she grabbed him by both shoulders and mercilessly dug her thumbs into the sensitive area between the top of his collarbone and neck. While her thumbs sunk deeper and deeper, she maliciously shook him back and forth. A forceful tugging on his full mane of hair usually accompanied this act of unwarranted rage, and today had been no different. Brian never fully understood what he had done to bring on these vicious attacks; however he accepted them and imagined something in the way he walked, talked, or breathed the air justified her response.

His hair had been gripped, tugged, and mangled so many times, he imagined he would soon lose it all. Many a night he woke up kicking and flailing in his sleep, thinking it was morning and he'd waken up completely bald. For now, he was a young victim who was in no position to fight back. Not yet, anyway. Instead, he was content to lose himself in the blissful music the world created around him and for him.

"There is no pain in music," he told himself over and over, and he determined to fill his life from that day forward with music. Beautiful music. Touching music. The kind of music that could bring cheer to a troubled soul and comfort to one in times of distress. And, Brian already knew a lot about trouble and despair.

His younger sister, Pamela, had been his partner in life up until the time he turned four years old. Then, one day she disappeared. Pamela looked very much like him, with blue eyes and light-colored hair—although, not as platinum as his. His hair color was unique. Nevertheless, her hair had its own beauty, what was called a dark ash blonde.

He and Pamela had been inseparable. Where he ran and played in their parents' comfortable middle-class home, she ran and played. They were as one from the beginning, and then she disappeared.

Pamela used to cough a lot. He remembered that. He also remembered that at times his parents had acted annoyed or put-upon by having to fuss and worry over her. At least that's the impression with which his young mind was left. Regardless, he remembered dear Pamela coughing throughout the night, on many nights. Once she left, the quiet arrived.

"Where's Pamela, Mummy?" he had asked, once he gave up hope she was ever coming back.

Instead of turning to him with a gentle, comforting word and touch, Louisa—or Louise as she preferred to be called—turned on him with a look of contemptuousness that he soon learned to expect. "Pamela was a bad girl, Brian, so she's gone and never coming back. If you don't learn to be a good boy yourself, you'll disappear and never come back, just like she did!"

A cold shudder ran through his fragile body, and he ran out of the house to the solace of his favorite tree and listened for nature's music. He swore that some day he would make his own kind of music that would soothe and cheer the troubled soul. "In music there is no hurt. No pain," he repeated over and over, while rocking back and forth on both knees. He didn't doubt that he would reach his goal of composing beautiful music. He was bright and he was talented, and he just knew from his earliest of years that he would make the music the world would never forget.

Brian also knew beautiful music wouldn't be his only destiny. His near-genius IQ told him he would never live to a ripe old age—whatever old might mean to someone of his tender years. He knew he was destined for an unplanned and untimely death, and someday—not that far away—he would disappear just as Pamela had. The question that troubled him was, could he prevent it? Was there anything he could do to stop this horrible prediction from coming true? Deep in his heart, he didn't think there was.

But before that time came, he promised himself, he would create his fantastic music.

As he continued to feel burdened by these strange thoughts, he buried his face in Rollader's purring body. Rollader was always there for him during his times of loneliness. While he would sit for hours under his favorite tree, Rollader would sit and purr beside him. Rollader understood him and loved him.

If only his mum and dad would…. However, that option seemed less and less possible each day, as mum and dad's abuse grew with each day. He believed, and continued to believe 'til the day he died, that his parents had killed his beloved Pamela.

Mr. & Mrs. Lewis Jones had reported the official cause of death for their two-year old daughter as leukemia. Others said the death could've been due to tuberculosis. However, during the 1940's, a child's death wasn't looked into as carefully as it is today. If a highly regarded, church-going family reported their daughter's death a result of an incurable illness, no one questioned their pronouncement.

Brian questioned it, though. With his innocent young mind, the fact that his father had simply stood by night after night and watched sweet Pamela cough herself into oblivion was enough for him to believe his parents had killed her. This belief played a major role in forming the absolute fear and dread he had of being abandoned and deceived by those who should love him. This fear followed him throughout his entire life—whether it was the fear of abandonment and treachery at the hands of some woman whom he might someday profess to love, or at the hands of the rock band he formed and created, the Rolling Stones.

The sum of all these factors was young Brian's major awakening—from the knowledge he would create music that the world would never forget, to the fact he would never live long enough to truly enjoy the recognition of his creations, and to the fact that the world—which at that time was in its totality his mother and father—would never understand or accept him and would continue to hold his memory in contempt and scorn.

# CHAPTER TWO
# The Murder, Part I

*"I faced death so many times that
I thought I'd grown numb to the event."*

Brian Jones

On July 2, 1969, Brian sat on the floor of his home at Cotchford Farm and played Creedence Clearwater Revival's *Bad Moon Rising* over and over. He sat on the cold floor with his arms tightly knit around his knees and rocked back and forth. He had turned twenty-seven years of age only four months earlier and knew his life was now coming to its end.

In a way this knowing was a relief, especially since he'd been certain of his upcoming demise for quite some time. He was tired of fighting the odds and fighting against life in general. Life had been hard enough when all the loneliness, betrayals, and constant threats had come from his blood family—his parents. However, now those same ugly threats had resurfaced among his second family, the family that he had personally chosen—his band mates, the Rolling Stones.

At first, he had tried to fight off the feeling of his impending death. He had telephoned numerous friends and asked for their help, and especially asked not to be left alone. He knew "they" were coming for him, to murder him. He once had the choice of reasoning with them, of negotiating terms with them—terms for his life.

The phrase sounded bizarre to his ears—negotiate terms for his life. His life...or his death. The words continued to repeat themselves in his mind as often as CCR's song spun on the turntable. As founder and leader of one of the most successful rock groups of all time, the Rolling Stones, he had chosen death rather than surrender to the bastards who wished him harm. His decision was based entirely on principles, the principles of right or wrong, justice or injustice, honor or dishonor, and betrayal or loyalty.

Brian had chosen to go with the principles he'd always believed in and fought for—righteousness, justice, honor, and loyalty. To him, the decision had been simple. He would never give in to threats and humiliation—especially where his band and his music were concerned.

His band and his music—that's what it was all about. Music had seen him through his lonely, often despondent childhood and his parents' abuse—every form of abuse. Music had seen him through his early years as a student, being chased, slammed about, called a fag, ridiculed for being too skinny, too puny, and laughed at for having to wear his oversized, horned-rimmed eyeglasses.

Music had seen him through his early teen years, when he was still skinny and scrawny, couldn't defend himself, and had his genitals abused by the bigger, stronger bullies in school. Music had seen him through the degrading year of living on the streets of England and the Continent as a homeless, destitute teen, who had to prostitute himself in order to survive. Music had seen him through the continuing years of hunger and near homelessness until his newly-formed band, the Rolling Stones, earned enough money to at least buy a few meager groceries.

Lastly, music had brought him the fame and fortune he had worked so hard to attain for so many years—all the years of unbearable pain and hardship, including no food and no heat during the bitterly cold British winters. The fame and fortune had only just come, though. Sadly, he hadn't really had much time to reap the benefits and rewards of all those years of struggle, as he worked his way out of the bottom and up the ladder of success.

He would never turn his back on what was rightfully his—his name as one of the world's best musical composers and arrangers, and brightest and most diverse musicians of all times. The Rolling Stones was his band. The Rolling Stones name was his name. He had registered it—no one else. Yes, the name and the band belonged to him.

Now they wanted to take all that away from him, and he would have none of it. If not giving in meant losing his life, so be it. Without his music and his band there would be no life for him. At first the choice appeared simple—there was no choice. He had cast his fate to the wind and now it was blowing back and hitting him squarely in the face.

The words and music to *Bad Moon Rising* continued to resonate in his ears, as he continued to rock back and forth on the floor that fateful day.

Yes, he had called out for help many times during the past several days, but no one seemed to hear him. *Was he invisible?* he thought to himself. *Could no one hear him?* Why was it so hard for everyone to understand his plea—they're coming to kill me! Please don't leave me alone....

But, he was very much alone that fateful day. "Stop worrying, Brian. You're just being paranoid again!" his so-called friends and acquaintances had said to him over and over. Why didn't they get it? Why didn't they believe him? Now, it was too late.

He walked over to the mahogany-framed wall mirror and gazed blankly. He saw Death gazing back. His lustrous hair, which had been the rock upon which his fabulous looks were carved—now hung limp and unkempt. What had been his piercing, vibrant eyes now appeared red and dull, and puffy bags bulged beneath his lower lids. His once-creamy complexion was now pockmarked and dry.

Death was closing in on him. Death was closing in on his once beautiful, fair-haired countenance with the still innocent blue-green eyes.

# CHAPTER THREE
## A House Is Not a Home

*"My rage was because I suffered enough from the day I was born, and I deserved better. I had put up with so much that, finally, I wouldn't put up with anything from anyone."*

Brian Jones

Brian Jones (a Piscean) was born during the early morning hours of February 28, 1942 in Cheltenham, England. He was the first of three children and only son of Lewis and Louise Jones. He was born prematurely and showed signs of fetal alcohol syndrome—a condition not yet recognized by the medical community.

Cheltenham was a small country town whose residents considered their lives genteel or rarified. The privileged lifestyle suited Mr. & Mrs. Lewis Jones well, since they considered themselves above the fray of everyday trials and tribulations. Of course, outwardly this was the appearance they chose to give their neighbors, friends, and relatives. Inwardly, Lewis and Louise Jones suffered from both alcoholism and gambling problems.

From his earliest days, Lewis Brian Hopkins Jones—or Brian Jones as he preferred to be called—didn't fit in with the pompous, privileged, or rarified lifestyle. There was nothing pretentious about the attractive, platinum-haired, but on the other hand, scrawny youngster. Adults who liked him described him best as precocious, while those who weren't as charmed by his angelic, sweet demeanor called him insufferable. One thing everyone, especially his teachers, agreed upon was that Brian was an exceptional student and very bright, with a well above-average IQ.

For Brian having a high IQ was a double-edged sword, mainly because he found living, what most boys considered an average life, tedious and boring. He constantly strove to amuse himself and liven things up—but unfortunately not for his stiff-upper-lipped parents—by experimenting with assorted hand-made, small explosive devices in the family's kitchen. He laughed with glee when toy plastic soldiers, and anything else he could get his hands on, either melted or exploded in a heap on one of his mum's baking pans. He tried to explain away his actions with a mischievous smile, "Blowing things up in the kitchen was an accident of sorts, and mum soon disallowed my experiments. I guess I would have blown up the entire house if I'd been allowed to continue. I was very curious, you know, although to blow up the house wouldn't have served me well, eh?"

He detested wearing his horned-rimmed eyeglasses almost as much as wearing the obligatory school uniforms. He stripped both off as often as possible, which led to further feelings of vexation on the part of both his teachers and parents.

\*\*\*

Unfortunately for Brian, back in the 1940's and '50's, hardly anything was known, understood, or diagnosed about what are considered everyday ailments among today's children. He suffered from attention deficit disorder, clinical depression, hyperactivity, and to make everything worse, bi-polar disorder, which was and still is common among extremely creative, ultra-intelligent individuals, and those in the entertainment world.

As he grew into young adulthood and later became leader of the Rolling Stones, his bi-polarism (or manic depression) remained undiagnosed and untreated. In many ways these disorders permanently crippled him, in that they altered and extinguished his ability to cope with the many stresses connected to his duties as leader of the band. The disorders also hindered his ability to interact with his band-mates or anyone with whom he might begin a loving, personal relationship.

***

While attending primary school, Brian continued to suffer from severe bouts of nervous asthma, which he had developed from approximately the age of four. Despite his various ailments, he developed the most magnetic smile and realized, if he cocked his head to the side and smiled innocently—while using his piercing blue-green eyes as bright lanterns—he could charm and ultimately get whatever he wanted from almost any adult man or woman.

Most people said he was manipulative, which was a term that unfairly clung to him his entire life, without understanding why a youngster would behave in that manner. The truth was, in his case, being manipulative became a necessary evil and the only way he could survive in an atmosphere that, nearly since his birth, was lacking in basic love and mutual respect between parents and child.

Whereas in the vast majority of households, the eldest son has always been thought of as the apple of mum and dad's eye, to Louise and Lewis Jones, Brian was thought of and treated as an undesirable child. He sensed their inability to bond with him, too, and because of that taught himself to be happy with any form of acceptance the couple chose to show.

One example of the disconnect between the sides was the fact that Lewis and Louise lacked the ability to empathize with Brian's fear of being alone and sleeping in the dark. After his sister, Pamela, had disappeared during the night, he developed the fear that if he closed his eyes and allowed himself to sleep soundly the "dark forces" would come and take him away—the same as he believed happened to her.

Naturally, his fear stemmed from Louise's comment that, if he didn't behave, he would disappear the same as Pamela had.

In spite of all these adversities, by age eleven he graduated from primary school with honors and was accepted into the prestigious Cheltenham Grammar School for Boys. He could excel at any subject he wished and was so versatile, he managed to compose original stories each week for his English teacher, without any effort. Additionally, he excelled in chemistry, math, and naturally, music.

However, he only excelled when the mood suited him, because he would often become bored with the pace of everyday school life. When bored, he would design unique ways to cut class, or purposely get himself suspended for a day or two for some minor infraction, just so he could run off and swim at the nearby pool.

Regular, organized team sports didn't interest him either, since he found it difficult to be part of any group for a period of time. Even though he was competitive by nature, he didn't like being bashed and battered by the bigger boys. "I didn't take to their cheap shots," he explained. "To me, it was silly to chase after a ball on a field, especially if you were going to be beaten up. My mind was broader than just a physical competition in which I knew I'd get battered. I'm a good strategist and prefer telling others what to do. I never really felt as one with any group."

He preferred to be the individual who worked alone or—if he did decide to take part in a team sport—had to be the leader. The only exceptions were a bit of badminton, rugby, and cricket, which he thought fun because of their quick action.

Among the activities he enjoyed performing on a solitary level were swimming, diving, table tennis, and judo. Even though he didn't remain with judo long enough to earn his black belt, he did gain his green belt. He was proud of this personal accomplishment, which combined the physicality of the martial art together with the required cerebral discipline.

Cerebral activity of any kind was what stimulated him and what his brain needed most—a strong mental challenge. He questioned everything instinctively, including the when, where, how, and why things worked or didn't work. Inwardly, he knew he had a sharp mind and depended upon his gut instinct to tell him whether any judgment call he made was right or not—whether that call was in sports, exams, or later on and most importantly, agreeing with and signing contracts for the group he created and perfected, the Rolling Stones.

For Brian, this serious look at what made the universe work and how everything on the planet came together had begun as a youngster. Because of his asthma, he hadn't been able to take part in hours of sports activities, like the other boys. He had to always keep an inhaler nearby, which became a necessity associated with him for the rest of his life. He learned to sit back and relax in order to breathe and took advantage of all this private time to contemplate the world's many mysteries.

From the age of six, his mum began to give him piano lessons. Thereafter, he went on to play the clarinet, managed to excel at guitar by twelve, and then moved onto the alto sax. By fourteen he was practicing sax day and night, and claimed Charlie "Bird" Parker as his first jazz idol. Neighbors recalled hearing Brian playing incessantly during the warm summer nights, when families normally kept their windows opened.

He began to compose his own music on piano at the age of ten, when his parents hired a more advanced teacher to give him private lessons. However, within a short period of time, she said he had advanced well beyond anything she was capable of teaching.

By the time he reached puberty the headmaster of his school, Dr. Arthur Bell, recalled Brian being well-mannered but introverted and went on to say that his young pupil was an intelligent rebel whose father, regrettably, was constantly after him to do better.

*\*\**

Brian didn't quite understand what an intelligent rebel meant but did know that in his own mind he had to buck the system wherever and whenever possible. At times he would bring brown ale to school, to drink in place of the milk and soft drinks provided. Nevertheless, he didn't consider that anything out of the ordinary and explained, "Heck, the ale was there, and so I tried it." At age eleven, he started to drink more often but again didn't think anything strange in his behavior. "Enjoying ale wasn't unusual among the kids I knew," he said.

Moreover, his mum drank often enough and his dad imbibed regularly too. He frequently witnessed his friends' parents stumbling around their own homes after having drunk too much from their bottle of spirits, and he clearly smelled it on their breaths. "Many of the mothers drank but did so by hiding the activity in their homes. The women were often loaded," he said frankly.

When he and his friends witnessed their parents drunk, no one said anything to one another. The boys simply looked at one another and smiled, as if to say, "Oh well, another day with mum and dad feeling no pain, except for what they choose to dish out to us."

Brian chose his own group of friendly blokes to hang with, who were almost as studious as he. He enjoyed being the leader of this small pack of youngsters who had grown up together, and said, "There were two or three blokes…good blokes. I didn't want any more. One was studious like me and studied bugs and such. He'd have them crawl on his fingers; but the other bloke wasn't as adventurous.

"My friends stuck by me because my mind was entertaining and amusing, and they always wondered what I was going to do next. I'd send them off into outer space with thoughts of all kinds of fun things, like putting a frog up a teacher's dress. That was all talk, naturally. Although, it was my gift to be able to smile my way out of my wrongdoings. It surprised me later in life when that ability stopped working for me.

"I wasn't a fancy dance man, but I knew I could captivate my audience with my mind, and I always kept them entertained, happy, and amused. I was the king of the nerds!

"But, I was young and oh, so skinny! All of me was skinny—especially my legs. Some of the bigger blokes hit me and called me fag."

He learned to ignore the bullies' jabs and mean-spirited words. He was quick and would often run his way out of jams. On the flip side, he was a natural entertainer and kept his close friends' full attention by making up stories and acting out all the parts himself. He had a great imagination and was both wise and intuitive well beyond his years. Later on, as a Rolling Stone, he would tell acquaintances that he felt aged right from the beginning, as if he were born one hundred years old.

As part of the entertainment Brian provided his chums, he practiced playing drums on anything from which he could get a beat. He'd bang on metal tins, used cans, and worn-out trash bins. He soon became expert with anything that could provide a sound and a rhythm. The fact he didn't have a regular set of drums to practice on didn't matter. His energy was incxhaustible when it came to creating his own brand of original music.

Getting sounds out of mouthpieces came next. Any type of horn, whistle, or jar he could fit into his mouth became an instrument for him to create even newer, original "Brian Jones" compositions. His young band of brothers sat in awe and with rapt attention to their fair-haired, lanky leader. He said, "I didn't sing songs for them, but I played my music."

In turn, he loved the adulation, attention, and admiration his spellbound audience heaped upon him. This feeling of wanting and needing love and adulation stayed with him his entire short life. Once he discovered that the only sure way he could get love and attention was by entertaining others—so be it—that was how he would get it. He knew he would never get any real love and attention from where it should have come first and unconditionally—Louise and Lewis Jones.

There weren't many hugs and kisses passed around the Jones' household, and Brian explained, "I never saw my parents hug or kiss. There was one time, mother kissed me right on top of my head. Since I was going off to school, I imagined she was saying, 'Glad to get you out of the house, Son!'"

\*\*\*

A majority of parents have always been proud to say their young sons were mentally sharp and interested in learning how inanimate objects work, and when discussing animate objects, what makes each one individual and have its own nature and personality. Alas, that was not the case with Mr. & Mrs. Jones. To them, Brian was an awkward embarrassment who not only should be seen and not heard, but preferably not seen at all. For his father's taste, Brian was much too girlie in both his appearance and the way he moved and talked. For his mother's taste, Brian was much too…well, he was a boy, a male, and that said it all.

He explained his parents' convoluted thought processes this way, "I felt my parents really didn't like me. Mother wanted a girl, and if I were a girl, my dad also would've been happy because then I wouldn't have been such a girlie boy."

Consequently, the couple ridiculed and criticized everything their son did and made fun of everything he said. While the vast majority of parents encourage their young children to talk and praise any effort at self-expression, the Jones couple did everything possible to minimize and ignore Brian's attempts at early verbal communication. This type of parental condemnation usually results in some form of speech impediment in a child, and in Brian's case the end result was no different. Therefore, he started speaking with a lisp from an early age. Instead of encouraging his young son to talk, the senior Lewis became frustrated when Brian couldn't automatically form sentences. "Spit it out, Brian!" he would yell, or "Speak up, I can't hear you!"

Naturally, such badgering and humiliation would only serve to stunt correct developmental speech patterns in any child, but especially with one as sensitive as Brian, this was a disaster. Before long, Louise became irritated whenever her son didn't automatically acquiesce to her every wish and command but instead innocently questioned her decisions. Rather than patiently answering him, she backhanded him across the mouth.

The combination of both parents' lack of basic human understanding as to how to encourage vocal communication in their son led to Brian's becoming self-conscious whenever he spoke. This also led to the awkward habit he developed of over-thinking anything he said. This awkwardness became apparent to many in his life, including his one-time girlfriend, Anita Pallenberg, who said Brian "was always a perfectionist in the way he was talking, choosing his words. He did want to catch your attention when he was speaking, to captivate you."

At least that was the impression with which she was left. What was more accurate was the fact that, Brian was so self-conscious of possibly having his speech ridiculed, he carefully chose each word uttered.

In his book *Stone Alone* Bill Wyman claimed that Brian also had the habit of self-consciously placing his hand in front of his mouth whenever he spoke publicly. Bill said this was due to the fact Brian had to have a front tooth replaced after an auto accident, but this was also due to his being self-conscious over his speech in general. How could it have been otherwise, when Brian had none of the usual parental support and guidance the average child receives from his or her parent during the very important formative years of developmental speech?

Additionally, Mr. & Mrs. Jones chose to overly scrutinize and ridicule other traits in their young son. "Stand straight, for Heaven's sake! Can't you do anything right, Brian!" the senior Lewis would yell. And, from his mum he heard, "Stop stooping over and stand with your shoulders straight. You look silly!"

Many a child would have succumbed under all this parental criticism, but not Brian. He swore he would never allow the constant barrage from both sides to break him. Plus, he decided he would overcome the deficiencies that his parents pointed out and would better himself. He couldn't correct the small lisp, but he was successful as the great storyteller, entertainer, and folk-singer he eventually became.

Constant badgering didn't end with those examples, however. After the death of his younger sister, Brian was turned into Louise's little servant. She was now pregnant with the couple's third child, who would be born nine months after Pamela's demise, and she relied on four to five year old Brian to tend to her needs. Nevertheless, instead of making him feel that he was an important, contributing member of the family by assisting her, he was ordered about and spoken down to as a menial servant who—when he wasn't helping out around the house—was a burden, a nuisance, and generally troublesome to have around.

Despite everything, he tried his best to please Louise. She was his mum and always would be. He used his naturally pleasant smile and quiet manner to cheer and comfort her, while he picked up around the house and served her milk and fruit during the trying pregnancy.

During this time, Lewis senior became more and more withdrawn from the family circle. He showed little interest in his young son and made no effort to get to know Brian for who he was. Professionally, he was a successful aeronautical engineer, but privately and personally, he was insecure about his ability to live up to his image of what a man's man should be. Lewis had never been good at physical sports himself and originally had ideas of grandeur by reliving his own pathetic life through his son.

Sadly and disappointingly for him, though, as soon as Brian began to grow into himself, Lewis realized that Brian was in many ways mirroring him. This epiphany ran a chill up his spine. No, he thought, he simply couldn't raise a son as inept as he felt he always had been! In his mind, his son was nothing more than small, weak, and frail—a complete disappointment. Therefore, nothing Brian could ever achieve would amount to anything in the senior Lewis' eyes. Brian couldn't walk right, talk right, study right, or live right.

During the times he wasn't feeling physically well, Brian's eyes and nose would run, and his eyes would appear even more red and swollen than they normally did. Simultaneously, if his bi-polar disorder was taking a downturn—when combined with his clinical depression—the two illnesses would cause him to either act lethargic or completely fall over and pass out. Lewis found these traits in his son pathetic and made a point of telling him so.

To top off his loutish insensitivity, Lewis frequently chastised Brian for being as pitifully thin as he was and poked fun at his scrawny, little shoulders. Among the phrases Brian became accustomed to hearing were, "Don't be a hunchback! Stop slouching and stand like a man!"

Since he was so afraid of the dark, Brian often went to his parents and begged to be allowed a nightlight; however, his innocent request was met with their usual cold, offhanded responses. "Stop acting like a girl!" Lewis snapped, or, "You're a little crybaby, just like your mum! Be a man, for Heaven's sake!"

***

Even if Brian had come from the best of families, growing up with the untreated ADD, clinical depression, and bi-polar disorders would have been extremely difficult. He experienced radical up and down mood swings. When he was up, especially because of his brilliant mind, he ran the gamut of finding interesting, fun things to do. When he wasn't teaching himself to play music with any type of instrument he could invent, he'd run amuck bursting with uncontrollable energy, whooping and hollering, like the proverbial hurricane.

These incidents threw Louise into a tirade of anger, since she insisted on keeping a quiet, orderly household. "Why can't you be more like your sister, Brian!" she would yell. Brian and his younger sister, Barbara, would exchange quick, little looks and smiles. Barbara so much wanted to be part of Brian's world, just as he wished to be part of hers, but both parents discouraged it. They felt Brian would only be a bad influence on their daughter's more sedate, genteel nature.

When Brian did run completely amuck, Lewis would charge after him and pound on him. One day the confrontation between father and son became even more intense. As eleven-year old Brian attempted to run full speed across the upstairs hallway, to escape his dad's rage, Lewis caught up with him and cornered him. Lewis pointed his finger menacingly in his face and screamed for the youngster to calm down. Brian started to back away in fright, one step at a time. Neither saw the staircase getting closer with each step that he took, and he fell over backward, tumbling all the way down. As he continued to tumble, his groin hit the edge of the steps, striking him hard.

He was terribly hurt, and then panicked even more when he saw Lewis dashing down the stairs after him. He tried to stand on wobbly, trembling legs and cupped his sore genital area; however, he couldn't control his lips that quivered and the tears that rolled down his face. Instead of taking his son in his arms and comforting him, Lewis grabbed him and violently shook him. "Don't you dare cry, Brian! Do you hear me? Don't be a baby, for Heaven's sake! Be a man. Now, go to your room!" he pointed up the staircase.

Brian was barely able to stand on his legs. Nevertheless, he wiped away his tears and stoically climbed the stairs, once again banished to the isolation of his tiny room. He couldn't understand why he was there, alone, and couldn't understand why he didn't feel part of his own family. He knew parents were supposed to love and cherish their children because he saw his chums' parents coddling them and talking softly to them, whenever they were hurt or injured. *What's so different about me?* he wondered. Was he that ugly, was he that horrible a boy that both mum and dad couldn't bear to show him a kind word or a loving hug? What could he do to make them love him? He had no answers and none came from the universe that he implored for answers. All he knew was, he felt even more numb inside with each day that passed.

With the bedroom door closed behind him, completely alone, he picked up his clarinet and began to play a little tune he had earlier composed. Life didn't hurt so much when he could drift away into the world of wondrous music that he slowly was making his own.

\*\*\*

Mr. & Mrs. Jones couldn't understand, or perhaps didn't care to understand, why Brian acted as unruly or hyper as he did, and the medical profession as yet had no explanation for such behavior in children. "Mum and Dad didn't believe I belonged in polite society," was all he could think of to say.

However, since that time child psychologists have concluded that, when exceptionally bright children are ignored and not praised for their attempts at self-expression, the children often turn angry and act disruptive. The professionals believe the rationale of the children is—if behaving nicely doesn't get them the much-needed love and attention—the opposite should work. Acting obnoxious always brings attention, and even if it's not the type of loving attention the children crave, it's better than nothing.

In dealing with Brian's crazed behavior, Louise had finely tuned her own methods of handling him. From the time he was a youngster of no more than three years, whenever she became frustrated with him, she'd taken to grabbing him by the genitals, and squeezed and twisted them. (Photo #801) This was done as a means of punishment and also for sadistic pleasure, since she despised the male body in general. She also chose to grab and rip at him with her fingernails, choke him, shake him, and whip him about. Afterward, she would get right in his face and yell, telling him how worthless he was and what a burden he was to the entire family.

When she would get this close and scream at him, he flinched and backed away. Since he was naturally quiet and introverted, this type of verbal barrage at times frightened him more than any physical beating could. He couldn't understand why he was worthless or why he was a burden. He tried as best he could to please his parents, but his best was never good enough. When speaking of his mother's attitude toward him, he later said, "She wished I were dead, or meant it without saying the actual words. She felt that way when I didn't do what she wanted—and I rarely ever did. She hated me and wanted me to have a hard time of it. She didn't understand anything of me and tried to squash my free spirit."

When Louise and Lewis spoke to one another about their son's dreadful behavior, they did so in his presence, as if he weren't there. With a heavy heart, Brian said, "Often I thought I was invisible, or worse that I had no soul at all because of the things that were spoken about me. Did they have no idea how much it hurt? How their words penetrated into my heart, how they stung me? They worried about others' feelings but never my feelings, as if I didn't count and didn't have any feelings.

"I tried to cover up and act like nothing bothered me, and eventually I became very good at hiding and not showing my feelings. I never felt safe when my real feelings surfaced, and I became angry with myself when they did.

"Later, I tried to hide my feelings with drugs and alcohol, so I could try to act superior; but ultimately, I'd crumble, cry, and expose my true self and show what I really was. I was a mess!"

*** 

Many times, Brian would catch himself in the middle of one of his bursts of energy and hide under his bed. There, he'd curl up in a fetal position and force himself to relax. Considering the fact he wasn't being medicated for the ADD, it is a testament to his own resiliency and inner strength that he had enough control to place himself in that quiet, submissive position.

Nevertheless, those times weren't often enough for the Jones parents and many a time he would be tied to a chair in the kitchen, bound securely, and unable to move. This set him into a state of panic, and he'd cry and beg for his parents to free him, promising to be good and do better. "I was tied up hands and feet, and then all around my body. They'd stuff mush and stuff into my mouth. Yeeooow! I can remember being tied to the chair at least three times for several hours each time. That's when I'd later hide under my bed, when I knew I had too much energy. I learned when to shut it down."

If she didn't tie and bind him, Louise would threaten to send him away for good. She would go to the front door, open it, and tell him that he and his belongings would be tossed onto the street like so much garbage, if he didn't heed his parents' orders. These threats held an especially sinister meaning for him, since he could never forget that dear Pamela had disappeared from the Jones' household. He wondered whether he'd meet the same fate as she, disappear, and never be heard from again.

For his part, Lewis senior was not the type of father to toss a ball or play catch with his son. He wasn't into outdoor activities such as fishing or camping. As a result, father and son spent little time together. However, at times he offered to help Brian with his studies. The irony in this was, Brian soon required little help from his father—he was well beyond being taught much, since he automatically gobbled up every bit of learning offered him.

Although, many times he so much wanted his father's love and attention, he purposely pretended he was stumped with one lesson or the other and politely asked his dad if he would help him. Lewis would sit and begin to go over the lesson with him but soon became either perplexed or exasperated with the schoolwork. Eventually, father and son found themselves butting heads.

Brian couldn't decide whether to laugh or cry. He had purposely dumbed himself down just to get Lewis' attention and make the older man feel important, but instead of feeling proud to help his only son, Lewis became flustered and annoyed when he felt Brian hadn't appreciated his efforts.

Dinnertime in the Jones' house wasn't an uncomplicated or trouble-free affair either, for Brian or his sister. Their parents had no time in their lives for human warmth or humor and expected their children to behave as a little lady and gentleman should, while at the table. For Brian, this was usually an impossibility, since he was a natural comic and loved to make funny faces. He would turn to Barbara and crunch his face in the most peculiar shapes, which caused her to burst out laughing. As a result, Lewis would pound the table with his fist, while Louise would give her son a sharp look that showed how displeased she was.

Nevertheless, as soon as his parents returned to their meal, he would resume his comedy routine. When his behavior wore too thin, he was sent up to his room without supper, and made to sit in the corner and not move. If he did move, he was put into the tie-down position in the chair until he calmed down.

***

Since Pamela's, death, Louise had turned more and more to drinking alcohol. This was in opposition to their local Christian church's teachings that frowned upon imbibing in spirits, gambling, and smoking. Nonetheless, the pastor's admonitions didn't prevent his flock from turning to such activities, if the mood called for it.

Since Brian had watched his mum drink and smoke in order to soothe her sour moods, when he approached puberty he naturally sought comfort in the methods he had observed for so long. Consequently, when he brought a bit of dark brown ale to school to share with his chums, they, in turn, shared their cigarettes with him. Within a short period of time, he was actively enjoying two adult forms of self-medication, drinking and smoking. He wasn't doing either to a great degree; however, this was the beginning of what soon became two constants in his life.

Lewis senior began to stay away from home more often and used the excuse he had to work late. However, his real reason for not wanting to remain at home was the increased feeling of emptiness, or deadness, that he felt in his relationship with his wife. Neither parent had ever been outwardly affectionate toward the other, but they instead maintained a civil and reserved tone with one another—similar to the way they treated their children. Brian explained, "They behaved nicely to one another, yeah, but they were also two conspirators. They were always stiff and polite towards each other. Mum would direct precise orders to me and then shriek madly at my antics! Father was quieter, but when he was on a roll, he'd stomp around. Mum took over the household until father got really angry…then he'd become the aggressor."

Unfortunately, the more Louise was left alone, the angrier and more explosive she acted toward Brian—who now blamed himself for his father's absences. His level of self esteem had been so lowered that he imagined all the ills that lay within the Jones' household should rest upon his tiny shoulders.

For someone like Brian, who had an outgoing, lively personality, the rigid, lackluster atmosphere his parents demanded was unbearable. He began to seek his own methods of expressing who he was on the outside, to ease the need for emotional relief.

As his early teen years approached, sex soon occupied his mind. Even though outwardly he was thin, petite, and short for his age when compared to the other boys, inwardly his appetite for sexual experimentation was in full bloom.

However, Lewis was afraid his only son would grow up gay and thereby further—at least in his mind—the shame and humiliation he had personally suffered during his own formative years. Because of that fear, he went overboard by not giving Brian even the tiniest margin of respect, love, and affection a father would normally share with his offspring.

When it came to the issue of whether Brian would possibly turn out effeminate or gay, Louise was the complete opposite. Since she had her own issues with the male sex and wasn't comfortable around manly men, she preferred a man with a more feminine approach.

She had never wanted a son and was disappointed when Brian was born. Naturally, she was thrilled when she next had Pamela, but Pamela died so soon. In her mind, she believed all she had left was Brian. But then, her second daughter was born, and Barbara was immediately and unconditionally held up as her ideal child.

Brian fit in with neither his mum's nor his dad's lives. He didn't fit in at all.

Nevertheless, making either or both of them happy was a tall order that he strove to fulfill. To please Louise, he acted as girlie as possible and learned doing so brought a smile to her face. She was happy when "her girls"—Barbara and Brian—played house and dressed-up for her. She encouraged the youngsters to don her dresses, shoes, hats, scarves, buttons and bows, all of it. She followed by giving them make-up lessons and taught them how to adorn their hair with ribbons.

Brian both enjoyed and easily took to the dress-up game. On one hand, those were the only times when the interaction between him and his mum wasn't vitriolic. He said, "When we were 'the girls' everything was fun, and she made it seem as if everything between us was okay."

He especially took pride in her make-up sessions and had a natural flair for reaching into and drawing from his more feminine side. He possessed the natural grace, charm, and beauty with which only very beautiful and seductive women throughout the ages have been born. Although, he never thought himself particularly good-looking, or pretty, as some men and most women believed him to be. "I tried to look the best I could," he once said, "but contrary to popular belief, I didn't feel a beautiful person on the outside. I know my preening and posing later seemed like I did. I thought I looked okay and thought I was doing all right, but underneath it all, I never felt really pretty. In my mind, my real gifts were my music and my mind."

Louise further taught him the right way to wear accessories and perfumes. She owned a pair of lime green gloves that he was attracted to, and he wore them together with her hats and strings of pearls. As an adolescent, from time to time he'd walk around the house in kimonos, high-heeled slippers, and lipstick. That was his private, closet life, and none of his friends ever knew he dressed in that manner.

The dress-up game usually continued pleasantly until the youngsters made a mess of Louise's bedroom. When she noticed her talcum powder strewn about, together with her fine laces and hats, she went crazy. Brian claimed, "We always cleaned things up for her, though. Dad would have killed us all if he should come home and find us like that!"

However, Lewis did arrive home early one day and caught Brian wearing a silk blouse. He went into a tirade and called his son a sissy. Brian said nothing and quickly changed into a shirt. Years later as a Rolling Stone, he gleefully said of his father, "He was a puny, little man with a fat ass." Then, to Lewis personally, he hissed, "In your face…fat ass!"

While the three, mum, son, and daughter, were well-adorned in that fashion, they spent hours watching films from the silver screen era. Brian practiced mimicking glamour queens such as Marilyn Monroe and Jean Harlow—who, in later years, he successfully dressed as for one of the Rolling Stones more widely-publicized press shots. (See Chapter 18)

Moreover, as a Rolling Stone, his ability to gaze seductively at anyone, male or female—while tossing his hair to the side and tilting his head in the most provocative manner—became second nature for him. Of course, back in those early, adolescent years no one—including mother, son, or daughter—had any idea that this simple, innocent game of dress-up would shape and mold the most famous rock star and musical icon of the Sixties' generation.

***

Since Lewis believed Brian and Barbara were finally old enough to keep his wife company, he continued to purposely absent himself from home on many nights and gambled his time away. Louise, left to her own devices, gradually turned to her young son for companionship. Since she found the male gender's aggressive nature repulsive in general, she sought solace in Brian's gentle nature and non-threatening appearance.

Because Louise believed her husband had abandoned her, and with the loneliness she felt, she now took to drinking excessively. The playtime she and her children had enjoyed ceased, and she lost herself in an alcoholic haze. Her emotions and thought processes became blurred, and what had once been her innocent, little dress-up sessions with Brian now turned into more intimate playtime. Barbara wasn't present during those times, as Louise made sure the young girl was asleep in bed.

Louise began to stroke Brian's face and hair, and told him—as she always had—how pretty he was. He had always welcomed this type of attention from his mum because those were the only times she wasn't screaming, hitting, shoving, twisting his testicles, or calling him names and telling him how worthless he was.

Since he was still chaste, he didn't know what actual sex was. The only experiences he'd had were the usual games of slap and tickle with other blokes his age, and the occasions when the local bullies cornered him and copped a feel of his genital area. As his early teens approached, his body began to feel what every normal, young man's body begins to feel. Consequently, as Louise's loving touch turned more intimate his body reacted automatically, even if against his will.

When he first realized he was getting aroused, he felt revulsion, panicked, and attempted to pull away, but Louise reassured him everything was all right. Her seductive energy was strong, and her gentle touch gradually turned incestuous. Soon, he wasn't able to resist or stop the feelings she had awakened in him, and their relationship went in a direction neither planned nor imagined.

Afterwards, Brian felt dirty and disgusted about what had happened. He blamed himself, as usual, even though no blame was necessary. He had done nothing wrong, other than to react to stimuli that had come unexpectedly and from a direction he had no way of foreseeing, until it was too late.

Louise found Brian satisfying because he didn't intimidate her, since he was so young. However, she taught him well how to feel sexual and taught him the true ways of seduction. She had always wanted him to be a girl, look like a girl, and act like a girl. At the same time, she wanted him to feel attracted to her, and in turn, she desired to use him and his body. Once he understood how far their little game had progressed, he was sickened.

By the age of twelve, he finally gathered enough strength to forcefully push her away. He said, "Mother came onto me. This happened a few times. When I ended it, we had no further contact and never spoke about it. That was how we handled things in our house. Father didn't know of anything. He managed to shut down any reality. He knew mum was weird but didn't really want to know how weird."

The fact that Brian finally ended their private time led to a horrible confrontation between mother and son. Louise screamed epithets and charged at him, to hit him. Panicked, he ran from the house and out to the safety of his favorite spot under the tree, with Rollader purring by his side. He bowed his head in shame and with feelings of remorse and horror vowed to never let such an act of intimacy happen again.

***

These experiences were his first introduction to the world of sex. Tragically, his first experiences were comprised of confusion, self-degradation, and self-loathing toward both himself and the female body. Since he had been a child, Louise had struck at him and emasculated him emotionally and physically. She had dressed him like a girl to humiliate him and also for fun. She had taken pleasure in grabbing his genitals, twisting, and hurting him as a sick form of discipline and control.

Her actions became the foundation for his later confusion and rage toward the female gender, and what ultimately led to his striking out at women during his adult life. He forever associated sex with women as a combination of pleasure, pain, humiliation, and uncertainty with regard to what love actually was.

***

While all this subterfuge was taking place within the Jones' household, Brian's friends in town, girls and boys, were themselves coming of age and learning what sexuality was all about. He never told anyone what had happened between his mum and him; nevertheless his sexual appetite was now highly aroused to where he needed to find release.

When any of the local boys approached females with thoughts of experimenting sexually, the girls would generally run from them in a panic. But with Brian, the girls' reactions were different. They weren't afraid of him and welcomed him with open arms. His petite frame and girlish looks worked wonders for him. The lasses were not intimidated by his presence, as they were by the rowdier and pushier neighborhood boys.

All Brian had to do was gaze at the girls in the seductive manner his mum had taught him, cock his head to the side, and smile sweetly. That automatically caused the girls to ask, "Want to see what we've got?"

"Sure!" was his enthusiastic answer.

He already knew what the boys had, the same as he, and there was nothing mysterious about that. However, the girls' bodies were very different, and he was eager to find out how the female body worked. The fact that he was enthusiastic about learning the mysteries of the female body was a further testament to his strength of character. More than anything, he wanted to develop into a "normal, healthy" young man—despite the odds against him.

The sexual contact he had with his mum was the only physical touching to ever have occurred between them. There never were any loving mother/child hugs or kisses. The majority of boys who are sexually molested as he had been are forever closed to feelings of lust for a female, but this was not the situation with Brian. He said honestly, "If I was turned on, I was turned on. What had happened between my mum and me didn't shut my body down."

With his mother, he had mostly closed his eyes and let the act take place, but now with the girls, he was open to learning what their bodies were all about and what made them sexual. In a way this was comical, because the skinny boy—who had been teased and called a "poof" or fag by his bigger, burlier peers—was now the first and only male to be actually getting some from the local girls.

Between bringing ale to school, smoking, and now having sex with the lasses, Brian's reputation turned for the time from being the puny poof to being the local hero.

He now had two things in his life that gave him love and comfort, his music and sex, and his interest and passion for both were equal in their intensity. His enthusiasm and love for creating music hadn't diminished since he reached puberty—in fact it had increased, along with his ability to experiment with and play many different instruments. The amount of time he spent studying, listening to, and appreciating American jazz also grew. He now spent his days and nights mimicking the sounds he heard on British radio and whatever records he could acquire.

An old blues standard contains the lyric—*If I didn't feel pain, I'd feel nothing at all.* Brian believed these words could have been written for him. Up until this time, he had felt no human emotions other than physical, mental, and emotional pain. Nonetheless, he believed there had to be more to life than that. He knew that somewhere out there in the real world there was love, and he determined to find love in any form or shape he could. Although for now, at thirteen, fourteen, and fifteen years of age there wasn't much opportunity to actually go out into the world and find that love. For now, he remained content to work with the only human emotions he had available to him, his love of music and his passion for sex.

***

Life outside the family home may have brightened for Brian but certainly not things at home. The struggle to get along with his parents by any means possible remained a constant. At age thirteen, he was found guilty of another major infraction, and this time his parents' threat to toss him to the outside world turned real. The front door was opened, his father's index finger pointed the way out, and out he went.

At first he was stunned and thought surely the door would open again, and he'd be allowed back in. But, that didn't happen, and he spent what would later become the first of many solitary nights out on the street. He said, "My parents much earlier had said to me, 'Get out, Brian!' but I wouldn't go. They were always trying to let me go or get rid of me. This started when I was around seven, when they began threatening to pack my things and make me leave. It's truly hard to remember the first time I was kicked out, but I certainly felt I'd been kicked out before the age of thirteen. In my mind, I was always being thrown out and never wanted at home."

Lewis had forewarned him—if and when he were tossed out—not to embarrass the family by seeking shelter at a friend's or neighbor's house. Therefore, Brian felt he had no choice but to suffer the indignity of sleeping somewhere far away from his neighborhood, out on a stranger's doorway. He returned home the next day and begged to be allowed back in, promising not to do ever again whatever the hell it was he had done in the first place—even though the horrible nature of his crime continued to escape him. He said, "I really don't know what I did. They were trying to show me that I needed to behave and follow their orders. You see, their arbitrary rules didn't always stay in my mind, which was off on other things such as music or what I was or wasn't doing. They'd say, 'Brian, I said this twenty times! You aren't listening!'

"I guess many times I didn't hear them. I wasn't trying to be naughty or bad, but it was more like I wasn't even in the same place of mental connection to them. It tended to piss them off, you know."

This scenario continued to repeat itself for the next couple of years, and with each occurrence the amount of time he spent on the streets—while his parents refused to allow him back in—increased in length.

During these times, he learned to forage for food in the neighborhood trash bins. At first his stomach turned, as he forced down whatever leftovers he could find. Eventually, he taught himself to disassociate from the horrible reality before him, and he pretended it was not really he who was foraging and eating the dried out, soured food—but some other pathetic, homeless child.

Unfortunately, his body was wholly into the important growing stage between puberty and young, male adulthood, and—as thin and frail as his body normally was—these days on the streets began to take their toll on his immune system. However, those issues were out of his control, and he remained content to eat whatever he could find.

He was quick and agile, and taught himself to swipe an occasional apple, orange, or banana from the neighborhood grocer's shelves. Thankfully, this little bit of energy saw him through some of the hours in which he managed to survive the cold, starvation, and being horribly frightened.

If school were in session during these days of living on the streets, his parents telephoned the school and gave illness as the reason for their son's absence. When he was allowed back into the house and returned to class, he naturally had to make up for the lost days of learning. Luckily for him, his studies never suffered from these absences, since he was always far ahead of his peers in his studies. He explained, "Yes, I was absent a bit. I'd hang around the park and look for food. I was terrified, but no one seemed to notice me. I never told anyone about this."

While he may have been years ahead of his classmates scholastically, he was that far behind in the ways of social interaction. Since he was never treated as an equal, loving member of his family circle, he didn't know how to get or receive the affection and acceptance the average person expects from life. He felt the need to constantly prove himself worthy of the air he breathed—so sadly lacking was he in basic self-esteem.

Whereas no household on the planet is entirely happy, there is a certain amount of love the average child receives from at least one parent or grandparent. In Brian's life, there was no such love available to him. Whereas many a child has overcome this debilitating start in life by carrying on and brushing off the indignities heaped upon him or her, Brian was exceptionally sensitive and vulnerable, and he couldn't ignore or forget all those inequities.

However, extreme sensitivity isn't necessarily a bad thing, because that quality was and is common among gifted, talented, and creative individuals. Brian already seemed destined for a life creating music, something he had believed in since a child. This belief only increased and never diminished as he matured, and his ability to create and perform music became more obvious with each passing day.

***

Fate hadn't finished taunting Brian, since one day while returning home from school, he spotted his beloved Rollader dead in the family's yard. He could see that the cat had been purposely killed, either choked or hung. He held his dear pet in his arms and sobbed. Rollader had been the only one there for him throughout all his years of loneliness.

He didn't know who had committed this heinous act but imagined it was personal. A few of the neighbors didn't like the fact he played music so loudly, and they had complained to his parents. He thought, perhaps, he hadn't acted remorseful enough for his neighbors' sensitive natures, and anyone who lived near the Jones family knew how close he was to his pet cat.

While his mum looked on dispassionately with her arms folded across her chest, he solemnly dug a hole in the yard and with much care and love buried Rollader.

# CHAPTER FOUR
## The One-eyed Cat

*"My world would be a world without sickness…a world where sickness of the body and of the mind would cease to exist. I'd like money spent on neuro-research, to find out what causes mental illness."*

Brian Jones

Aside from the fact that chronic asthma would be a lifelong problem for Brian, he also suffered from numerous, undiagnosed physical aches and pains. As a child, even though he was outwardly agile, quick, and extremely mobile, inwardly he had learned to live with the fact that on any given day his little body ached horribly. By now he knew complaining to either mum or dad would be an exercise in futility, and so he carried on as best he could pretending to be the fun-loving, carefree, and playful youngster almost everyone in Cheltenham saw.

Marbles and hopscotch were two of his favorite games, and his nimble body allowed him to regularly beat the other boys. At the same time, his teeth ached and his jaws hurt, along with his neck, shoulders, arms, and legs. Years later, Rolling Stone bass player Bill Wyman mentioned that, with each new day, a standing joke among the band was to place bets on which particular ache and pain Brian would show up with and whine about incessantly.

Mick Jagger eventually took to teasing Brian, calling him "whiney briney". While the others laughed, Brian wanted to cry. Even as a man, he still couldn't get his band mates, or anyone for that matter, to believe how badly he truly hurt.

With what we now know of modern-day medicine and diagnosis, and by putting together the constant, assorted aches and pains Brian complained about on a regular basis, we can safely say that he suffered from arthritis at an early age, together with the most elusive ailment we now know exists—fibromyalgia. Sadly for him, the medical community would not recognize this crippling condition for another forty-plus years.

The one sport that provided him the most enjoyment and soothed his many physical pains was swimming. While he attended secondary school his passion for swimming grew, and he would often take full advantage of his ability to get himself suspended for the day by purposely breaking whichever rules he could. He would take this free time away from class to run off to the nearby pool and spend the day swimming and diving.

The reputation he had earned as the popular, local rebel was enhanced when he would return to school the next day, looking tanned and totally refreshed. His bright smile and animated appearance clearly made obvious the fact that the suspensions hadn't hurt him at all.

His sharp interest in American jazz also grew along with his collection of jazz and blues recordings. While he listened to his favorite music on the local radio, he sang and played along with the tunes. What was clear to all who knew Brian was that nothing could ever stop or hinder his enthusiasm for what he had early on decided he would do with his life—become a professional musician, composer, and all-around entertainer.

At age fifteen he joined the local skiffle group and played the washboard. His energy level was literally bursting at the seams, and all who witnessed him entertain couldn't help but comment on the bright sparkle in his eyes and the big smile on his face. He had found his niche.

With his newly-found confidence and dreams of approaching independence, he began to spend less time at home, except to come home to study. He continued to take pride in his scholastic achievements and promised himself he would never let his intellect take second stage to any activity.

Home had little to offer him, except for a place to sleep and a place to complete his studies while he developed his musical skills. By now, his parents had successfully managed to separate him from his sister, Barbara. The couple vowed to keep their daughter pure, pristine, and untouched by whatever bad influences their unruly son could rub off on her.

Despite the fact he was striving to make his own way through life, his heart ached from the everyday isolation he continued to feel within the family circle. His constant depression bore an ever deepening hole into his soul, along with the knowledge he was unloved and considered a burden that his parents had to endure.

To his dismay, there was no one at home with whom he could share his enthusiasm for the world of music or his plans to perform as a professional entertainer. Whenever he did try to talk about his plans for the future, Louise and Lewis stared back at him with their own feelings of dismay. "We raised you better than that, Brian," his dad would say with a look of contempt.

Lewis originally had hopes that Brian might someday follow in his footsteps in the professional world, but his dream seemed to be slipping away.

*\*\*\**

To add to Brian's natural dislike for the majority of organized team sports, at age fifteen he experienced for the first time a disturbing incident that occurred while he was in the showers with his classmates. As had happened to him in the past, the bigger, tougher, rowdier males singled him out as the pretty one. They began to tease him and called him their pretty girl, and—the expression he learned would stick with him the rest of his life—their "blonde beauty".

But the name-calling wasn't what bothered him. He was already accustomed, since the day he could walk and talk, to being called skinny, puny, and later on, gay. So far, as long as he knew he wasn't, those names rolled off him. What alarmed him and caused him to beg out of playing team sports was the fact the boys began to grab and tug at his genitals, and rub his butt.

What had started out as a simple game of slap and tickle after a short amount of time grew into a few of the boys becoming overly exuberant, and now these attacks in the showers were entirely different from simple teasing. Because their sexual libidos continued to grow daily, some classmates took lust-filled pleasure in touching him in both his genital and butt areas.

He realized he had become the prey for the teen boys' sexual cravings and experimentation. He tried to back away and push the boys off but learned that, as small as his was, he was no match for permanently holding them off. He now believed he had two reasons to get himself excused from regular sports activities in school—one was to beg out because of a limp or sore leg, which often was very real—and the second was from fear of being sexually attacked.

This would be his first experience as the object of the larger males' sexual desires. He was horribly confused and frightened and had no idea what led to his classmates treating him differently. He explained, "There were a few such attacks in the showers, and I'd get out of there as fast as I could. I didn't actually mind if they touched me but couldn't understand why it had to be violent. I was afraid of getting hurt or even killed."

What confused him was the fact these young males continued to chase after their female counterparts, and therefore, he couldn't understand why they also desired him. Nonetheless, he was still the only male to continue receiving firsthand sexual experience with the teen girls—primarily due to the fact they didn't find him a threat as they did the bigger, rowdier boys.

Another discovery he made was, if a boy was gentle with him and fondled him sensually instead of grabbing, tugging at, and hurting him, he actually enjoyed the feel and touch of the boy's hand. This would be the dawn of his realization that the gender of the person with whom he interacted didn't matter to him—what mattered was the pleasure he received from the interaction.

Since he had constantly felt physical pain in one part of his body or the other from the beginning of his life—and also felt the emotional pain of never being held, coddled, or pampered by his parents—the gentle touch of another human being was a welcome relief to the nothingness he ordinarily felt. At least he was experiencing something good for a change, something that didn't hurt and cause pain. However, what continued to horrify him and what he couldn't understand, from age fifteen and on, was why the average males had to be rough and hurt him. If only they would be gentle and caring, he would welcome their attention.

To those boys who were kind and caring, he selectively gave his shy, furtive smile and batted his eyes in their direction. He had originally taught himself to do so—without really knowing why—while he watched his favorite femme fatales of the silver screen, together with his mum.

He would have liked to tell someone, anyone, about the frightening sexual attacks but knew he had no one. Sadly, since Lewis had told him he was pathetically girlie and warned him against turning into a full-fledged poof, Brian knew that if he confided in his dad and told him about the unwelcome touching, the older man would only say, "See, I was right. You are homosexual, and those boys would never touch you if you weren't! If you'd only act and look like a man, then that wouldn't happen!"

He was so sure that would be his dad's reaction to his plight that he complained to no one and learned to once again pretend nothing was happening. He said, "I couldn't tell my father. If he would've found out, he would have killed me himself."

He found himself caught between two worlds. On one hand, the girls loved him and found him attractive and desirable. For this, the average schoolmate admired Brian and was jealous of his successes with the fairer sex.

On the other hand, with some of the regular jocks at school, he was thought of as the pretty one and the object of their teasing about his natural femininity and their lust. To prove to both himself and the teen boys that he wasn't a poof, he dove headfirst into seducing as many girls as possible. He believed he had a lot to prove—between his father telling him he wasn't a man and his mum dressing him like one of the girls and then seducing him. He also believed, if he could prove his manliness by showing the jocks what a stud he was with the girls, maybe they would leave him alone and stop treating him as if he truly were gay.

*** 

Another reason Brian had no trouble attracting and keeping girls was that he was not only great looking—with his full head of platinum blonde hair and expressive blue-green eyes, which they claimed reached into their souls—but he was also attentive to their needs, polite, and well-spoken. He enjoyed conversing with them in many areas, including his plans to create music. They welcomed this difference in his personality, when they compared him to the boring, monosyllabic way the average teen boy had of expressing himself.

At sixteen, he met a pretty fourteen-year old local girl named Valerie. She was very mature for her age, both mentally and emotionally, and he found it easy to talk to her. Within a period of only three months, they believed they had fallen in love, and Valerie became pregnant with his baby.

He had absolutely no idea nor made any connection to the fact that, by constantly having unprotected sex, he might get a girl pregnant. As brilliant as he may have been when it came to scholastic matters or creating his own music, when it came to everyday matters of one on one relationships with another, he had in many ways the emotional equivalent to a young child.

He had heard stories that other young lasses, who had gotten themselves in the family way, had gone off to have abortions. At first he thought that would be the most practical and efficient way to deal with his problem. Valerie, for her part, had traditional views of family and insisted on having their baby. Brian was so naïve that he explained unabashedly, "I knew about the birds and bees but didn't equivocate what I did with the birds and bees. For me, it was about free love and easy availability. I expected the girls to handle all of that…not getting pregnant."

When Valerie's father learned of her condition, the older man became violently ill and eventually suffered a major heart attack. Because of that and because she re-evaluated the fact that Brian had requested she have an abortion, she broke all ties with him.

He came around, though, rethought their situation, and offered to marry her. In his simple way of looking at such a complicated issue, he thought that by ultimately doing the right thing—providing the child his name and offering the young lady the respectability of marriage—that would smooth everything over. That wasn't the case, and Valerie still refused to see him. She believed his—at least in her mind—condescending marriage proposal insulting.

Her parents sent her off to have the baby, away from the small town's prying eyes. After the birth of her and Brian's son, she put the baby up for adoption.

As far as Brian's parents were concerned, Lewis and Louise refused to allow their firstborn child to further humiliate the good Jones name. Lewis yelled, "You think this makes you a man? You think you know what you're doing? Get out!"

They ordered him to pack a few meager belongings, pointed the way out the front door, and abruptly slammed it shut behind him. This time, he knew, there was no chance they would allow him back in after a few nights on the street. This time, he knew, he was officially homeless. Brian described the situation, "I realized this time was serious. Mum and dad had taught me not to care about babies. They taught me that having feelings for my baby was bad, and I should disconnect from all of that. It was very confusing. All they cared about was their shame and their reputation, but they never cared what happened to my baby. Valerie and I were so young, but all my parents wanted was for everything to go away. They wanted me to go away."

***

At sixteen years of age and still very small in stature for a young man, Brian was on his own. With only one tiny suitcase that contained a change of clothing for a couple of days, his guitar, inhaler, and a few shillings in his pocket, he hadn't the foggiest idea where to go or how to get there.

He spent the first several days and nights going from one friend's house to the next, but this still was in many ways postwar England, and the average family wasn't financially suited to take in another's child. He explained, "I had friends I stayed with, but that was just temporary. No one had the space, money, or food for another. I enjoyed charitable family situations at times, but they were rare and only for a night or two. My looks got me by because they believed I looked kindly and not menacing or threatening. I guess blondes look less intimidating."

Sadly, once word of Valerie's pregnancy spread, his reputation was soon ruined in the small provincial town, and many considered him a ne'er do well. He was found guilty without a trial of having no consideration for anyone else's desires except his own.

Naturally, nothing could be further from the truth. Nevertheless, Mr. & Mrs. Jones were successful in pretending they had always provided a stable, secure, loving environment for their only son, and that he had always been the one too self-absorbed to appreciate their efforts. Brian said, "They colored reality to their friends about their real relationship with me."

As a result, no one blamed Lewis and Louise for the pregnancy or questioned them about Brian's lack of consideration for Cheltenham's young ladies.

Since he had never spoken aloud about the complete lack of love and emotional support from his parents, there was no sympathy now offered him for his plight. No one ever knew about the fact he had been constantly beaten, callously tied down numerous times, and tossed out onto the streets several times—not to mention the sexual molestation perpetrated upon him by his own mother.

As he looked up and down the narrow streets, he wondered where to go next for food and human companionship. He realized his greatest fear had come true—he was completely alone in the world. He had not yet finished his secondary school education and had no means available to earn money for his next meal. He took to doing what he had done so many times before when he had found himself out on the streets—he ate from trash bins and scurried off with whatever he could steal from grocers' shelves.

Soon, though, his body and the few clothes he had were dirty and unkempt. Brian had always been very meticulous about his appearance, even if he didn't believe he was good-looking or the blonde beauty that he often had been called. He detested feeling dirty, and the simplest things such as where or with what to brush his teeth, shampoo his hair, or wash his body now became impossible to perform.

He implored shopkeepers to let him clean their stores and clean out their toilets or storage areas—and whatever else he could do to assist them—in exchange for food and possibly a place to spend the night. This included permission to use their bathroom and wash facilities. Any help was temporary, though, because people weren't open to offering continued housing to anyone's homeless child. "Those were hard times and very scary," he said. "I didn't know when or even if I would eat. I had some degree of pride, but that soon left me. I didn't like to be dirty or unclean, and I now found myself without the necessary accoutrements with which to clean myself.

"There always was the sense of dread around each corner in that I might get slapped down. I had to come out of my own paranoia for fear that every stranger might bite my head off, step on my feet, and take what I had in my pockets—however meager that may have been."

He traveled further and further away from the only home he had ever known and the friends and classmates he had ever known, into the strange and very frightening world of the unknown. He never had been hard-nosed, and whereas many a sixteen-year old young man may easily have taken to the rigors of life on the streets, Brian was sickly and extremely sensitive to the harshness and cruelties of life.

Despite the fact he had earned his green belt in judo, he'd always felt vulnerable when confronted by bigger, tougher boys. Now, he was totally defenseless when pit against the hardened street mongers who lived that style of life day in and day out. He quickly realized how dangerous it was to be among the world's predators and knew he had to use all the wit he could muster to survive another day.

For the first time, a stranger offered him money in exchange for sex. The man could easily see that Brian was homeless and in dire need of warm food and a place to sleep, and he eagerly took advantage of the youngster's plight. Brian was still very much in a state of shock, but knew he had to survive no matter what he had to do. So far he'd never had actual sex with any man or boy. Nothing at school had gone beyond the slap and tickle or erotic touching of his genitals. This, now, was entirely different, and he really didn't know what to do or how to perform.

The man guided him through the ugly process, and Brian had his first experience with being treated as a male hustler. The term, hustler, had been completely foreign to him, but now it was to become—for as long as necessary—a way of life. He said, "I never thought sex would be my occupation, and I never imagined I'd suck cocks for food and money."

This first experience of giving a man oral sex nauseated him, and he vomited. But, at least he got paid for his time. It wasn't much, but enough to see him through a couple of meals and to pay for lodging, if only for the night. This also gave him the chance to wash his clothes—even if he could only wash them in the bathroom basin—and bathe himself properly.

He realized he could not do this on a regular basis and once again panicked. Fortunately, as he journeyed through parts of England that were closer to the Continent, he began to witness men and women busking on the street. The revelation was a salvation for him, especially since he had experience entertaining Cheltenham's young people and had composed his own little ditties. He eagerly watched the buskers and soon began his own version of singing, dancing, and playing his guitar for whatever monies were tossed in his direction.

He now had a brighter outlook as to how he could survive the horrors of life that he faced. With every hour that passed and with every song he sang, he felt rejuvenated and felt his spirits rise. Between busking and doing whatever manual labor he could find, he managed to put together enough money for a trip by ferry over to the Continent itself.

With nothing and no one in England for him, he felt the need to get away for a while. He believed he stood a better chance of survival in a completely different atmosphere. Since he was well read, he was somewhat familiar with the background of Europe's other countries. He looked forward to meeting new people and learning the customs of peoples from varying backgrounds.

Once on the Continent, he began a several month journey through parts of France, Germany, Denmark, Holland, and Scandinavia. Regrettably, by the time he set foot on the Continent, he had already run out of the little money he had. He couldn't very well plan from day to day, or even from hour to hour, but kept an inner faith that he would earn enough money to see him through many new days.

He had used the last of his savings for his first train ride in France and was sorely aware that he needed to raise additional monies, immediately. He was not fluent in any language other than English but knew enough German and French to get by. On the other hand, by now he understood the language of sex quite well, and sex for sale did not require any proficiency in the spoken word. He had spotted a man watching him on the train, sized him up, and knew the man was interested.

He used the sly smile and sideways glance that he had learned over the years while playing dress-up with his mum and sister and let the man know he was available. As he explained, "I made eyes while on the train. This man would be my first official 'John'."

The man took Brian to his private compartment and paid him for his time. Even though communication was difficult because of the language barrier, when they arrived at their destination, he and the John came to an agreement for him to stay over for a few days.

This was another first for him—exchanging sex or his companionship with another person for a living arrangement. But, at least he was in a warm house for the first time in a long time. As long as he gave in to the John's wishes, he had food and lodging available to him, not to mention everyday necessities such as soap and water—and toilet paper. He laughed to himself at the thought of how grateful he was to have toilet paper once again. "Try wiping your ass with wood!" he said with a grin.

The littlest things that the average teenager took for granted had now become his prized possessions.

He was still lacking, nonetheless, in the one thing that he never had available to him—real, unconditional love and understanding from another human being. He could sell his body for food and lodging, but he had no idea how or if he could ever sell enough of himself to get someone to truly love him for who he was as a young man, and nothing else.

***

Brian was hesitant about leaving his John and once again striking out on his own, to either busk or find some sort of regular job. He was fearful because he was in a foreign land, knew nothing of the layout of the streets, what sections of the city were friendly or not, and spoke little of the language. He realized early on, though, that most of the people he met spoke English, and that was a blessing.

John was proud of his personal blonde beauty and took the young teen out to his favorite haunts. There, he introduced him to a few of his acquaintances. Brian finally met other young street hustlers and learned where to go and how to get there. He also learned how to find a good corner on which to entertain by playing guitar and singing.

Unfortunately, John had become much too possessive and demanded Brian stay with him—an ongoing problem Brian experienced with nearly all his customers. He had his own mind and was determined not to ever let anyone own him. He waited for the man to leave for work, grabbed his belongings, including his inhaler, and left the flat. Before escaping, he discovered where John kept his cash and felt not the slightest bit guilty about taking every cent on which he could get his hands. He figured he had earned it, and more, by allowing John to use him the way he had.

Back on the streets, he felt carefree and happy, at least for a while. He had enough money to see him through several days and didn't have to worry about food. He met up with a few other hustlers who were also working the streets and felt he had something in common with them. He learned there was an unwritten rule that the young males worked separately from the females. Each gender hustled different areas of the town.

He watched and learned from those more experienced how to pick a few pockets from the wealthier passers-by, and how to "snatch and grab" small items from the local stores that he could sell on the streets, such as watches and small electronics. These experiences were entirely new for him and something he wouldn't have imagined doing under normal circumstances—but there was absolutely nothing normal about the current situation in which he found himself.

Once he felt more relaxed, he started to visit the local clubs. He didn't generally have a problem being allowed entry, despite his young age and despite the fact he didn't look older than he actually was—unlike so many teens who easily passed for twenty and above. He looked young, mainly due to his small stature and innocent fair-haired, almost angelic appearance.

On the other hand he was very well spoken, and with the quiet, pleasant way about him, he managed to charm nearly all he met. These people gave him access to the clubs, where he further taught himself to play and entertain in exchange for money, food, or a brief lodging.

The more he entertained, the more he realized his natural ability to compose original lyrics and music on the spot. After some time he didn't even have to think about it—the tunes came to him as if he'd sung them his entire life.

He later said the times he spent singing and dancing for his many audiences were among the happiest of his entire life, despite the awful hunger and deprivation of life's everyday comforts. He was coming into his own, carefree and genuinely happy. While reminiscing years later as a Rolling Stone, he said, "Back then, I never gave myself the chance to enjoy the freedom of the streets, although there were times when I felt free, and there were times when I felt joy. And now, when I'm successful and have money, I realize that the streets weren't so very different from the world I've grown accustomed to. Even though good food, drink, and all manner of entertainment, including drugs, are available to me at will—it's still much the same thing. I don't know who's going to be around the next corner, to knock my head off or step on my foot and take what's rightfully mine.

"At times I think about my days on the street and see them for the opportunity for freedom that I hadn't been able to appreciate when I was in that situation. That's my point—that one doesn't appreciate the situation that they're in at the time because of all the bad things it seems to bring. And then, later it all seems much better. You know what I mean.

"For example, no one actually starved to death, no one was beaten to death, and no one froze to death. In spite of everything, I managed to live, didn't I?"

*** 

As he continued to entertain whenever possible at the clubs, Brian managed to earn money, but not enough to get his own quarters. Because of that, a constant, sad theme began to repeat itself. Whenever he met teenage boys or girls with whom he got along fairly well, they usually had homes to return to. They'd part ways and say good night, but in his case he had no home to return to.

Since he didn't have permanent lodging, he was back to sleeping in doorways, park benches, and the occasional car—when he could find one that was unlocked. Once again, the problem of being dirty and not being able to properly wash either himself or his clothing reared its ugly head. This lack of permanent domicile posed many problems. One problem was he couldn't find a proper job, even as a manual laborer, without having clean clothes and a neat appearance. His lustrous blonde hair had lost its glisten and shine, and his beautiful countenance had taken on a solemn, gaunt expression.

He explained, "There was no dignity living on the streets; it was dirty. When the weather permitted, I took every opportunity to wash in streams or even in the water that had collected on the streets. I urinated and defecated in alleyways and sometimes in streets. When I saw others dining out, I felt like the one-eyed cat staring in the seafood store."

Because he was never one hundred percent physically well, the bags he'd had under his eyes since a child became even more pronounced. He was very much in the growing stages of life, when proper nutrition and sleep are so important. Unfortunately, the fact he had neither good food nor decent rest proved disastrous to him, both then and later on, when he desperately needed the stamina to stay on the road as a Rolling Stone.

***

Brian attempted to phone home a couple of times while on his journey through the Continent. His father answered twice, and as soon as he heard Brian's voice on the other end, he hung up. One time his mum answered and she, too, hung up without asking her only son how he was or where he was.

He couldn't fathom why his parents didn't worry about whether he was dead or alive, but they obviously didn't, because with all three phone calls no inquiry was made as to his health or well-being. This caused him to weep, but not so much for himself. The reason he had phoned was not only to ask if he could return home, but also to see for himself if they were alive and well. No matter what despicable acts they heaped upon him, he would always love and respect them as the only parents he would ever have, and he could never understand how they, in turn, did not or could not worry about him.

He explained, "There were times very early on when I tried to reach my parents, but then I stopped. I sickened myself for all the times I cried tears because I just wanted to go home. Then I realized I had no home to go to and knowing there would never be any home made me sicker. I was homesick for a place that didn't exist for me.

"You might say that sweetness I possessed of worrying about others who didn't worry about me was a real drag. My dad had to know what life on the streets would be like for me. He wasn't that naïve, and so he simply didn't care what happened to me. I have to believe that he chose to prostitute me; however, in my life that wouldn't be the last time he did so."

Nevertheless, he pressed on. If nothing else, he still had his dream to fulfill of creating wondrous music.

When the weather permitted he would awaken early each day, before people were on their way to work. He'd wash his face and hands, and clean his teeth wherever he could find running water, and combed through his hair as best he could. He had studied the paths the average folk took along the city's bustling streets, and from there he entertained them, singing songs and strumming his guitar during the early morning hours. These endeavors didn't earn him much money but generally enough to buy food for the day or at least part of the day.

When the weather wasn't conducive to outside entertaining, he resorted to his other means of making quick cash. Regrettably, because he currently wasn't clean, he couldn't approach the wealthier clientele who normally paid him well for his time. Therefore, he had to contend with selling himself to the seedier populace of whatever town or country he was in.

From time to time, though, he lucked out and met customers who were wealthy and wanted his company full-time. He eagerly took advantage of these temporary homes, acquired new clothing, and a fresh start on his journey to where he did not know.

Brian never gave up on his dream to become a professional entertainer and continued to listen to and study music whenever possible. Naturally, protecting his guitar was of paramount importance. He said, "There were times when there was money, and there were times when there wasn't. It's not that I hadn't a single penny for the whole experience of being homeless. There were places where I stayed, places where I camped, and places where I did a lot of things. I worked here and there but also turned tricks.

"My guitar and inhaler stayed with me at all times. One bizarre experience that I remember was playing something that you might call a shell game but with bottle tops, to earn a few coins. When I became bored with that, I walked around the park and played my guitar, hoping for coins in my cup. This day, I sat to rest for a while, and some kid ran by and stole my guitar! He started to run off with it, and I had to run him down to get it. When I returned to my spot, my little cup had been emptied. There wasn't much in it anyway. That little bastard!" he said with a grin.

Then he continued with his tale, "You see, that morning all I wanted was to walk among the cobblestones and enjoy the fresh air. It was early, and I'd just come from sleeping in a doorway. I was hungry and trying to earn some coins so I could eat. I didn't need a lot, but I needed something."

He could easily have stayed permanently with one or more Johns over the months, but eventually they all wanted to own him, and he would have none of that. He said he thought of getting a full-time patron to take him in but didn't think that would work out over time. "If I were good at relationships, I wouldn't have been kicked out of my own home, now would I?" he asked rhetorically. "Besides, I wasn't looking for a cage, and to me remaining free was all part of my journey. It was about adventure, it was about survival, and part of it was a lark. There were days when I was happy.

"Sweden was wonderful to me. Sure, most everything was hard and stressful, but there were times when I laughed. I was utterly alone, and it was a strange and wonderful feeling all at the same time.

"I'd already been evicted from the comfort of my home, so it didn't matter what I did or where I went. I stayed with friends, and I stayed with strangers. I lived on streets, benches, cars, and then some rooms. At times things were cool and when I hitched rides, I felt invincible. I'd hitch a ride and go."

There was a more serious reason why he refused permanent lodging, which was, the more time he spent with many clients, the kinkier they became. Several wanted to experiment in sordid ways that he found impossible to perform. He left every one of those situations but sometimes not before he was injured or terribly frightened.

Again, because of his small size, there were times he would encounter the customer who beat him down, forced him to perform a sexual act, and then left him laying in the street injured and bruised. During those times he not only wasn't paid but also had stolen from him—as a lesson in total humiliation—whatever meager pocket change he might have had.

***

Brian would have preferred only having sex with women in exchange for money or goods, and frequently older, well-to-do women eagerly paid for his time. On many occasions—when he wasn't able to keep himself looking as good or clean as he would have liked—he felt too ashamed to approach these women because he believed himself unworthy of being touched by a feminine hand. "Women of that class preferred their boys clean," he explained forlornly.

After a while, though, he believed his female clients mistreated him as horribly as their male counterparts. Many women demanded that he engage in sado-masochistic activities, which included tying and binding him. He normally ran from these situations, since they reminded him so much of the tie-downs his parents had forced upon him. However, there were times when he was too hungry, too cold, and too tired to care. During those times, in order to endure the abuse, he used the technique he had taught himself to disassociate from the situation. He pretended it wasn't actually his body being used in that manner, but instead another hapless lad's.

Married couples, too, paid for his services. Each experience afforded a new insight into life's uglier side, which was radically different from the provincial lifestyle of which he had grown accustomed. This look into the darkest acts, of which the human mind and body were capable, both scared and fascinated him. Nevertheless, as long as he could pretend it wasn't really he participating in those sordid, seamy acts, but instead another desolate young man, he was able to withstand their touch.

In order to tolerate the merciless lifestyle thrust upon him, he experimented with an assortment of drugs and now considered them part of his daily routine. His clients frequently gave him cocaine, upper's and downer's, and anything else available. The average client's theory was that young boys, such as Brian, were more easily managed or handled while under the influence of drugs.

He welcomed as many drugs as his thin, young body could withstand, since taking them made pretending he wasn't actually a part of "the life" much easier. Many times, days and nights became a complete blur, and he was grateful for these respites from the realities he had to face.

When he had no choice but to sleep in filthy hallways, doorways, or outside on park benches, he had to fend off predators of every sort, both human and animal. Among the animal predators, who had to themselves survive in that bleak world, were rats, vermin, and blood-sucking, disease-carrying mosquitoes. Many mornings, he would wake up with big, red blotches and bites that covered his body.

Among the human predators were not only the sexual hunters—who would grab him and attempt to carry him off when he was too drugged or too tired to care—but also the other young hustlers who lived the same sordid lifestyle as he. These boys and girls, sometimes in groups of two or more, would search for a lone, solitary figure like Brian, and try to rob him of everything he possessed. Amazingly, he managed to cling to his guitar and inhaler but often enough lost his meager earnings and any extra clothing.

Occasionally, he got into serious fights in order to survive and said, "I got beat up a time or two by the other homeless."

One man pushed his head down into his crotch and forced him to perform oral sex. Then he wouldn't pay Brian, but instead beat him mercilessly around the head. Brian didn't attempt to fight back because he believed himself overpowered and much too weak to fight. He remembered spitting the man's cum back up. He couldn't afford rubbers, he said, and as far as not catching any sexual diseases, he explained, "I was very lucky in that I never came down with that sort of thing. I did many drugs and took whatever was offered and available, just to feel good about myself.

"I kept reminding myself that music was my destiny. I don't know why, but anyone I got too close to on my journey wanted to own me, control me, and keep me for their own uses—which is why I kept moving on. I'd stay with them until they became too violent or too fucking bizarre. They tried to put the noose around my neck too quickly.

"When you're considered their plaything, they're not too kind. In turn, I stole from them whenever I could."

Some of the other junior hustlers were jealous of his exceptional talent and ability to earn money by singing and dancing, and—because of that jealousy—they singled him out to prey upon. He learned not to make close friends with any of them. Originally, he had taken a few into his confidence and shared his bounty with them; however, they looked upon his kindness and generosity as a weakness and eventually stole whatever meager possessions he had.

He did make friends with one girl in particular, however. While talking about her, he said, "I really liked her, but she was homeless too and got very physically sick. I had to move on and couldn't help her. I think I was lucky in that the lung disease she had didn't kill me. I also felt lucky in that I never got cut by anyone and lost my looks. I needed my face to get as far as I did."

Additionally, the boys on the streets were jealous of the territory each considered his own, as far as where to solicit paying customers, and Brian had to fight to keep his section of the street. He was daring and not afraid of mixing it up to protect himself; however, the sad fact still existed that, no matter how brave he might be, he was often too small to win many battles.

He had and always would have the heart of a lion and had no fear of fighting for his life, or for his rights. The tragic reality that he had to contend with 'til the day he died was his lack of size. Despite that, with sheer determination and agility he could protect himself from the average man but when confronted by someone extremely big and strong—or when outnumbered by two, three, or four at a time—protecting himself was an impossibility.

His body ached from the bruises, kicks, and jabs thrown at him. He cried so hard and so often that he couldn't remember days when he didn't. He cried not only from the unbearable physical pain but also from the emotional pain of knowing he was completely alone in the world. He asked himself over and over what had he done to deserve this horrible a fate, and what could he do to improve his lot. He could have succumbed to the elements and to the predators, and simply let himself lay down and die. "In death there is no pain," he repeated over and over—the same phrase he had first taught himself as a youngster, when even back then he had been mentally and physically prodded, kicked, and bruised by many around him.

In spite of that and just when he thought he would give up the ghost, he remembered his goal in life—to become a professional entertainer, musician, and composer, and someday have his own band. Once he remembered, he straightened himself up, picked himself up, and went on with the daily struggle to survive. No! he promised himself, he would never give up his desire to succeed. He possessed a natural dignity, and that natural dignity wouldn't allow him to give up the intense fight to succeed.

***

During the times Brian felt especially upbeat and earned extra money by performing manual labor, he visited the local bars and pubs of whatever town or country he was in. For him, the time he spent in Germany was the most satisfying of the entire journey. He got along well with the German populace and was especially popular whenever he entertained the friends he made with his music. In turn, he enjoyed their warm acceptance and the company provided. He truly felt as if he belonged in Germany, and his spirits were once again reborn.

He said, "Germany was rockin'! The beer always flowed, and in return for all the beer, I played music for my friends. The place was really neat, and I could have just lodged there for a long time. But, I realized I couldn't simply continue to live off people."

Among the friends he made were some who had their own apartments, and he designed his own ways of getting invited to spend the night with them. Those nights were important, because they afforded him a place to sleep and bathe. The system he used was to stay at the bars late and then pretend he was too tired to make it home to his "own" flat. Other times, he'd say that his roommates were expecting their girlfriends over and had asked him not to return for the night, so they could have their privacy. "So…you don't mind if I crash with you a bit, do you?" he would ask with his pleasant, non-contentious manner.

They normally agreed and were more than happy for his company and the chance to share their homes with him. He dearly welcomed, even if it were temporary, these safe, comfortable dwellings in which to rest his weary body. However, after a while he believed he had to move on and said, "It became time to go, and the friends that I'd made were going off to do other things. For example, one was becoming a student."

Indeed, Germany was the highlight of his travels. He felt more mature there, rather than the boy he actually was. However, he'd grown into his maturity quickly. There, he acted like a chameleon, as if he were the one going off to college and easily played into the fictitious, vacation playtime story. That felt good to him. He acted boisterous and partied among the populace. Besides, the German people were much less stodgy than the Brits. "They and their country were really neat!" he said with a broad smile.

No matter which country he may have been in, he easily captivated girls and talked them into spending time with him. As with the girls in Cheltenham, the ladies felt comfortable around him and were enthralled by his natural charm and quick wit. He had a fantastic, spontaneous sense of humor. The young women freely gave themselves to him, and more often than not he didn't have to seduce them, since they lusted after him. As a matter of fact, he was a bit awkward when it came to approaching a female for sex. But luckily for him, he found he didn't really have to pursue anyone, other than to stand straight and smile sweetly.

His natural ability to attract others for sex, whether male or female, had begun with puberty and continued 'til the day he died. He possessed a grace, charm, dignity, and allure that easily drew others like a magnet.

Nevertheless, the habit of accepting money in exchange for sex hadn't come quickly or easily for him. At first, he had accepted money in exchange for busking, and from there—in order to survive—he began to accept money, drugs, and every form of creature comfort in exchange for sex. Without knowing it was happing at the time, those experiences, the lusting after him and paying him for his time—that started out on a small scale, in small clubs and with small audiences—magically led within a short period of time to be multiplied a hundredfold onto the very large stage of the real world.

***

As winter quickly approached, Brian still had no permanent place to live. He became increasingly tired and cold with each passing day but still tried to keep his income growing by working as hard and often as possible. He was aware that, by the time the snowstorms relentlessly struck the continent, he had to have a permanent home.

His fragile body, unfortunately, wouldn't cooperate any longer, and he became violently ill. At first, he thought it was a simple head cold that would quickly pass as had the others, but this time his infirmity was very different. Within a couple of days his temperature rose, which led to an intense fever. His body alternated bouts of shivering from the cold and trembling from the deep sweats. He was too weak to forage for food, not to mention busking.

He curled up in an alleyway and tried to cover himself with newspapers and cardboard, but realized he had no fight left. Throughout his entire ordeal, he had always kept his hands and fingers protected with as many clean cloths, newspapers, or bandages as he could find and kept his fists tightly wrapped. As an entertainer, he knew that no matter how dirty, hungry, or weary he might be, if he were to live to realize his dream as a professional guitarist and musician, he had to safeguard his hands. He now looked down at them and cried when he saw how red and swollen they had become. He said, "My bones ached from the cold and the dampness."

This time, he believed, he would not live to see another day.

The next thing he remembered was waking up in a hospital ward with tubes running in and out of various parts of his frail body. He was told that he had run a 105 degree temperature and had been diagnosed with walking pneumonia. He felt lucky in that the hospital system had enough funds to take in wayward teenagers, such as he, and they treated him until he was deemed healed and expected nothing in return. The staff was friendly and supportive, and he recovered over the course of the next couple of weeks.

When the time arrived to discharge him from hospital, panic once more set in for Brian. The climate was still winter, and he was still weak and hurting, and had no place to go. The doctors provided him with whatever prescriptions he needed to last him through the next several days, but aside from that, he had nothing with which to survive.

At any rate, he left the facilities with clean clothing and somewhat of a fresh look about him. Fortunately, he lucked out and fate finally smiled down on him—he met a married couple who invited him into their home. Naturally, his stay wasn't without a price. He had long ago learned there was no such thing as a gift without strings attached, and the husband and wife team expected him to satisfy their cravings. However, this time it was different. This couple actually treated him as if he were human and with a degree of kindness.

To them, he explained his desire to return home to England. He had faced death firsthand and felt, if he were to die, he wanted to and needed to be among the people he had more in common with than any others—the Brits. In exchange for doing some menial work around the premises and entertaining the couple with his conversation and his private time, within a couple of weeks he managed to put together enough money to at least begin his long trip home.

Now at seventeen years of age, Brian still had his guitar and inhaler by his side and embarked upon the return trip to England. Before leaving the Continent, however, he took a moment to reflect on whether he was making the right decision. He could stay in either Germany, Sweden, or Holland. All three countries had welcomed him and treated him well.

After proper reflection he said, "I knew if I stayed, I couldn't continue to be homeless. The illness and near-death experience I suffered caused damage that I knew was long lasting to my overall health. So, I would have to find someone to take permanent care of me, whether that was a man or a woman. I had a real aversion to marriage, though, or living with anyone who would have a say in everything I did.

"On top of that, the longer I stayed away from England, the deeper and darker I traveled into my soul. I'd become really homesick, even though that feeling of loneliness and of not fitting in had been with me from the very beginning of my life.

"In the end, what made me most upset was knowing I had no real home to return to. Heck, even when I was home, I was homesick! There seemed no place for me anywhere and from that came my predominant feeling of permanent darkness."

# CHAPTER FIVE
## The Dawn of a Dream

*"I felt my experience while living with my parents was always very tenuous. If I visited them, I knew it was just a matter of time before I was made to leave next—so I made sure I always had a place to go."*

Brian Jones

The long journey home should have been dull and tiresome, since Brian certainly didn't have money for airfare but had to once again depend upon the Continent's rail system and a ferry ride to take him back to the place he longed to be, England. Conversely, these days were a welcome relief since for the first time in a very long time he didn't have to fight the elements, or worry over his next meal and where he would sleep.

He said he had to come back to England "out of sheer desolation. I didn't want to be adopted by anyone, and if I had stayed on the Continent, I'd have succumbed to that temptation."

Therefore, he felt a free man, and his face beamed with joy at the thought of returning to his native land. Nevertheless, when he imagined actually walking up to the front door of his house, a chill ran through him. He looked down at the clothes he wore—shoes that were well-worn through, with their soles and heels tilted to one side, and a jacket and pair of slacks that had lost all of their natural color. His outfit looked like something that had barely survived the London Blitz.

His calloused hands showed signs of having seen much hard labor, and his fingernails had no luster but were instead filled with cracks and crevices. His beautiful platinum blond hair lay like burnt straw, and the bags under his eyes set prominently on a young face whose skin looked more like it belonged to a man forty years older.

However, the one feature he had that still maintained its intense fire and glow, despite all the suffering and deprivation they had seen, were his magnificent blue-green eyes. Whenever he smiled at his fellow passengers, they couldn't help but smile back. Behind his vibrant smile lay a natural radiance that would never be quashed.

Unfortunately, what had caused that sudden chill to run up his spine was the prospect of once again standing face to face with the very righteous Lewis and Louise Jones. He understood the possibility existed that, instead of welcoming him home with open arms, they would cringe at the sight of their only son who looked absolutely horrid. The couple would never want their neighbors to see him in such a substandard condition.

He was a realist and couldn't imagine that his stiff-lipped parents might have changed their outlook on life, and he understood that the way he looked made him totally unsuitable to be seen in public. "I was very thin and a mess!" he said.

"No," he said to himself, "mum and dad would never want to see me looking and smelling so foul." He sincerely believed that because, during the time he had lived on the streets, he could barely stand to look at or smell his own body. Even if his parents hadn't been firm on the subject of maintaining proper hygiene, he still would have felt repulsed by anyone whose body was as filthy and smelled as rank as his so often had, while he was homeless.

Even though he didn't smell or look dirty when he approached England, he felt unclean. He knew what he had been through and what he had been forced to do to survive, and he believed no matter how much he may wash or how expensive his clothes may some day be, he would forever carry the stain and stench from the life he had lived.

Before making his grand entrance at home, he would have to acquire better clothing, plus a pair of shoes. Consequently, his stomach turned inside out when he decided to wait a while longer before entering the refined atmosphere of Cheltenham. That decision brought him back to where he originally was—homeless and with little money to survive.

Therefore, he started to slowly work his way back to Cheltenham, one town at a time, and performed whatever manual labor he could find. Once again, he had to earn enough money for food and perhaps a cheap room—but more often than not he was back to sleeping on park benches, or in cars or doorways. Something as simple as finding clean water to drink became a problem. Whenever possible, he was happy to spend a night or two at a bus station just to use their bathroom facilities in which to wash.

Finding work that paid daily was difficult though, and he needed quick cash. Unfortunately, the only sure way he had of getting quick cash was to again prostitute himself, and he supplemented that income by picking pockets and stealing from grocers' shelves. After doing so he would run off, hoping not to be seen, after stuffing his bounty under his bulky coat.

Within a couple of weeks, he lucked out and managed to get part-time work washing dishes and sweeping floors at a local pub that he liked to frequent.

The near-death experience he had from double pneumonia mightily scared him, and he now made sure he ate as often and as well as possible. He needed to gain weight and understood that, if he were to realize his dream of making the world a better place through his music, he had to keep his body healthy.

The ability to earn money through prostitution had become second nature to him, and he could easily spot a John or a Jane. He would take care of business quickly and effortlessly, as long as he was able to disassociate and pretend it was some other lad doing the deed. The threat of getting robbed, beaten, or forcefully raped was always with him, but he had no alternative—he had to exist by whatever means possible.

That was the one bitter pill he found impossible to swallow—that his parents, by tossing him out onto the streets so coldheartedly and callously, had literally forced him into a life of prostitution.

Although, in his sweet, naïve way of looking at things, Brian made himself believe that maybe mum and dad had also changed their outlook on life and would now look at him differently. If he had changed and grown over the past months, perhaps they had, too. Surely, they had to be worried about his well-being by now, because he hadn't called home for months. He prayed his parents, and his sister Barbara, were all right and that they thought fondly of him. Barbara would be thirteen years old by now and entering young womanhood, and he looked forward to acting as her older brother and protecting her.

\*\*\*

Three months after returning from the Continent, Brian felt ready to hitchhike his way back to Cheltenham. He now wore a new set of clothing, the natural brilliance had returned to his face and hair, and he looked in the best physical shape of his life. During the months he had been away, experience-wise, he had matured a lifetime. All the same, the one thing that never changed was his innocent, angelic look, which anyone who ever knew him commented upon and could never forget.

He walked up the path to his home and hoped for the best but also braced for the worst. He wondered—since his parents had hung up on him the three times he tried calling home—whether they would also slam the door shut on him.

He had purposely timed his arrival for when he knew both would be home. The door opened, and there stood his father. In his mind, his father looked an impenetrable giant, even though both stood about the same height—no more than five feet, six inches.

"Hello, son," Lewis said offhandedly. There was no embrace and no bursting-with-joy sound of, "Welcome home, son!"

But at least the door remained open. After Brian was allowed entry, his mum met him. She offered a brisk, "Hello, Brian."

He next spotted Barbara and started to run towards her. Louise stepped between the two, and said, "You can greet Barbara from over there, Brian," and pointed to the other side of the room.

Barbara was embarrassed by Louise's action and looked down, while Brian attempted to give her as big a greeting as he could. He now realized nothing had changed and never would change. To the uncompromising, rigid Mr. & Mrs. Jones, their only son would forever remain a pariah in their eyes.

Nevertheless, he stood firm and upright and refused to allow them to destroy the self-confidence he had acquired during the past months. He had left Cheltenham a young boy and come back a man, and knew if he had survived the streets, he could survive anything.

During these first few moments of seeing his parents, he had already decided to no longer think of that house as his home. He spent the remainder of that initial visit talking politely and even stayed for dinner. Afterward, he went upstairs to his old bedroom, gathered up whatever belongings he might need, and left. He explained his feelings this way, "I knew I was much more reflective and withdrawn than when I left. I knew my abilities and felt assured with what I planned to do with the rest of my life. My energy was very different towards my dad, even though he still thought I was worthless, stupid, and no good. They were trying to break me."

\*\*\*

Perhaps the most important decision that had come out of Brian's journey to the Continent was one to pursue a course of action, which he planned to follow as soon as he settled in. He had decided that his purpose in life was to educate and entertain the world with the majesty and ethereal pleasure that could be derived from learning about and listening to the Black roots music that had come out of America's Deep South.

He had always felt, since he could walk and talk, that great music was life's one saving grace, and the one constant beauty in a world filled with pain and rage. His all-too-real visit from the Grim Reaper weeks earlier had proven to him that the reason he didn't succumb to the nothingness, but had survived, was to realize the goal he had been sent to Earth to accomplish—entertain the masses through the wondrous music he would create for them.

During the several months he had spent traveling, he witnessed countless instances of man-on-man cruelty or man-on-animal cruelty, and he couldn't understand why any human being would find the urge to hurt, injure, maim, or double-cross another, pleasurable. He had even witnessed men and women reach orgasms from such premeditated, calculated acts of depravity and vindictiveness.

Additionally, in 1959-60, most of Europe was still reeling from the effects of two world wars that had been fought on its soil. Countless towns and cities were still in the process of rebuilding, and innumerable families were barely getting by. Too many citizens led desolate lives, with little to cheer them.

Brian believed he had overcome the horrific situations in which he had been forced to live during the past months in order to grow internally and then be able to reach out to the masses with his newfound knowledge. The knowledge he had acquired was that music could sustain the human spirit through any hardship or adversity. While he, personally, had survived starvation and countless assaults on the streets, music had been his friend...his only friend. His ability to strum a guitar, play harmonica, and beat out a sound or rhythm on his leg—or anything else from which he could get a sound—helped to ease the pain of the reality he had to face day after day.

However, at this time, the average European still wasn't open to listening to the gospel of the Delta Blues, and many weren't even aware of their existence. The only exceptions were the few referred to as the beat generation who hung out in coffee shops and jazz clubs.

Before having been sent away in disgrace, Brian had already visited some of these clubs in his hometown and was fascinated by what he had seen. He could feel the pain and anguish represented in the rich heritage contained in the original Blues. He honestly believed that he, too, had personally felt the anguish contained in their legendary songs and felt just as misunderstood, ridiculed, and looked down upon as any Blues performer had been in his or her lifetime. He felt a real kinship with the Black soul expression and longed to achieve that same depth of expression through his own music.

He believed he had the ability to help heal much of the inner pain that everyday people experienced and to make them feel that they were not alone in their misery and suffering. He would do so by giving them the opportunity to see, hear, and understand the feelings of relief and bliss that could be derived through his idyllic style of music.

*** 

In addition to following through with his plans for a life of music, Brian had also promised himself that he would finish his schooling and earn his diploma, once he returned. He had been only a few credits short of graduating before being thrown from his house, and for that reason he didn't believe it would take him long to reach his goal.

However, one unexpected problem arose between him and the local school system. To be recognized as a current student, he had to show a permanent home address, and he had none. Fortunately, he was temporarily staying with an old chum from school and successfully talked his friend's parents into allowing him to show their address as his own.

He also began to work at a series of part-time jobs and managed to acquire as good a collection of jazz and blues records as he could afford. One job he especially wanted to keep was that of clerk for a local record store. He found it difficult to give customers his full attention, though, because he wanted to spend all his time listening to every jazz record in the establishment. After a while he was let go, an occurrence he discovered happened with nearly every job. Primarily due to his untreated Attention Deficit Disorder, he didn't have the ability to concentrate on any form of work he considered menial or that wouldn't bring him closer to his goal as a professional musician.

Years later, he was asked why he hadn't taken on a permanent, wealthy lover who would take care of him until he was able to get his musical career going. His answer was both frank and startling. "I guess I just wasn't that smart—but it was also about my freedom. Having a benefactor wasn't my main goal and trying to find what you would call a 'normal lover', even a temporary one, didn't occur to me."

He spent every waking hour practicing on the alto sax his parents had bought him, plus his acoustic guitar, and he soon became expert in both.

His great looks and silken blonde hair continued to attract the young ladies, and he didn't have to put much effort into finding beautiful women who were eager to bed him down. Time and again, they approached him and sexually stimulated him. His quick sense of humor, pleasant manner, and enthusiasm for music kept them captivated.

Sex became an addiction for him, and he freely experimented with various forms of giving and receiving pleasure. In many instances, he enthusiastically allowed his body to be used as a playtoy. His liberal attitude towards sex and his sexual acumen had been finely groomed—from his early experiences at home and at school—and later perfected during his days working the streets.

Now that he was on his own, he was finally free to choose his sex partners—a welcome change from either feeling trapped at home or from prostitution. He swore he would never again put himself in a position where he would have to sell his body for money, or anything else life had to offer.

He had become a chain smoker and preferred his "cigs" strong. Rarely was he seen without a smoke or an alcoholic beverage between his fingers. For now, he wasn't doing any heavy drugs, except to smoke weed. On the other hand, pot wasn't considered a drug in the world of which he was now a permanent resident. Evenings, he hung out at the local coffee shops or jazz clubs and was regularly invited to play guitar and sax.

All the experience he had acquired while busking on the streets now turned into a huge asset for him. His naturally lithe body moved sensually to the rhythm and sounds he and his fellow musicians created. He possessed a grace and beauty that transcended anyone's, and he quickly became the object of desire for all who saw him, both men and women.

He used the time spent in coffee bars chatting it up with the older regulars, who had much more experience with the business end of the music industry. He knew there was more for him to learn in addition to playing several instruments. He composed much of his music at the keyboard, but then used the guitar to play those same original tunes and entertain his followers. Additionally, he used drums, or anything else on which to pound a beat, to achieve his inimitable tempos.

Brian valued the input he received from the older musicians, and also found he had much more in common mentally and emotionally with those well into their thirties. He had little in common with anyone his own age, especially within Cheltenham's stifling atmosphere, since he was in many ways now a man of the world. Once he had crossed that threshold of surviving on his wits and nothing else, there was no turning back the emotional clock for him. Even so, had he the choice he would have loved to regain some of that lost innocence, but his destiny had already been cast, and he never looked back.

He became well known for his natural talent to entertain, and more and more people began seeking him out and pleading with him to perform.

These weren't paid gigs, although he did begin to sit in with the groups who were being paid. He was now considered a semi-professional and hour by hour he perfected his knowledge of the in's and out's of the entertainment industry. He knew he was destined for greatness but at the same time realized his journey to greatness would not come easy.

***

Towards the end of his seventeenth year, Brian was listening to a band play at the Wooden Bridge Hotel in Guildford, when one of his chums approached him and said a woman was asking about him, and that she would like to be introduced. Brian looked in the direction his friend pointed and was pleased to see a beautiful woman smiling back.

After formal introductions were made, he took her aside so they could talk in private. He wasn't surprised that such an attractive woman wanted to meet him, in view of the fact many beautiful people had solicited him from his days on the streets. Nevertheless, he could tell there was something special about this twenty-three year old woman, who carried herself with grace and self-assurance.

"What can I do for you, Angeline?" he said coyly, with the small lisp that so many found irresistible.

"You may call me Angie," she smiled back. "And…what you can do for me, Brian, is to give me some of your time." She explained honestly that she was married, but that she and her husband had a falling out of sorts and were separated. She was lonely and desired the company of someone who presented himself very much like Brian.

He felt his face turn a shade of red. Despite the fact he was considered a pro, he retained a high degree of wholesomeness and integrity, which no amount of sordidness could tarnish.

Angie sensed this in him and appreciated these qualities. She invited him to spend the night with her. The next morning she paid him well for his services, as she continued to do the next couple of times they met. He was happy for the money, especially since he had no permanent home in which to live and was currently staying with friends. Those arrangements were temporary, however, and he came to realize that everyone had their own problems.

Outsiders were never welcome permanently in anyone's house. Sadly, he was the one with never a home to call his own, and his relationship with his parents would forever remain tenuous at best.

After his third encounter with Angie, she told him there would be no further meetings—she and her husband had decided to reconcile their differences. That was fine with him because he never wanted a permanent relationship, even a paid one, if it could lead to some form of permanence.

As a result of these clandestine meetings, nine months later Angie gave birth to a beautiful baby girl. Luckily, her husband was fine with what had happened and raised the daughter as his own. By the summer of his eighteenth year, Brian had become the father of two children.

A few months earlier, he had met another local girl named Pat Andrews and began to date her on a regular basis. Pat was different from the usual girls he knew. She was serious for her sixteen years and worked a regular, steady job. As for Brian, there still was no regular, steady job in his life. He was hell-bent on his musical career, which moved ahead steadily step by step.

Regardless, he was by no means content with life. His parents constantly pressured him to follow in his dad's footsteps, attend university, and work towards a respectable career. He was well aware that, with his high IQ and the ease with which he mastered any subject he set his mind to, he should strive to become a highly-paid professional. No profession suited him, however, except for his study of music.

Pat Andrews soon discovered she was pregnant with what would be Brian's third child. He continued to live a nomadic lifestyle, at times with his parents, but more often than not with friends for a few days at a time. The fact that, since the age of thirteen, he never really had a permanent home—from which he might not be tossed out at a moment's notice—had a permanent effect on him. He believed he didn't deserve a home, and he must be a horrible person—because if he weren't, he would have a regular family who cared for him and cared about what would become of him.

He knew that the caring attitude his parents showed the outside world about his future was for show purposes only. They wanted bragging rights to a son who would either become an architect, engineer, or any professional. From the outset, Brian could never be any of these—he was on his personal mission to entertain and enlighten the world through his music. The more life reared its ugly side and spat in his face, the more determined he became to be the one who would make the world a better place for his having lived in it.

At the same time, he resented the fact his parents had told friends and family that the reason their son had absented himself for several months was due to their sending him off on a paid holiday, to tour Europe! They said they believed doing so would give Brian a fresh outlook on life and change his mind about having sex outside the boundaries of marriage. Of their story, he later said, "It sounded good, didn't it? Such a pretty, little story that they manufactured. Let's see…did they throw me out of the house, or did they send me away on holiday as a reward for getting Valerie pregnant? I pleased them so much that they sent me away to the south of France!"

Lewis and Louise further claimed that Brian was now happy to be home fulltime, and that they were maintaining his living expenses until he settled on a permanent career. He angrily described his feelings, "Does anyone believe that I would go back to sucking up to my parents, so I could live with them again, after they threw me out the last time? Does that make any sense at all? I lived by my wiles on the streets, sucking cock, and now I should worry about what they thought about anything I should do with my life?"

He had been living with them a day or two at a time since returning from the Continent, mainly due to the expediency of whatever living arrangements he could find. Basically, he no longer lived under their domain. The last time he actually tried living with his parents was during the Christmas of 1960.

He had brought Pat around to visit his family for the holiday. When he and she arrived that evening, they found the lights turned off and the doors locked. Outside lay his suitcase, which his parents had packed for him together with a brief note saying they had decided to visit friends for the holidays, and therefore, he was expected to fend for himself. He said, "Yes, they did lock the house, but I hadn't really told them I was coming for sure—although, they didn't stick around to see, either."

Brian wound up breaking into the house to get some of his things, and neighbors called the police to report a break-in. No charges were pressed, and he retrieved some of his belongings that still remained behind. "When you get kicked out on the street, you don't take everything with you on your back," he explained. "There were still things that I had left behind and needed. Most of my clothing didn't fit, but I took a few of my father's shirts that did fit."

He moved in with Pat's brother for a while but was unable to pay rent on a regular basis, due to his not having steady employment. Once Pat announced her unexpected pregnancy to her family, he was asked to leave—or rather, was unceremoniously tossed out.

Once more, he found himself without a place to live. Regardless, more than ever, his enthusiasm for his musical career increased with every passing day. He tried to juggle working at whatever odd jobs he could find while perfecting his craft, and he added the electric slide guitar to his list of instruments.

He could never find that same enthusiasm for regular work, as he had for composing music. He sat barefoot and cross-legged for hours on the floor practicing guitar and listening for new sounds, which were constantly being created in his head. He often stayed up late, either composing music or playing for the public in coffee shops and clubs. As a result, he would often forget to show up for his regular job 'til later in the day, or not at all. The list of odd jobs he took on, and quickly lost, ranged from working at a bus company, on a coal lorry, or as shop attendant to various business establishments. None came close to a career for him, and none lasted longer than a few weeks. To him, it was all work and without meaning—a common trait among those whom the world typically considers creative or artistic geniuses.

***

Brian worked his way up to a few paying gigs at the local jazz clubs. For economic reasons, he decided to share a flat at an establishment called Selkirk House, together with Dick Hattrell and Graham Ride. Dick was a music enthusiast, if not an actual musician, and

Graham was both an architectural student and a musician. Dick and Brian were already close friends, and Graham had just recently been introduced to the pair.

Dick was the only one of the three with a regular paying job, and Brian quickly and shamelessly took advantage of his generosity. For his part, Dick had what could be called a crush on Brian, and Brian had enough experience knowing when someone was attracted to him and how to take advantage of it. Even so, nothing sexual ever took place between the two. Nonetheless, Brian believed—if he gave Dick the privilege of hanging around him and being entertained by him both musically and with his antics—Dick should pay his way.

Dick groveled at Brian's feet, something that grated on Graham Ride's nerves. However, Graham saw the musical genius that lay within Brian and chose to ignore what he considered Brian's constant bullying of their hapless roommate.

Also, Graham couldn't help but bond with Brian when he learned—at least from the tiny amount Brian chose to divulge—about his having been tossed onto the streets, having the tenacity to finish his schooling, and now, again tossed out from Pat Andrew's household because of her pregnancy. He personally witnessed Brian's physical frailties, such as his chronic asthma and the other, assorted daily ailments that forever afflicted him. Those ailments included the very real aches and pains in his joints, which included his arms, legs and feet, and up to his neck and head.

Moreover, his untreated and undiagnosed bi-polar disorder continued to hound him. His moods swung from being a bundle of energy—which many described as a raging, intense fireball—to moments later crashing onto either the bed, the floor, or anyplace he happened to land. Once he crumbled, he would fall into a deep sleep. Many who witnessed this phenomenon ridiculed him and often poked and prodded at his defenseless body, leaving black and blue marks that he later couldn't understand how they came to be.

Today's medical profession describes these symptoms as all attributable to the bi-polar disorder, and others compare his behavior to a form of narcolepsy.

The chronic depression that mentally tore him apart since childhood further contributed to his debilitated state. The only respites he found—from his many physical pains, his emotional up's and down's, and the never-ending loneliness—were in playing music, engaging in frequent and frivolous sex, and partaking in whatever drugs on which he could get his hands.

The drugs he took ranged from uppers, downers, cocaine, or anything that might blissfully numb him, if only temporarily. While he fought all these demons that lived inside him, he remained the carefree prankster and jokester, always wanting to make those around him happy. Simultaneously, he continued to plunge head-first into enlarging his repertoire of musical instruments—all of which he quickly mastered—and to expand his knowledge of the inner-workings of the music industry.

While Dick worked, and Graham attended school and also worked part-time, Brian—at nineteen years of age—remained in their tiny flat, content to practice, arrange, and compose his own music. He cheerfully sat barefoot and cross-legged on his bed hour after hour and studied his favorite albums, whose artists mainly consisted of Johnny Cash, Bill Haley & the Comets, Jimmy Reed, Muddy Waters, Julian "Cannonball" Adderly, Count Basie, Howlin' Wolf, Elmore Lewis, and Robert Johnson.

While he spent hour after hour studying the blues, he formulated a plan to start his own band, which would bring all the joy and passion of the world of music to the forefront of the British populace. Up to now, the public had only been stimulated by either pop ballads or what was known as traditional jazz.

Since he had no steady job, he couldn't afford to buy a majority of these albums for himself. Occasionally, he received money on the dole—akin to unemployment compensation—from the many jobs in which he'd been let go. As a result, in order to acquire these valuable recordings, he sweet-talked Dick Hattrell into purchasing them for "their house". Whether Dick ever realized Brian felt free to take advantage of the former's personal feelings for him didn't seem relevant. Dick was happy with Brian's friendship—and if that meant he paid for much of Brian's food and other living expense in exchange for this friendship, so be it.

Brian's other acquaintances helped him through these tough times, as well. Whenever they invited him to join them for a night out, or for a simple dinner, he would put his hands inside his pants' pockets and pull out their empty lining, signaling how devoid of funds he actually was. He followed that with a meek shrug of his shoulders and an innocent grin. Invariably, they softened, paid his way, and never expected reimbursement.

In his mind, he wasn't taking advantage of Dick or the others. He did what he had to, to survive. He had learned to use his feminine wiles to survive on the streets, and to a great degree, to survive his childhood. He could never forget the days having to eat disgusting, spoiled food from trash bins or steal from grocers' shelves, just so he wouldn't perish. He could never forget the days of being in hospital on the Continent, when he believed he had died—if only temporarily—from the 105 degree fever.

He was never selfishly manipulative, as he so often was accused. All he wanted was a chance at life, and he wanted a fair shot at someday realizing his dream, and nothing more.

He was still in the budding stages of a highly-successful musical career, and because of the charismatic manner about him and his fantastic good looks, people were drawn to him. He never had to work at receiving attention from anyone, to get people to offer him money or buy him the things he needed. They did so freely, just to spend time with him, be close to him, and enjoy his company.

He possessed the subliminal energy of entitlement and walked with a regal bearing that helped him get through many hardships. He admitted, "I was lucky, and my friends were very charitable."

People sensed something special in him. He had an innocence and childlike aura that made them automatically want to take care of him. During these early days of his career, to his benefactors he seemed similar to a stray puppy or kitten that begs for food and needs a warm place in which to snuggle up and rest, if only for a while.

For a majority of the time what these people desired wasn't Brian's sexual company but his personal company. He was blessed with a quick wit and ease of manner, which enabled him to poke fun at the most ordinary of things and get everyone to join in and enjoy his outlandish jokes and flamboyant mannerisms. He could take his spectacular face and contort it into grotesque shapes, simply to get and keep everyone's attention.

He had always been a great storyteller, even as a youngster, and his days on the streets provided him with ample fodder for a never-ending stream of unique stories with which to entertain. For all this—to hear him sing and play, and perhaps see him use his sensual body to dance a step or two in their direction—men and women eagerly shared what they had with him. They wanted to be near him and touch him, and when he was a Rolling Stone, they hoped to have some of his fame rub off on them.

***

Even so, the persistent lack of funds became an ever-increasing problem for the three roommates, and Dick's meager earnings could only carry them so far. Since there were no late-night bars open and since Brian was well known at the local joints, Graham initiated the idea to invite the local musicians up to their flat to continue partying, after the bars closed. In exchange for a place to drink booze and jam, each musician was asked to kick in a couple of dollars. These parties quickly became popular and then became bigger and noisier, once the musicians' fans joined in. These events became known as rent parties and helped to sustain the trio for a time.

In spite of that, the parties didn't provide much funding, except for basic rent and to pay a couple of household bills. The lack of quality food still was the major obstacle facing Brian. He often resorted to eating plain mayonnaise sandwiches, with nothing else to fill the hunger pangs that continued to haunt him. The other staple he ate nearly fulltime were potatoes. He and Graham became incredibly inventive on the many ways to fry, boil, mash, hash, dice, and slice potatoes. Years later, Brian was heard to say he didn't think he could look another potato in the eye ever again.

Graham recounted the first time he saw Brian and Dick together at their flat—the two young men were aggressively fighting one another for the last slice of bread in the cupboard. Since the age of sixteen Brian hadn't had decent meals on a regular basis, except for the occasional times when he ate at home or with friends, or when he managed to scrounge up enough money through odd jobs and the occasional paying gig to buy some of his own groceries.

Additionally, he needed money for various sundries, clothing, and basic spending money—some for the clubs he attended almost nightly. Finding clothes of any sort that fitted him properly became an exhausting task. He hadn't had new clothing for years but had managed as best he could with second-hand, used garments. Even though he wasn't vain, his appearance and good looks were of the utmost importance. He had learned early on that his looks and overall appearance would see him through the worst of times. He was well aware that if it weren't for his handsome features and smart looks, he would most likely be dead. For him, this was a serious issue and not one he took lightly. "I needed that face in order to survive," he often said.

While he lived with Graham and Dick, he had to borrow their clothes from time to time, even though neither men's bodies matched his, not by any stretch. Graham was taller and bigger, while Dick was shorter and much more rotund. Nevertheless, Brian smiled through all this and was often seen wearing ill-fitting jackets and slacks, usually when he went out on a date or performed in the clubs. He'd roll up the sleeves on the oversized jackets and do the same with the all-too-long pants' legs. "I wasn't trying to make a fashion statement," he said in his self-deprecating manner. "I believe I looked more like Charles Dickens' 'poor boy'." (Photo #802)

He actually was frustrated that he couldn't hold down any job for a period of time—mainly because he found it impossible to keep track of the time and keep anything close to a fixed schedule. Unfortunately, he never knew why he had these problems—the disorders of bi-polarism and manic-depression had yet to be named—and so he tended to agree with those who said he was a ne'er do well.

When he had exhausted the charity of others, he occasionally resorted to the one thing he knew would bring instant cash, exchanging his sexual favors for money. He didn't do that often but often enough when things had gotten especially tight for him. He was very much ashamed of returning to this lifestyle, nevertheless it was the only means he knew to see him through the hard times, until his musical career took over.

Because of his small size, many Johns continued to see him as an easy target and tried to force him into performing sexual acts without paying. For his personal safety, there were times when he thought it necessary to take his clients home for the "date".

During those times, in deference to Brian's feelings, Graham would pretend nothing out of the ordinary was taking place. Brian appreciated this and thought of Graham as one of the few honorable friends he had. He explained, "Graham was clean, and I didn't want to bring my dirt into his life. He was a friend and would look the other way at times, for me. I could have been the worst of the lot or the best of the lot. Graham never knew, but he stood by me as best he could."

Unfortunately, their landlord noticed the quality of some of the guests that Brian brought into the building, and also noticed that after those visits the roommates suddenly came up with the overdue rent money. Soon, Brian and Graham were evicted and had to find a new place to live. Brian said, "Occasionally, when it suited me to get by, I did a few tricks. I had tried to get away from it but couldn't manage. What I hated was, they'd want me to talk to them, care about them, and stay with them. Yikes! I'd have none of that."

Despite the many hard times he had already faced throughout his short nineteen years, he continued to maintain his inner dignity. Graham saw this in him and tried to understand why his friend had to do some of the things he did. He saw that Brian had an insatiable craving to be noticed and the center of everyone's attention—to be adored, worshipped, and hopefully, loved unconditionally.

Children normally take those natural gifts—such as unconditional love—for granted, and they receive them from their families. However, Brian never knew of nor received any of those gifts from his own family. That void in his early life left him with the never-ending feeling of inadequacy, a feeling he forever had to prove himself worthy of human warmth and love—or even the air he breathed.

The times he felt compelled to resort to performing sexual acts in exchange for money only added to his feelings of being unwanted and unloved, and reinforced his determination to succeed as a musician. As time after time he forced his mind to block out the reality of what he was allowing to be done to his body, he swore to himself that things would change for the better, and that his dream of becoming a great musician and composer was his destiny.

***

Graham and Brian fed upon each other's enthusiasm for rhythm 'n blues and American jazz. Graham became the coaching partner Brian needed, to work with him and encourage him in the pursuit of his dream career. Years later, when speaking of his friendship with Graham and his musical development during that time, Brian said fondly, "Graham knew me better than Mick (Jagger) ever could. He was the good friend who enabled me to move in the direction that I needed to go, even at his own expense at times. He understood that to get where I wanted to be, I was only playing a role, and he supported me in doing that. And for that, I was very grateful. Our friendship was mutual."

Indeed the several months that he and Graham lived together were probably the most important and stable of times that Brian had ever known. Even though the men were continuously lacking in funds to do anything extravagant, they were secure in their friendship and in the fact they looked out for one another. This time of safety and comfort—to know he wouldn't be tossed out onto the streets again on a mere whim—was pivotal for Brian. He now had the opportunity to study and refine his musical abilities, the time to heal from the traumas of the past years, and the chance to solidify his resolve to see his musical ambition reach fruition. He now realized he had the ability to compose his own music and write his own lyrics. Additionally, he now realized he had the talent to arrange his own music, plus the talent to take another's finished score and twist it and bend it, giving it a completely new sound that made it his own. He also realized he could learn and master any instrument put in his hands.

He needed this private time to gain confidence in himself as a musician and composer. At this point in time, he first realized the significance of adding exotic sounds to either existing music or to his original music. He and Graham would sit for hours and relish what they heard coming out of the Indian music that contained exotic instruments, such as sitars and tamburas.

Almost on the opposite end of the musical scale, Brian took to teaching himself a multitude of original sounds that he was able to draw from various blues harps, also called mouth organs or the harmonica.

All the same, he came to believe that his dream career wasn't materializing as fast as he wanted. He blamed that on the fact he wasn't living in London—and thereby have the opportunity to mix it up with the more sophisticated jazz musicians. He had no doubt he would eventually succeed and succeed very well; his problem lay in the fact he wasn't sure how to become as one with the more innovative players, unless he moved to London. Although, while still at the age of nineteen, this would be a major move for him, especially since he had no financial stability.

The problem that he faced while homeless once again reared its ugly head—the ability to acquire some form of work that paid a consistent salary and still left the time he needed to pursue his true calling in life.

His financial woes increased in October 1961 when he became the father of his third child. Pat Andrews gave birth to his second son, Julian Mark. Brian insisted that his son be given the name "Julian" after one of his favorite musicians, Julian "Cannonball" Adderly.

# CHAPTER SIX
## The Birth of a Musical Legend

*"That Guitar Player Ain't Bad!"*
Muddy Waters, as he referred to Brian Jones, Chicago, June 1964

While still living with Graham Ride at Selkirk House, Brian and friends once again stayed late and closed one of the pubs, where a blues band had been playing. As was their custom, they invited the group back to their home for booze and partying. Among the band members who accepted their offer was legendary blues guitarist, Alexis Korner. Alexis was already known as a blues evangelist in the United Kingdom, and Brian felt he needed the more experienced man's approval, friendship, and backing if he were to get to the next level.

Alexis—who was fourteen years older than Brian—was immediately taken in by the younger man's fire, dedication, and non-stop talk about Chicago Blues. He was intrigued to hear Brian's opinion of the direction in which he believed R&B would eventually move. Alexis also noticed an inner passion in the thin, shaggy-haired young man who would soon become his protégé, and this made him pay attention to what Brian had to say. He even went so far as to invite Brian to visit him and his wife at their London apartment, and to stay for a while. The intention was for Brian to get himself acquainted with the jazz scene in Britain's capital. All agreed that if he were to ever progress to leading his own band, Brian would have to make that move.

Another legendary British jazz musician, who at times played together with Alexis, was trombonist Chris Barber. Chris had his own band that Brian would go to see and hear whenever possible.

Shortly thereafter, all three—Alexis, Chris, and Brian—became the foundation for introducing the British populace to rhythm 'n blues and true American jazz.

*** 

For the present, however, Brian wasn't quite ready to take the final plunge and move to the big city. In the back of his mind there remained a lingering doubt as to whether he could make it in the fast-paced world of a professional musician. There was no question he had the raw talent and creative genius to perform the music he heard being played over and over in his head. However, he worried that all the chronic physical, mental, and emotional pains—from which he suffered—would gather together and mount an offensive against his frail body, which he would not be able to overcome.

Years later, when he reflected back upon this time, he said, "Despite those worries, I knew music was my destiny. I knew I would persevere—I was going to be on stage and would take my band with me. There were moments when I felt fire in my eyes; I could see the future so clearly…I could feel it and taste it. And yet, how I was going to accomplish these things—that part I didn't know.

"I felt as if someone other than me was orchestrating what came next in my life, making the plans, the dates, and the gathering of the band members. Much of the time, I felt as if I were looking at someone else moving through me. That evolution bewilders me to this day."

Before long, he and Graham decided to officially team up and perform together before a live audience. The duo would have no backup such as drums or keyboard, but instead chose to rely on their own ingenuity. Until this time, Brian had only played sit-in with other bands and never as his own man. For his debut, he would perform on acoustic and steel guitar, and Graham would play alto sax. They didn't own an amplifier, which was a must if they were to be taken seriously. However, Brian talked a friend into loaning the duo his.

They decided to pick stage names rather than perform under their own. Since Brian was primarily playing steel guitar, he chose a combination name derived from two of his personal heroes—Elmore James, the "King of the Slide Guitarists", and Furry Lewis, the consummate Mississippi bottle-neck guitar player. Brian Jones became Elmore Lewis. The fact that his legal first name was also Lewis was a mere coincidence and not by any means planned, especially since Brian wanted no remembrance of his father's name.

Neither Graham nor Brian felt sufficiently confidant with their individual singing voices, and so they decided to stick with only their instrumental sounds. They managed to put together a forty-five minute set, playing many of their personal rhythm 'n blues favorites.

When the night was over, Brian felt enormously confidant. The audience had enthusiastically welcomed the unique arrangements he gave to existing hit songs. He had managed to skillfully bend and tweak their sounds, to make them sound original, and as a result he turned them into his own.

This early success brought him a renewed spark of confidence, and he decided to take the initiative and stay with Alexis Korner in London. Alexis had informed Brian that he could put him up for the first few days, but after that he would have to rent his own flat. Brian had originally asked Graham to move to London with him and become a permanent part of the new band he planned to create. He assured Graham of their future success and that there was no need to worry about their future.

Even though Graham thought this move was the best for Brian's future, he decided becoming a musician full-time wasn't for him. He wanted a more secure future than what he could see coming out of a blues performer. Architecture was his forte, and he would stick with that profession.

Brian took his friend's rejection good-naturedly and decided to make the trip on his own. As usual money was a problem for him, and he asked Graham to loan him enough money to cover the train ride to London, plus living expenses for at least a couple of weeks, until he could get a job and be able to rent a flat.

Despite the fact Graham was a student and only working part-time as an architect, he managed to put together the money Brian needed. Days later he helped take Brian to the train station. Brian's big move was jam-packed with instruments, equipment, and anything else he had accumulated over the past several months. The two shook hands, and Brian promised to repay Graham for his selfless generosity in financing his venture into the unknown.

When he later spoke of his friend's noble act, Brian said, "Graham was my good friend, who enabled me to move in the direction I needed to go—even at his own expense—and for that I was very grateful."

For his part, Graham was confidant that if anyone would be successful at bringing true American jazz and rhythm 'n blues to the Brits—twenty-year old Brian Jones was the one to do it. He respected the tunnel vision and determination in Brian's eyes, and wished him nothing but the best.

Neither man, however, could foresee the aftermath this simple act of kindness would bring—the creation of the greatest R&B band the world had ever known.

# CHAPTER SEVEN
## The Band Without a Name

*"The name popped into my head and made
my soul feel free, like a buzz that shot through me."*

*Brian Jones*

As brilliant at playing R&B music as Brian was and as tenacious as he was in deciding to lead his own band, he was as equally ill-suited and unable to settle down to a regular paying, full-time job. Everything he tried working at eventually turned into a dead end. Nevertheless, he did manage to find enough work to sustain him, at least for the time needed to establish himself within the community of professional musicians.

Personally and professionally, Alexis Korner was as enthusiastic as ever in his decision to invite Brian Jones to join the world of London's R&B music scene. The younger man's ability to play guitar as well as any of the older, seasoned musicians was quickly recognized among the inner circle.

He was introduced to another young entertainer named Paul Pond (who eventually became Paul Jones, creator of the highly successful Manfred Mann). At that time Paul was the blues singer for a group called Thunder Odin's Big Secret. When Paul's guitarist quit, he asked Brian to become part of his band. Brian said he would but only if he could lead, because he had his own vision of where he wanted to take his music. Since the band already had a leader, an arrangement couldn't be worked out; however Brian continued to sit in and play whenever possible.

In the meantime, Alexis persuaded the proprietors of Ealing Jazz Club to allow rhythm and blues to be played there. They agreed, and Alexis' band, called Blues Incorporated, performed there for the first time in March 1962. Their sound became an instant success, since the number of British fans of the blues increased with each day. As Brian had predicted, the younger generation soon yearned to dance, play, and make love to the sensual rhythms and beats of this form of music.

Because Alexis held Brian's steel guitar playing in such high regard, he invited him to play with his band during their second session at the Ealing Club. The date was March 24. On that date, for the very first time Brian met Alexis Korner's new drummer, Charlie Watts—who Brian would later invite to become the Rolling Stones permanent drummer. "From the moment I first saw Charlie, I knew he was the one, without a shadow of a doubt," Brian explained. "He had the raw talent I was looking for because I knew we (the band) were going to create something that hadn't been out there before. I thought Charlie and I could work together…yeah! On hearing his sound, I was more on fire than I'd been in a long time."

Brian was asked whether, instead of being as determined as he was to start and lead his own band, would he have been happy to simply continue playing along with Alexis' group? He answered, "There really wasn't room for me with them and for where they were going. I never asked to join them because I instinctively knew this was the beginning of other things that were yet to come—but still, I was happy as hell! The fact was, I was destined to lead my own band.

"The same way you get led to certain outlets, I was pulled and pushed in different directions that, when combined, formed the early days that eventually led to my band."

During this time, his old friend from Cheltenham, Dick Hattrell, moved up to London and became part of what one might call Brian's first entourage.

Alexis was so impressed with the direction Brian was taking that he invited him to play alone at the Club in April. Brian asked Paul Pond to accompany him as singer. Luckily, Brian had saved up enough money for a fresh suit of clothes for an occasion such as this. Since this would be his first gig at flying solo, he decided to revert back to the stage name he had used with Graham Ride months earlier—although, he altered it a bit to Elmo Lewis.

Regardless of what his name might be, Brian 'Elmo Lewis' Jones became an immediate hit with the crowd. He took bow after bow and perhaps for the first time in his life felt he truly was within his element. He belonged!

Not only did he belong, but he was quickly becoming a star. Something about the way he moved, the way he talked, and the way his platinum blond hair and sparkling blue-green eyes glowed, made him stand high above the rest. To the audience listening to him, he wasn't the introverted, far too short, far too thin, and unable to hold down a steady job reprobate that his parents thought him to be. To them, he was someone to fawn over and adore.

Among the group that night who looked at Brian, as someone who deserved to be fawned over and adored, were a pimply-faced wannabe singer named Mick Jagger and an up 'n coming guitarist named Keith Richard. Mick and Keith were already playing together for another new group, in which a musician named Dick Taylor was a member. So far, this band had been playing on its own without achieving any great success.

Mick wanted to be a part of the world that Brian Jones was already a part of—and very successful at—Alexis Korner's inner world. Mick and Keith understood at once that Brian could become a part of anyone's successful group—the doors were opened to him. Nevertheless, that wasn't what he wanted. He told the pair that he planned to form his own R&B band. More than ever, he was determined to lead his own band, with his own vision, and to play his own music.

On that fabled night in April 1962—when Brian Jones', Mick Jagger's, and Keith Richard's worlds collided—destiny or fate, or whatever one wants to call it, truly stepped in.

Keith was salivating over Brian's first official performance at the Ealing Club. With his often funny way of expressing himself and looking at things, Keith got Brian's stage name of Elmo Lewis mixed up and went around bragging to everyone that he had met the legendary Elmore James! Brian would soon learn that this was a typical trait of Keith's—however, a trait that Brian soon learned to very much enjoy.

Mick and Keith thought of both Brian and his playing that night as having been performed by a "musical God". With his new, dark suit and wearing oversized, dark shades to hide his eyes, Brian had played much of the night with his back to the audience. Keith thought this was a stroke of genius and gushed over how cool the blonde entertainer was. The two newcomers couldn't get enough of Brian and followed him around the club, talking to him, and observing him every second they could.

Actually—something that no one knew, but that Brian later admitted was—the only reason he had worn those dark, oversized sunglasses and played with his back to the audience that night was because he was scared out of his wits. He was truly shy, quiet, overly sensitive, and all-too-often unsure of himself. "Those sunglasses were just a bit smaller than my face and a little squarer, but they were really black," he said self-consciously.

*** 

Naturally Brian still had a personal life to think about, which for the time included Pat Andrews and his son Julian Mark—or 'Mark' as he was always called. Not long after Brian moved to London, mother and child made the trip to join him and become a family.

Since he could barely survive himself, he wasn't thrilled with the prospect of having to be responsible for the lives of anyone else. On the other hand, he wanted to do the right thing and tried harder than ever to hold himself accountable for fathering another child. When he later reflected about his son, Brian said, "I felt I was acting a role that I didn't know how to get into, since I'd never been fathered myself."

Pat easily obtained employment, while he continued to jump from one mind-numbing job to another. The couple soon learned that finding an apartment was nearly impossible. During the early sixties, society frowned upon unmarried couples who lived together and especially upon those who carried the extra baggage of a "bastard" child. Because of that, they settled for whatever they could find. The three moved into a cramped, broken-down flat, whose windows were so encrusted with filth from the years that barely any sunlight was able to seep through.

For Brian, living within that type of environment—with a young woman who wanted his love and attention and a baby that naturally needed his love and attention, in a flat that possessed such a gloom and doom atmosphere—was akin to forced imprisonment. The need to work as many hours as possible in a dead-end job, in an attempt to support everyone, only added to his stress. Nonetheless, he never complained to Pat about their situation and accepted it as best he could.

However, he could feel his spirit being crushed with each day that passed. For any musician, and especially one who was attempting to create his own magical, truly unforgettable band, this situation proved extremely traumatic and noxious.

Adding to his problems was the fact that his and Pat's salaries couldn't meet their needs, and so he often pilfered extra money from whatever cash register or till at which he worked. Most times he wasn't caught, but often enough he was, which automatically resulted in his being sacked from another job. He was lucky, though, in the fact that no one ever pressed charges against him for petty larceny.

Only Alexis Korner knew of Brian's personal problems, since Brian had learned to never share what actually was going on with anyone else. He preferred to pretend everything was progressing smoothly and that he was leading a charmed life. In his mind, if he pretended hard enough perhaps it really wouldn't always be so bad—and perhaps the brighter side of his future was closer to his reach than he imagined.

Additionally, his sense of pride was gargantuan. He could never let anyone think small of him—or give anyone ammunition with which to belittle him—which he anticipated would happen if he fessed up to what his own private world was really all about.

***

Upon seeing how hard his young protégé was working at remaining both a companion to Pat and a proper father to Mark Julian, Alexis constantly tried to encourage him and finally talked him into auditioning musicians and singers for his new band.

Brian really wanted Paul Pond to continue on with him and become his lead singer, but Paul didn't think the world was ready for a true rhythm 'n blues band. He explained his misgivings to Brian and added that he believed no one would ever take this new band seriously. However, true to form, Brian insisted that his gut instincts were correct, and he resolved to continue with his quest for success, even without Paul.

He posted an ad in a jazz journal that stated he was currently auditioning new talent for a still unnamed R&B band. A gutsy blues pianist from Scotland, Ian 'Stu' Stewart, answered the ad at once. Stu was impressed with Brian's shrewd insight of the music industry, especially for someone that young. He was also impressed with Brian's basic understanding of the history of music and the who's who of the jazz world.

When Stu first came around to Brian's flat, he was struck by the stark existence within which his new band mate lived. As had become his norm, Brian was satisfied to eat what the everyday person would consider inedible foods, or even things that didn't count as food—just to get by. Among these were meals consisting of the ever-present mayonnaise sandwich, ketchup soup, or some form of unembellished spaghetti dish.

All the same, Brian continued to be Brian, and so—when Stu came to visit—he pretended nothing was amiss, and the men continued to chat about their future.

Auditioning potential band members and having a place to rehearse cost money, and Brian needed to come up with the cash to do it all. These expenses left nothing over for any extras, even cigarettes. But, Brian had to have his smokes. At times he reverted back to getting whatever he needed the way he had from his days living on the streets. He snatched packs of cigarettes from countertops and ran off, or merely stashed whatever he could get his hands on into his pockets.

One day, however, he was caught going behind the bar at the rehearsal hall he had booked, just to get his daily supply of smokes. He and the group he was auditioning were all tossed out into the street.

This was not exactly an auspicious beginning for the future Adonis of the rock industry—but then again nothing does come easy....

***

Alexis continued to help Brian, and whenever he heard of a good musician, he would send him Brian's way to be auditioned.

Dick Taylor was the bass guitarist who had been playing along with Mick Jagger and Keith Richard; however, he also wanted to become a part of Brian's new band. Together, he and Mick went to Brian and asked to be heard. At first Brian thought Mick's voice was much too weak, and he continued to audition other singers.

At times Mick sang with Alexis' group at the Ealing Club—while in the back of his mind, he intended to wear Brian down and eventually win the top spot as lead singer. He brought Keith Richard along with him. He and Keith were life-long, boyhood chums and where one went, the other followed.

Keith was a natural follower, which suited him fine. He was basically shy and reserved in most things and preferred taking second place to anyone he considered wiser or grander than he. Because of that, he and Brian quickly bonded.

Among Keith's heroes in the music industry were Chuck Berry, Bo Diddley, Jimmy Reed, and Muddy Waters—while Brian's first loves were Muddy Waters, Elmore James, Howlin' Wolf, and John Lee Hooker. However, the more Keith introduced the sounds of Jimmy Reed and Chuck Berry to Brian, the latter eventually became enthused with their musical styles and began to incorporate them into his own sounds.

As Brian allowed himself to bond with Mick, Keith, Dick Taylor, and Ian "Stu" Stewart, his more sophisticated, accomplished fellow players—from Alexis Korner's inner circle—began to show their contempt for what they believed Mick and Keith represented. To these jazz purists, or bluesmen as they were called, Brian was considered their brightest new star, and they couldn't understand how he appeared to be settling for the likes of those other, wanna-be entertainers.

Their distaste for Brian's choices grew into loud resentment, and a dispute erupted between the two factions. To these professionals, Mick and company were freaks, not to be taken seriously. For whatever reason, Brian stood by his new band mates and defended their abilities, even if it meant going against the better judgment of the more seasoned musicians.

These men decided to show Brian the folly of his ways and concocted a plan to humiliate the one they considered the weakest and the one with less musical talent among the group—Mick Jagger. Ginger Baker, then considered rock's ultimate drummer, together with two other musicians decided to throw Mick off his timing when the group next played at Alexis' club.

They knew Mick and Keith were plebian when it came to any form of advanced, stylish beats, and they determined to show Brian the error of his ways by continuing to jam with them. When Mick started to sing with Ginger and his musicians, they purposely advanced onto a more rapid, progressive beat, which they knew Mick had no way of following. Mick was successfully stonewalled.

Instead of looking the other way and letting his new friend be humiliated in front of the gathering, Brian jumped onto the stage with him and counted the beats aloud, thus giving Mick the opportunity to finish the song. When the night was over, Ginger Baker and friends still didn't think any more highly of Mick, but they did indeed admire even more their dedicated colleague, Brian Jones.

\*\*\*

After they had rehearsed together for a few months, Brian believed his new band was ready to get its feet wet and perform for a more widespread audience. Alexis offered Brian's still unnamed band a one-night gig at the Marquee Club in July 1962.

The band consisted of Brian and Keith on guitar, Dick on bass, Mick as singer, Stu the pianist, and temporary drummer Mick Avory. (Avory would later become drummer for the Kinks.) Brian still opted for Charlie Watts to be his band's permanent drummer, but Charlie for now remained content to play with Alexis' Blues Incorporated.

In order to play at the Marquee Club that night, Brian's hand was forced to choose a name for his fledgling band. At first he was stunned; he had spent all his time preparing them, rehearsing them, and gathering them together—and at last, when a live performance was scheduled, he had no name for his band!

To honor Muddy Waters, he selected the name from one of Muddy's hit songs, *Rollin' Stone*.

"The name just popped into my head, right then, right there, and it was like…Yeah! It happened that fast," Brian said. "Deep in my soul that name gave me a sense of being free, of not being constricted or confined by what was acceptable or what was normal. I wanted anything but normalcy for my life, and this band would be beyond anything that had come before.

"The name made my soul feel free like a buzz that shot through me all of a sudden. When I first spoke those words, Rollin' Stones, when I heard it and understood its meaning—everything connected in that one, split moment."

That day twenty-year old Brian Jones gave birth to his fourth child—a band called the Rollin' Stones.

# CHAPTER EIGHT
## A Love Affair Gone Wrong

*"I wasn't ever really close to Brian Jones."*

*Mick Jagger*

In mid 1962, nineteen-year old Mick Jagger was still attending university full-time and aimed for a degree in economics. The only income he had was an allowance from his parents. Keith Richard (whose last name still had no 's' at the end) was enrolled in art school. He had no clear picture of what to do with his life but did have a meager allowance that routinely came in from his family.

With still no financial or familial support from Lewis and Louise, Brian Jones, clearly the most creative, intellectual, and worldly of the three young men, had his mind set firmly on his calling to make the world a happier, freer, and better place to live through his music. "I wanted to bring the history and sound of music to the entire world and move it forward globally," he explained.

Even though he seemed preoccupied with the success of his new band, Brian's private life actually did revolve around his son, Mark. The toddler was already exploring his own tiny world and scurrying around as best he could. After Brian arrived home each night from whatever job he had, he would get on the floor and play with Mark, until the child fell asleep. He bonded with the boy the way he never knew his own father to bond with him. In a way, he was finding his own lost, inner child and allowing that child to finally fly happy and free.

Monetarily, though, things were at their worst—if that were at all possible. Pat wasn't making much money, but whatever there was went for the rent and electric bills. Any money Brian brought home was put towards groceries and the never-ending supply of guitar strings that every musician needs. The family's grocery budget was stretched thin. He often went without food for himself but made sure Pat and their son had enough to eat.

As the band's leader, he still had to come up with money to pay for the Rollin' Stones' rehearsal halls, and this usually came from any monies he could pilfer from the petty cash drawer of whichever job he had. "Those jam sessions cost money!" he often said.

Between juggling a job, finding time for his son, and time for whipping into shape his latest baby—the Rollin' Stones—Brian managed to wear his fragile physical state much too thin. Pat would find him passed out on the floor—while he still lay in the barefoot, cross-legged position that he had become known for—with his guitar resting between his legs.

Dick Taylor and Keith Richard also witnessed this glitch in Brian's psyche. They remembered seeing him passed out in that same cross-legged position during the middle of rehearsals. They couldn't tell if he had literally passed out or was simply tired. When later asked if he remembered feeling sleepy, Brian would say that he briefly remembered being tired, but before he knew what was happening, he had fallen into a deep, narcotic-like slumber.

The fledgling band's piano player, Ian "Stu" Stewart, became bitter, because Brian would often show up late for the band's rehearsals, and when he did show up, he was often so tired he could barely play. The real reason he'd show up late was because he was holding down a job to support his family—but no one knew that, and he would never complain to anyone, even his own band.

From a child, he had learned not to complain aloud about all his physical ailments and all the emotional up's and down's of his undiagnosed manic-depression, because no one ever cared to hear about them. "It never occurred to me to complain or even discuss my situation," Brian explained. "I'd rather make a joke of my falling asleep or let them think whatever they would, rather than to let them know the mess my life seemed to be. I imagined that a regular, ordinary bloke would've been concerned about his woman and his babe, and how to take care of them, right? But for me, my dreams were much bigger, and I had to push forward in spite of all that. To admit that would make me seem like a very bad person, like an uncaring man and father. Regardless, I had this thing I had to do with my music, and I guess I had a lot of things backwards.

"It was more that I didn't want the guys to think I couldn't handle everything, that I couldn't continue to juggle everything...the family and the band. I didn't want to make excuses but just wanted to show up and perform. It had to do with my pride, which wouldn't allow me to admit my overload of responsibilities."

As a result, the sad fact remained that he never told anyone he was juggling several lives. Because of this admirable stoicism—he was misunderstood and criticized from the beginning by many around him, including his newly-found band mates.

Nonetheless, they couldn't ignore the severe bouts of asthma that debilitated him from time to time. They learned to keep alert as to where Brian kept his inhalers—or how to quickly obtain a new one—whenever breathing emergencies occurred. At times the Stones would panic when they witnessed their leader fight for air, while in the midst of one of these critical attacks.

***

Pat Andrews could tolerate the couple's financial woes and their cramped living quarters, but other situations were taking place that became too much for her to accept. While she desired a monogamous, loving relationship with Brian, she could tell he had no intention of ever remaining faithful.

Beautiful women continued to flock around him and openly flaunted their bodies. No matter how thin and how frail he may have felt and looked at times—with the ever-present bags under his eyes—he was constantly sought out for sex. If anything, his frailties made him even more sexy and desirable in everyone's eyes—both male and female.

Once Pat forced herself to see the couple's one-sided relationship for what it really was, she packed her things, took their son, and returned to her parents' home. For Brian, this was a mixed blessing. In one way, he felt remorse that he hadn't been able to take care of his little family, plus, they had brought a feeling of solidity and comfort into his life. He would naturally miss being a father and cared very much for Mark Julian. But in another way, he didn't love Pat—at least not in the way a man should love a woman—and he was relieved to see her go.

Now he was able to concentrate full-time on his lifelong dream of leading his R&B band into musical history.

\*\*\*

In spite of the fact Brian spent every waking moment working toward his band's goal, that did not mean he had no desire for real love in his life. Quite the opposite was true. Perhaps even more important to him than his love of music was his yet unanswered search for that once in a lifetime, all-consuming love for another human being.

Finding that one love was vital to him. He had been alone all his life. Sure, he always had friends, but deep in his mind that old saying remained true—friends are only there for you when they want to be. He had witnessed that fact many times—since he was a youngster, when he was tossed out of his parents' home—that friends or acquaintances will help you to a certain degree. But, when his needs interfered with anything else they considered more important, sadly his needs always took second place.

He couldn't remember ever being number one in anyone's life and certainly not in his mum's or dad's. Maybe he had been number one with his dear, departed baby sister, but that was for much too short a period of time. Since then, his life had been empty.

Still, he knew deep in his heart that he had so much love to give. Proof of that was the fact that his utmost wish for the world was to help provide solace to the suffering masses through his music. If he were the coldhearted bastard or nihilistic, self-absorbed lout that his future enemies portrayed him to be—he would never have put that wish before his own lifelong dreams.

\*\*\*

Shortly after Pat and little Mark moved out, Brian moved in with Mick and Keith, into a small two-room flat in a place called Edith Grove. The place was literally a cold-water flat with absolutely no amenities. "I thought I had moved into a freezing Hell!" Brian later joked. "Only one word could describe the place—squalor. Aside from the ceiling and four walls, I was back to living on the streets. But, it was exciting, too. We could now get together and make it happen. This would be our make it or break it time, and I knew we were going to make it. In these starving, cold days our bond was formed."

The three were without funds, and any money they did put together had to go for their musical careers. To continue with their study of the Blues, especially Chicago Blues, they had to purchase any and all record albums in that genre on which they could get their hands. Some of these albums were so rare in England that they carried a high premium.

Regardless, they had to have them. Brian and Keith spent twenty-four hours a day—or at least the majority of that time—practicing the sounds they heard, and more importantly, they improvised and improved those sounds to make them fresh and original for the Rollin' Stones band.

The boys also needed money for equipment, including sheet music, amplifiers, and even more sophisticated guitars and a variety of harmonicas. The cost to rent rehearsal halls was a constant, plus the cost of transportation to get them from one place to another.

They had no funds for electricity, and the three made do a majority of the time with one light bulb. On top of everything, the winter of 1962-63 was bitterly cold, and the trio normally couldn't afford heat. They spent night after night huddled together, under whatever blankets and sheets they managed to accumulate.

As had become the norm for Brian, food came last, and whatever food they could afford wasn't of the highest quality nutritionally. On the other hand, since the three were young men who shared the same experimental, partying personalities—if they had to decide between food or cigarettes and booze—they generally opted for the latter two.

With his unique style, Brian explained, "Unless I was bloody crawling on the floor, about to pass out from lack of food, our money went for rehearsal halls, smokes, guitar strings, and booze."

Another reason they preferred booze was so they could erase some of the horrors that surrounded them in that squalid flat. Even soap had become a luxury and having to bathe with cold water was intolerable. Despite this, Brian could not go back to feeling as grimy as his days living on the streets, and so he bathed often—shutting out his mind to the horrendous shivering his body had to endure. As for Mick and Keith, they preferred to put up with the stench from their own bodies.

"Mick had this habit of lifting his arms above his head and sniffing his armpits," Brian said, amused, "and he'd say, 'Hmmm, manly!'"

On the other hand—from out of that cold, miserable winter of 1962-63—one unexpected and quite remarkable occurrence took place. While the three huddled under the same coverings, they shared secrets, ideas, and dreams with one another that they probably never would have, had the circumstances been different.

For Brian, Keith—even though he was a year younger—turned into the big, strong brother he never had. Despite the fact Keith was a bit dyslexic and not nearly in the same league as Brian when it came to sophistication or mental acumen, he had the opposite qualities that Brian lacked and wished he had extra. Whereas Brian was overly-sensitive, given to emotional up's and down's, and bouts of extreme energy and exuberance—Keith was quiet, almost monosyllabic, and calm, hardly seemed to move at all, and extremely introverted.

Whereas Brian needed to be the center of attention, worshipped, and adored by everyone—Keith seemed happy for any attention tossed in his direction. He liked to be the follower and supporter, opposite to Brian's desire for total leadership. The two meshed well together and found a camaraderie with one another that they never expected.

As Brian explained, "We were all in the same situation and were struggling together. Quite naturally, there was a bond that formed. It was who we were and what we were, and we had to have that strong bond together. Keith and I were different, in that we had a friendship, brotherly kind of thing. To me, he was my brother."

When it came to their sexual libidos, Brian was overly sexual, with traits of androgyny, and fascinated with any pretty face and nicely shaped body he encountered. Even though his body was entirely masculine, his androgynous qualities allowed him to be attracted to, and be found attracted by, both men and women. All his life, he had been told he was pretty—not handsome, but pretty, even gorgeous.

Women found him irresistible, with his boyish charm and great looks. To them, his slender body wasn't menacing or over-bearing. They found him safe to approach for sex, without the threat of being overpowered or held down against their will.

Men found Brian equally irresistible, even though most men—who considered themselves heterosexual—couldn't understand why. Their sexual attraction to him typically had nothing to do with whether he was male or female. He was pretty and he was sensual, and he had a lithe body that they were drawn to inexplicably. Brian had the charisma that the majority of Hollywood's male stars possess. That charisma is something they're born with and not something that can easily be learned or acquired.

Even more than sex, Brian enjoyed simple cuddling and being held tenderly, with both males and females. Most often he chose women, but when he did meet the occasional male who possessed the qualities he desired, he—without any feelings of shame or guilt—showed his feelings for them. With men, he preferred those who were mainly free of body hair, similarly slender, and "pretty". He preferred men who weren't overly loud or sexually aggressive—since he had been brutalized so many times by those who possessed those traits.

On the flip side, he also knew enough not to flaunt his bi-sexuality. During those years, being either gay or bi-sexual was looked upon as a sin and perverse, and he would never endanger his well-being by outing his own sexual preferences. He was also very discreet in his encounters with the male sex and careful not to engage in any sexual touching while in public forums.

Keith was once again the complete opposite of Brian when it came to his sexuality. He was just as laid-back and reserved when it came to sex as he was when he spoke or joked aloud, and in public. Keith wasn't sure how women perceived him. He didn't think of himself as sexy or even attractive. At nineteen years of age, he had a bad case of acne and was often teased about his large ears that stuck out. He purposely wore his hair long to hide his ears but was still self-conscious about this flaw in his appearance. He was not the type of young man that women pined for or sought out. Here again, he was content with taking other blokes' leftovers when it came to partying. If no female was available, Keith was content to be alone and take care of his own needs.

Conversely, Mick and Brian were both very much alike in many ways and totally opposite in many ways. Both were sure of their sexuality—although Mick 'til now had not experimented with bi-sexuality. He was well aware, however, of the sexuality of his body. He had a strong sexual libido and didn't think twice about having sex with women in public, if that were the only place available. He'd have oral sex in hallways, elevators, or wherever he found himself, and he liked to be the sexual aggressor. In his own way, Mick had a pretty face—at least to some. He, too, suffered with severe acne that erupted from time to time.

Brian, on the other hand, had beautiful skin for a man. His skin tone wasn't coarse or rough like so many men.

Mick's body, like Brian's, was lithe and slender, even though he was at least five inches taller. His eyes were dark and penetrating, while Brian's eyes were pale and yet sparkled like bright lights. Mick's hair was dark and his appearance somewhat brooding. Brian's hair was platinum, and his appearance innocent and—in many a person's eyes—angelic.

Mick was laid-back and at that time still soft-spoken, but he was well educated and good with words. Brian hid his true introverted nature well and often came across as explosive. Mick was serious about most things, and Brian was often the jokester, wanting to please and amuse others.

Both men shared the vital qualities of being mentally astute, with razor-sharp instincts, and they were willing to fight for what they believed. The two could perceive strengths and weaknesses in others, and automatically knew how to use those traits against others—especially business rivals—in order to get what they wanted. For Brian and Mick, those assets were crucial to attaining their ultimate goals.

Whereas Mick was a bit rough around the collar and appeared gruff, Brian came across like a male model. However, both looked and spoke in a refined manner. Even though Brian's clothes were always well-worn and hardly ever new, he possessed a regal bearing that made most people not even notice these shortcomings. Mick wore newer, expensive clothing that his parents bought for him. Then again, even with his new wardrobe, he had no fashion sense or awareness as to how to create the type of appearance that would make him stand out.

When Brian walked into a room, both men and women turned and smiled in his direction. When Mick or Keith walked into a room, people either looked the other way, or frowned.

Regardless, in that cold, dreary winter of 1962-3 while Brian and Keith bonded as brothers—Mick and Brian bonded as lovers.

"Guys will experiment, same as girls do," Brian explained. "It was the times, too, the freedom, and the experimentation. But initially, Mick and I only huddled together to keep warm." His frank statement indicated the beginning of the close, physical relationship that quickly blossomed between the two men.

***

Mick and Brian's unexpected affair started with the simple exchange of a smile—nevertheless it was the type of smile a couple exchanges when they know they're ready to take their relationship to the next level. In Mick and Brian's case, the next level was a strong desire for sex.

For Brian being a vamp and flirting with a man was comfortable. He was confidant with his own sexuality and was open to trying out almost everything. When asked about his adventures, he said with a mischievous grin, "Calling me experimental was minor!"

Testing the waters came natural to him, and he acted upon whatever felt good. Since he knew no sexual boundaries—due to his experiences at home and on the streets—he felt both mystified and confused when it came to making judgments about what the average person considered normal.

As for Mick, up 'til then he'd never had a sexual experience with another male. And yet, he didn't really think of Brian as another male but simply a beautiful, extremely sensual person with whom he wanted to enjoy sex.

Brian understood what Mick wanted when he smiled back at him that night, and that smile wasn't one that would normally be swapped between brothers. Mick had clearly signaled his intention.

They waited for Keith to fall asleep, after giving him one beer too many. The electricity was cut off as usual, and so a solitary, glimmering candle lit the small room. Mick sat naked atop a woolen blanket that lay crumpled on the floor, and with much anticipation he watched Brian walk over to him and hold out his hand. Brian didn't have to say anything. He never did.

Mick reached out with his own hand and took hold of Brian's, pulling him down on top of him. Both felt they had waited long enough to be close in that way, and both felt the need to show their feelings for one another. They laughed with the blissful relief that comes from realizing they were about to satisfy one another.

Afterwards, the three band mates slept huddled together for the rest of that night, just as they had all the previous nights. However, this time for Brian and Mick, the closeness was very different. While Keith slept the contented sleep of the innocent, the other two held onto each other as lovers—in a tender, warm embrace.

The next day, Mick felt even more drawn to Brian's open femininity and took hold of him once more. Now awake, Keith stared at his two mates with his jaw hung open in total disbelief.

When the pair finally separated, they stared back at him and burst out laughing. Keith didn't laugh back but shook his head back and forth, almost sadly.

Brian later explained, "Mick felt like love, although I didn't want to admit it at the time. I couldn't help but love him. We were both very confused by it, but yeah, it was deeper than either one of us wanted it to go. The feeling was there on both our parts. For me, it was just like that moth to the flame deal. You know it's gonna singe your ass, but you can't help but be drawn and attracted."

From that day forward, Mick and Brian's sexual flirtation grew more and more intense. The reciprocal touching turned into mutual oral sex. This lasted for a time, but then they found that not fulfilling enough.

Brian already had anal sex in the past, both willingly and unwillingly. He'd been raped several times while on the streets or had given into anal sex in exchange for money, just so he wouldn't starve. In any event, he didn't count that as real sex since he felt nothing but dead inside when it was over. Occasionally, when he needed someplace to live, he had sex with male acquaintances that he liked but still didn't feel any close connection. Those were consensual in their own way but not nearly close to full orgasmic sex.

Now, finally for him the thought of having anal sex with Mick seemed entirely natural, and he looked forward to showing Mick how much he cared for him by giving into his lust. After a while, he wanted to transfer his own love to Mick by giving him anal sex. He waited until he knew Mick's love for him was mutual and then said what he wanted.

Happily, Mick wasn't fearful of being in this subservient position for the first time—he trusted Brian and loved him in a way that he'd never felt for anyone. He wanted all of Brian and wanted Brian to take all of him. "Mick couldn't resist me," he said shyly. "I told him we made a cute couple."

When the weather wasn't too cold, Keith would take off for a long walk, whenever his band mates began their heated sessions. He didn't want to be privy to their affair but still wound up knowing all. Still, as the true friend he was, he kept his mouth zipped.

None of the other Stones or their acquaintances actually knew of Brian and Mick's affair—although some suspected. No one needed to know and most likely wouldn't have understood. Brian explained, "Mick didn't mind 'going there' but didn't want anyone to know. Plus, he thought I had a cute ass!"

***

Reciprocal sex between band members was common during the sixties. The sex was normally done during drug and sex fests between both males and females. However, when the bands were on the road touring for what seemed like unending weeks and months—without a break to return home and visit loved ones—the members would at times seek comfort and solace with one another. These incidents were never spoken about aloud, or even generally acknowledged privately, and once the bands took a break and went back to their regular lives, the extraneous sex was erased from their minds.

Hardly any turned into true love, but Brian and Mick, without ever thinking it could happen, did fall in love—true love—with one another. Neither had ever fallen in love before. This was a real attachment that the two—although poets in their own way—couldn't put into words. They communicated their desires through their eyes and that special look, but not with words.

Whenever they did feel the need to express aloud their dedication to one another while in the presence of others, they'd simply say to one another in a joking manner—"I love you, brother."

On the other hand, even privately they felt stilted or uneasy in saying aloud the words they actually felt. In their minds, they very much were macho men, who were entering a career as hardcore rockers. Although, during the times they were alone in their small flat, they would smile and say to one another—"I love, you sister."

That was the closest they ever came to acknowledging both to themselves and to each other the deep devotion they felt. For this special time in their lives, Brian and Mick enjoyed their affair entirely behind closed doors.

# CHAPTER NINE
## A Dirty Business

*"There was a Mafia-like control of the bands…"*
Bill Wyman, 1990

As creator and leader of the Rollin' Stones, Brian had to also take on the unenviable role of part-time mediator. This task would not be easy, since he was dealing with the assorted oddballs who were now a part of his band. To further complicate things, each musician had his own theories as to which musical direction the band should take. When the group got together for rehearsals Mick, Keith, Stu, Dick, and Ian immediately butted heads, with no one willing to back down.

With his normally quiet way about him, Brian stepped in and took control. He spoke with the band mates first individually and then collectively, and explained away the strengths and weakness of their views. He wanted to ensure that no one felt left out and that each theory was respected and taken seriously.

Dick Taylor credited Brian with being exceptional at merging the divisive group into one. Since his musical background was all-encompassing, Brian was able to recognize the value of each position, and with ease and civility he managed to blend their varying opinions into one. Had he not taken the time to do so and allowed their arguments to continue unabated, the band would never have turned into the cohesive unit the public ultimately saw.

As docile as he might have seemed when it came to mediating their opinions, he was equally as strict when it came to how long and how often they had to rehearse. He pressured them to work hard and to learn as much of what he already knew about the music world. He willingly shared his dream and his vision with them.

He saw the raw ambition and talent in each and ordered them to get off the couch and play. He prodded them on relentlessly, especially during the times the group was demoralized, feeling they couldn't make it. "Yes, we're doing this! We can do it!" he insisted.

While he made final plans to present his band to the town's club owners, he and Keith continued to perfect their guitar playing. Their unity became so sharp that they developed an almost symbiotic relationship. Each created and played off the other, and hours would pass in which neither man said a word. Verbal communication wasn't necessary, since Brian and Keith shared the same language, the language of the Blues.

Nevertheless, he had to sadly admit that it was sometimes too hard to concentrate on creating new musical sounds, when the sounds coming from their grumbling stomachs were much louder. He said, "We made music and talked about how damned hungry we were. And how cold the water was."

He, Mick, and Keith scraped bits and pieces of food out of the bottoms of empty cans, just to get something to eat. His ability to shoplift bread and potatoes from stores could only go so far before the local shopkeepers recognized him. "But I was really good at getting away with it!" he joked years later.

In addition, he and Keith wore their fingers down to the bone from hours of practice. Between fighting to ignore the hunger pangs, and playing until their fingers were ready to drop from their hands—the pair welcomed the brief respite that finally came when they fell asleep on the cold, hard floor.

But with each new day that passed, Brian was pleased that he was turning into a maestro, as he worked to an even greater degree with various guitars and harmonicas.

He believed the time had come for the industry to take the band seriously, as a viable, commercial product. As the band's leader, it was up to him to get the many club owners enthusiastic about auditioning them. He soon learned that the welcome mat wasn't automatically rolled out for upstart bands, especially those who looked as out of sorts as the Rollin' Stones. As a matter of fact, the band didn't start out as "the Stones". Instead—as Brian later described it—"We were just blokes playing for our supper in grungy, dingy places."

Even though the traditional jazz scene was changing rapidly, true rhythm n' blues still wasn't recognized in Britain as anything that would bring in the money-paying audiences. There actually was an almost Mafia-like grip on the clubs, and the owners weren't open to new sounds and new sights. Most were old-fashioned in that they believed in sticking only with what had a proven track record to bring in the big bucks. However, the truer story was that the traditional jazz scene was no longer bringing in the big bucks, and Brian—who was still only twenty-years old—determined to get the club owners to understand this and take the plunge into rhythm 'n blues. This was his greatest challenge so far—to get his band seen and heard. Without the big break, no matter how good they might be, if no one got to hear them, they would never get anywhere.

A few clubs went far to show their disdain for the "long-haired freaks"—as many considered them. For amusement, the owners would book the band to play, wait for them to show up, and then tell Brian and his mates that their gigs had been cancelled, due to unforeseen circumstances. Instead of allowing these incidents to destroy his confidence in his band, these events made him even more determined to succeed and be recognized.

He said, "I had to pull the band along in every way to get them up to speed with what I expected—in order to get them into the clubs and be recognized. It wasn't just my charming personality that worked for me. I was persistent and determined, and I knew that I was going to do this and succeed. Yes, I flirted with the club owners, if you want to call it flirting. I could sense who would respond to that, even though I didn't promise to do anything for them. I expressed the suggestion, though, in my look, in my demeanor, in my smile, and in all ways to make them think we were pretty tight and everything was okay between us.

"It's not as if that type of action never happened before me and never happened after—you see, I was off the streets and becoming a music star—so if I had to give a kind of false suggestion to get the job, I would. But, I didn't want to actually be beholding to anyone in that way."

***

With his months and years of studying and absorbing the in's and out's of the music industry, Brian had learned—for a newcomer to be given a fair shot at success—one of two things had to be offered before any doors were opened. The first was money. If a performer, be it actor, singer, or musician was to be taken at all seriously, and he or she came from a wealthy enough background to offer a big-enough payoff—that was one way. If they didn't already have a wealth of available cash but were willing to offer the producer or club owner a larger share of their earnings in exchange for the right to perform—that was another way.

In situations as the one with the Rollin' Stones—where they had no ready cash to offer and no ability to show that they were capable of bringing in the big bucks, from which they could pay back a larger share of any and all profits—a third offer had to be given. That third proposal was the offer of sex.

Brian knew this option lay out there all along, but he also believed his band was good enough, and as a result he wouldn't have to consider the alternative. Normally, any sex offered by an entertainer came from members of the female sex. But if the up 'n coming performer happened to be male, then he would offer up a pretty girlfriend or pay for a high-class prostitute that the producer or club owner desired.

Again, the Rollin' Stones had neither to offer. Nevertheless, none of the band members knew Brian's actual background. He was very good at keeping the dark, shocking side of his pathetic life private, and no matter how close he and Mick might have become, he would never fully divulge the life he had been forced to live for the past few years.

When he and Mick once compared their teenage years, during some down-time they spent while living at Edith Grove, Brian had no real story to tell. He talked briefly of having to live for a time on the streets but never went into detail. He did say that he had to forage for food and a warm place to live, but nothing more.

To that, Mick's response was, "That must've been really tough!"

And, Brian answered, "Yeah, Man, it was." Nothing more was ever said, and Brian kept his mouth zipped.

Now that he was forced to play the hand he was drawn—he decided to explain to Mick and Keith the tricky situation of getting the band into the clubs. One important lesson he had learned while on the streets, he told them in confidence, was how to act sure of himself when he actually wasn't. He knew how to step up to the plate when it was necessary and push forward no matter what obstacles were thrown in his direction. After all, he said, the creation of the Stones was all about "my music, my way, and my vision." There was no question of his leadership and his gut determination to see it through to the end.

Any time he had approached a club owner to be auditioned, his experience so far had been that—while they were taken in with his fire and enthusiasm—when they met the rest of the band, to say they were turned off would be putting it mildly. He was the only one among the Stones the club owners were interested in considering. In those days, Mick wasn't even noticed.

But again, Brian had the innate ability to tell when someone was even mildly attracted to him, and he knew all too well how to play off that energy. Some of these club owners had shown enthusiasm to simply have him around to talk to. With the time he had spent hunting for food and money, he'd become a terrific hustler, in addition to being street wise. Now all those hard-earned talents were about to be put to good use, for the future of his band. He said modestly, "I'd usually go in alone at first and discuss my band. I waited as long as possible to have the clubs draw the curtain and see the entire band. You see, they didn't come across as well as I did."

As honestly as possible, he explained to Mick and Keith his plan to flirt with the owners in order to get them to audition the band, despite the fact he had no intention of taking it a step further. This had to all be kept quiet, he further told them, and none of the other band members would ever know what actually had taken place.

True to his nature, Keith looked away and said nothing. He'd come to think of Brian as his brother—not brothers in the blood, naturally, but something even stronger than that—brothers in the heart, bound forever with a common destiny. And because of this, Keith couldn't deal with having to see his brother put in a position to offer something as tawdry as what he was describing.

However, Brian remained fearless and said, "I dared myself to do what the others were too afraid to do, or didn't have the balls to do."

For the first time, Mick showed his true colors. "Go for it, Brian! Do what you gotta do," was his answer to the dilemma that the vulnerable young man, who was his full-time lover, faced.

***

The fact that Mick cold-heartedly sent his lover out to face the wolves should not seem incomprehensible. Mick had been raised in a relatively normal household, wherein his parents treated him kindly and with much consideration. He was used to having almost anything he wanted handed to him. Over the years, he had come to expect others to do things for him.

Even as a teenager and now as a young man, the seed had been planted and continued to grow for the pimply-faced, wannabe singer to someday be crowned by the music world as "King Mick". To him, everyone was disposable. One of Mick's favorite phrases was, "use them up and spit them out!"

Even though he loved Brian, as much as he could ever love anyone at that time, when tough choices had to be made regarding who could be sacrificed and who could be spared, Mick would always choose himself as the one to be spared. He had a strong survival instinct to crush anyone who might get in his way, even when such a drastic decision wasn't necessary. His theory seemed to be to seek and destroy anyone who may eventually be a threat.

At the time he cavalierly sent Brian out into the streets to prostitute himself not for money, not for ultimate survival, but merely to get himself seen and heard by the public—Mick probably wasn't fully aware of his deadly primal instinct to outdo any and all competition. Unbeknownst to anyone, as the years progressed he would finely tune that instinct.

As for Keith, he did have a somewhat rougher upbringing, which fit in with the street fighter personality he had now come to enjoy. His family wasn't as well off, but they treated him with love and compassion. Brian said, "Keith was poorer compared to Mick—that's my take. But he also had this thing about him that he didn't feel a strong connection to his family. Like a lost boy kind of thing."

He was making reference to Keith's feeling of isolation within the Richard family unit. Of all the Stones' backgrounds, if any were at all similar, Keith's and his were—but not by any means identical. While Brian had to screw and rob for his supper, Keith had to merely play guitar for his.

***

At first Brian felt pleased that Mick had agreed with him, and that he should "go for it," especially since the band needed a break.

Before leaving on his mission, he took in a deep breath and squared his broad, but clearly overburdened, shoulders. As he reached for the door handle, he took one last look back at Mick. By now he had reconsidered and so much hoped Mick would tell him not to go, not to do this, and that they could work it out some other way. However, Mick stood firm and said nothing. Brian opened the door to their cold, squalid flat and walked out into the even more frigid, bitter wintry night.

Stu had been using his old van to drive the band from place to place, and that night Brian needed him to drive him to the first club. While Stu drove, Brian sat back and reflected. He couldn't help but wonder whether, if the situations were reversed and Mick was the one expected to offer up his body in exchange for the right to perform, would Brian have told him to "go for it!" Hell, no, he decided. He would never want nor expect someone he truly loved to acquiesce to such a filthy, degrading act. He covered his eyes with his hands and continued to ponder.

Why was it different for him? Why was it okay for him to debase himself over and over for the greater good of getting the Stones recognized? Why should it be necessary to prostitute himself, just so some filthy freak of a club owner or producer could hear how great his band actually was?

He knew how damned good the Stones were. He didn't have to prove it—he knew! Therefore, why was it all right for him to put his body on the line like this, but not Mick?

He felt the warm tears well in his eyes. He was a good musician—no, actually he was a great musician and leader. Plus, he was a good person. He had never unnecessarily hurt another human being, unless he had been forced to defend himself.

Nevertheless, for some reason he couldn't understand, he felt everyone, including his parents, continued to think of him as a disaster and treated him like a pariah. He wondered whether perhaps Lewis and Louise had been right all along, and he deserved to be treated like shit. Perhaps everyone who seemed to want to destroy him was right—maybe he was a piece of shit. Therefore, it shouldn't really matter if he let himself be treated like this. Hell, even Mick—the man he loved more than anyone—was now treating him as if he didn't count, as if he didn't really matter, as if he felt nothing and didn't deserve to feel anything.

Why else would Mick have watched him walk out the door and not tried to stop him?

He felt so alone. He had been alone so much of his life, with no one to support him, look after him, or protect him. And now, things were no different. He only had himself to depend upon and to lean on. He rested his head against the van's headrest and moaned aloud.

"What? What's wrong?" Stu asked, concerned.

"Nothing. Nothing at all. Everything is fine," was his only answer. He would never admit aloud the inner angst he felt.

However, he had to force himself to push all these worries—the thoughts of feeling demoralized and once again used—to the back of his mind. He would think about them some other time, whenever the time was right, and now was not the time. He had to formulate his plans for the best way to approach the different club owners whom he'd chosen to meet. Each man was an individual in his own way, and each had to be dealt with accordingly.

***

Naturally not all, or even a majority, of these men were gay or bi-sexual. Nonetheless, each had his own energy that needed to be stimulated, cajoled, and sweet-talked in the way Brian felt would make them receptive to him and his band.

The fact of having sex with a man didn't bother him, but doing it with a man who sickened him, did. Additionally, he felt like a lowly con artist who had to talk, beg, and plead his way into being heard. He hated the thought that manipulation was now being associated with his music—because to him his music was pure, as was his mission to share the joyful bliss that came from enjoying true rhythm 'n blues.

In his mind, to bow, scrape, beg, and plead to have his band seen and heard was a form of prostitution. Even though many performers thought this was a normal part of the auditioning process, for Brian to have to plead with these businessmen—whom he considered too inept to understand what great music actually was—this was an unbearable form of degradation.

Considering his innermost thoughts, the act of prostitution didn't have to include the exchange of sex. For him to sell his mind and his integrity in this manner was even more debasing than offering up his body for a couple of minutes. He hated to be any man's boy, or putz, as he called it. To exchange his body for a favor or money was less painful than exchanging his soul. When he offered up sex, he let his mind float free to another place, as if it weren't really he doing the deed. But, when it came to selling his mind and his musical integrity—that was the ultimate humiliation he could not ignore or pretend it didn't exist.

As he traveled from club to club and made the owners aware of his band's existence, the very real fear always lay in the back of his mind that he, at any given time, could be once again assaulted, beaten-down, and raped. This, naturally, was by no means a fear borne from paranoia—but a fear borne from actual past experience and common knowledge of what actually took place in establishments such as these. The type of man who either ran or frequented these clubs was often less than human. And to them, the type of musician who walked in off the street and begged for the honor to play was less than human.

When he spoke of the clubs in which the band would eventually perform he once confided, "Some of them were really rank places, you know."

In light of that, he had good reason to be fearful for his physical safety, while he stood alone and defenseless in the dark, barren wasteland that many of those clubs encompassed.

***

When sex wasn't part of the equation, Brian had his own unique method of negotiating terms. While club management and the various producers automatically dismissed the vast majority of entertainers who approached them, when Brian walked directly over and offered his hand, something about his presence captured their imagination.

He possessed a naturally contagious fire that ignited them. The drab lights inside the poorly lit clubs appeared to awaken as they danced off his full head of platinum blond hair. He had a grace of walk and inner dignity against which his vibrant blue-green eyes offered a stunning harmony.

These businessmen were turned-off by the loud talking, aggressive musicians they normally met. On the other hand, Brian was different. He spoke with an ease of manner in a calm, but confidant voice. His soft lisp only enhanced what he had to say. The men remembered vividly Brian as he stared directly into their eyes and announced, "My band is the best band in the land."

To their ears that simple phrase sounded like poetry—the best band in the land.

One such club owner, who had the foresight to see how good Brian's band actually was, was Giorgio Gomelsky, owner of the Crawdaddy Club. The Crawdaddy was unique in that Giorgio believed in presenting new, exciting sounds, especially the Blues. "The owners all wanted to make a name for their clubs and to bring people and their money in, and so, having a great band perform was also in their best interest," Brian said candidly.

Giorgio fell among the group of club owners who found Brian sensual and was immediately taken in by his charm. Giorgio was one of the first in the industry to refer to Brian as the little blond beauty. In his mind, Brian was neither a hot hunk of a man, nor a sexy fox of a woman. Instead, Brian was a beautiful individual whom he found irresistible, no matter what his sex.

However, Giorgio was not one to whom Brian offered sex. Simply knowing the man was attracted to him was enough for Brian to play off. Besides, Giorgio was an astute businessman and would never coerce one of his entertainers into offering sex. All the same, Brian kept him interested and flirted casually with him, as needed. Nothing happened more than he and his band performed time and again at the Crawdaddy Club—the place where the Rollin' Stones eventually got their first big break.

When speaking of this time in his life and the business people with whom he had to deal, Brian later explained, "They said I was gorgeous, even though I never felt pretty. I thought my face was coarse and rough looking, but to others I had appeal."

In saying that, he referred to the comparison often made between him and the beautiful women or ladies of the silver screen.

For whatever reason, whenever he met the men who had all the power to make or break his band, his beauty most often mesmerized them. Either consciously or sub-consciously, Brian reminded them of the gorgeous sirens whom they had lusted after their entire lives. Moreover, just as they had found those gorgeous sirens unobtainable, many thought of Brian as equally unobtainable. In a way, this illusion greatly protected him from the more depraved predators.

Sadly, though, it didn't protect him from all the predators. There were times when he felt his band needed to get into a particular club or heard by a particular producer, and he knew there was no other way to get the job done, other than to give into their perverse desires. During those occasions, he felt less than human.

He later said, "I was hit on everywhere, and I hated when someone exerted power over me. It was degrading. I hated the bastards! I felt dirty and shameful inside. My looks were a bloody curse.

"There were times when I was attacked, and I would disassociate from my body—when I didn't feel what was going on. I felt my spirit hovering over what was happening, as if it were happening to someone else. There were times I felt especially vulnerable to being attacked, even though I believed my mind could talk my way out of most situations. And, I knew I was smart and able to move pretty fast."

***

Just as he gave up food for himself to make sure that his son Julian Mark and Pat Andrews had enough to eat, Brian sacrificed himself for his band time and again.

Mick Jagger knew what was going on and coaxed Brian to "go for it." Keith Richard knew what was going on but pretended he knew nothing. Later, Bill Wyman and Charlie Watts would learn what was going on and had gone on—but chose to pretend nothing had ever happened.

Brian said Mick was "hard as stone," and then added, "The music industry is a dirty business. I didn't sleep my way to the top—like so many others. Instead, I slept my way out of the bottom."

# CHAPTER TEN
## Roommates & Other Strangers

*"Mick, Keith, and I allowed others to pay our way,
in exchange for our company. Entitlement—an ugly quality!"*

Brian Jones

The band was barely bringing in any money and certainly not coming close to paying the rent and other bills. Stu constantly needed gas money to get them from place to place, and monies were needed to maintain his worn-out van and pay for their meals, while the guys rehearsed. Naturally, the group also wanted to add varied, upscale instruments, and larger amplifiers to their collection.

To Mick, Keith, and Brian the solution sounded simple—bring in additional roommates. Brian's old buddy, Dick Hattrell, was in town and looking to share a flat. When he heard Brian needed another bloke to room with, he jumped at the chance to once again get close to him.

Under normal circumstances, Dick would have been a great, loyal friend to have around. Money wasn't a problem for him, and he was more than happy to provide Brian with whatever he needed. In the past, whenever he saw Brian about to go hungry, Dick had always been there to buy him a decent meal.

Now things were a bit different. Keith was with Brian full-time, and wherever Brian went—Keith was right beside him. Mick was still in school during the day, but when he was around, the three were inseparable.

Whenever the trio went out for the night—with Dick along for the ride—Brian purposely kept him in the background, as if he felt embarrassed to be seen with him. At the same time, he would call Dick to the forefront as soon as the check arrived. Brian would then walk out with Mick and Keith and offhandedly toss the check in Dick's lap. Dick didn't complain but graciously picked up their tab.

Additionally, during that terribly cold 1962-63 winter, Brian as usual had no decent coat or jacket to keep him warm. When Dick was around, he would tell Dick to take off his new, comfy jacket and give it to him. Dick acquiesced and spent the rest of the time shivering in the cold. One day Keith, too, was without anything to keep him protected from the elements, and so Brian ordered Dick to give Keith the sweater he had just put on, after loaning Brian his coat.

Brian would only acknowledge Dick's presence when the other two weren't around. Brian would then attempt to talk civilly to him, but once Mick and Keith returned, he reverted to treating his old friend as less than human.

\*\*\*

In Brian's mind there were good reasons he treated Dick so horribly. But—since he never spoke aloud about his real feelings or past experiences—he never shared his true story. Outwardly, he explained, "Dick did not inspire respect. He had no self-respect." In other words, if Dick didn't respect himself—why should he?

That was the explanation he gave aloud. Because Brian said that half-truth without realizing what repercussions it would bring, he once again gave his future enemies fodder to claim how coldhearted and cruel he could be. Inwardly, there were two untold, sad, and more profound reasons for his treatment of the young man, who should have been his good friend.

The first reason was that Brian—despite being aware of his superior ability to create great music and lead his own band—did not think much of himself as an individual. After all the years of being told by his parents that he was a loser and would never amount to much, he always had—as he put it—"a niggling feeling" in the back of his mind that they might be right.

The abuse he had suffered at the hands of merciless predators, while on the streets of England and the Continent, only compounded that feeling of inferiority. Those years, between the ages of sixteen and eighteen, were the most important for him to grow into a secure, mature young man. In order to grow into that secure, mature individual, he would have needed the support and guidance of a loving family unit, or even one family member. He never had that support and guidance.

As a result, he—even though he was a genius when it came to his musical abilities—was immature and wholly unprepared to face everyday life and regular, everyday interactions with people. Children are meant to be nurtured along by their parents—or others assigned to guide them—until the age of maturity, when they can leave home and successfully begin their lives independent of the family.

Brian never had that nurturing background. He had been tossed out onto the streets from the age of thirteen, and before that been mentally, emotionally, and sexually abused and confused—since he first learned to walk and talk. He didn't even know who he was or what was expected of him most of the time. His bi-polar disorder impaired him by bouncing him back and forth with major mood swings that—without the proper medication or counseling—left him emotionally crippled to handle any form of stress.

Interestingly, these characteristics are common among men and women who go on to highly-successful careers in the arts, either in entertainment or the more creative arts, such as painting and sculpting. The sad fact remains, however, that with no strong support from a close friend or loved one, these brilliant, creative individuals are crippled when it comes to surviving and interfacing with everyday life. Brian Jones fit tightly into this category of creative genius.

Tragically, his situation was far worse than that. He carried the extra burden of having been traumatized by the degradation he suffered, as a result of having to prostitute himself over a long period of time. He had been raped, beaten down, and sodomized numerous times. Many times he even felt this was his own fault, because he was either too small or too weak to protect himself. He felt dirty and unclean—as if he had to constantly wash the stench off his body—from all the people who had touched him in that way.

Because he felt unclean, he didn't believe that anyone truly pure should want to touch him or care for him.

Due to these constant feelings of self-doubt and inferiority—which Brian vainly tried to ignore and tried to pretend did not exist—he automatically felt that anyone who truly loved him or admired him for who he was had to have something horribly wrong with them. In his mind, since he was unworthy of being loved or admired, only those who were equally unworthy or unclean would ever choose to be with him.

***

Unfortunately for Dick Hattrell, he had a big crush on Brian. Brian tried as best he could to discourage that feeling in his friend, but wasn't successful. If anything, the more Brian treated him miserably, the more Dick groveled at his feet.

Brian actually did care for the young man—but only as a friend. And because they were friends, Brian tried to let him off the hook by not flirting back or accepting his advances. As a matter of fact, Brian actually feared that some day Dick would aggressively come on to him in a sexual manner, and that he would have no choice but to physically beat and hurt him. Despite his small frame, he was a pretty good street fighter, and he wouldn't give a second thought to pounding anyone who would not leave him alone. "It wouldn't have gone well," Brian said later, when reflecting on those times.

During those hard days when there was nothing to eat, Brian went so far as to talk Dick into stealing milk and groceries for him and the others. When Dick got a new electric guitar, Brian coerced him into giving it to him. With all that, the hapless young man continued to worship at Brian's feet.

Brian said of those days, "Dick worshipped and adored me. You would think he wouldn't have put up with it, wouldn't you? I wanted to tell him, 'Get some self-respect!'"

He further went on to say, "It was revolting!" He felt as if he needed to wipe Dick Hattrell's essence off him. He was too much in Brian's space and too much in his face.

All the same, the saddest and funniest incident—depending upon which point of view was adopted—between the two men occurred one night when Brian came back to the Edith Grove flat especially late and feeling especially tired. His body ached, and all he wanted was to climb into his own bed and fall into a deep, blissful sleep.

To his horror, when he approached his bed, he saw Dick sleeping in it! Brian went into a tirade. He was livid. He honestly felt Dick had sexually molested him by touching his personal mattress and pillows. Naturally, if he hadn't been molested by others, he never would have reacted in that manner.

Unfortunately for all, no one knew of Brian's sexual past, and all Dick and the others witnessed was Brian going into an unnecessary, vile frenzy over Dick's innocent act. On the other hand, Brian knew the real reason his friend was in his bed—it was because of the man's ongoing sexual frustration over not being able to touch him. Therefore, in Dick's mind, if he slept in Brian's bed, he felt he was getting as close to Brian as he would ever get.

During Brian's angry outburst, he grabbed two electrical wires—which in reality weren't attached to any outlet—and chased Dick around the apartment. He screamed that he was going to shove them up the unfortunate man's butt and permanently electrocute him. Dick wasn't aware that the wires weren't live and yelled for help, while he ran for his life.

Everyone else knew Brian wasn't really going to hurt the pathetic young man and all enjoyed a good laugh. Brian, too, laughed when the incident was over. And, from that day forward, Dick Hattrell never slept in Brian's bed again.

***

The second, and perhaps even more provocative roommate to share the Edith Grove flat, was an eccentric young man named Jimmy Phelge.

According to Brian, Jimmy was one of the most grotesque, weird-looking human beings he had ever met. He even said he believed the word "eccentric" was specifically created for Jimmy Phelge. Jimmy reminded Brian of the common street people he had encountered while on the Continent, who spent their lives rummaging among the garbage. Jimmy's clothes—when he chose to wear any clothes—were always soiled, and he hardly ever bathed.

The only reason the guys kept him around was because he had money, and he willingly shared his money with all of them. Brian said, "We took some money from Jimmy. We did what we had to do at times."

Mick and Keith now joined Brian in believing they were doing others a favor by simply allowing them to hang around. Even at this early stage of their careers, the three felt that special twinge of entitlement. Naturally, Brian had this feeling all along, especially when he accepted others' offers to pay his way. They willingly paid him, in return for the privilege of having him talk to them and be close to them. He never thought of a sexual exchange in these cases but merely offered his benefactors the privilege of his company—if only for a short time.

***

One bizarre result came out of Jimmy Phelge's rooming with the Stones in the cramped Edith Grove flat. Beginning in 1963, when the Stones officially began to compose and copyright their own music, Brian was the one—as leader of the band—to decide upon the name "Nanker Phelge" for their pseudonym. Brian declared that the group as a whole would share the writing royalties.

Naturally the name "Phelge" was in sardonic honor of their eccentric friend, Jimmy. But the name "Nanker" was purely Brian's. As a young boy and afterward, he was known for taking his beautiful face and contorting it into the most rubbery, creepy faces anyone could imagine. From a child, he told everyone he was making nanker faces.

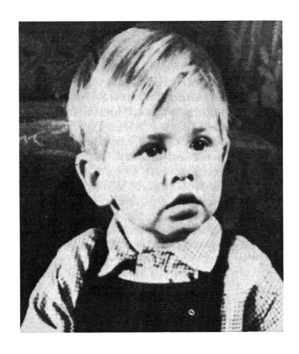

801

802

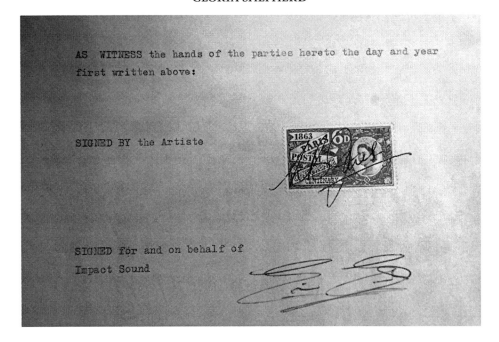

803

804

805

806

# GLORIA SHEPHERD

807

808

809

810

Dear Shandi,
     Thank you for your letter.
     As you said you can't make me write but I will, because I like answering my fan mail. I don't laugh at any of the letters, unless it is a joke and it's funny, but not about your feelings. I don't take fan letters for granted, or anything else if it comes to that. Peoples feelings aren't to be laughed at. Some things seem ridiculous, but you are all too kind towards us all,

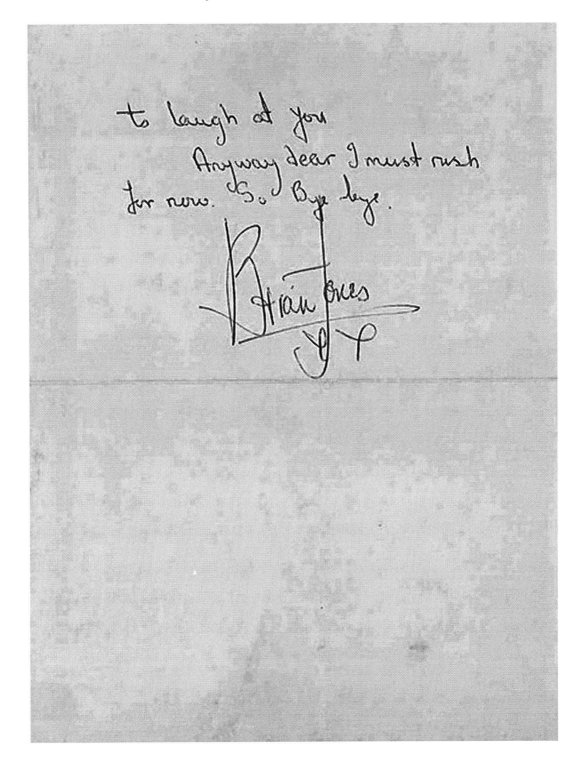

812

Dear Shandi,
      Hello again! Thanks for your letter.
      I am sorry to hear you don't much time to listen to the record player. I can see I wouldn't have got on very well at boarding school. When I am at home, my player is never off! If I'm not playing R and B, it's Bach! Anyway, I hope you have time, someday, to listen to all the numbers on the E.P. and I hope you like them!
      On the number "Satisfaction" there is no saxiphone. It is two

guitars working together, Keith and myself playing them to make that effect.

Yes, my four-poster is antique, very, and it is lovely and comfortable.

I must push again dear. So!
Bye bye,

*Brian Jones*

Dear Shandie,

Thank you nuts for your lovely letters. (I don't mean you are nuts, it's just an expression I use!)

Yes, I remember when I was very ill in America. Well, I remember feeling rotten in Chicago one night, but after that I don't really know what happened. Apparently, I had a load of tubes stuck up my nose and in my throat and I nearly didn't live, but I'm happy to say I'm still quite alive now!

I don't know if fans will be allowed on the set while we are filming, but I don't see why not, but I'll have to see what the others say.

I hope you like the

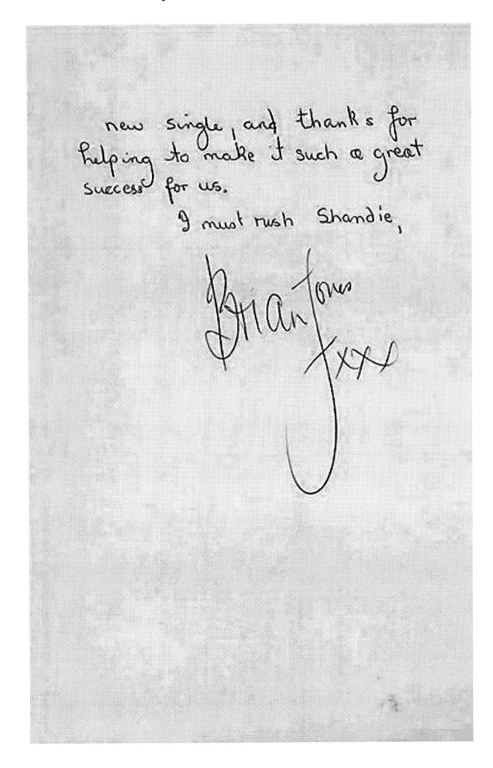

Dear Shandie,

Thank you nuts for your letters. Please forgive me for not answering before, but I have been so very busy lately.

Actually I like the name Shandie. I wouldn't say it sounded like a cheap lipstick. Mind you I'm not up on the names of lipsticks.

Nothing has been said whether fans will be allowed on the set, but there's no harm trying - eh!

I must rush Shandie,

Brian Jones
xx

Dear Shandi,
    Thanks for your letter. Nice to hear from you again.
    Yes, of course I'd love to meet you and have a good old chat, about everything. I always love meeting you all.
    I agree with you about R and B. You have to understand it before you can like. You can hope to like it if you dont understand it. These people who say it's aload of rubbish make me sick. Let's face it, if we all liked the same style of music the 'Pop World' would be dead.

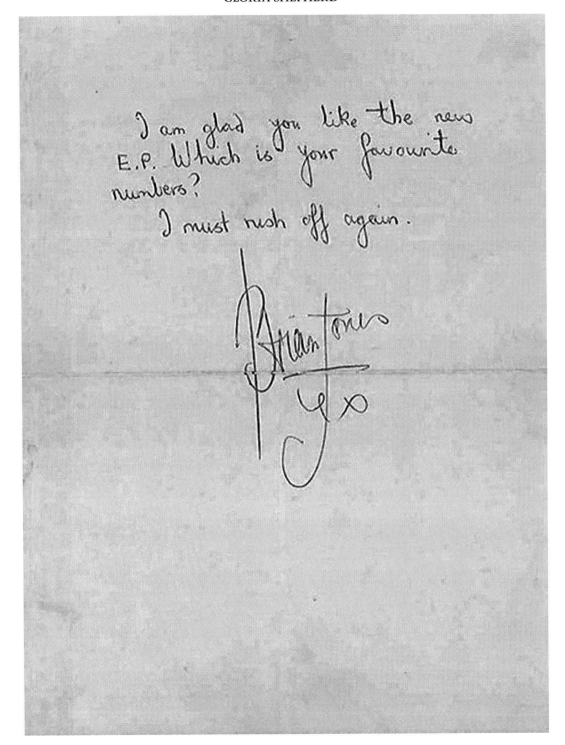

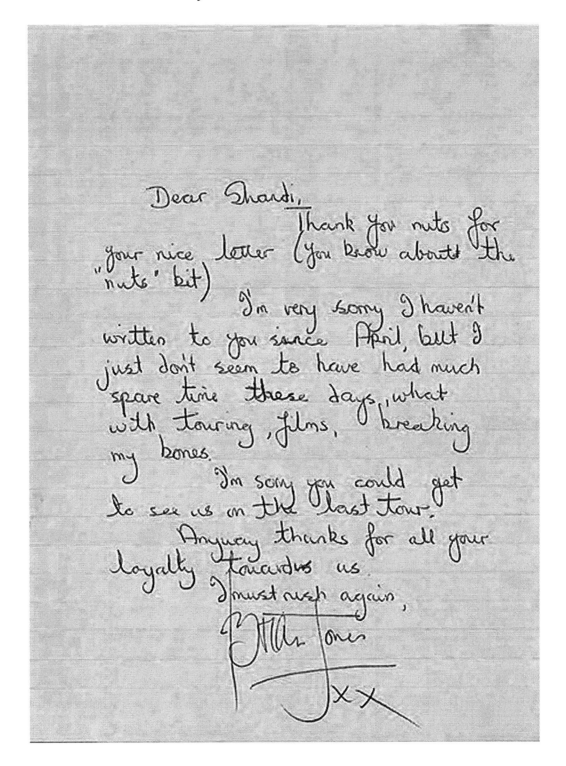

821

822

823

824

# CHAPTER ELEVEN
## Pas de Deux

*"Brian was really fantastic. Mick & I both thought he was incredible. He could have easily joined another band, but he wanted to form his own. The Rolling Stones was Brian's baby."*

Keith Richards

The general public and even the media weren't yet aware of the Rollin' Stones, but London's key jazz and Blues musicians were certainly aware of the band's existence. The one of which they were most aware was their leader, Brian Jones.

Raw energy, extreme talent, and a fiery imagination propelled his ever-rising star. Even though attendance at the small clubs they played during the 1962-63 season was sparse at best, those who did see them perform instinctively knew something special, something truly different, was taking place.

Brian described it this way, "Yeah, things were tough. But we were making history! We could feel it, Man! Something was really happening." The more the audiences reacted to his sexual energy, the more he poured it on.

Hell, he figured, in the beginning he'd taught himself how to shake his ass and strut his stuff just so he wouldn't starve to death, and now he could apply all those tricks of the trade to thrusting his own band into stardom.

Mick, Keith, and Dick Taylor couldn't see it happening quite that easily, and from time to time they fell into deep funks, when they came close to chucking it all in and going back to their regular lives. At times, their lackluster outlook would drag Brian down, however, he'd quickly reclaim his vivacious, boyish enthusiasm for his music and life in general. He told them over and over, "We're going to do it! It's happening." Within minutes his pie in the sky exuberance recaptured their imaginations, and they returned to his demanding schedule.

He was by nature a perfectionist and drove himself as hard as his band, seeing to it that they rehearsed hour after hour, as they fine-tuned their routines.

While musicians can rehearse their craft until they reach perfection, a band's lead singer, or frontman, cannot rehearse what he's not naturally born with. Stage presence and the ability to capture and hold the imagination of one's audience has always been a fine art that an entertainer either has or doesn't have.

Brian often called himself an actor, acting whether he was on stage or acting for the benefit of a different type of audience, such as producer or club owner. "Acting is acting," he said and applied what he knew to everyday situations in order to get what he wanted.

He never intended to be the frontman for his own band. He only intended to be their leader—to guide them as far as how well they performed and what kind of music they performed, to speak on their behalf with the press, and to negotiate and sign their contracts. Naturally, he wanted to be an integral part of their overall stage presence and to play as varied a selection of instruments as any professional musician—but he never planned to be their lone frontman.

He said the lead singer was normally the frontman and in their case, the frontman was Mick Jagger. On the other hand, Mick had no stage presence. When London's other professional musicians saw him on stage, they joked about having to look for him. He seemed to disappear into the background and could only be found by tracing the sound of his voice.

Mick had zero personal appeal as far as being the eye candy that any successful band needs. Ginger Baker, who continued to take a personal interest in the Stones progress, compared Mick Jagger holding onto the microphone to a drowning man holding onto his life jacket—too afraid to take a step out of his comfort zone.

While they performed, Brian was the one who danced, strutted, and beat out the sounds with his tambourine. Alexis Korner commented that their audiences—comprised of just as many boys as girls—became totally mesmerized by Brian's antics. Alexis described how Brian could act like a total bitch on stage. He'd strut, yell, and pound his tambourine in their faces, while sticking out his tongue in their direction.

All those mannerisms were finely honed from his days on the streets—but of course no one ever knew of their origination. Brian possessed the beautiful, sensual, combination of a great musician and the hottest bitch on stage. The females in the audience did a complete meltdown as they watched him, while the males reacted with a confusing mixture of jealousy and rage.

The jealousy was easy to understand, because their women were fawning over some guy who they thought was nothing more than a blonde bimbo. Nevertheless, the rage part was harder to dissect. Outwardly, they hated to watch Brian so openly flaunt his sexuality in their faces. Inwardly, they were frightened by their own feelings of lust for him.

His androgynous performance appealed to everyone, regardless of the gender of the individual audience member. He could be the gorgeous, seductive vamp, and at the same time, be the sexy hunk with whom girls dreamed about running off.

While he played guitar, he couldn't very well prance and strut around the stage. This was where the lead singer or frontman needed to shine, and so far, Mick hadn't been able to fill those shoes. Brian offered to work side by side with him, to coach him, and to nurture him, until he could take over for himself.

"That sounds great! Let's get started," Mick answered with enthusiasm.

Beginning late summer 1962, throughout the following year, and even beyond, Brian took over the reins to guide Mick in the fine art of audience seduction.

The two would stand in front of a large mirror, where Brian would go through his routines alone, and then he'd have Mick stand beside him and copy him. Mick wasn't naturally graceful, although—since the two found one another completely irresistible—Brian patiently walked him through the steps that he needed to master, in order to relax and feel more comfortable with his appearance overall.

Mick's acne made him self-conscious, and he thought himself unattractive. Naturally, in Brian's eyes, Mick was tall and elegant, and he taught Mick how to use his intense features to entice their audiences. To help loosen him up, Brian put on some of his more effective "nanker" faces, which soon had Mick rolling with laughter and relaxing even more.

Additionally, Mick wasn't proficient with harmonica, maracas, or tambourine—while Brian handled all three with ease and grace. Here again, he patiently guided Mick through his routines. The two continued to stand side by side, dancing together, while they worked those instruments in what could be described as a rhythmical pas de deux.

Brian taught Mick how to shake his rump together with the beat, even though Mick protested that his butt was too flat and not as hot as Brian's well-rounded derrière. The three all laughed, as Keith—with the ever-present cigarette hanging from the corner of his lips—accompanied the pair on guitar.

The inability to move to the music wasn't Mick's only weak spot; he also was unable to throw his voice to match the varied rhythm 'n blues sounds the band executed. Brian considered all those factors and once considered replacing Mick with another singer. (See Chapter Fourteen)

Looking back on those days, Brian reflected, "I thought Mick was really cute, but I knew he wasn't talented enough. He had more of a raw energy, which I thought would be appealing. Although, it didn't seem like he had any actual polish or control of his own voice then—for him, it was strictly learn or you go.

"But I couldn't just let him go, even though he, too, felt inadequate at times—and that was pretty obvious. But then again, simply screaming into the microphone seemed to be acceptable in those days. I wanted to let Mick go, but for me it was just like that moth to the flame deal that I've said over and over again. You know it's gonna eventually singe your ass, but you can't help but be drawn and attracted to keeping things the way they are."

Unfortunately, Mick discovered Brian was leaning in the direction to fire him. Brian explained, "It really pissed Mick off when he found out I was going to let him go, and he wanted to get even. Yes, I thought his singing sucked—but his attitude! Man! What was he coming off with that attitude for? He was a pain to deal with—like he was special. You see, I was the card dealer and the one to get things done.

"Mick always felt he was the real star of the band just because he sang, and he thought I couldn't sing. Of course, we did need him, but there were stronger singers for sure! He only had great appearance, being tall."

For the first time, Brian intimated the love/hate relationship that forever became a part of his and Mick's interactions. He had already begun to resent Mick for tossing him out into the streets to prostitute himself, just to get the band heard by the producers and club owners. In his mind, Mick's attitude was no different from his own parents, who had tossed him out at age sixteen and thereby forced him into months of prostitution, which included all the other degradations that came along with it, in order to survive. Just as his parents were supposed to love and care for him, Mick was supposed to love and care for Brian.

On the opposite end of the spectrum, in Mick's mind, once he learned Brian planned to fire him—he began to harbor a deep resentment for what he believed was a traitorous act on Brian's part.

Oddly enough, Mick would never accept blame for what he had done to Brian—offer him up, body and soul, in exchange for the band to be auditioned.

From this point forward, a vicious circle was drawn, from which neither man would back down.

***

During the bouts of animosity between the two men, the sexual energy didn't abate but instead grew with each day that passed. Mick and Brian apologized superficially to each other, so the band could continue rehearsals. One issue on which they all agreed upon was, the band's future success remained their ultimate goal.

Even so, for Brian and Mick the extra motivation for them to kiss and make up was so they could continue with their lovemaking. Instead of growing colder to one another due to the constant in-fighting, quite the opposite occurred. The temporary flare-ups only added to the intensity of their already steamy sessions.

Mick, Keith, and Brian continued to be thrown together geographically because of their inability to afford separate apartments. To keep their spirits up, they regularly enjoyed a plethora of drug taking—whether it be smoking weed, snorting coke, popping uppers, downers, and everything else in between. On top of that, a steady supply of booze was a prerequisite.

Keith discovered, if he got himself stoned and stayed drunk, the combination helped him ignore the confinement he felt, whenever Brian and Mick initiated another one of their sexual escapades.

During this time, Mick began to notice that—while he and Keith could do any form of drug and drink alcohol to excess—the combination didn't have any long-lasting side effects for them. Conversely, Brian's frail constitution couldn't stand up to the same amount of drinking and drug taking. Whereas, Keith and Mick easily shook off the drowsiness brought on by the chemical mixtures, Brian normally passed-out for hours and then couldn't remember what had taken place.

As Mick studied the effects drugs and alcohol had on Brian's well being—without even realizing he was doing so—an evil plan began to evolve in the back of his mind, which he planned to put into effect whenever the time was right....

***

Brian's tutoring of Mick wasn't limited to dirty dancing. There was much more for both Mick and Keith to learn. The need existed for them to walk, talk, dress, and breathe the air of a rock star. The image Brian wanted his band to portray had to eventually become second nature for them. Although for him, that image had been groomed from when he was a young child.

One of the things he had learned from his mum was the fine art of flirting and cross-dressing. He said, "Mum saw that natural feminine inclination in me and initially didn't try to shut it down. She taught me a lot."

Not only did Louise teach him how to flirt and dress like a woman, but she also taught him how to apply make-up, choose matching jewelry, and seductively shake his hips.

Back in those early days, she had no idea how that playtime at the family's home would later shape and mold the future Adonis of the rock world. All she knew, at the time Brian was born, was that she had wanted a daughter. When her first daughter died, she automatically began to think of Brian as her little girl. When her real second daughter, Barbara, was old enough to interact within the family circle, she, Louise, and Brian became the Jones household's three sisters.

The senior Lewis never knew any of this, and if he did he made sure to pretend nothing out of the ordinary was taking place. Whenever he would return home from work early—and the three were involved in a game of dress-up—young Brian would run to his room and quickly remove the powder and lipstick from his face, together with the hair ribbons, and throw on a pair of jeans and a shirt.

Now as leader of his own band, Brian had come to realize that the world of rock revolved around two things, money and sex. He wasn't a cynic; however, he realized that to succeed in the music industry, the band had to sell not only their music but also sell themselves—not in the literal sense but in the figurative sense.

The guys had made note of the audiences' exuberant reaction to their performances. The audiences always reacted with great enthusiasm to the style of Blues they played, but that reaction was nothing when compared to the unbridled fire and passion shown when Brian took the stage and strutted his stuff. He was the original rock star—and those credentials were never disputed.

More than anything, Mick wanted to do what Brian could do and believed he could eventually do it better. He understood that to become the true frontman he had to copy Brian, then become Brian, and lastly, bury Brian and forever erase his memory from the minds of the fans.

Brian had no idea what lay in the back of Mick's mind. All he knew was that he was thrilled to hear Mick wanted to move ahead full speed in learning how to imitate him. Brian said, "I saw Mick's and Keith's potential. There was destiny happening, Man! We could feel it. I saw them as 'my' people. I could take them somewhere and mold them. They were so receptive—they really wanted to learn."

Now the trio—Mick, Brian, and Keith—decided they needed to sell as much sex as possible, along with their musical image. Mick and Keith wanted to use sexuality to get the band noticed and were overjoyed that Brian knew exactly how to portray that image. They never knew and never asked how Brian had acquired those extra talents—they were simply happy he knew how to use them.

After the band had achieved its fame, Brian admitted, "Don't think I didn't turn on the charm whenever it suited me to do so. I was an actor, you know. I never called doing so wrong, and there were some who I came onto energetically, but they never acted offended—as far as I knew."

Mick already had a natural femininity that, up until now, he had not openly tapped into. Brian offered to open this still-hidden world to him, and Mick eagerly fell in headfirst. He came to enjoy the sensual aspect of almost everything—anything that smelled good, looked good, and felt good, including the sensual touch of silk and lace. Mick liked his make-up, perfumes, and to play dress-up.

When Mick wasn't rehearsing his dance moves, Brian taught him how to match his rugged voice with the R&B sounds the band played. They spent hours going over the notes and beats. Here again, Mick didn't have the ear at that early time to pick up the subtle tones of any given song.

On the opposite end, Brian was born with the ability to hear and play the subtlest shifts in beat or timbre of any song. "My gift was my ear," he was happy to say. "And I could make the sounds work."

Even though he spoke modestly of his ability, other musicians weren't as modest when speaking about Brian's unique gift, and they admired his ability to recognize when a note was no more than a quarter beat off.

The main reason he didn't take on the position as lead singer was due to the fact he had a mellow, refined voice that lent itself more toward folk music. Before Brian met Mick and Keith—while performing on the streets or playing solo in the clubs—he did sing. But, the songs he sang were more folksy-sounding. He didn't have the rugged voice needed to match the rhythm 'n blues his band played.

***

In addition to dancing, strutting, and perfecting the use of his voice, Mick also had to learn to move and walk sensually. He thought Brian's moves irresistible and pleaded with him to help him learn. He eagerly shouted to Brian, "You've got it! Work your wiles!"

Back then, he had no problem feeling and showing his passion and admiration for Brian—as long as no one else knew. As for Brian's thoughts at that time, he said, "Mick was a handsome fellow, and I found him quite appealing. Eventually the girls and boys found him appealing too."

Brian imagined the other Stones suspected the true relationship between him and Mick, but they never said anything. Keith was the only one to witness firsthand the goings on between his two band mates, and he would either look the other way, or roll his eyes with exasperation at their girlie antics.

Within a short period of time, the girlie antics between the pair escalated to full-fledged dress-up. They called it "costuming". Whenever they had spare money, Mick and Brian would run off to stores and buy women's clothes and accessories—scarves, hats, and all. Then they rushed back to their flat and dressed-up, trading off make-up and spraying perfumes on one another.

Of those days, Brian said, "We had great fun! However, Keith had little tolerance and didn't like our games, but then we'd get him really drunk and force him to join in—just a bit. He was a reluctant fellow."

Mick and Brian even did role playing. Brian would always be the glamour queen and mimicked the sirens of the silver screen. Jean Harlow was his favorite and when he "costumed" just right, he bore a striking resemblance to the femme fatale, especially since he was smaller boned, the same as Jean. "Marilyn Monroe was too fat for my liking," he explained.

He went on to say that when they costumed, Mick would portray "the socialite set or sometimes the haggard old aunt. He'd act worldly wise or tight-assed—the type of woman who would beat you over the head with her umbrella!"

A frustrated Keith often called his band mates "idiots!" Brian taunted him back by saying, "You could never be a drag queen, Keith. You've got no charisma!"

In one of his more campy moments, Brian placed a bowl of fruit on his head and mimicked Carmen Miranda. He danced around the flat, while cocking his hips up and down one at a time. Once, when he felt particularly open to talking about those escapades, he compared himself to the female go-go dancers of the time and said, "My moves were always better than theirs; I was smoother, sleeker."

A couple of years later when the Rolling Stones were famous, Brian had fun showing some of his own dance moves to these go-go dancers. He was proud of his androgynous traits and at ease with how he looked and how he moved. He admitted, "I felt comfortable and beautiful in women's clothing, as if I were just 'one of the girls'. Although, Mick was more girlie than I could ever be!"

Mick and he would sit side by side while watching black and white movies on TV. They studied the movements of the glamour queens of that day and of days gone by. When the movies were over, they would then take turns emulating their favorite sirens.

The two were in their element, and they were comfortable with who they were. For them, during those harrowing times of not knowing whether they would ever make it in the music world, the days of carefree playing and costuming were later looked on with much sentimentality.

# CHAPTER TWELVE
## The Leader of the Band

*"I was their leader, sharing my dream and my vision with them. I had to do it myself, see it for myself. My own vision was different from everyone else's in all ways. My expression had to be from me, as I saw it and felt it, and not dictated by others—once I was musically set free."*

Brian Jones

In 1948, six-year old Brian Jones would run from his house in times of turmoil and sit under his favorite tree and seek solace by listening to the music in thundering clouds, rustling leaves, and winds gusting through the treetops. He heard these concerts, complete with choruses of chirping birds, in the same way early man found his solace in those very sounds.

Interestingly, primitive man heard music in many other forms as well. Included among them were sounds heard in breaking waves, babbling brooks, water rhythmically dripping down cave walls, or sounds from crackling fires that also kept them warm, cooked their meals, and warned off predators. This early music was listened to, appreciated, and later on emulated throughout the world, from central Europe to native America, and onto aboriginal Australia. In their own way, sounds from the human heartbeat were considered melodious. As early as 45,000 years ago in Eastern Europe a bear femur was found, which had been hollowed out and then had four small holes carved through it—with each hole purposely spaced evenly for musical fluidity. This was believed to be the first human flute.

More advanced flutes, with either five or eight holes also evenly spaced apart, were later located in China. These were created from the hollow bones of cranes and dated back to approximately 9,000 B.C.

More uniquely, from a graveyard located on a small island in the Aegean Sea, two marble statues were discovered. These dated from 2700-2500 B.C. One statue was of a musician playing a double flute and the other was of a seated musician playing a triangular-shaped harp.

Humans, however, were not the first musicians. Monkeys were known to beat rhythms on hollow logs, and mankind soon copied their originality. Regardless of how, when, where, or by what means musical sounds have been heard or built upon—they've always proven an integral part of both human life and the animal kingdom. The reasons for the desire to create sound, especially hauntingly beautiful, captivating sounds have varied. They ranged from the desire to attract others who might be too far removed from the human voice to hear, an attempt to seduce a lover, or the inherent need to find peace and tranquility of the soul.

Playwright William Congreve's quote, "Music has charms to soothe a savage breast," may just as well have been personally written for Brian Jones. The passage had to be on Brian's mind when he first envisioned making the world a better and happier place to live in, if people would listen to and enjoy the fantastic music he planned to create and play for them.

***

Part of Brian's noble vision included taking his title as the Rollin' Stones leader to heart. He selflessly took upon himself the responsibilities of not only guiding their musical integrity and rehearsal schedules, but also performing the never-ending and sadly unappreciated duties of public relations, booking gigs, locating places to rehearse, and, as he put it—"Did I mention writing songs?"

The public and the media didn't one day simply wake up and realize an R&B band such as the Stones existed. They had to be painstakingly nurtured and led to the awareness of the band's existence. Solely on his own and with no back-up Brian accomplished this task, one of the most important for the band's future. He relentlessly made the time and expended the energy to write, cajole, and pressure publications such as *Jazz News* and media sources such as the *BBC* to come, see, and hear the Stones play—refusing to take no for an answer.

Additionally, he laboriously and with great flare wrote to assorted publications, and detailed his vision for where the sound of rhythm 'n blues was heading. In his opinion, outdated traditional jazz didn't connect to the masses, but instead the earthy, sensual, and soulful sound of the Blues was what the everyday audience desired. He foresaw the future of rock 'n roll heading in the direction of rhythm 'n blues—the type of R&B that his band played.

He also claimed, whereas traditional jazz was mostly comprised of improvisational sounds with almost no emotional basis, R&B related strongly to the inner pain and hidden passions of people in general. Unfortunately, he knew all too well the feelings of anguish and despair, which only the sounds of unforgettable, rousing music could quell.

During his personal visits to the club owners and producers, Brian tirelessly and unashamedly sweet-talked and bragged about his band, which he said was the brightest star for rhythm 'n blues' future. He said, "I was devoted to making the creation of my band into something special. I saw the Stones going all the way to the top."

At the end of 1962, the Rollin' Stones finally came into its own when two significant events occurred. Bill Wyman took over as bassist after Tony Chapman was let go, and—to Brian's great joy—his persistence in hunting down and luring drummer Charlie Watts finally paid off. Charlie decided to leave Alexis Korner's Blues Incorporated for the newer, more innovative R&B sound of Brian's Stones.

As a result, on January 12, 1963, the official band known as the Rollin' Stones played on stage together for the first time at the Flamingo Club. The only difference was that this version of the band included a piano player, Ian "Stu" Stewart.

***

Throughout the many months that Brian worked one on one with Mick—helping him improve the range of his voice, his harmonica playing, and overall stage presence—he continued to juggle his many other duties. He worked on the band's routines and directed the sounds they played. At the same time, he tended to the aforementioned, often unappreciated, and mostly unseen duties as manager, public relations spokesperson, and bookkeeper.

In his books, Bill Wyman openly states that Brian at that time was unquestioningly the band's business manager. He took care of finances and paid the band members equally, after deducting expenses, plus took an additional sum for himself. At that time no one questioned the fact he took a tiny, extra percentage for himself. After all, he was giving freely hour after hour from his personal life to promote the band, in addition to calling, visiting, writing, and otherwise begging, pleading, and cajoling anyone who would listen to the fact that he had put together the greatest R&B band the world would ever know.

The Stones also didn't question how he split their meager incomes. They knew all too well they would not be playing anywhere professionally—and certainly not with promising futures on the horizon—had Brian not been as eager, energetic, and farsighted as they knew him to be.

He had accomplished all this while the rest of the Stones enjoyed their free time or continued with band practice. He didn't need actual practice time because he had already spent much of his life perfecting and creating the groundbreaking sounds, which only he could perform on any instrument put in his hands. His other band mates were content with, or limited to, playing one or two instruments each, with varying proficiency.

Brian did, though, spend much time rehearsing the band—ensuring they were in sync with one another. He rehearsed them as a music teacher rehearses his pupils, giving them what can be compared to work or study assignments. He would say, "Okay, now let's try this…" or "Show me this…do that," and then leave the group to go onto his other managerial chores. He later returned to see and listen to the results of their rehearsal time.

Even with all this guidance, Keith admitted that Brian never spoke down to or treated them as subordinates. He was happy to say Brian treated them all with respect and cheerfully shared his musical knowledge with them as equals.

During this time, Brian had another major brainstorm that he decided to implement, which later became known throughout the industry as pure genius. His idea was that he and Keith should play their guitars duet-style, but instead of matching note for note, they would offset one another. While one guitarist would play music going up the scale the other would play going down the scale. To his dismay, he found it impossible to get Keith excited about any new idea. As a result, he had to literally shove Keith off the couch to wake him and make him work at getting the intense imagery he wanted from the dueling guitar composition.

Once more, his hard work and pitbull tenacity paid off and within a couple of months his brazen idea received rousing success. Both critics and audiences alike said his and Keith's playing together was so harmonious that they couldn't tell whose guitar played which part, or whether the sounds were even coming from one guitar or two.

Brian's theory to put together completely different sounds in an R&B band was highly original and farsighted. As yet, hardly anyone in Britain had heard true rhythm 'n blues music or knew of stars such as Jimmy Reed and Bo Diddley. Audiences had been accustomed to sit and listen politely to regular bands. Now, as they watched the Stones perform, they found themselves dancing, whooping, and hollering, and experiencing sensations in parts of their bodies that they never knew existed.

At the center of each gig—receiving non-stop raves and accolades—was the platinum-haired, petite, and ever-so-sensual leader of the band, Brian Jones. Since personal safety was not yet an issue, at times he would jump into the audience and perform, which drove both males and females into frenzied displays of erotic bliss.

After having lived on the streets for so long, and later starved himself just to have enough money to put food in the mouth of his baby son, or to pay for his band's rehearsal halls, Brian finally felt he had achieved success. No longer would he shiver through the cold European winters without proper shelter or clothing, or relive another near-death experience from double-pneumonia, as he had in France not that long ago.

He had achieved his hard-earned success completely alone and with no family support. The strong support he did have, though, came from the brotherhood of his band. He thought of himself as the driving force pushing his train—the band—uphill all the way. To him, his band mates were cars on the train rushing full speed ahead, striving to reach a vital destination—musical success. Each member of the band played a major link that connected the train, while they followed behind him, their engineer.

At this moment in time, despite feelings of loneliness, he believed he had a reason to live. He was realizing his dream to bring joy to the masses, to whom he felt strongly connected. His dream included forever sharing feelings of joy, laughter, and youthful exuberance through his music. Much later, while reminiscing about his dreams, he said poignantly, "I saw the Stones going all the way to the top. The difference is—I saw myself forever being with them and leading them."

***

Brian's unique, lively stage presence was completely self-taught. He didn't have a model to follow, as Mick had with him. When he was asked why he never wished to attend formal college, he answered, "I had another mission and another type of job in mind. Where was the school to teach me to be a rockstar? At that time I didn't have the words to describe what I intended, but I knew I would take the band someplace really big!"

While he was on stage, he was truly in his element. He lived for the applause and the recognition, but not for himself personally. He never believed that he was something special for his own sake. The recognition for which he thrived was for his music and to finally feel free, to share the joy he felt while playing spectacular music with others, in what he felt was mostly a joyless world.

In December 1962, Alexis Korner—forever Brian's number one fan—clued in John Mansfield, owner of the Ricky-Tick Club in Windsor, to the Stones existence and invited him to watch them perform. Straight away, Mansfield recognized Brian as the band's absolute leader and admired his raw edginess and ability to capture an audience. He quickly signed the Stones to his club, and as they continued to perform at the Ricky-Tick, they developed an avid and wild fan base. The enthusiastic boys and girls who came to watch them night after night helped spread the word of the band's amazing gigs. Some audiences fondly remember seeing the Stones nonchalantly play each evening, while coolly smoking their cigs and sipping their beers in between songs. This was all part of Brian's grand scheme to have his band appear confidant, giving the audiences the impression they were seasoned professionals.

Throughout the years, John Mansfield maintained great respect for Brian and said, had he lived, he could eventually see Brian's soulful personality taking an active role as protector and spokesman for animal rights and the Earth.

***

Nonetheless, despite all the regional attention, the Stones still hadn't made it big in the music industry. They were close but still far from realizing their dream of stardom. Brian realized the importance of making and keeping the right contacts, and he continued to meet with the press and with his letter-writing campaign on the band's behalf. When asked if writing so often to magazines and the press helped, he said, "Yes, and I thought it was necessary. It made them aware of our existence, and that's what I was trying to do."

He had an easy manner of speaking with people in positions of power. They found him believable, were taken in by his charismatic personality, and of course, his sensuality. Naturally, he was the consummate actor and would stroke them along when necessary. In these instances the stroking wasn't sexual but the stroking of the mind that was necessary when he had to appeal to men in positions of power, which in itself was a fine art.

On the other hand, Mick Jagger had neither the flair for doing the same, nor the basic knowledge as to how best negotiate with and ingratiate these people—which he knew Brian could do effortlessly. Nevertheless, Mick did know enough to assiduously study Brian, memorize his techniques, and eventually strive to make them his own.

Another businessman, Glyn Johns owner of the Red Lion Club, also took special notice of Brian and his band. Additionally, Glyn was senior engineer for a recording studio and was happy to arrange for the Stones to cut their first official five-track demo and present it to Decca Records. Brian was proud of this achievement and thought of it as a major stepping-stone. Decca, though, didn't share the band's enthusiasm and turned the tape down. Regardless, Brian remained especially upbeat for what he considered a landmark event. Of this he said, "Yes, that was a big deal! I was happy, scared, and nervous all at the same time."

Brian's Rollin' Stones stood on the threshold of stardom. They could feel it; they could taste it. Of them all, however, no one deserved to feel the euphoria, the sweet smell of success, and at the same time, the intense pressure more than the leader of the band.

Brian had fought and clawed his way, as he put it, "from out of the bottom." He had been on his own since the age of sixteen and had very brief respites where he enjoyed any family life. For most of his years, he had gone cold and hungry. Those years of deprivation would have destroyed the healthiest and sturdiest of young men, let alone someone like Brian who was born with many infirmities—both of mind and body. He explained, "I coughed blood from time to time from the beginning of my life, and I weakened as time passed. I remember my sister, Pamela, dying from tuberculosis, and that kept the fear of dying from respiratory ailment and infection within me."

Tragically, at the still tender age of twenty-one and at the dawn of a totally new era—not only for him personally, but also for the world of R&B music—Brian began to feel the oncoming breakdown of his body. With the hours upon hours and days upon days that he had spent, and continued to spend, trying to get the band recognized—these all added to his already debilitated state.

Unknown to any of his band mates, he possessed a deep fear of falling apart. Nevertheless, keeping leadership of the band that he dreamed about for so long was of the utmost importance to him. That leadership was proof that he deserved to live and that he had earned the right to live.

He gave unto others probably the most brilliant acting performances of his life—when he felt they were needed, in order to keep that leadership—that of a healthy, young, adult male, who was in charge of his faculties.

## CHAPTER THIRTEEN
### Between a Rock & a Hard Place

*"In the beginning Brian ran the band. But he really wanted to be called the leader of the band. I didn't particularly want to be the leader.*
*There WASN'T a leader."*

Mick Jagger, 1979

*"The Rolling Stones that I joined was led by Brian Jones. There was no doubt who led the group in every way. Brian called the shots…."*

Bill Wyman, 1990

*"Mick was now my pimp in sending me out to do the job, including giving sex. Everything was okay as long as I did all the dirty work."*

Brian Jones

By the Spring of 1963, Brian had known Mick Jagger and Keith Richard for one year. The trio's complex relationship began with Brian seeking musicians for his new band, and with the latter two looking to hook up with him, after watching him perform. From the beginning, Keith was hypnotized by Brian's ability to put together great music, while Mick was also taken in by Brian's irrefutable charisma and talent, but to a lesser degree.

The three had now also lived together for several months, during which time the bonds among them had changed drastically. What started out as nothing more than sexual chemistry and playtime between Brian and Mick soon turned into full-fledged love. The love wasn't intentional and not even desired—but both men could no longer pretend it didn't exist.

Brian wasn't as opposed to these strong feelings as Mick. Brian had never known the strong ties of family life or love, whereas Mick had come from a strong, stable background. Because of his stable background, Mick was independent by nature, while Brian displayed independence that had been thrust upon him by what could laughingly be referred to as his family. At this stage of his life, he was tired of being alone and tired of having to make personal decisions for himself. He needed someone to lean on and someone he could give his trust to, unconditionally.

Mick had proven his love to Brian by demonstrating it physically. Hell, he had freely given his male virginity to Brian! When Brian was later asked how Mick felt about allowing another male to penetrate him for the first time, he answered, "It was hard on Mick initially, but he wasn't scared at all. He was eager to experiment by that time of our relationship—although he would never admit it out loud."

Brian loved Mick's free spirit, forceful nature, and the fact that Mick was—at least in Brian's eyes—strong, stable, and grounded. Mick's overall appearance was aggressive and masculine. Brian admired those qualities in him and wished that he possessed more of those traits. He was always fearful, as he put it, "of coming undone, going over the wall, and completely unraveling." Hiding this inner fear was a constant struggle—all part of his manic-depressive disorder that no one knew existed. Brian lived each day hiding and trying to manage, as best he could, what he sadly thought of as his major weakness.

Simultaneously, Mick came to adore Brian as his lover and wanted to share all his time with him. Mick would gaze at Brian, and—as a mutual acquaintance once said—"He looked like he wanted to eat Brian up! He couldn't get enough of him." (Photo #804)

One major trait that both men shared, and that they respected in one another, was that they were extremely bright and able to measure up other people's strengths and weaknesses. Unfortunately, as time passed one would use that trait to destroy the other.

But for now, Mick looked upon his petite, blonde lover as a doll or toy that he could be passionate about and at the same time play with. For him, his feelings of love for Brian were especially confusing because not only was Brian his gorgeous lover to enjoy and explore, but he also was Mick's leader and teacher. Mick had to accept that he needed Brian for career guidance, and needed him badly. At this time of his life Mick had no imagination and no lively spirit with which to experiment and broaden his horizons. He could never be the risk taker. For all these special qualities that he desired more than life, Mick desperately needed Brian's tutelage.

Additionally, Mick was very jealous of Brian's every move and didn't want him to see anyone else. For Brian, that was impossible. No matter how much he might care for Mick, he would never give up his freedom to pick and choose who he wanted to see socially—whether that person was male or female. When it came to selecting whom to bed down, Brian said, "The world was my oyster!"

Outwardly, he chose to only be seen with girls, since he knew all too well how dangerous showing signs of bi-sexuality or homosexuality could be. Interestingly, he never flirted with another male by stating his desires aloud. He had taught himself well how to say what he wanted with his eyes and with his gaze. His mum had taught him the fine art of female seduction. Naturally, had he not been born with androgynous qualities, he never would have responded so openly to her tutelage.

To many who knew him, he appeared as not belonging to either sex at all times. When he felt masculine, he was very masculine. He had a deep voice, a perfectly firm "T" shaped body, and possessed intense upper-body strength. He was aggressive and explosive when it came to getting what he wanted.

But on days when he felt especially feminine, he could easily play, flirt, and move as gracefully as any femme fatale. His long blond hair, lively blue-green eyes, and exceptional skin—together with his small physique—made it easy to imagine him girlie. And, it was this girlie presence that Mick fell in love with. When Mick refused to share Brian with anyone else, the two men began to fight a battle of wills that grew in intensity with each day. Brian was naturally flirtatious and couldn't help how attractive he was to either sex. If Mick even thought Brian was returning another's advances, he would go wild with anger and threaten to break off all further ties with him, unless he promised to stay faithful.

Brian said, "Mick mostly didn't want me seeing other men. He didn't mind women so much, as long as they didn't take up too much of my time. It wasn't too big a deal, as long as I didn't spend too much time with them. But, if Mick even thought one of his girlfriends was looking at me, he'd crush her silently with his looks."

***

During that year Brian's relationship with Keith Richard had also changed into a strong bond between brothers.

Keith was the consummate heterosexual male and found Brian and Mick's love confusing to deal with and understand. Keith and Mick had been friends since childhood, and each understood the other implicitly. Now that Brian had come into their lives and turned the relationship into a threesome, things became complicated. Nevertheless, Keith truly welcomed his new feelings toward Brian as a brother, especially since he admired Brian for his musical genius. In those days, Keith couldn't brag loudly enough to anyone who would listen about Brian's musical prowess and his business sense.

For his part, Brian thrived on having Keith as his big brother, despite the fact Keith was one year younger. Age had nothing to do with his feelings toward Keith's acting as his long-lost, big brother. Brian longed to have someone just like Keith as protector, friend, and confidant. The two didn't need to talk much to one another in order to understand what the other was thinking or wanted—which worked out very well for them since Keith's method of speaking was mostly monosyllabic.

For Brian, Keith was the protector he had needed all the years when he was alone on the streets and when he'd been unable to protect himself and defend himself against the bigger, stronger predators.

Conversely in Brian, Keith found someone to look up to, want to follow, and learn from musically. Keith saw the musical genius in Brian, as everyone did. Fortunately for him, since he and Brian worked together so closely, he became the immediate recipient of Brian's genius, became inspired by it, grew from it, learned from it, and played off it. Brian said, "One thing I can say about Keith is that he's very good at jumping into a sound, getting inside it, and working with it."

Keith's connection to work with Brian was an extraordinary opportunity for him, because without Brian's influences his playing would have been dull, boring, and unimaginative.

On the other hand, Mick's jealousy toward the newfound friendship between his band mates was obvious. He wanted to keep Keith's friendship all to himself and at the same time wanted to keep Brian's love all to himself.

***

Regardless of how the interactions between any two of the three may have been reshaped and rewritten, one basic truism existed. They were now a band of brothers, not three individuals playing in a band, but three brothers playing in a band. They were a family who ate together, slept together, hurt together, and played together.

For Brian, this feeling of family had the most meaning because he never had brothers to lean on, talk to, and depend upon. In Brian's mind they were a brotherhood when Keith was included in the equation, but when the equation was between Mick and him, the two became a sisterhood. Therefore, that was how they took to saying to one another, "I love you, sister." When speaking to Keith, it was always, "I love you, brother."

Brian said with a laugh, "Keith was always the brother among us. It was fun! But me, even when I was at home, I was always one of the girls."

Like true sisters, when Brian and Mick argued or disagreed over how things should be done, they didn't fight like men but like women. "We were totally bitchy to each other. We were vicious," Brian said honestly.

\*\*\*

Although the relationship among the three may have changed, the one constant that remained was the fact Brian was the leader of the band. Because of that, Brian was the one to first approach Giorgio Gomelsky (see Chapter Nine) owner of the successful Crawdaddy Club for the chance to have his band play. He held nothing back with Giorgio, when he begged and pleaded to be heard. "We're the best band in the land, Giorgio," he whispered time and again.

Not only was Brian confidant in the Stones ability to gain a large fan base, but he also knew Giorgio harbored a certain feeling for him personally. "No sex was ever exchanged between us," he said candidly, "but Giorgio wanted it bad!" As a result, he played Giorgio along and soon had his Stones playing the Crawdaddy as the house band. Here, the group's following reached numbers they never could have imagined.

With each performance, Brian's hot-blooded harmonica, or blues harp, playing grew in passion and intensity, and he held everyone mesmerized. The fans found him raw, earthy, and completely irresistible.

Up 'til then Mick hadn't played much blues harp, but Brian wanted him to be able to take over whenever they had to perform live. Since Brian would also be needed on guitar, he had to teach Mick to play. Eventually, Mick became proficient enough to perform on the blues harp, but he never could attain the sounds and emotions that Brian could. To anyone who watched the band perform, it was clear that Brian didn't simply play the mouth organ—he ate, breathed, and lived the sounds he so masterfully generated. The instruments came in different sizes and shapes, and he drew sounds from each that no musicians had previously heard.

Giorgio was among those who saw the genius behind Brian's playing, and to show his true admiration, he arranged for the already-famous Beatles to come to the Crawdaddy and hear the Stones. Since John Lennon and Company's presence would make any new band nervous, Giorgio decided it best not to inform Brian, until right before the Beatles were due to arrive, that he and the Stones would be performing for them.

Even though Brian at first felt awestruck, by the time the Beatles arrived he was completely relaxed and performed at his very best. John Lennon couldn't believe what he saw and heard coming from Brian's blues harp and immediately became a huge fan, approaching hero worship. Even though Brian had outwardly appeared relaxed and sure of himself while Lennon watched, inwardly he felt the opposite. He said, "You know, I nearly shit my pants! I hope, from John's perspective, that he enjoyed hearing me play. He said very little, but the joy on his face and the light in his eyes thrilled me. He said, 'Good job, Man!' and I took it to heart. It's something beyond description—to be idolized by your own idol."

Brian had the ability to suck and manipulate a harmonica as if he were giving oral sex, and Lennon wasn't the only one to feel a sexual experience taking place while watching him perform. His ever vibrant, penetrating eye contact with the audience made the imagery of watching a porno film experience a fait accompli.

When the Stones were finished for the evening, the Beatles accompanied them back to their Edith Grove flat. For the first time, what would later become known as the world's two foremost rock bands got together to discuss their careers and enjoy a spontaneous jam session.

Soon after, Giorgio invited the editor of the Record Mirror, Peter Jones, to watch the Stones perform. Peter was also taken in by Brian and said he recognized him as the one who "reigned over every single move" the band made. In turn, Peter arranged for a relatively new nineteen-year old public relations representative, Andrew Loog Oldham, to visit the Crawdaddy. Andrew brought Eric Easton along to share the experience. At the time Eric was a full-time agent for mildly popular musical artists.

Both Eric and Andrew were so impressed with what they saw and heard, they immediately decided to talk management with the Stones. At first Andrew spoke for Eric, and he walked over to Brian to discuss business. He approached with the attitude that he was doing the band a favor, which didn't sit well with Brian. When Andrew offered his hand, Brian glared him down. Andrew felt so intimidated that he turned on his heels and talked to Mick instead. He found Mick much more approachable, without realizing he was trying to negotiate with the wrong spokesperson.

\*\*\*

The truth was that by the time Oldham and Easton approached the Stones, Brian was feeling worn down. He was physically sick from the many aches and pains his thin body continued to fight, and mentally and emotionally tired from the many months of doing all the managerial work. Added to this was the fact he still guided the band's musical development, along with tutoring Mick to properly sing, speak, and walk the walk of a pop star.

Additionally, he was sick and tired of having to grovel at the feet of the club owners and other "mackies"—a phrase he personally developed that referred to assorted gofers and assistants. Many of these men went so far as to insist that the band act as procurers for the drugs they wanted. Rock bands who hadn't achieved any degree of stardom were expected to perform such subservient acts. As Brian put it, "We were expected to provide drugs—pot, coke, and amphetamines—at different times for different workers in the clubs. They would give us the money, and we'd pass it on to whomever we knew would hook us up. It was all part of getting along."

Brian never used drugs himself when dealing with the clubs. He explained, "I had to have my faculties about me. It was business. I couldn't make the mistakes then that I wound up making later on." Even so, he was bitter about the way he was treated. "I had to have all the confidence, all the wherewithal, the determination, and the drive to hold the group together and to sell the band to those idiots. And then, I had to act beholden for the opportunity to play in some dive!"

When asked if Mick and Keith realized he had to put himself through all this groveling, he answered, "They just assumed that I would, and they knew I had finesse in handling things. They were naïve and in a world they never even imagined—but they got over that really quickly. Mick was now my pimp in sending me out to do the job, including giving sex. Everything was okay as long as I did all the dirty work."

However, Brian came to realize he couldn't do it all any longer and do any of it well. Always a perfectionist, he feared that wearing too many hats had worn down his level-headedness, and he might fail his band musically unless he let go of most of the managerial and bookkeeping duties. As a result he decided, after meeting with Easton and Oldham several times, to sign the band to a three-year management contract with the pair's newly formed company, Impact Sound. He signed "L B Jones"—his legal name, and Eric Easton signed on behalf of management. (Photo #803)

Brian found Easton—despite the fact Eric was approximately fifteen years older—much more agreeable to deal with, and whenever possible he bypassed Oldham and went directly to Eric when business matters needed to be thrashed out. Something about Andrew turned Brian off, whereas something in Eric made him feel comfortable and secure.

Due to Brian's uneasiness in releasing any of his decision-making powers, he studied the contract offered the band over and over. He felt caught between the proverbial rock and a hard place. On the one hand, he knew he couldn't do everything alone any longer and be everything to everyone. On the other hand, he was naturally fearful of relinquishing any of the authority he had worked so hard to attain. He said, "I had a good business eye and good business sense. Even though I had a strong creative eye for music, I also instinctively knew what made good business sense and what did not. I was destined to lead my own band—but then I felt pulled and pushed in different directions.

"Part of me resisted and resented needing other managers to handle the money and the situation, because I wanted to keep control. I wanted to still handle things, but it really had gotten too big for me, and I had to let go. It was a cyclical thing and meant to be just the way it was."

He was gifted in that he had the talent for music and also knew how to put it all out there, promote it, and be on the cutting edge. He possessed the knowledge as to how to dress the band up, make them up, and teach them how to seduce audiences. He was at the forefront of knowing which buttons to push, to make his band more and more popular.

During this important time, two major decisions with regard to name changes were implemented. The first was to change the band's name to the Rolling Stones and the second was to have Keith add an 's' to the end of his name, making it Richards.

One of the first business decisions Oldham made was to have Ian "Stu" Stewart dropped from the band. His reasoning, which he explained to Brian and the others, was that six on stage was too many for an audience to focus on, and more importantly, that Stu did not fit the band's raw, rebellious image. (Photo #823) In Oldham's opinion, this move was a necessity that left no room for debate.

Brian grudgingly agreed, but then had the bombshell dropped on him by Oldham that he should be the one—as leader of the band—to tell Stu he was no longer a Rolling Stone. Brian dutifully did the dirty work and promised Stu he would always receive a share of whatever monies the band made—as recognition for all he had done on their behalf. He asked Stu if he would stay on—travel with the group and act as a roadie—and also fill in on piano whenever the band needed him. Naturally Stu was stunned, but he accepted the paltry offer Brian made. This was partially due to the fact he was too embarrassed to admit he had been let go and partially due to the fact he truly loved the band.

The other Stones—Charlie, Bill, Mick, and Keith—didn't show much emotion in seeing Stu treated so shabbily. According to Brian, "They were all too star struck after witnessing the Beatles success."

***

For Brian Jones and the Rolling Stones, the years 1963-64 were pivotal. Many changes were taking place, and the band was receiving recognition from the press, media, television studios, and most importantly, the recording studios.

In May '63, Brian personally signed the band's first recording contract with Decca Records. Since he had been negotiating the deal on his own, he completed the transaction without input from Impact Sound.

During this time, the band recorded their first single—chosen personally by Andrew Oldham—entitled *Come On*. However, none of the Stones, including Brian, liked the song and were so ambivalent to its existence that they refused to play it at their live performances.

Between June '63 and May '64 several single records and albums were produced and sold in the United Kingdom, and beginning with March '64, the Stones' first United States hit single *Not Fade Away* was released.

Television had become the most popular medium for the bands to attract large audiences, and the Stones made countless live appearances on *Thank Your Lucky Stars* and *Ready, Steady, Go!* among others. (Photo #805) During these appearances, Brian sang, danced, and camped his way through several improvisational sketches—among the most noteworthy and humorous was one in which he mimicked "Sonny" from Sonny & Cher.

He and Mick shared microphones and center stage equally. Mick was by no means ready to take the position of frontman yet, and Brian was thrilled to continue fronting his band. Critics said of those times that, when being interviewed during live performances, Mick would look down or away from the camera and mumble incoherent, juvenile-sounding sentences, while Brian spoke with warmth, finesse, and ease.

During the year 1964 and thereafter, innumerable color and black and white magazines were published dedicated to the lives of the Rolling Stones. Brian personally arranged for much of this publicity, despite the fact Easton and Oldham represented the band. He explained, "I worked my butt off. I kept in contact with everybody around who would give us publicity or do anything about us. You know, I was our own press agent. I enjoyed it, and it worked."

He further joked, "I had more personality than management. Tell me, who would you rather talk to, me or management?"

In all the band's camera shots Brian took center position, with a meek-looking Mick Jagger staring off into the distance. Brian had the most sensuous of poses ready for any occasion. One in particular stands out with the group standing outside in line formation, with Brian at the helm—left hand posed seductively on his hip, head tilted to one side with its full mane of hair glistening under the sunlight, while his sultry eyes played coquettishly for the camera.

The Stones spoke proudly of their leader and felt proud of the heights to which he was taking them. August '63 saw the Stones perform at England's renowned Richmond Jazz Festival. Brian personally selected the outfits for the band to wear, after the disastrous results they had when Oldham earlier selected horrid hounds-tooth jackets for them.

From July through September 1963 the band conducted their first domestic tour of the UK, which consisted of seventy-six days at various clubs and ballrooms, including the prestigious Studio 51.

Eric Easton also arranged for the Stones to be part of the Everly Brothers 1963 UK tour that included celebrated entertainers Little Richard and Bo Diddley. The New Musical Express (NME) of August '63 quotes Brian as saying, "For us, the big thrill is that Bo Diddley will be on the bill. He's been one of our great influences."

Brian's respect for Bo Diddley was reciprocated when the Stones recorded their second song, the Lennon/McCartney composition, *I Wanna Be Your Man*. For the first time ever on a British recorded disc, Brian pioneered the unique sound that emanated from this recording, when he played bottleneck guitar. Not only was Keith, as usual, taken aback by Brian's inventiveness by stating, "Brian made that record with that bottleneck!" but Bo Diddley was also greatly impressed. He described Brian as, "A little dude that was trying to pull the group ahead. I saw him as the leader. He didn't take no mess. He was a fantastic cat and handled the group beautifully."

The 'B' side of this recording, called *Stoned*, became the first official production of Brian's original music publishing company, which he named Nanker-Phelge Music, Ltd. (See Chapter Ten)

The connection between Brian's Stones and the Beatles continued, when the former band was asked to open for the Beatles on September 15, 1963, at London's Royal Albert Hall. After the resounding reception the Stones received, their popularity and ability to capture an audience was never questioned.

In October '63 Brian contacted Eric Easton and requested on behalf of his band that Eric arrange their first United States tour.

November '63 saw the opening of another extensive tour in the UK, in which the Rolling Stones were featured for the first time as headliners.

There was no longer any doubt among the Stones that Brian's dream of putting together "the best band in the land" had reached fruition. Interestingly and to his credit personally, the Kellogg Company commissioned Brian in 1963 to write a jingle for their Rice Krispies commercial. The ever-famous thirty-second tune *Wake Up In the Morning* was composed entirely by him.

***

All within the music industry saw the Rolling Stones, and especially their leader Brian Jones, as the bright new stars on the horizon. 1963 had been an exceptional year for the band. For Brian, this rush to stardom was proof positive that, by following his gut instinct all those years, he had been right on. His fans loved both him and his band. (Photo #807) He was destined to spread the harmony and exhilaration that could be derived from R&B music.

While the radiant light of musical genius cast upon his handsome outward appearance, so too did the dark, sinister light of physical and emotional turmoil take permanent seed within his young soul.

Towards the end of August '63 and into September of the same year, he began to miss a series of live performances. The excuse given was that he had collapsed from nervous exhaustion. At the time that was the only term the medical community could give for all the debilitating symptoms that attacked him simultaneously.

He had just come to realize what was only the beginning of all his future successes, and for which he had worked so hard to attain, despite the odds that continued to work against him. Among these early successes were the management and recording contracts he had signed, together with the band's well-received soundtracks, and most importantly, the personal praise and recognition he began to receive from renowned entertainers such as the Beatles and Bo Diddley.

Tragically, Brian's deepest fears of coming undone appeared to be materializing—fears that he had hidden away so well from the rest of the Stones and his girlfriend of the past few months, a dark-haired and dark-eyed beauty named Linda Lawrence. The only way he could explain away the collapse that so weakened him—and that prevented him from doing the one thing in the world that brought him great pleasure, playing music—was by saying, "I felt like I was losing it. I felt sick inside like I couldn't move one foot in front of the other. I felt like I was losing my mind—deeply depressed and physically exhausted. There were times when I had deep paranoia about the whole process, like I was going to be consumed or eaten alive, as if a foreboding. I felt they were going to consume me, like it was a bad nightmare that I couldn't wake up from—the crowds, the public, the world."

He had fought the good fight for so long, alone. Now, he decided that in order to keep his sanity and his health he needed to get away from living with Mick and Keith, at least for a while. He wanted, as he said, "a semblance of normalcy in my life," and decided to move in with Linda and her family. He further added, "I went there in part to rest and have something that felt normal. I did what I thought was best, but it ultimately proved to be a bad chess move. I didn't want to always be under Mick and Keith's constant scrutiny, at least for a while. It was very awkward, to stay together with them. We needed the separation for sure. It was hard to maintain relationships, plus the music. Stones morning, Stones nights, Stones days—it was all too much.

"I needed to maintain my own individuality. I felt suffocated, smothered, absorbed into the pack instead of feeling like myself—separate and whole. Not that Mick or Keith were trying to make me feel any certain way. I just couldn't be in the same place with the same people all the time. You have to remember that I had spent so much of my time in isolation, whether it was in my head creating music, while on the streets, or making plans for the future. For me to be with others all the time, as ringleader, teacher, master—all those different roles—it was just too much"

# CHAPTER FOURTEEN
## A House Divided

*"Every kingdom divided against itself shall be made desolate:
and every city or house divided against itself shall not stand."*
Matthew XII.25

Tightly knit rock bands were and always have been a brotherhood like any other brotherhood, whether they were formed from police officers, baseball and football players, or military units. For Brian, the firm belief in brotherhood and family was the foundation upon which he had built his band. Within this belief system he placed a strong sense of responsibility on his leadership and loyalty towards his group, the Rolling Stones. The band didn't start out as five or six guys who wanted to form their own band, but with Brian, individually, who wanted to form a band of his own.

When Eric Easton had suggested to Brian that Mick's voice wasn't good enough or strong enough to last performance after performance, and therefore he needed to be replaced, Brian disagreed. (See Chapter Eleven) At first he had given it some thought, since Eric was the one to make the suggestion, and he wanted to show his new manager the proper respect by mulling the pro's and con's. Brian was still troubled over the fact that he had earlier been forced—at Oldham's insistence—to let Stu go as the sixth Stone (See Chapter Thirteen) and so this time he stood firm and refused to acquiesce to Eric's proposal.

Regardless, somehow Ian "Stu" Stewart overheard the initial discussion between Eric and Brian over whether to let Mick go, and he ran to Mick to inform him of Brian's imminent act of betrayal. This was Stu's small-minded, malicious attempt to get even with Brian for firing him. Once again, Brian had been caught between a rock and a hard place, and Mick—instead of coming to Brian directly and talking over the situation—decided to forever harbor a resentment against his lover and forever seek retribution. For Brian, this misunderstanding continued to snowball and would later on have disastrous consequences for his future, and ultimately for his life.

Of that time Brian said, "When Eric first suggested it, no, I didn't say it was okay. I knew there were better singers, but I wanted to work it out with Mick. Think about it—if I had wanted to let Mick go and I had said 'yes,' to Eric—Mick would've been gone. Don't you recall that I chose Mick? And, I didn't want to let him go. I knew he didn't have the best voice, but so what? We weren't about the best voice; we were about raunchy and bluesy. What's more, I never wanted to let Stu go either. For me, it was all about loyalty, but that also meant I had to do what was best for the band."

Andrew Oldham also backed Brian in keeping Mick, and the decision to let him go for a more seasoned singer was never acted upon.

***

Once Brian moved away from Edith Grove and moved in with Linda Lawrence, Mick and Keith took up residence with Andrew Oldham, at a separate flat on Mapesbury Road. At the time Brian made the move to separate from the pair, at least physically and emotionally, he sincerely thought it best for everyone. Normally, whenever he followed his gut instincts they proved accurate, but sadly not this time. Had he the choice to reconsider that living arrangement, he never would have separated himself from his band mates.

He said that, yes, the five continued to tour together but, "I still needed a reprieve of some sort. I was trying to get my personal life back on track, and unfortunately, it wound up serving a different purpose than what I thought. Moving away made me the outsider."

Once Brian was out and away from Mick and Keith, Oldham—who harbored a not-so-secret passion for Mick—took full advantage of that time to backstab, falsify, and exaggerate everything that Brian said or every move he made.

One such exaggeration was that Brian was full of himself, jealous of the Beatles fame, and determined to overtake their success and their fan base. Nothing could be further from the truth. Brian said, "No, I didn't personally seek the fans' adoration. Plus, the screaming girls were a painful price to pay for the fame. Of course I wanted our band to be on top of the heap, and my driving motivation remained music and communicating through music. The fact I wanted us to be successful did not mean I was envious of the Beatles in a negative way. Did I feel competitive with them? Yes, absolutely yes! But, it was a business matter, and I respected them musically, wanted their respect for our music as well, and hoped to attain it. And, I believe we did."

Those weren't the words of a man who was full of himself, but the words of a man who was objective and sought a healthy, competitive relationship with another band that he admitted to idolizing.

From the beginning that the two men—Brian Jones and Andrew Loog Oldham—set eyes upon one another the die was cast, although subtly at first, that the latter would set out to destroy the former. Despite constant rumors put out by what was later called the "Stones machine", Brian was never a conniver, schemer, or a traitor, and because of that he never saw the bullet coming from Oldham's well-oiled gun.

Brian felt secure with Eric Easton's decision-making from the beginning but never felt the same with Oldham. On the flip side, he did have a definite reason for bringing Oldham on as co-manager. He said, "Andrew was a fast talker and at that time there weren't many people who had any actual experience of taking anyone (a band) anywhere that we were trying to go. My decision to go with him felt okay at first, but then—call it my intuition, gut instinct, whatever—caused it not to feel as good. With Andrew, there was no warm and fuzzy. It was like he was looking down his nose at me, as if I wasn't so much. Just something about my attitude or arrogance, I think."

In reality Andrew saw much of himself in Brian, and what he saw he didn't like. Andrew was extremely feminine and immediately felt the need to compete with Brian for Mick's attention. "Oldham saw Mick as the stud, for sure. He acted more like a bitch than a man," Brian explained. "Andrew's a slimy, greedy bastard who masturbated with the thought of being subservient to Mick."

He perceived Oldham's attitude as laughable at first and tried to ignore it. Unfortunately for him, Oldham wouldn't let go and from this a personal vendetta against the man he perceived as his fair-haired, blue-eyed rival was born.

Easton and Brian both shared the view that the best way for the Stones to compete with the Beatles for fans was to highlight the differences in both their music and their appearance. The Beatles portrayed a more conservative appearance in their choice of clothing and hairstyles. They had nicely kempt, trim hair and were always seen wearing perfectly fitting suits or sports jackets.

Brian and his Stones preferred the appearance of just getting out of bed with their hairstyles—except for Brian, who was called Mr. Shampoo by his mates for having the most meticulously kept, luxurious hair of any rock star. Even so, his hair still looked unruly—as if it were having an argument with the rest of the world. Brian had a mysterious air about him, in which his long, blonde bangs shadowed much of his face, at times even covering his brilliant eyes. Whether consciously or subconsciously, he didn't want the rest of the world to ever see the well-hidden tight fuse that held him together.

The Stones attire was mostly comprised of high-heeled boots, jeans, and pullover shirts or sweaters—very casual and not meant to look uniform. Ties, suits, and sports jackets were worn when necessary for formal photo shoots or TV appearances. They didn't smile much or look directly into the camera, except for their leader. Brian liked to pose smartly, wanting always to give the appearance of the one in charge of the band.

Both the Beatles and their fans gave the appearance of supporting the more conservative lifestyle and outlook of the time, whereas the Stones made a particular point of demonstrating the rebellious aspect of the day's youth. They were anti-government and anti-establishment, and were proud to let their fans know it. While the Beatles music was wholesome and grounded, the Stones preferred the raw, earthy sounds of the Blues.

In many ways there was no competition between these two super bands, since their fan bases were entirely different. More often than not, Beatles fans would never buy Stones music or attend one of their concerts, and vice versa.

Even though Easton and Brian wanted to portray the band as anti-establishment, they knew the benefits of maintaining the proper etiquette and decorum needed when they dealt with the press and their fans. Brian spoke with ease and grace when addressing both and ensured his band mates did the same. He wanted the Stones fans to look upon them as if the band was on their side, and said, "We were the leaders of the revolution against the established norm."

Andrew Oldham had quite the opposite viewpoint of what he wanted the band to represent. As soon as Brian became physically separated from Mick and Keith, he started his campaign to undo everything Brian had worked so hard to uphold over the previous year and a half.

"Every single thing about my story and the Stones story has two distinct sides," Brian took time to explain. "It was all a dichotomy, because I wanted to put my best foot forward to the public, and yet I agreed to be the leader of the 'bad boy band', and so it was hard to tell which was the act and which was true. Still, I never wanted it to go down that I would actually be this degenerate, this idiot who couldn't form sentences—so everything was the dichotomy. Oldham wanted us to be the rebellious, raunchy rockers, but he didn't want to deal with the personal repercussions of that either—and so, the conundrum was our outward projection toward the public versus what was actually going on internally with the band. Oldham and I constantly battled over that in many, many ways—personally and individually."

Once Oldham got his claws dug into Mick's and Keith's psyches, however, their outlooks quickly changed. Without Brian there to constantly guide them, they fell under the spell of Oldham's theory that the band needed to act as stupid, loutish, ornery, and mean-spirited as they possibly could for interviews, and the public in general. Charlie Watts and Bill Wyman didn't necessarily subscribe to that theory, but that didn't matter since they hardly ever acted as frontmen or spokesmen for the band. They did, however, act as sheep in following Mick and Keith's antics, which got worse and more despicable as time went on.

Brian, as the still-recognized leader of the band, found himself having to defend the Stone's actions to the press and television reporters. This was an unwelcome and uncomfortable task for him, since in reality he didn't agree with that code of conduct. At the same time, he felt fiercely loyal to the Stones and vowed to defend them, no matter what he actually felt inside. Of course he was no angel, either, and at times he did act as rudely and crudely as any of them—especially later, while he was under the influence of drugs or alcohol. However, up until then such behavior had not been his usual code of conduct or the one with which he felt most comfortable.

Oldham began one of his cruelest and most overly-exaggerated campaigns against Brian's integrity when he whispered, behind Brian's back, to the other band members that Brian insisted upon being paid the exorbitant sum of five British pounds per week. Yes, that was true but never true in the sphere that Brian though about himself special in any way.

As stated, he still conducted many extra duties and accepted many extra responsibilities on behalf of the band, of which he was so fond. He happily kept up with press releases, writing to the media, handling the all-important fan mail, booking expenses, and the constant everyday expense of getting the band from one place to the other. He and Easton had an open agreement that he would receive this extra sum to compensate for all his time—of which he had given freely for so long.

Before Easton was put in charge of handling the band's finances, Brian had done it all on his own, and at times he had taken out extra money to compensate for his work and his time—that is, when there was any extra money. Most of the time there had been none, and Brian had resorted to literally stealing and pocketing money from whichever establishment he worked. (See Chapter Seven)

Sadly, once Oldham framed his accusations the way he did, the rest of the Stones forgot all the dirty work Brian had performed on their behalf, since the day they met. Naturally, he felt extremely hurt over the shortsightedness on the part of his brothers. To him, family loyalty was above all, and he never would have taken anything he didn't think he deserved. Plus, he surely didn't think he was stealing money from his own band!

Unfortunately for Brian, being so wrongfully and heinously accused was only one of many cruel cuts that he would begin to suffer at the hands of the man—Andrew Loog Oldham—who considered him a threat to his personal goal, which was to have Mick's attention all to himself. Quite bitterly, Brian said, "Taking the money was my way of trying to maintain the leadership position over my band. I was still doing all the extra work. The leader is the leader, and I was still trying to be the leader. It was my band, and I created it.

"There were band expenses that still had to be covered. But, it did give them a reason to feel negatively about me, and it was fodder for the whispering and the rumors. It was something they could take and say, 'Yeah, yeah, we aren't getting our fair share'—but no one looked at why! They regarded me suspiciously, and I would say, 'I'm booking this; I'm doing that.' I thought they should know everything cost money. And yet, they called me self-absorbed!

"I explained things often by saying, 'covering expenses, covering expenses.' I was devoted to the concept of turning the band into something special, no matter what the cost. At the time, I was frankly relieved when Oldham took over. But I didn't realize what was coming; I just saw hiring management as a burden off me, and then the guys couldn't blame me for what they thought were discrepancies. Of course, they didn't mind paying Oldham for doing the same work!"

To accuse Brian of pocketing extra money for himself back then was akin to what many spouses often do to their significant others, when one person takes responsibility for paying all the bills from a mutual bank account. Then, when the significant other doesn't understand where all the money has gone—instead of calmly going over the budget with the person who pays the bills—that person automatically accuses the other of stealing.

*** 

Another shock to Brian's psyche came when he discovered his leadership of the band had been diminished even more, when Impact Sound took over control of their finances, shortly after he signed with them. He explained the process this way, "We had them working for us as managers, but it turned out to not be a democratic society after all. I signed away my rights to be the one who handled the money, which was the same as signing away the rights to be the one who had the power. I didn't realize at that time how true that was."

As far as who set the band's touring schedule from then on, Brian said, "The dates were set at first with only my approval, then with the entire band's approval, and then without our approval. The managers just did it. We said, 'Set up our tour dates, and schedule and book for us,' but I had no concept of what we were really signing up for.

"Here's the thing—I knew it had all become too much for me. I was no longer able to be the musician, poet, writer, and performer because I was going crazy with handling all the business details, too. And frankly, the band couldn't progress further unless someone came in to handle all that. After I signed, I went back to being 'just an ordinary guy' and it felt great! In my mind, I was still the Stones' leader, and I thought I still was in theirs—but obviously not," he added sadly.

For Brian, to take part in creating music or to make significant improvements to existing songs—and to do that together with his band—was his greatest satisfaction. To his sorrow and disbelief, Oldham dealt the deathblow to his world when he deliberately told Mick and Keith to compose songs on their own and without input from Brian. At first he was stunned by the suggestion and told Oldham the Stones were still his band, and he was the one to decide what music would be played. Oldham's inane answer was that he was experimenting with Mick and Keith's writing ability, and for Brian to leave the process alone for now and let the duo do it.

When Brian was asked why he didn't simply take the initiative to join Mick and Keith and continue creating with them, he said, "Mick told me it was private, and I wasn't to bother them. How could I explain that answer when I didn't understand it myself?"

When he was further asked if he reminded Mick whose band it actually was, he explained, "I did, but it was all part of how everything started to go wrong, with Mick put in charge and me being put on the outside. Management (Oldham) set it up for Mick to take over.

"I was so tired, and I stopped fighting back. That was a deep blow to me emotionally—to feel so disregarded after everything I had done for the band. It hurt very deeply, but hurting deeply and having the fire to wage the battle were two different things. It was demoralizing, weakening, and I had nothing left to fight back with. The facts were, they started writing together, and I became less and less included. I felt so ill, like an old, old man—that was, except when I started to do drugs and drink heavily. That was what bolstered me to continue on.

"Had the band and my leadership not been stripped from me, I never would have gotten so deep into drinking and drugging. Without the ability to direct my band my own way, I really had no motivation or momentum to keep myself together."

Either sadly or comically, Brian's mania must have clicked in, when he went on to say, "But this was still a great and fun time for me and the band!"

His untreated bi-polar disorder and the manic-depressive episodes gave him a range of high exuberance as the band continued to tour, and he continued to receive more and more acclaim for his musical contributions. Performing music was all that mattered to him. Music was his life, and without it he had no will to live.

At times, the reality of losing control of the band he had created would hit him hard. He said, "All of a sudden, I'd not be able to cope with the depression and had no energy to do anything. It was like a sudden darkness came in on top of me. Everything seemed wrong and frightening, and I couldn't go on. But the band thought I was nothing more than a hypochondriac, and they thought I complained a lot. They didn't understand. Hell, I didn't understand it myself!"

When he missed performances and important rehearsals, the band never knew the deep despair that had taken over his body and overwhelmed him. Since he believed, as a man, he had no right to complain, he never honestly explained what he was going through. Besides, at the ages of twenty-something, chances were very strong that none of the other band members would have understood or cared what their leader felt—even if he had told them.

They were all strong, healthy, strapping young men who never had to live the years of deprivation from lack of food and warmth, as Brian had, and never had the near-death experience Brian had due to the 105 degree fever he ran while in France.

When he would return to the band, after taking days off for health issues, instead of sincerely asking how he felt, his mates—especially Mick, who now took the lead and spoke for the rest—would mockingly utter these bitter words, "Feeling better, Brian?" Those words were said with contempt and scorn.

***

Ultimately, the convoluted love/hate relationship between Brian and Mick played the major, decisive role in dividing the house that Brian built—the house of the Rolling Stones.

By the time Andrew Oldham first decided to separate the three—Brian, Mick and Keith—the latter two had already spent months and months studying Brian's musical techniques, the way he came up with new ideas for existing pieces of music, how he incorporated his original Blues beats to the music, and how he created his own unique sounds and rhythms.

Mick had assiduously incorporated Brian's dance routines, his sensual style of moving, and most importantly, had learned from the master himself—Brian Jones—how to seduce an audience. Had Brian not been so in love with Mick, at least for that period of time, he'd never have allowed Mick to completely imitate him and eventually become him.

Therefore, when Mick and Keith began to write together, they already had Brian's imprint and his energy on their minds, with which to work. They knew Brian inside and out, as far as his musical style and abilities. Mick's strength was in knowing how to take someone's good qualities and make them his own; Keith's strength was in knowing how to follow a lead—whether the lead came from Brian or Mick. As Brian had so rightly noticed, "Keith's role was to follow and serve."

Mick planned to take over Brian's power and leadership much earlier and knew he could do it, when he realized how much Brian cared for him. In Mick's mind, to feel such deep feelings for anyone was a weakness—a weakness he determined not to have. Initially, he cared for Brian as much as Brian cared for him. But in order to destroy Brian, Mick had to make himself lose all feelings for the man. Brian accurately said, "Mick resented me for making him feel things he was never ready for or ready to admit—even to himself."

Mick had to hate Brian for loving him.

When Mick and Keith—under Oldham's direction—first began to shut Brian out from the writing process, Brian threatened to leave the band and once more go on his own. Mick panicked, because he had not yet finished absorbing all of Brian's talents and energy. He cried and begged Brian to stay, saying how much he…oops! the band…needed him. Brian said, "Yes! It was always about himself, Mick."

Nevertheless, because of his still-soft spot for Mick, Brian acquiesced and returned to perfecting, arranging, and filling in—with whatever instruments were needed—the songs that the duo created. Nonetheless, this was a position he considered demeaning and secondary. Actually "created" was an incorrect term, because all Mick and Keith would do with the majority of their new music was to put together the bare minimum of an original melody and lyrics. Then they would go to Brian—and would occasionally include Bill Wyman in this equation—and ask him to work his magic with the skeletal pieces that they had begun.

The onset of making Brian feel an inconsequential part of the Rolling Stones was what first turned him to drink and take drugs to excess. He was the one to have created the band, named the band, hired its members, and made the press and public aware of their existence. He was the one to have stolen and prostituted himself over and over to get his band proper recognition. He was the one to have taught Mick and Keith how to act, talk, walk, and dress like rock stars. And now, because of Andrew Oldham's insane obsession with money, fame, and Mick Jagger's body—and because of Mick's growing obsession with his own money, fame, and power—Brian was tossed aside like the proverbial rag doll.

At first, Brian couldn't believe his eyes when he saw Mick look and perform identically to him on stage. Brian compared it to looking at himself in a mirror. "The change was so gradual that I never saw it happening," he said. "It was a mind fuck. Mick took everything from me. To watch your own persona being played out so fully and so completely right in front of you makes you feel as if you don't exist. It was my own identity that was being stolen by Mick. I felt almost hypnotized. I felt like to stay alive I had to change! The change was so slow on Mick's part, but all of a sudden he was becoming me. Then he was me! It was a shift of reality.

"Mick began to tell me I was nothing. When we were alone, he would yell at me for being lazy and slacking off. At times I fought back; at times I was dumbstruck by it; at times I did the attack on him myself. Mick telling me that I was nothing. Mick being Mick!" he said bitterly.

"To become me, Mick had to tear me down completely," he added and looked away.

When they first started out, Mick was a frumpy looking, conservative wanna be accountant. "He had skinny legs and big feet," Brian joked. He dressed and walked like an older man who wore nerdy-looking tie-up shoes. After Brian finished polishing him, Mick had been turned into a full-fledged rocker. Mick came out with full-face make up, sequins, multi-colored boas, pointed toe shoes, and his favorite—silk kimonos. He loved the combination of the masculine and the feminine.

In the early days, the two had enjoyed their own private playtime together. As Brian described those times, "The main things were developing the band, our closeness, our living together, and clinging together. The whole idea of jealousy was beyond us. The experimental nature of our music and our lives was what I was very keen on.

"Originally, the sex between Mick and me evolved naturally from our being in such close proximity to one another, and alone. It was more like a dance between us—who could say who started it or who carried it through?

"I cannot say with certainty whether Mick had it in his mind to take over initially, but it just seemed to be the natural progression. And then, at other times it seemed he had plotted it from the beginning, even though I don't think he's really that smart. It's so gray…so many shades of gray…not black and white."

Unfortunately, the big division between the two occurred when Mick first decided that he knew more than Brian about what was better for the band, even when it came to creating music. When the band got together to rehearse, Mick began to tell the others what chords or riffs he wanted played and how he wanted them played. When Brian took Mick aside and reminded him whose band it was, Mick used the sexual relationship between the two to punish Brian and teach him who really was in charge. As Brian described those situations, "If I wanted sex from Mick, he'd withhold it from me to teach me a lesson or because he was

Sadly for Brian and his present and future fans, his story didn't have the fairytale happy ending in which good ultimately wins out. For some inexplicable reason, in Brian Jones' life evil won the battle.

***

The following chapters will tell the story of Brian's ultimate, heart-breaking struggle to survive and keep whatever happiness and musical success he had worked so hard to attain.

Losing all control over his life wasn't a new experience for him but one of his most terrifying that he desperately tried not to relive. All the years he had spent studying music, working towards his goal, fighting odds to the contrary, stroking whomever needed to be stroked—advancing inch by inch to the top—the rewards from all those years appeared to be slipping away from him.

And, he could think of nothing, for the present, to stop it from happening. He had the monstrous feeling that losing his control, losing his leadership of the band, was only the beginning of many horrendous experiences he would be dealing with, and he didn't know how much time he had to turn the odds around—at least one more time.

# CHAPTER FIFTEEN
## On Top of the World!

*"Little Red Rooster provided Brian Jones with one of his finest hours. It realized a cherished ambition to put Blues music at the top of the charts."*

Bill Wyman, Stone Alone

As 1963 came to a highly-successful end, 1964 opened with an even-brighter future materializing for the Rolling Stones band. Even if things weren't entirely copasetic between Mick and Brian's personal lives, professionally the band was running full-speed ahead, under the direction of Eric Easton and Andrew Loog Oldham.

Each new single record and new album that the band released reached higher up the music charts and stayed on the charts longer. Within the music industry, longevity has always been a prerequisite for everlasting success, and so far the band showed every sign of maintaining their rank on top of the charts.

Every new TV appearance and live performance continued to show Mick as lead singer, with Brian standing beside him, playing whichever instrument each song required. Brian also served as back-up singer on numerous occasions, along with Bill Wyman and Keith Richards.

The band's rigid touring schedule continued as January 31, 1964, opened a twenty-nine day show schedule. During the early to mid-sixties British touring buses and trains didn't travel at such a high rate of speed—which made the hours of getting from one destination to the other especially long. There was also a lack of eating facilities that served both quick and still highly-nutritious meals necessary to maintain proper body strength. On top of that, as soon as the band arrived at a new destination, they had to unload and deliver their instruments to the show site, set them up, and begin rehearsals. Only the strongest could survive that fast-paced, strenuous schedule.

Many times the Stones drove themselves from city to city using their own vans or cars, again allowing them only minutes to grab a quick meal wherever they could. But no one complained, especially Brian, who was thrilled that the band he had dreamed of was reaching even greater recognition than he could have imagined. "I was happy we were finally recording and making money!" he said ecstatically.

Oldham's theory to have the Stones act as loutish and unruly as possible backfired in certain cases, though, especially when the band needed comfortable hotels to stay at during their travels, decent restaurants to dine at, and shops from which to purchase everyday necessities and equipment. Often those establishments—once they recognized the group—refused them service or even entrance. The business owners were afraid of having their regular customers chased off by the scraggily looking, weird-sounding band.

Many nights the Stones settled for second or third-class sleeping and eating facilities, which put an additional strain on keeping their morale up while they traveled those long days and nights on the long and sometimes lonely road.

To help break the monotony of the endless miles, Brian took on the position as the band's official clown or monkey, as he called himself. Whether they were in planes, trains, buses, vans, or another monotonous hotel room, he'd act out, in an attempt to make the time pass more quickly and keep spirits up. He said he acted this way to counter the years in which he had to act as an adult while at home, when he was still a youngster, and even while living on the streets—when he had to suddenly mature in order to survive. So now as a Rolling Stone, he felt free to let loose, act like the kid he never was, and regress into the rebellious childhood he was never allowed to have.

Actually, he had a fantastic, unusual sense of humor and was a natural prankster, both facially and with his actions. At times he'd grab his guitar and pick out strange, bizarre sounds that frightened the other hapless travelers. More often than not he'd use his ability to twist and mash his sultry face into the most outlandish shapes—again scaring fellow travelers—as he ran from place to place or down hotel hallways, with his misshapen facial expressions seemingly ossified.

Other times he would use his ability to contort his face and body to mimic monkeys. He'd hunch up his body and jump, run, or bounce from chair to chair while chirping imaginary monkey sounds. He said, "I was seven years old all over again during these moments. Touring would get so fucking boring! You'd think traveling would be the glamorous life all the time, but no…no…no! Trains, buses, planes, all of it boring.

"I'd drum on anything I could get my hands on to make the time pass. The other Stones would put plugs in their ears and covers over their eyes. Some would just stare into space."

When his manic state wasn't in full bloom, his depression would take over during their journeys, and he would go into what appeared a coma. All of a sudden he would pass out, whether the band was on a bus, van, or whatever. The other guys couldn't wake him and just thought he had overdosed on something, or perhaps was simply lazy. That wasn't the case—the problem was neurological. Brian had what he described as little firing mishaps in his brain that would knock him unconscious. He described the feeling this way, "I couldn't really feel it coming on, even though I tried to. By the time I thought my passing out was about to happen, it was too late, and it just happened." Those moments both embarrassed him in front of his band mates and made him exceptionally tired.

No one ever realized the extent of his bi-polar condition, including Brian himself. But when he was back in full manic condition and continued with his clowning, after a while the rest of the Stones would begin to feel agitation towards his antics. He said, "At times they were amused by me, but at other times—no. Sometimes they saw me as their entertainment; at other times they saw me as the clown. For me, that was fun."

During the countless hours of travel, the rest of the Stones took turns feeling like hell themselves, in their own way. They suffered headaches, hangovers, and assorted ailments. Brian tried to read, but "being on the road wasn't conducive to sitting and reading. I had my eyeglasses, yes, but my eyes bothered me a lot from being tired and strained from smoke. Also, my eyes generally burned from allergies, even though I used eye drops."

Many times his knees got dreadfully sore from the hours of sitting in whatever mode of transportation they were using. "I got so restless and couldn't sit still. My legs seemed like they were always asleep, and I felt one hundred fifty years old at the age of twenty-three. I also had a bony butt and got the sore ass," he said and laughed.

He got tired really quickly, because his constitution was weaker and more fragile that the rest of the band's. Consequently, while on long tours he felt bad most of the time. "The road was especially hard on me," he said.

***

One night while back home and close to his roots, Brian gladly sat in at his old haunt, the Crawdaddy Club, and played harmonica for the Yardbirds' Keith Relf, who was out ill.

During this time, an unwelcome phenomenon in the world of rock music had begun to occur during the Rolling Stones appearances—their overly enthusiastic fans caused riots to erupt from city to city. Originally, police escorts or other tight security hadn't been needed for performances, but now their presence proved a necessity with each new day. On more than one occasion, due to the fear of riots occurring, the Stones appearances were cancelled before the band even played one song.

Audiences soon realized that they had to maintain some form of proper decorum if they wanted to see their favorite band, the Rolling Stones, perform. From this time forward, security that included specially trained police personnel was sent out to maintain the peace before, during, and after each scheduled performance. Brian described the band's feelings, "As Stones, we all wanted protection around us. There was always some drunk in whatever house or theater we were playing in, who would want to get it on with the 'queer guys'." (Photos #806 & 830)

Nonetheless, despite the added security, the band never knew what to expect from their audiences, and they began to approach every performance with extraordinary caution. Having their jackets, shirts, and even their slacks and shoes torn from their bodies by overzealous fans became the norm.

Countless times, Brian had clumps of hair literally ripped out of his head. Because he was about the same height as many of his female fans, he was at times hard to differentiate. This led to disastrous results for him—as he would disappear into a sea of swarming arms and grasping hands. He always had a deep fear of being ripped apart by "the flesh eaters"—as he called them—and now his most lurid nightmares appeared to be turning into reality before his very eyes.

With each new tumultuous playing date, he found it necessary to brace himself before going on stage with various and sundry uppers, downers, or anything else he could swallow—and still be able to stand upright and perform.

He frequently found himself stranded alone after performances and unable to get away—while the rest of his band somehow managed to magically make it off stage and out of the building without him. No one seemed to find it necessary to backtrack and look for the band's founder, who they knew was the most fragile and vulnerable to physical attack, and the weakest in terms of self-defense.

Nevertheless, by the time he managed to fight his way back and rejoin the rest of the band, he played off all the terror he had felt and laughed about the fans' craziness as loudly as the others—at least on the outside. Inside, his heart ached when he realized this form of terrorism might now be a way of life for him. The physical pounding he took time and again, all for the sake of educating the world to the wondrous sounds of Blues music, took a painful toll on a body that was already racked with countless, never-ending pains.

*** 

One of the memorable journeys the band took in the Spring of '64 was a trip from London to Geneva, Switzerland, to film a special version of their favorite TV program *Ready, Steady, Go!* The band was treated royally, further establishing and affirming their status as a highly successful rock band.

Brian took as much time as possible to relish the acclaim he witnessed his band receiving. No matter how fatigued he may have felt, to see first-hand the approval and joy in the eyes of his audiences made the effort all worthwhile for him. In the back of his mind, the love and adoration he received from the fans made up—even if only in a small way—for the years of having no real family love or acceptance, and for the years of enduring the public humiliation by having to prostitute and steal in order to survive.

The constant traveling, which now wore heavily on each of the Stones physical and emotional stamina, had an adverse effect on Brian's asthma. Not only was his regular breathing erratic, but now he was also experiencing severe asthma attacks that disastrously weakened him. He had to keep several inhalers within reach day and night, including during performances and rehearsals. Each of the Stones knew where to quickly get his hand on one of Brian's inhalers, should he see Brian gasping for air.

He described the ordeal this way, "There were times when the asthma attacks happened a lot. Sometimes I could get through nearly a whole performance without inhaler use. But it had to be with me all the time. I'd turn my back to the audience in between songs, or when switching from guitar to harmonica, maracas—whatever—just to take a hit. I got to be really good at getting a quick hit, but when my fingers and hands were occupied, I had to do the best I could. Harmonica playing made the ordeal worse."

One night in May '64, he unexpectedly missed the first of two shows in Bristol. The rest of the Stones had left for the show earlier without him, and by the time he was ready to leave by private car an auto accident had closed the road, which prevented him from getting through. "These were thrilling times!" he joked. In speaking about why his band mates went on ahead, he said, "They were ready to leave—and without me if necessary. I wasn't moving as quickly as the rest of them, I suppose, and told them I'd catch up. They were rushing around, but I preferred being alone. That was a way for me to get some down time, to get back into myself before a performance or before getting in front of a crowd again."

The mauling crowds frightened him so much that he had to mentally talk himself into making further appearances—unless he heavily medicated himself. As a result, he found it necessary to self-medicate more and more to get passed the panic attacks, which grew in intensity each time a new set of clothing was ripped to shreds off his body, or a newly-grown clump of his luxurious hair was torn from his scalp. "The booze and the drugs fortified me," he said gloomily.

The rest of the band, though, wasn't happy that they had to move on without him many times, and that he had to have private limos take him from place to place. According to him, "They'd say, 'Get off of your arse, Brian!' 'Come on!' or the more common—'To Hell with You!' But I was working on my own timetable at times, or a lot of the time!" he said with a laugh.

He did make it back in time for the second Bristol show, with the help of a police escort and was happy to see his parents there. Mr. & Mrs. Jones found it hard to accept their wayward son's success, but they still showed up for the band's performances whenever they were in the area. When time permitted, Brian would spend a day or two back at home visiting with them. Things were very different now, in that he was no longer a needy child seeking their shelter but an independent, adult male who had made it on his own. He said, "I did see them a couple of days here and there from time to time. I mean…they were my parents. They were intrigued, I think, for the success that was happening with the band. Not that they understood it or had ever anticipated it. It was them wanting to be part of the pomp and circumstance. I always wanted to feel that my parents cared about me, and I guess it took becoming a famous rock star.

"But I didn't want them interfering with the music or my freedom, now that I was completely out from under their control. And, I felt that they were interfering by showing up at the times they did. There was also the part of me that, if I wasn't too inconvenienced, I could give some form of reconciliation a chance—if I didn't have anything else going on.

"Actually, I didn't mean their interfering so much with my music, but with my life. We (the band) had a lot going on, and one doesn't always want mum and pop showing up to insert their energy and thoughts into the situation. I mean—it's quite a different thing from being at home in front of the telly."

In having said that, Brian tried hard to sound as if he truly could care less what his parents did or didn't think about him any longer. But, nothing could be further from the truth. In the back of his mind, he desired and prayed for their real love and devotion, but he never felt they ever gave it willingly or freely. "They took my money, though," he said with much bitterness. "Although, they acted as if they could care less that I offered…but still, they took it."

Also in May '64, the band took the required smallpox vaccines for their upcoming first trip to the United States. As usual, Brian ran a high fever as a side effect of the vaccination. However, happily—or whatever you want to call it—this time he wasn't alone in being ill, because Charlie and Keith also ran high fevers along with him.

Two weeks before their departure for what would be the most important trip of their lives to the States, Brian was once again left to fend for himself during a show in Bradford, and once again he had most of his clothes torn off by swarming female fans. Riotous shows followed quickly in several cities up 'til their send-off time for America, on June 1.

***

When asked to describe how he and the band felt arriving in New York City, an animated Brian said, "I thought we were on top of the world! America! The United States! It was a dream come true." In comparing the city to London, he said, "Similar in ways, but with a totally different feel. You know—New York has all the hype. We thought we had really arrived and were welcomed with open arms."

As for the screaming fans in America, he said candidly, "They were a shock to us. We joked to each other and said, 'Hold onto your pants!' But the losing hair part was really frightening and made me have animosity towards the fans. It was unforgivable to be attacked. What—through love of our music they attack us? I don't think so! It was too bizarre. But it was only the girls—the boys weren't trying to hunt us down. We thought it was going to be fun, but it was totally scary."

The magic and excitement of having thousands of adoring fans worship every move they made were diminished by the moments of feeling trapped by the very same fans. The band had security, police, tough-looking, muscular stagehands, and professional bouncers protecting them, as they made their way through restaurants, shops, and to and from shows. Getting everyday necessities such as shaving cream or a new toothbrush became literally impossible, once a band member was spotted. Brian, because of his magnificent golden hair, was usually the one spotted first. During these days, he gained the moniker of being called the Golden Stone—a name he forever cherished.

On this trip to America, he and his mates either became reacquainted with or got to meet several of their personal heroes, which included Bo Diddley, John Lee Hooker, Chuck Berry, and Muddy Waters. The difference now was that these legendary performers accepted the Rolling Stones as their peers. For no one was this acceptance more important than for Brian. If it weren't for these entertainers' existence, his dream—to form his own band and spread the music of rhythm 'n blues throughout the world—would never have originated.

He repeatedly claimed that there was no comparison between American Negro Blues and what was called the British take-off of the same. Mick wholeheartedly agreed with Brian that there would be no British R&B without the original American music born decades earlier in the Deep South.

On this first American tour the Stones traveled through several states giving radio interviews and making TV appearances, in addition to their live stage performances. The press recognized Brian as the band's spokesman, and his voice, face, and persona were the driving images behind the group. No one, including Mick at this time, had a problem giving Brian his space and letting him represent the message the band wanted to depict. The Rolling Stones image was that of a band of rebels who were selling freedom. And, that message of freedom was for the youth of the world to rise up and speak against the hypocrisy of the lawmakers and government leaders throughout the world.

The Stones wanted to stand for the freedom of the days' youth to not be ashamed of showing public displays of love and affection, and to feel free to dress and wear their hair and make-up in whatever style they felt comfortable. The theory, as Brian had long envisioned it, was to demonstrate that outward appearances did not make the man. What made the man or woman would be what the person ultimately achieved and stood for during his or her lifetime. "I wanted to tear down the codes, removing the uniform aspect of dress—the suit, the tie, the neatly-pressed white shirt, the tied-up lace shoes on the males and the self-imposed, laced-up frilly females. I was crossing gender boundaries and revolutionizing all forms of expression. We now wore the frilly laces," he said. (Photo #831)

"Average young males thought we were queer. They laughed; they made fun and thought we were outrageous. But, of course, we were trying to be! We found this loose style of clothing very comfortable. Mick and Keith felt comfortable with it, too, because we were breaking down another wall and helping to break down sexual restrictions and norms. We wanted to prove that we didn't have to be like all the rest, that we could do anything.

"The females didn't know what to think of our dress at first. In our earlier stages we looked rather normal, I suppose, but then we began to give the impression of cross-dressing. And so, the girls became attracted to our music and then to us—and that was really hot! By then, we were all dressing girlie fulltime. We were pretty much into the era, weren't we? We were making new fashion statements all the time, and the rest of the world was just trying to keep up with us, or so we thought.

"Sure, I knew you couldn't go to the office dressed like that. So—don't go to the office!" he joked. "Besides, the office workers weren't really our target audience. The wealthy, spoiled teens were the ones who could afford to buy our music, the clothes and such. They wanted to look like us, to be like us—actually, they wanted to be us."

Brian envisioned his music being free and leading the way for a new society of youth who would live life to its fullest and be happy to dance, make love, and show love for one another without fear or hang-ups. When he had his band demonstrate their carefree, uninhibited performance on stage, he succeeded in setting a precedent for a world that would nevermore be held back by the shackles of a hypocritical and morally decrepit adult society. "I was there to excite and insight passion from and through music. Absolutely! I wanted to wake people up and bring them back to life."

The more the band appeared and performed, the more they took the lead in what the public demanded to see. Even though the Rolling Stones weren't headlining each American performance, they were the ones the audiences chanted to see and hear. Thus began an unwelcome rivalry and jealousy among the established entertainers, who were either headlining or performing along with Brian's band.

There was a rumor that Chuck Berry felt a certain amount of animosity towards the Stones in general. About this Brian said, "No, I never heard that. We met, and I didn't feel any animosity. We all loved his music, and he knew that. There was some competition, but not something we'd openly display to one another. Chuck was confidant in his own right, in his own way, and in his own skin. But you see, we could go in the front door everywhere, and there were places where he had to go in the back. It was an unspoken irony, as if we wanted to say, 'Sorry, Man! That's the breaks.' But, no one said it. Even with bands that had Black back-up or Black members, to be treated differently was beyond what any of us could fathom."

That sad reality of race was something that no one ever saw, at least among the public or the fans. As for himself, Brian had a part of him that wished he were of African ancestry—even if only by a small percentage. He felt if he were, he'd be better able to interpret and compose more realistically that style of music.

During this time he enjoyed his first sexual experiences with members of the Black female bands with whom they toured, such as the Ronnettes and the Supremes. Of this he said lightheartedly, "Why not? We were tasting all of the treats! With the Black women we had only one thing in common, and it wasn't about talking!"

He felt he was actually the conquest for their lust and their curiosity—they wanted to be sexual with a gorgeous, blonde, blue-eyed guy. "I was the candy for them to eat. Everything was a lark, and I wanted to try everything available. I didn't know who I was half the time but just knew what felt good. Also, the drugs changed everything. With fame everything became available, and the drugs changed my reality."

Before they returned to London, this first American tour was made especially unforgettable with the band's closing performance at Carnegie Hall in New York City. The show was hosted by famed disc jockey Murray the K and attended by screaming, adoring fans.

Once back home, the band filmed Top of the Pops and ended the evening with an extravagant bash held at the Alexandra Palace. The gala didn't end until daybreak the next morning. Brian described his feelings on being treated so royally, "Words escape me! But it was knowing we had arrived, feeling honored and welcomed. And, we had a damn good time!" He went on to say with his self-deprecating manner, "There was actual coherent conversation that evening, insofar as I was coherent myself. I was recognized as leader of the band, but we were all approached to speak. I had my share, and I was in my glory."

Management signed the band on to form a company called Rolling Stones Limited. Brian said, "It was their desire to take the band to the next step and included the right to sell other items like tee-shirts, posters, and photographs. Anything that would be associated with us."

Despite the fact the band was now recognized worldwide, ironically, actual spending money was still a problem. "It was tough," Brian said. "We were constantly amazed at all the expenses required to get us to and from performances. We felt childlike in a way that we had to ask for spending money. We assumed the bills would be taken care of, but it was very inconvenient not having access to our own money."

Normally the men tried to bill their personal expenses to management's charge account, and Brian explained, "Yes, that's what I did until they put a screeching halt to that. Management would say, 'It's not in the budget,' or 'We didn't know you purchased that.'"

July '64 was extra special to Brian individually because Vox Music Company created a one-of-a-kind teardrop guitar for him. No others were put up for sale, and this version was meant to be used only by him. He explained his feelings, "I felt immortalized! I held the guitar to my chest and melted around it." (Photo #829)

The end of July through the month of August presented the Stones with their first full-fledged European tour. In comparing this to their earlier tour of the United States, Brian said, "In a way performing in Europe felt much better because we were on our own turf. It felt like we were conquering our own land. We had fans showing up to see us, where in the past I could have walked passed them on the street and no one would've noticed."

Being on the Continent once again brought certain worries to him that only he knew and would never share with any of his band mates. He feared that perhaps a former "client" might inadvertently recognize him from his earlier days on the streets. He said, "Returning to the Continent as a rock star felt really cool. But I felt worried, too, cause I didn't want anyone to recognize me from the past. Although, I didn't look much the same in my finery. My hair was much more ragged back then, too. No one put it together, but at times I'd be very paranoid. I sweated it, and then I'd take something to ease my pain." He laughed at his own metaphor to taking drugs in order to chase away his personal ghosts.

***

That year the band released a new album and several new singles including *It's All Over Now, You Better Move On, Not Fade Away, Heart of Stone, Time Is on My Side,* and *Little Red Rooster*—all of which reached either number one in the States or England, or high up on the musical charts. *Little Red Rooster* became Brian's trademark piece, in which his magical electric slide guitar playing received accolades worldwide. Sadly, because of the song's sexually explicit lyrics it was banned on many radio stations in the United States or simply not made available for sale.

However, there were and still are video tapes offered that depict the band performing this piece, including their performances carried on England's TV stations. Perhaps in no other song available on video was the sexual chemistry between Brian and Mick more evident than on *Little Red Rooster*. According to Brian, he claimed the song was typical of the interaction between him and Mick. "That was us all the time," he claimed. "Each wanting to be the top cock." (Photo #844)

And, it was this very sexual chemistry that sparked and fired their audiences. Mick and Brian's natural sexuality for one another was what made the band notable. Later on, after Brian's death the band was never able to rekindle that type of sound or appeal.

Not only was the sexual tension between the two evident during the *Little Red Rooster*'s performance, but also Brian's purposeful seduction of the television camera was not wasted on the audience. He cocked his head to the side and vamped for the camera lens, showing the hidden twinkle of sexual promises never to be kept radiating from his eyes.

One of Brian's crowning achievements was the day *Little Red Rooster* became the first Rolling Stones record to beat out both the Beatles and Diana Ross' Supremes for number one position on the record charts.

Unfortunately, the Stones recording successes were marred by the eruption of newer, more vicious riots that took place during the band's performances. The worst of these occurrences was the infamous incident in July at Blackpool, England, in the Empress Ballroom.

Riotous scenes such as this had been brewing for some time, especially with Brian's increasingly sexual gyrations on stage. He and Mick played the sexual chemistry off one another brilliantly, and when the sexual tension reached a high point, Brian turned all that energy onto the audience. He explained it this way, "I don't know how the Blackpool riot got turned around the way it did. What we (the band) were doing on stage is what we had been doing. We were evolving, I guess you could say, into something more sassy, sensual, precocious. Anyway, something sure as hell erupted that night. There was actual anger and violence against us. Almost like we struck a chord with the males in the audience, and we struck something that they were very uncomfortable with. They decided to take their anger and frustrations out on us.

"I don't think this ever happened with the Beatles, but they didn't have the overt sexuality that we were bringing. Yes, I started all that sexuality on stage—but it worked! It was fun, and it pissed some people off."

He was asked if he had gone over the top that night with his act. "Well, it could've been my sort of come on, come hither appeal with my hips gyrating in the direction of the males in the audience. But I wasn't trying to get the guys worked up the way they got worked up. Was it supposed to be a sexual come on—bottom line, yes! I was trying to tease the guys and obviously it was part of the performance. I wasn't going to try and take on the whole crowd in my bed, now was I? My performance just really got to them in a way I hadn't fully expected."

Whether he tried to tone down his performances after that experience wasn't clear, even to him. He said, "God knows! It was such a freak show during those times. Toning it down? No—I got a reaction and a response. I guess it was something that both terrified me and made me feel very powerful, to be able to get that reaction. I wanted to tell them all, 'Relax! It's only a performance!'"

He further explained, "When all was said and done, the band and I—we all had a good laugh. We had lived through it! We thought yeah, we were cool. The band said to me, 'Man, you were really crazy out there! What were you doing?' We agreed it was something that hadn't been done before. They said, 'Hell, Man, are you trying to get us killed?' And I thought it was kind of cool to get everybody riled up like that. The males realized it was because of my seductive, girlie thing. You know—the macho men of the world, what were they doing at a Stones concert anyway? Let me ask you that!

"But, they didn't like my come on. It was all very confusing and complicated in those times, what we were doing—the bisexual revolution. And there were the Billy Rednecks there, wanting to be the bad asses, the pub brawlers, the macho men...."

There was the actor in Brian and the imaginative genius that only he among the Stones could be. Mick never could have pulled off on his own the seductive poses that Brian did. Mick never could have affected the pure sultry, sexual energy. Brian explained, "I liked to appeal to those who might have a more vivid imagination. I was feeling very camp and realized that my audience came from both males and females. These things were very hidden—or not so hidden—even then in the sixties, and not that open."

He would walk to the edge of the stage and stick out his tongue, while smashing his tambourine in the audience's face. He was the precursor to KISS and Alice Cooper without ever realizing the far-reaching effects of his act. Brian's goal was to horrify the audience and appear sexy at the same time. He said, "Getting that close to them with my tongue and hitting the tambourine in their faces was taking a stab at their sexuality. It was the shock effect, but I never hit them though, did I? It was a game, a show, and part of the act. But that night in Blackpool and for a time after, the audiences wanted to kill me. Keith always came to my defense, but still he thought I was going too far. He'd say, 'Don't get in the faces of the bulky men who want to run you over.' It was all right, short of having blows thrown and getting bloodied."

Brian was proud to see his brother, Keith, come to his rescue time after time. During the Blackpool incident, Scotsmen and other brawlers spat on Brian and grabbed at him from the stage floor. Keith ran to his side of the audience and kicked and stomped at the attackers. The band felt lucky to make it out of there alive that night; however the rampaging mob managed to climb onto the stage and break several amplifiers, and even smashed the large grand piano.

Having Keith, as a much bigger man, come to his rescue wasn't an unusual occurrence for Brian. Since he was petite and prone to being overtaken by larger males, he had taught himself to survive by using his naturally feminine wiles and—almost like a woman—he got stronger, brawnier men to protect him.

***

During the Fall of '64 a fourth tour of the UK was arranged, quickly followed by the Stones second trip to America for that year. The year appeared to have no end, and even Brian was astonished with its pace. He exclaimed, "Did we really do all that in '64?"

One of the more humorous events that occurred while in America was between the band and the ever-famous, number one rated Ed Sullivan TV Show. Ultra-conservative Ed Sullivan had a distinct love/hate relationship with the Stones. He detested everything they stood for, especially their rebellious attitude, dress, hairstyles, and even music. However, no matter how many times he swore to never again have them on his show, he always recanted and year after year had the band back for repeat performances.

Brian said of this phenomenon, "It was crazy, wasn't it? Our popularity was greater than what—his antagonism of us?" Ed kept his loathing behind the scenes, and as Brian explained, "We (the band) got wind of his feelings, but we both needed each other. Ed didn't want us to give a bad performance, even if he thought our music was bad. Because it was his show, or 'shew' as he used to say!" he added with a laugh. "Ed wanted to act like he loved everybody on his show, especially if the fans did. Even though we always looked and acted like gentlemen for him, he still thought we were arrogant punks. We spoke briefly in passing, he and I. Although, we (the band) were pretty full of ourselves; but I thought we were there to be pretty full of ourselves."

The band interacted with Sullivan's workmen in making final preparations for the show, and Brian said, "I thought we and the workmen got along fine. We told them what we needed as far as how we wanted to have things set up. And I guess they weren't used to that. Maybe I had a higher degree of professionalism."

During the TAMI awards show in California, the band got to meet up with the Godfather of Soul, James Brown. Brian said, "I thought James was a real stud! As to whether he was bi-sexual—not to my knowledge, and frankly I didn't want to have to compete with that!" he added as a joke, referring to the size of James' "member".

Like Brian, James was known for his sexual appetite and for the fact women expected sex from him wherever he went. And like Brian, James Brown was quite short—approximately five foot, six inches. In response to this, with a gleam in his eye, Brian claimed, "I believe I'm a smidge taller than James."

In November, the band made their second visit to Chicago's renowned Chess Studios to conduct another recording session. These were especially memorable for Brian, since he so much admired the true American Blues style of music. He said, "There was something special about recording at Chess. It felt fresher to me, like a different territory. I felt perhaps I had gone stale, and I really needed new input and freshness to light me up again. So I liked it; it was different in terms of how things (recordings) were done, but it felt good to me.

"I learned different techniques, and that's the thing I want to say—in that I saw myself as rather a sponge that soaks everything up. I'd see all these different techniques and equipment that they used at Chess, and so many things that were unlike what I was familiar with. I'd just take it all in. My mind worked rather photographically. I could recall how the set-up had been, what the licks looked or sounded like much later on, and it was like I just carried that all with me. It was really wonderful to be in that situation."

Mick also tried to absorb what he saw at Chess Studios, but he would focus more on what one particular thing looked like and how it worked mechanically—whereas Brian would soak up all the pieces, instead of focusing on only one part. He said, "I had sensory feelers, if you want to call it that. I say that as if I were the orchestra leader and could keep my eyes focused all around. Later on I could put myself back in the situation and recall each individual piece of what took place."

He especially was fond of the Black professionals who made the experience so different for him. He said, "Yeah, they were really cool! I always loved the whole Black, soulful, bluesy thing. Somehow I thought I had missed something by not having more Black in or around me as I grew up."

He wasn't sure where his musical genius came from, but he loved playing, and being open to all new things, and allowing them to come in and mix and meld though him. His willingness to be open to new sounds and new creations was the foundation for his genius. He opened his psyche up completely to bring in new sounds, which didn't have to be approved or authorized by others.

Unfortunately, one of the things along this same line that later brought him down was this same experimental, open personality that allowed him to over-use and over-experiment with drugs.

***

The joyous, second '64 tour of the States ended on a sad note for Brian, as he got so seriously ill that he suffered another near-death experience, very similar to the one in France not that long ago.

He once again ran a fever of 105 degrees and spent several days in hospital with tubes going in and out of his body. (Letter/Photo #815) He spoke about his serious illness, "I was out of my mind—not knowing what I was doing—with the delirium from the fever. God knows what I said! It was from touring too much, and evidently it was an infection in my body that continued to pop up whenever I was overly stressed or overly tired.

"I think Mick actually had the fear once or twice that I might die. Then he would get very angry with me for having him get that fear. As far as Keith—I sincerely felt he wanted me to get better. The other guys—they wanted to be supportive but there was also, I suspect, a part of their fear that if they were dependent upon me—and I wasn't going to be able to hold up—then what was going to happen to the band? So I suppose they ultimately figured they might as well take the band over, anyway."

As far as how upset Mick actually was over his condition, Brian further explained, "I think there was a little that he worried about me. The bloody bastard—he did love me, at least in a way and for a time. He knew he needed me and that I had brought him to where he was going. And so, it was that kind of love/hate thing as in 'I love you, so I hate you for it.' I think I scared him and made him think of his own mortality, as in, 'God, what could happen here?' and he was very uncomfortable with it."

He was pleased to say that when he returned to the band several days later, Mick personally greeted him. "Mick isn't that demonstrative, but I could say he gave me a little hug and said, 'Better, Man?' to which I answered, 'Yeah.' He then said, 'Okay, let's get on with it!'

"I was kind of shocked as shit myself to be back on the scene, alive. I knew how really disconnected I had been from life—as it's called near-death experiences. It is scary when you realize your body can be overcome like that and not from something from the outside, but from something that's wrong with you on the inside."

When he rejoined the band he was very weak and thin, but he pushed through. The doctors had told him, "You need to take care of yourself, Boy," because they realized he had not been eating well and continued to smoke and drink too much. Regardless, he never liked to admit his own frailties, especially to himself, and being the invincible person that he liked to think he was, he said almost flippantly in response to the doctors' orders, "I listened to them for a day, I suppose."

He didn't remember much about this second critical illness, but he did remember nearly dying the very first time in France. Of this he said, "The Chicago trip really killed me, and I nearly died—or so they tell me. Yeah, I believe it is true. But the time before (in France) seemed a bit more dire in that I was totally alone. I had no personal resources of my own to bounce back from that first time, as opposed to now being a Rolling Stone in Chicago."

That statement was especially pathetic in that it once more pointed out to him how important the reality of not having any family to back him and support him actually was. The nightmarish health emergency in Chicago seemed better to him because he felt the support of his new family, his band.

For Brian, living through this second experience and actually seeing—at least in his subconscious mind—the Other Side was a reassurance for him that he would not be alone when his time actually came. He did suffer some brain damage as a result of the high fever and was delirious for a couple of days. Overall, this experience renewed his desire to push forward with his band and in a way gave him a sense of peace.

With his complex nature, and despite his constant inner sense of despair, he determined to remain upbeat and believed everything would be all right. What he didn't realize was that this latest illness eroded a bit more of his decision-making abilities and weakened his ability to handle drugs.

# CHAPTER SIXTEEN
## Fans, Fatherhood & Friends with Privileges

*"I'd like to say that I loved all the mothers of my children, even if the love may have been in a very fleeting, momentary kind of thing. I liked them or loved them in the time that I was with them. But I was moving very fast and wasn't intending to settle down and get the white picket fence."*

Brian Jones

Throughout the months and years of touring, performing live, and recording new material, the band had free access to sex and drugs wherever they went. Brian often claimed that money and fame opened doors they never knew existed. While they were on the road, dating in the normal sense of the word was impossible, so the guys took advantage of whatever companionship they could find.

Brian said, "No, I didn't take the time to flirt with anyone. We were always so preoccupied. Everything was moving so fast—besides, being the Stones and so well known, I couldn't just flirt, pick up anyone, and go out for a quiet dinner, as on a normal date. There were no regular flowers and dinner dates. I liked going to shows, but unfortunately found little time for them.

"For me, a typical date was going to a pub, having food, booze, drugs, and sex. I saw cute guys and cute girls, but I didn't connect one to one that often. Also, I couldn't take the chance of that information coming out about my possibly being gay or bisexual."

Fans sought out the band, who couldn't escape the outstretched arms that longed to grab, grope, and fondle any part of their bodies that they could reach. Ordinarily the guys laughed at the unexpected adulation, but there were other times when it became downright annoying. They had no privacy for themselves—except for when they were hunkered down in a plane, train, or bus.

During their travels, normally Mick and Keith shared a room, while Bill and Brian shared another, with Charlie, Stu, and Oldham taking a third. At the beginning of this divide, Brian felt the most uncomfortable since he was the one—who along with Mick and Keith—were the foundation and creation of the band. But again, Oldham proved the deadly poison to that early relationship, which originally had worked so well.

Feelings of confusion as to why he was being so isolated ebbed and flowed through Brian's consciousness, throwing his already vulnerable mental state into deep paranoia. He was often teased and put down for his feelings of paranoia, but—as he clearly stated, "They all proved true, didn't they?"

Mick even started the heartless rumor that the only reason Bill wound up bunking with Brian was because, "We'd all cut cards to see who got stuck with Brian, and Bill lost. The luck of the draw, you know."

Normally a person would laugh off that kind of joke, but Mick knew very well what he was saying. He knew that Brian carried lifelong scars that would never heal, about being unwanted in his own home. That's where the cruelty of that statement hit so hard for Brian, and in his weakened state of mind he believed it and took it to heart. He believed no one ever wanted him around just for himself.

At times it appeared, but was more often rumored, that Brian and Bill engaged in as much frequent, frivolous sex as they could make time for. Bill bragged about his sexual conquests while on the road, despite the fact he was married. Somehow, since he was traveling and his wife wasn't with him, he didn't equate having sex with fans as cheating. On the other hand, Brian earned the unwelcome reputation of at times being a woman beater, or even in certain instances, a rapist.

This part of his psyche took many complicated twists and turns, and he tried to explain it away the best he could. "They claim I was either impotent or a rapist. I wish they'd make up their minds! I was usually too tired while traveling to care what was going on, or even to enjoy sex—which was available to me freely and easily. I took advantage of it when I was in the mood and had them (the fans) do things to me. I preferred receiving oral sex, mostly because I didn't have to do any work. Lips were lips, and it didn't matter whose they were as long as it felt good. These were all faceless people with no names and no faces.

"Some, though, who looked or appeared special to me—those would inspire me, and I'd have actual sex with them. I didn't have the energy to rape anyone and more importantly didn't have to, as they were more than willing to knock down the doors and rape me."

He went on to say, "I tried everything out and acted upon whatever felt good, especially group sex. I was sexually immature in that I didn't know what was expected of me or what was considered right or wrong. I took many drugs to enhance the experience and make it more intense.

"So often I couldn't feel anything and simply preferred cuddling and having someone be around just to hold me. I prefer men for that; with women, you always have to perform and do for them. Women actually have it so much easier—they can always fake it, fake the orgasm. But blokes, we have to perform, and I was just too tired, too depressed, and too confused. For the public, I strutted and preened but in private I was more quiet and submissive, especially with men. I wanted women to love me and adore me, worship me, and then leave me alone. But they wouldn't.

"Once women got into my room, we're talking mostly about fans now, they wouldn't leave. They always wanted more than I was willing to give. That's where the rumors of my beating them came into play. I never started hitting on them. They were the ones who wouldn't leave me alone and would get into my face, screaming and hollering because they wanted to own me, live with me. The only way to get rid of them at times was to strike at them, especially when they backed me into a corner. I'm not physically aggressive, but felt I had to protect myself at those times.

"They only decided to scream rape when I wouldn't let them stay—then I was a rapist! Of course all the drugs twisted me and twisted what I saw taking place. But they were doing drugs, too, and that's when everything went bad."

When he had been tossed onto the streets at age sixteen, he was basically naive and innocent. Therefore, the majority of his sexual skills or outlooks were shaped during and after that time—some good and many not so good. Add to that his incestuous experiences at home at such an early age, and he—as a rockstar and still a young man in his twenties—never had a chance to form what would be considered a normal, healthy, sexual relationship. Because of his confusion, he would engage in frequent group sex, since it had no rules and no boundaries. He said, "What should you believe? The stories of my being the constant stud horse or the crying, cuddly boy? Everyone wanted to have sex with me, and I was constantly sought out. They all wanted to use me; they wanted my energy. To them I was the Golden Boy, but I was always physically smaller than the others."

In his mind, his height was an embarrassment and a weakness. Because he felt diminished next to the bigger, stronger men, he felt the need to act tougher, bigger than life itself, and more wicked, meaner. "I felt very vulnerable much of the time," he explained. "I felt a little guy like me had to act big and overbearing, but I wasn't proud of it."

He had a very sweet nature, and so he had to work hard at being mean. As a result, when he forced himself to act mean he became so obnoxious that no one could stand being around him. "What can I say?" he tried to explain. "At times utter irritation would flood up out of me. I was always under a lot of pressure…pressured in everything I said or did. I had to keep the band up to speed, too. I was the perfectionist and didn't always act right."

All the drug taking and group sex the bands frequently experienced shaped Brian Jones the rockstar, as well as the person he truly was. He said, "I was basically shy and introverted, but when I'd meet someone, it was their expectation that it would be about sex anyway. The groupies were there for that purpose. There was no romancing, no hearts and flowers. Our romancing was drinking, drugging, and getting naked."

***

Brian had been the happiest when he first began entertaining audiences in the smaller, intimate clubs. He loved the one on one interaction with fans who were there to live through, dance with, and make love through the music he played. He missed the simple days when he could reach out to an audience member and say something like, "Can I bum a smoke?"

Those were the happy times, and now they appeared permanently over. Now the fans couldn't hear anything the Stones played, as all they did was scream, yell, and holler louder than any speakers or amplifiers could carry the band's music. Brian said honestly, "It was distracting to have the fans screaming and acting negatively during our performances. I felt I could just as well play my music alone in my room, and sometimes preferred it."

As time passed, the band's live performances took on less and less meaning for him. Even though he may have outwardly acted as if the money, fame, drugs, and sex had taken over who he was, inwardly that wasn't true. Seeing the joy on audience's faces from listening to his band's music still was and always would be what mattered most to him. When they stopped listening, but only wanted him and his band for their bodies and their fame—that's when he lost himself in the sea of drugs, group sex, and escapism. He explained his feelings this way, "The audiences were all screaming. It was crazy. The rest of the band tried to maintain a serious posture and continue playing, even though no one could hear us. I then decided to blow the audience off as they'd blown my music off. So I took to playing the song *Popeye, the Sailor Man* during shows. Yes, it made the rest of the band angry with me, but so what? No one was listening anyway.

"I'd be stuck on stage when the performances were over, with fans storming us, and me having my guitar strung around my neck! I couldn't move and felt queasy. It was frightening, and I felt claustrophobic having them rush me. I thought I wouldn't get out alive."

As scenes like those became the norm, he became angry at the entire situation, with the fans, the managers, and anything he could lash out at. He felt numb, and waves of fear and dread flowed through him as he imagined what his life had seemingly turned into—a circus. He pictured the band as monkeys performing for a crowd. No one seemed to care about the music, even sometimes his own band mates. Their concentration was focused on record sales and money. Brian described his feelings, "When the audience showed no respect for our music or even any desire to hear it, and we played anyway—what more could you say other than we were just monkeys who were entertaining for what reason—to sing for our supper?"

He was especially angry with the fans, the "flesh eaters" as he repeatedly called them—the fans who tried to eat him up in pieces, rip him apart, and tear out his hair. He was also angry with himself and felt horror with the choices he had begun to make, such as embodying all the materialism and pleasures of the flesh to such an extent. His heart and soul remained the purist, the musician, and he now believed he had sold out.

He shouted, "It was the bloody popularity thing that derailed the focus of the music, and for that I was very angry! I was angry because it all turned into a carnie, but that's what the audience wanted. It was demeaning! That's also why I strutted so boldly and flashed my tambourine in their faces, and basically acted so poorly.

"What it all came down to was making money—and they insisted I strut. It was from Mick, Keith, and all of them. And, I let them play me into doing it."

Many times he retaliated by acting especially sensual and then pulling it away. "I used my sexual energy on stage to entice all who saw me. As if I were telling them, 'Worship me, want me, love me, but don't touch me!' I wanted to be adored and at the same time hated being worshipped. It was never me they really loved but who they thought they were seeing. People just saw what they wanted to see, and it was never the real me."

He developed a disdain for the fans and was annoyed and scornful of the adulation. All he wanted was for the audience to concentrate on his music and his ability to play, but he hated them for worshipping him as a false idol. As time passed he acted with arrogance and snobbery towards everyone—the fans, the band's assistants, the workmen, the private photographers—everyone and anyone with whom he came in contact. He went so far as to claim that photographer Gered Mankowitz was "nothing more than the hired help, and so I didn't have to be kind to him if I wasn't in the mood. We paid him for his services."

However, once Brian had time to reflect on his actions, he softened. "I'd snap at people and sometimes I'd judge them really harshly in my own critical mind. I'd see them as being inept, inadequate, stupid…and you know, that wasn't the way to be. But, I'd really get annoyed when people couldn't get the point of things," he said honestly and then added, "I have to admit that when Mick and I were getting along, I'd be in a better frame of mind. But when we disagreed on so many things, I'd get annoyed. I would pick at Mick, and he would pick at me. That would make me feel annoyed with the fans or crowds, and as a result I'd show my contempt for everyone."

Even though he was a Stone—whatever that meant any longer—he felt he was back to prostituting, but now he was doing so for the crowds. Sure the money was grand, but the premise was still the same—exchanging himself, whether it was his sexual favors or now his musical favors, for money. He said, "I realized I behaved badly at times and hated being that way, but I was emotionally so young and couldn't handle what had become of me. The success brought the drugs and the feeling of invincibility. I'm sure it looked that way—that I had gone mad with excesses and drugs. I did some pretty crazy things and was full of myself for sure. But that offset the times of deep depression. I needed the courage to continue, and drugs provided me that courage.

"You have to know that, standing there in front of thousands of people, all looking at you, all wanting something from you, all expecting you to be great while you're shaking down into your bones, but wanting to deliver regardless—it was tough, it was very tough. Then you start to buy into your own press that you're wonderful, that you're mad, or that you're any of what's being said. And you wonder if it can be true—maybe you're really nothing at all, and you're making it all up."

Brian constantly faced the huge problem of being terrified to perform in front of large crowds. This gave him another reason to become more and more dependent upon the heavy use of drugs, to get him up on stage. He said, "It's a process of becoming okay in front of a few people and then many people. The drugs really helped me to face the audience. I had to brace myself and shore myself up, including at times the use of heroin. There was the shy side of me that others didn't know. The whole band tried heroin ultimately, but I had to be the first. I was the leader, the founder, in the know, in the groove. And, there were those in the industry who respected me for being that. Hell, it was fun and games!

"Who was anyone to judge me at that time? In my mind it was a guy thing, a 'who's the most manly' thing—*Quiene es mas macho* thing. I did things that were very stupid, silly, and crazy. I took handfuls of amphetamines as if they were jellybeans. Yes, it was adolescent. Stunted emotional growth, I believe it's called," he said honestly.

As they toured, and he continued to act out by whooping and hollering to make the time pass, Mick found Brian hard to deal with. Brian explained, "I acted like the clown, like an idiot, to break the monotony. Even the drinking, drugging, and the girls became a monotony, and we needed something to break the cycle. But Mick couldn't deal with my act. He would turn very dark and brooding. His eyes would cloud over and darken up, and he'd speak in these wicked tones. He was trying to stay in charge of all of us—like the schoolmarm—and we rebelled like kids. Hell, we were kids! I felt the oldest most of the time, but I had the other side—the boy in me was always very much alive. Mick took himself too seriously, and we'd all make fun of his seriousness, which made him even angrier."

The press, with whom Brian had a polite, close association at first, turned into another nightmare for him. Of them, he said, "The press—holy shit! Originally I had to suck up to get the band exposure. But later on they asked inane questions, and the media jerks wanted to dig us a hole for every little 'oops!' we might do.

"You know, we did some good songs and made some good records, and we finally had some money coming in. Suddenly the press thinks they own you, and you have to be a certain way and kiss their ass. Yeah, they were annoying. Maybe I didn't always act right; maybe I wasn't always the graceful rock star for the media. But hell, I tried!"

*** 

While the fans and press were driving Brian to madness, while Mick and Oldham were playing every mean trick in the book to take his band away from him, and while Brian dealt with his everyday physical, mental, and emotional up's and down's—there were still many bright spots taking place in his personal life. In July '64 Linda Lawrence gave birth to his fourth child and third son. They named the baby, Julian Brian, and Brian admitted to having serious thoughts of marrying Linda and finally settling down.

Ultimately, a final decision had to be made, and he decided not to pursue marriage. He said, "My life was evolving so fast with the fame and with the whole Stones gig that I couldn't maintain a homebody lifestyle in the midst of all that, and it was a problem for me. At first Linda thought traveling with me would be fun, but then she wanted to stay at home, and she wanted me to stay there, too. I couldn't do what I had to do with the band and stay home.

"I couldn't be 'Brian Jones, rockstar' on the road and then be faithful homebody, perfect husband/father at the same time. It wasn't in the same arena. Looking back, those were good days, and I was pretty satisfied with the home part of it. But I was also restless to get out and complete my ultimate destiny as well."

While he was enjoying his relationship with Linda, he also began dating and traveling a bit with another beauty named Dawn Malloy. Dawn, too, became pregnant after a while, which meant Brian was facing fatherhood for the fifth time. Of this he said lightheartedly, "Who knew it would take every time! I suppose I sound like the arrogant man who thinks it's the woman's responsibility to not get pregnant. Certainly I cared for Dawn. I'd like to say that I loved all the mothers of my children, even if the love may have been in a very fleeting, momentary kind of thing. I liked them or loved them all in the time that I was with them. But I was moving very fast and not intending to settle down and get the white picket fence.

"Dawn wanted much more than I was willing to give. Things became complicated when suddenly the issue of pregnancy arose. I don't mean to sound heartless or cold for the fact she felt compelled to put our baby up for adoption, but I felt that was a decision she needed to make. I know I sound like an arrogant asshole. She was more hurt with me than angry, I believe, but I knew I couldn't stay with her."

In March '65, Dawn gave birth to a son she named Paul, whom she did put up for adoption. Unfortunately, in those still-conservative days of the mid-sixties, unmarried mothers were not looked favorably upon and faced rejection.

Moreover, Brian hadn't forgotten Pat Andrews and their son Julian Mark, and specifically instructed Impact Sound to give her support money whenever she needed it. Because of his basic gullibility and misplaced trust in his fellow human beings, he never questioned Easton or Oldham as to how much money from his share of the band's earnings they passed onto her. It wasn't until much later that he realized they had constantly turned Pat away, the numerous times she had pleaded with the Stones' office for monetary support. This cold-hearted act was made worse in that—because of management's treachery—Brian was labeled heartless and a scoundrel by Pat, who thought he had abandoned her.

Despite all the misunderstandings, all of the women in Brian's life cared for him and loved him, even though he couldn't fully appreciate it or understand it at the time. He forever carried the scar of believing he wasn't worth loving, but hardly anyone ever knew that. His lovers cared so much for him that all they wanted was to be with him, adore him, and put up with his moods—just to stay with him a while longer.

What was sad for all, especially Brian, was that since he thought himself unworthy and undeserving of true love—whenever someone showed they did care for him—he believed he had to prove them wrong and acted as mean or loutish as possible. Then, once they finally turned on him, yelled and screamed at him, and told him how selfish he was, he could say, "See, I knew you never really loved me. All you care about is my fame and who you think I am. But I'm not that person!"

On the flip side and what no one else knew or could see was that at this very same time—when he had just become the father of two new sons by different women within a very short period of time—Mick was using all of his energy to tear down whatever was left of Brian's self-confidence and self-esteem.

Not only was Brian's leadership of the band being tested, but also his ability to write and compose music was being relentlessly questioned. On the personal side, what further tore down his confidence in himself was Mick's constant prodding and poking fun at Brian's weak spot when it came to his physical appearance—his height.

Mick, who was inches taller and also somewhat bigger when it came to his sex organ—at least according to Brian—told Brian he wasn't a real man because of his stubby legs, short neck, and tiny cock. Naturally if the latter were true, Brian would never have kept all his male and female lovers longing and begging to forever stay with him. However, he was too insecure and beaten down by drugs and anything negative thrown at him to clearly defend himself. He said bitterly, "It's one thing to be the same height as most women; it's another in your strong testosterone days to have someone imply you're not a man. Mick just knew how to get to me.

"He was also cutting the microphones off on me in the recording studios. (See Chapter Seventeen) I would find out when we played the tape back, and I realized I wasn't on it! Again, his way of diminishing me within the band. Whether the rest of the band knew he was starting to do this—who knows what they knew or thought? They just went along with what Mick said by this time."

Pitifully, he was unable to see himself as others did. There were so many who could have given him the love, understanding, and comfort he so much desired, but he managed to shut himself off by self-medicating his many pains, and numbing himself with alcohol and drugs to the real world around him. Others saw him mostly as well-spoken, quiet, gentle, well-dressed, funny, and personable.

He dressed to perfection and wore many assorted colognes, which he preferred squirting all over. Like many Europeans, he didn't personally like deodorants. However, he was meticulous about bathing and keeping his thick hair well-trimmed.

He highlighted his hair, which to him was his crowning glory, and used women's dyes, preferring as he said, "the sun-kissed look." Everyone adored his quiet lisp and appreciated the many antics he would pull just to make them laugh.

What no one saw was, when he looked into the mirror, he saw none of these fine, endearing qualities. He was akin to the anorexic woman who sees herself the three-hundred pound Amazon; but in Brian's case, he saw himself the sawed-off, pathetic dummy.

*** 

In mid-1964, Brian moved from Linda Lawrence's home into his first, official apartment in the upscale Belgravia section of London. He detested living alone and from time to time took in assorted male roommates with whom he shared his dwellings. He found members of the male sex easier to get along with, and they found him fun and easy to live with—at least when he wasn't going through one of his manic-depressive episodes. These would hit him unexpectedly, and without any medication to control the occurrences, both Brian and his guests had to deal with the consequences of whatever took place.

Some of his roommates worked as assistants to the Rolling Stones or were entertainers themselves, and some—but not by any means all—were his lovers. He normally treated his houseguests with great generosity and said what was his was theirs for the time they were with him. Occasionally, his male acquaintances complained that they couldn't give him all the attention and understanding he needed, especially when he was feeling very insecure and paranoid about his interactions with the Stones. Brian said, "My friends wanted my gifts but not my angst. That really hurt. I suppose I was kind of demanding, especially when someone let me think that we were in a mutual closeness and had a mutual affection for one another. The reason it hurt me so much was, you could say, my feminine side coming out."

The decision to live alone, or have someone around, was a lifelong dilemma he faced, and it didn't matter if the choice were based on whether the prospective houseguest was male or female. He explained, "There were times I had my own place but also stayed with others for a time. Then I was, in my own mind, hiding out in two different places! It all boils down to the roles we have to play in life, doesn't it? The constant dilemma of wanting to be alone, hating to be alone, wanting to get along with others, and resenting the contortions you have to go through in order to do it gracefully. It's all very fucked up, isn't it?

"I always had hopes of being able to pick and choose when to be with others and when to enjoy being alone—but it never seemed to happen."

Even though he benefited from the close sexual bond with a few of his male roommates, none turned into a lasting relationship. The main reason was both Brian and his associates chose to remain discreet about their sexual appetites. Some of his guests had a desire for him, but he only wanted to remain friends. As he said, "I wasn't mutually attracted to everyone. I liked to remain only friends with most of them."

Among the more amusing reasons he came up with, to not connect permanently with the males with whom he actually did enjoy sex, were—"the timing wasn't right," "the place wasn't right," "we were only brief, temporary playmates," or "the guy was gorgeous, but we had scheduling conflicts." Of those whom he truly wanted to stay—but knew it couldn't last—he said, "our relationship was condemned from the start."

A favorite joke of Brian's, to explain why he didn't have sex with the majority of musicians and entertainers who sought him out was—"It's not as if I had this big rocket between my legs that was always ready to enter whatever opening came along!"

There were a couple of men that he was especially attracted to, but for whatever reason they couldn't be seen living together, even as roommates. During these times, the two would maintain a separate hideaway where they would go to meet and enjoy each other's company, whenever possible.

An especially close friend of his was Prince Stanislaus, called Stash by everyone. Brian freely said, "Oh, yeah! We had a mutual attraction right off the bat. We connected as much as we could, but we were both so busy. With us, it was the opposites attract thing. I liked my men darker usually and my women fairer usually. Of course some of my women were fairer by choice," he said with a laugh, but then quickly added, "I'm not being critical, since I use the (dye) bottle myself."

He was proud of his time with Stash, as in, "Uh hum, I did that. I conquered a prince. Or, you could say—we conquered one another." (Photo #836)

***

Brian's next succession of female lovers was of a different variety from the gals with whom he had previously hooked up. He began to date a French model, actress, and singer named ZouZou. A unique feature about the couple was that she barely spoke any English and Brian's knowledge of the French language was also practically nil.

He was heard to have boasted lightheartedly, "ZouZou was dark-haired originally but made herself lighter for me."

He saw her for a few months and really liked her company. "She made me laugh, and the chemistry was really there," he said. "We liked to eat out together a lot, and I felt free to be me around her."

Regrettably, his depression and manic-depressive episodes hurt their relationship. He was suffering insistently from feelings of helplessness, because he couldn't get Mick, Keith, or Oldham to create the kind of music he'd always envisioned. He felt defeated professionally, and consequently, his emotional state was on another up and down roller coaster ride. And, at this time of her life, ZouZou wasn't ready to handle that type of volatile relationship.

Another woman Brian truly cared for was a beautiful gal from Sweden named Mona. They had met while the Stones were touring the Continent. He had strong feelings for her, and she felt the same for him. He asked her to return to England with him and marry him, and at first she gave his proposal serious consideration.

He explained, "Why did I ask her to marry me? Not an easy subject. You could say I had always been afraid of the dark since a child and never wanted to be alone. I know that sounds unmanly, but it's true. And, I needed someone around for companionship. There are all kinds of love, and I did love her in a way. You have to understand—I tried as best I could to find true companionship and comfort."

Regrettably, Mick was on one of his one-upmanship trips and decided to play mind games with Brian, as soon as he realized Brian cared for Mona. The band was attending a party Mona hosted, and Mick made sure to give Brian the impression that he and Mona had something going on between them. As susceptible to betrayal as Brian was, he fell prey to Mick's ploy, and afterwards a huge fight erupted between Mona and him. He accused her of cheating with Mick and carried on so poorly that she turned down his proposal to return to England.

Once he calmed down, he begged and pleaded with her to reconsider, but she had witnessed a side of him she didn't like and refused to continue seeing him. Mick relished this victory over Brian, which once more embarrassed him in front of his band mates, making him appear even more weak and hopeless. Brian seemed his own worst enemy during these episodes, but again no one ever knew what his life was like. Whereas he might have appeared weak, cowardly, or even a defeatist—in that he didn't fight back all that hard against those who determined to take him down—what should be considered were both his young age and his life's experiences.

Because of his heartrending experiences, he believed he was doomed from birth. And, because he never had the proper psychiatric care or even confided the true nature of his neglected childhood, he lacked the ability to understand why he behaved the way he did or why others treated him as they did.

What cannot be overstated was the fact he had grown up in a home where both parents had no love or support to give, and the fact he had grown up with several physical, mental, and emotional ailments. Added to that were the two near-death experiences he suffered, in one of which there was proof he died for a short period of time. The high fevers that resulted from both those experiences had to have caused some brain damage, to what otherwise still was a brilliant mind.

Therefore, by the time he met Mick, Keith, and the rest of his band, his body had already been beaten down. His only wish for life had always been to create and present to the world the gift of music that would inspire. Nonetheless, just as he appeared to have reached that goal, he saw his dream being ripped from him.

If all this information were taken into consideration, one must agree that Brian Jones wasn't a coward or a defeatist when confronted by the bigger, stronger, bullying Mick Jagger—but that he had long ago lost the battle against life and had limited stamina with which to fight back.

# CHAPTER SEVENTEEN
## The Music Makers

*"Bill definitely added to the music, but let's give Mick & Keith their due. They became very proficient at turning a phrase & coming up with some very key ideas. So, yes, each one added to the band or they wouldn't have been important. But I still was the maestro, the director, the one who knew which sounds needed to come in, which needed to fade away and come back as a crescendo, and really stir the emotions. I could call it stirring the soul, but it was really more stirring the loins!"*

Brian Jones

History has proven that the pressure, which stems from the force to create, has driven many insane. Musicians have been the angels of sound, with music being part of the creation of the universe. As a species, the human race was originally opened to receive these wondrous sounds; however, the numbing agents—drugs and alcohol—quashed much of music's beauty. Musicians, the true poets, have consistently endured great pain in order to create their gifts of sound.

Brian realized his genius for music at an early age but didn't realize how difficult such genius was for a young man to handle. He had composed songs in his head as far back as he could remember. "Not formally written down," he said, "but saved inside myself all the time." Once he formed his band that concept never changed. He continued to compose in his head, however, he didn't realize the importance of continuously sharing his ideas with the rest of his band.

He knew that the importance for the Rolling Stones to initially gain a strong foothold, plus recognition, within the industry lay with their ability to take established hits—and then twist, bend, and change them by utilizing different arrangements and instruments—before they actually recorded them. He had the perfect knack for listening to something and then making it his own. He could interpret what he heard, absorb any sound, and turn it into music. That was his gift. "It's who I am," he said. "I suppose it was a genetic gift that came in from the Heavens."

He also had the fantastic ability to perform live and teach others to perform. He did a great job of explaining to each, individual Stone his role in playing and working together as a unit, and ultimately making it all harmonize. Most importantly, he taught the band how to do all that and still be in sync.

His theories proved successful in that the band realized a string of gold and silver albums and numerous other awards, within a very short period of time. What he never imagined was how quickly the band would rise to superstardom, with the Stones eventually considered equal to the Beatles as the world's two foremost rock bands. During these early years no other band came close to approaching either band for supremacy.

One constant that no press, critic, reviewer, or fan could argue was that what had propelled the Rolling Stones into superstardom was the raw energy and charismatic presence of their golden-haired leader, Brian Jones. His charisma and style hypnotized all who saw him perform.

His wish was to free the soul of his generation. "At that time there was a big movement for depth of heart, consciousness, and awareness—including the need for peace and love. An entire generation seemed to be crying out for the freedom of expression," he said. "The movement was solid; it was real, and I wanted to help make it real. I couldn't express the serious nature of my heart with my words, but I could do it with my songs, and that was for me the healing and release of my spirit."

Those weren't the words of a narcissistic, money-grabbing egomaniac—as the Stones later described him—but the words of a young man whose heart lay within his music.

He loved his band as much as his music, and said, "It was really super, being with all my band mates! To me, it was everything it could be and even more. There were times when our ideas were very bright; it all meshed, and we thought we were great. Yes, at first we were inspired and very motivated to be artists and to use our genius."

A rumor he wanted to dispel was that he was unhappy with the band's first big hits. "Yes, I may have felt that Mick and Keith's first efforts were pretty weak compared to the soulful blues music that I loved—but I was never contemptuous of these recordings. It was fun being part of it all, and if that's what they liked—then okay! We had to do what we could to get our music out there and make our name," he said unashamedly.

When the band created new music, Mick and Keith would normally come up with an outline and then present it to Brian for completion. He'd bring in the orchestral arrangement and intensity by introducing many different instruments. He compared himself to the orchestra director who says how the music should go, puts in the unique licks and turns, the stops and starts, and the combination of instruments. This method included how each instrument would speak to the other and which instruments would be highlighted at different times during each song.

He was also the one to, at first, direct how the band should represent itself. They all agreed that to compete with the wholesome Beatles, they had to adopt the bad boy image. He described it this way, "It seemed a good show, yes! The main high for us was getting others to believe we were the shocking bad guys. But in reality we were skinny young guys with penises, who had to be larger than life. We wanted to act like the tough guys—it's the masculine dream. Like, 'We're tough; we're bad!' We even stuffed our pants to appear bigger, especially Mick—he could never be big enough. It seemed outrageous, because we were all skin and bones. We portrayed sexy, dangerous bad men. And it worked!"

He foresaw the importance of combining great music with great visual appeal. "The theatrical appeal certainly played into it. We caused a greater sensation by being outlandish, by wearing the boas, hats, and playing up the androgynous thing," he explained. "It was all about staging and opening up new territory with our performances.

"Think about the clean-cut boys who used to stand right in front of the microphones, with their ties and clean-cut shirts, and just sang their songs. That was boring! We were bored with that, and so we pushed the edges.

"Imagine my parents having to lay claim to me, strutting around and doing anything I could dream up," he said with a laugh.

***

Initially Brian had many ideas for songs himself, ideas that he had probably saved for decades. Whenever he tried to present them to Mick, the latter didn't want to hear him. Brian said, "Sure, I tried presenting my ideas to him. But when Mick had his mind set in one direction, it was the same as talking to the proverbial brick wall. I encouraged him to look at different things, but all he'd say was, 'No, Man. No, Man, No!'"

What Mick and Keith never spoke of aloud, though, was that they often did listen to Brian's ideas but only put their own names down as the original composers. For example, when Brian arranged big orchestra pieces he would tell Mick to ensure his name was put on the album as "arranged by Brian Jones". Mick would always say, "Sure, I'll take care of it," but he never did.

Brian wouldn't see the end result until the record or album was released—and by then it was too late. He said that heinous act felt like, "Mick took a pen filled with my own blood instead of ink and put his name on my music. My name was taken off everything, even though I had done all the arranging. But, they erased me."

Typical of the problems Brian faced was, whenever Mick needed help in completing a song that he and Keith had begun to write, Mick—by taking advantage of the soft spot he knew Brian still had for him—would cozy up to Brian and ask him to pretty up the song. With his gentle lisp, Brian re-enacted those times, "Mick would softly whisper, 'Briney, (the name of endearment he often used) lend us a hand, would you?' Then, as soon as I put the revision down on paper, Mick would snap it from me. He needed me to write, create, and give it to him like a trained dog."

Even though deep in his heart he knew he was being used, Brian would still put pen in hand and work the magic that only he could. His love for the band that he had created and his love for music were always foremost in his mind. He said, "Mick and Keith would bring me the words, and I'd doctor them up. At times I'd be at a disadvantage, because the words may not have been something that really resonated with me. I changed them in instances when the words didn't fit quite right, were too pat, or wouldn't musically flow.

"It was like—they would begin the song—then we would co-write the lyrics together, along with my musical adaptation. I still was the bandleader."

He also went on to say, "Keith would have an idea for the melody, and I would expand on it. They always showed me what they were coming up with."

He was actively the maestro of the band's songs from its inception, through 1965, and thereafter. The entire body of works for the Rolling Stones entire career was seeded during Brian's most productive years. He participated in all of their hits and yet was taken aback by some of their awards. "I thought all our awards were wonderful!" he beamed, "I felt inside me all along that would happen some day. But still, in a way, I was surprised to see it come to fruition. The surprising part for me was that we were frequently awarded for the things that I didn't think were the best. And, for the things that I really thought were our best, those weren't the things the public acknowledged. That was just an interesting point of what at times took place."

The evolution of the Stones' music making went this way, "Initially my thoughts and feelings about how the music needed to go and progress were all taken into consideration, but as the band grew musically—it became very hard to tell who brought what to the table. There were sounds we had all heard before, but we wanted to do them differently. Mick and Keith came up with the basics to new songs, but I did all the enhancements and decided what instruments should be used. They came up with the themes."

Inwardly, Brian knew the genius he was, with all his incredible musical ability, but—because of his small size—he imagined he had to bark larger than life to get the attention of his rowdy band, and get them to listen to him. This irritated them and made them think he was overly dictating his wishes, but no one knew the unenviable reason behind his actions.

***

While the battle for supremacy of the band was taking place between Mick and Brian, management was also having its personal battle for supremacy. Andrew Oldham was doing his best to undermine Eric Easton's authority, despite the fact that Easton was the one who had gotten the Rolling Stones name synonymous with musical success.

Easton was consistently securing lucrative engagements for the band and ensuring them a larger share of the profits. Despite this, Oldham decided Easton's methods and views were outdated and undermined future bookings that Eric had secured. Typical of Andrew's treachery was his arbitrarily canceling three major radio shows that the Stones were already signed to appear live, unbeknownst to the band.

As a result, when the band didn't show up for their scheduled appearances, the BBC became livid when their switchboards lit up with disappointed fans who wanted to know where their favorite performers were. This debacle made Eric appear unreliable, which added fuel to the rumors Andrew was spreading that Eric was too old to continue managing their careers. Bill and Brian both stood by Eric, because they knew what he had done for them and would continue to do, but again Mick and Keith—siding with Oldham—prevailed, and they decided Eric had to be let go.

Unfortunately for Brian, he needed Eric's continued support in recognizing him as the band's leader. If he were let go, Brian would have no major voice to back him. A misjudgment for Brian, though, was that he had made the mistake of mixing business with pleasure and had a brief sexual fling with Eric. This was, according to him, a one or two-time thing that occurred during the times he had felt especially isolated and needed to seek comfort in another's arms.

Brian liked Eric as a friend and knew he could trust him—a feeling he rarely had with anyone. When the decision had to be made to let Eric go, Brian said, "I did like him; I definitely didn't love him, but it all got messy and weird. The sex interfered with business."

Actually the loyalty between Eric and Brian swung both ways—it started out strong and then eroded. When Oldham first started to ease Brian out as leader, in order to have Mick replace him, Eric backed Brian up. Brian said, "I think he tried to take up for me at first, but there was something that made Eric frightened about imposing his will too strongly. It was as if he got weaker in the face of defending me. There were things being said about me that were very negative. I feel that Mick, Keith, and Andrew were trying to convince Eric that I was no good for the band's image, because I was unreliable due to my illnesses. I think that was the big thing they were saying.

"They didn't care that I actually was sick—that interfered with their plans for making money. Did Eric want to take up for me? I think he did, but then he was convinced that he was going up against something too powerful, and he decided to let it go and backed away. It was more important to him to keep his position as manager than to keep me. It got to be all about money and what would work, and where the band was going—that was the important talk—'where the band was going.'"

What also had the band standing on edge was the bitter feud that had erupted over the musical direction they were taking. Brian, naturally, insisted on staying with the R&B sound and wanted to focus on creating new songs with that basic theme. Mick, Keith, and Oldham wanted to go for whatever would sell, whatever was more commercial. However, no one ever took the time to test Brian's theory for music making to see if it wouldn't bring in just as many big bucks. He said, "No, they didn't test my theories on music. But, by that time they weren't altogether sure that I could show up for all the performances, were they? Or, they weren't sure that I would do what they said, as they were then deciding what was or wasn't working. Suddenly, in their minds they thought, 'Who was Brian to know what worked?' In their minds I was just this drug-addicted musician...."

The question was—by the time Eric Easton was being let go and New York producer Allen Klein was making overtures to take over the band's management in the United States—was Brian actually too drug addicted to be dependable? His depression and paranoia over losing his leadership, together with the continued sniping by Mick and Keith, caused him to become more and more addicted to the heavy intake of drugs and alcohol. Additionally, being on the road constantly was deadly to him as far as his physical health. He couldn't keep up with the schedules and not face complete collapse.

He described his situation honestly, "At times I felt like I was trying to act my way into appearing normal or sane—God knows whatever that might look like! At times I felt very grounded and normal, but at times I thought I was holding on by a thread—at least I was afraid I was.

"Being sick took away my sense of confidence about what I was going to do or be able to do. So I would pretend to not be as sick as I was. And of course, I had the depression, and I'd get very bummed out at times. When I was in that place mentally, I would just try to pull back and not be around the band, rather than let them see where I was mentally. Then there were times when I had these spurts of creativity and passion that were just extraordinary experiences for me! I feared that others in the world might see my confusion, too.

"So you see, it was all a problem for me. Can you imagine Mozart or Beethoven having to pass their thoughts onto band members first and having to run everything by for approval in order to create their sounds!" he added metaphorically.

He could have created his own one-man band like a Bob Dylan or Gene Pitney and thereby ensure the music he really wanted was recorded. However, he hated to work alone;

he thrived on reassurance and backup. On the idea of flying solo he said, "There are so many good things about having a band with different members playing different parts, which makes it much more interesting—to have the mixture of all these ingredients to work with. Besides, Gene Pitney isn't the Stones, anyway, is he?"

***

Once Eric Easton was replaced and Allen Klein took the band over, Brian's fate appeared sealed. Originally, Klein recognized Brian's musical genius, but then "he regarded me rather suspiciously, it seemed," Brian said sadly. "Like 'who is this weird kid, and is he really that important to the band? Can we do without him?' Allen thought the rest of the band was brainwashed about my talent and my performance, and he didn't feel that their loyalty toward me would serve the future that he envisioned. He thought Mick and Keith had already wrung out all of my musical genius.

"Mick and Keith obviously knew that I brought them to where they were and that I had taught them most of what they knew. I don't think they were hiding that fact from Allen early on. But then—it also seemed that from the beginning they were looking for a way to take what I had to offer and then get rid of me, because I was the loose cannon."

Allen eventually did consider Brian a loose cannon—someone who had too much of his own mind for Allen's taste. Allen preferred "yes men", like Mick or Keith who were mainly interested in making as much money as possible and—if that meant producing commercially-trite recordings—so be it.

Brian said bitterly that all Klein and Oldham cared about was what sold records and what still was selling records. "That didn't sound like a musical direction to me. It was more like being crushed through a meat grinder, being formed, and then spit out like the other music that was selling—as if management knew anything about music at all!"

Klein finally decided that Brian was too much of a problem. As he explained, "I guess it was my attitude as leader—that was a conflict between us. We argued and I'd say, 'We're doing it this way, Allen!' to which he'd glare into my face and sometimes even hold his fist up to me, and say, 'Really? We'll see about that!' You see, I figured I was still in charge.

"Then Mick and Keith specifically told Allen that I wasn't willing to do the music their way. I started bucking the system, as it were. But I thought the system was mine to buck or create! It was more about the general direction the music was taking, and it was more that I didn't want Allen dictating the music we were to do. He wanted us to be monkeys performing in the circus. He thought he knew better than I what music to create. Allen cranked out music like a hamburger grinder; he was a butcher."

Allen didn't want to gamble with Brian's style of music making. Then again, Brian pointed out that "Yes, the Beatles had some pieces that will be considered classical, but they had some crap as well. It's more like a crap shoot when you're experimenting with new sounds and what the public will accept, like, and buy—and what music feels good to the artist. Besides, Lennon had already gone his own way and was doing that horrible music with Yoko!"

He was asked whether the Beatles or other bands ever considered themselves as monkeys performing on stage, as the Stones sometimes felt. "I suspect they did. Although, most bands didn't cause quite the stir that we were, did they? Of course, the Beatles did cause quite a stir, but they weren't inclined to be the bad boys of rock. Hmmm, were they then the 'choir boys of rock'?" he joked.

***

Brian's position as the senior member of the band was being diminished with each new song he created. One example was a single he put together called *Sure I Do*. He expected it to be turned into a commercial record and explained what occurred, "The song was a little fun effort, but they (Mick and Allen Klein) made it pretty insignificant because it never came out, did it? Let's just say it was held back. It was my effort on several instruments with some voice tracks that I laid in as well. I did have some backup from the band, but they're very much in the background in this original version. Mick isn't singing on it, and management didn't think it should be released—since being more of a solo effort made everyone uncomfortable. So they held it back."

On *Sure I Do* Brian played harmonica and even sang a bit; Keith strummed guitar, and there was some drum. The song had a very bluesy sound, and both Keith and Brian liked it. Mick didn't like it simply because he wasn't a part of it. As Brian said, "Mick runs a totalitarian form of band, not allowing other members to suggest new songs or material. Afterwards, he remembers the melodies and words we proposed, makes them his own, and puts them under his own name.

"In this case, Keith thought my song was cool and okay. We were just playing around together, coming up with the song. At the time I wasn't sure what they were going to do with it, as I had other things on my mind. But I thought it was going to be released and thought they'd release it at the right time—at least that's what they said. Then, it never came out."

Today, Bill Wyman has proudly displayed on his restaurant's wall a framed copy of Brian's original composition, *Sure I Do*.

***

Brian felt badly that he and Mick couldn't continue to work closely. "We should have worked perfectly together, what with my genius and Mick's ego—or what he calls his stage presence. We could have meshed perfectly and complemented each other. In the beginning, we were very excited about the differences between us, for we thought that was what would make us great. But what made us great was what eventually destroyed us."

Brian was asked if his stubbornness in not relinquishing his leadership was partially due to the fact he felt he had already suffered so much of his life—and because he had struggled and worked so hard to get the band where it currently was. He said, "That was it, yes, but also I knew much more about music, and how to create it and arrange it. Music had always been my heart, my soul, and my being. For me, it wasn't just a performance taking place on stage—but with Mick—it was all about the bloody fame!"

***

The evolution of how the Rolling Stones created new music over the years, plus the evolution of Brian's rise and fall as the band's leader during those years, took many unique twists and turns. As stated earlier, Brian continuously composed songs internally and never shared his thoughts with the band. When asked if he ever told the band when he planned to have them begin recording their own music and stop recording other's established pieces, he said, "Not exactly, but there were many things brewing within my own mind that I didn't share upfront with them. But, I could see a direction taking place and forming. In retrospect, many things weren't communicated and should have been."

Even when Andrew Oldham separated him from Mick and Keith, to create new songs, Brian didn't speak up at first. He explained his lack of vocalizing this way, "Because planning on creating new music and actually creating it were two different things. I had envisioned us (the band) doing it together, of course. I was always playing around with licks, strumming, doing lines and absorbing, but I wasn't at the place of presenting songs to them that were fully my own compositions. Then everything started moving so fast, now that I look back, that I could never see my foot in a steady place.

"Yes, the bi-polar disorder stopped me from focusing completely, and yet there'd be times when my creativity would just pour out, and then it would be gone…it would disappear." Once again, fate—who had given Brian the genius of music—had for some inexplicable reason robbed him of his ultimate creativity by shutting him down with immeasurable frailties.

He enjoyed a quick laugh, though, when he spoke of a business venture that Mick, Keith, and Oldham struck on their own in 1966—without consulting the rest of the band. They called this new enterprise Mirage Music. Brian said tongue-in-cheek, "That was their secret little work that they were doing. But—it actually turned out to be a 'mirage' and disappeared! It's not like they asked me whether it was okay, and yet they were supposed to be the Rolling Stones. They were thinking of having a solo career, or in their case it would've been their duo or duet! Interesting how that never took off. Can you see Mick doing anything musically without the backup of the band?" he asked rhetorically.

There was a time when Oldham callously challenged Brian to write a song on his own. Brian said, "Under that pressure I floundered. It was more about being separated from the group. Mick and Keith had each other, and I was put by myself, alone. We needed each other's input to really do something great, which would work for everyone.

"At times I tried working with Keith, but it never worked out. Times, dates, and places—it just didn't work out. I didn't have the overview of their chessboard, I imagine. There was one incident, then the next, and I didn't realize that the incidents were supposed to lead to the overall separation of me from the band. In ways I was a great chess player, but with the illnesses that came over me, I lost the ability to fight. Between my personal life and my family at that time—the Stones—everything became so clouded."

He simply didn't know who he was or what was expected of him any longer. His comfort level was never that he desired to be the public front person—the lead singer could have that position. Nevertheless, he had to be the power behind it all, the director, and the one who called the shots—that's where he was comfortable, creating music. He had to be the one to say how it should go. The only times he felt at peace with life and with himself was when performing or playing music. Music was in him, around him, part of him, and who he was.

In a way, he subconsciously allowed drugs to destroy him, when he lost his position within the band and felt as if his creativity had been shut off. What further crushed him was the belief that his band was forced to perform like monkeys on a stage, for the screamers who didn't even care about their music. That was heartbreaking for him, in that all they wanted was to see the outward performance and not to hear their music. He said, "If not for my being such a music purist, I could've been happy just being a money maker. With fame I figured I would get both laid and paid—and I did. But I found that wasn't enough.

"It became my tendency to even question whether I was giving enough of myself to earn the air I breathed. I felt very insecure, very hurt, very wounded, and very angry about losing my voice in what the band did. I knew that the one precious, best thing about me was my music, and when they were taking my music away, and not allowing me to express myself musically—or let it grow in the way it should have—that was the cruelest cut of all."

Taking apart and destroying the last remnant of Brian's self-confidence by teasing and playing mind games with him had become a great sport among the Stones. It became a game of one-upsmanship against a man who already felt he was slowly dying inside. His many illnesses—especially the bi-polarism—crippled him and pulled him away from reality, and before he realized what had happened, he would discover he had missed many rehearsals and performances because they had already taken place. For those unplanned absences, his band labeled him selfish and egocentric—without understanding that he had no idea how those absences occurred—and he couldn't even muster the strength to conform to everyday life, no matter how hard he tried.

He never attempted to explain to the band, and even to his girlfriends, what he was going through because he couldn't understand it himself. He knew something was going horribly wrong with his mind and his body, but he had no words to explain it. He could only tell the story of his life at that time through his music, which was his only voice.

He had begun "composing little ditties here and there, mostly freestyle" for the first time when he was on the streets. He knew he had the gift to speak through music and said, "Of course when I was working around established musicians, they would tell me how good I was, and I always knew when sounds were even a bit off or when they were right on."

***

Hollywood producer Edward Bass said, "Look at any star, from Marilyn Monroe to Vivian Leigh—all the greats—what do they have in common? Pain. It's what gives them their edge." That phrase applied perhaps to no one more than Brian Jones. Like all the entertainment greats who have suffered much inner pain, he suffered from both deep pain and depression, and that was what gave him his edge. On the other hand, even with all the pain, he was both inwardly and outwardly as beautiful and sensual as any legendary star or temptress. He was pure, raw energy combined with the appearance of angelic innocence. (Photo #809)

The Rolling Stones was Brian's band and his creation, no matter how fanatically Oldham, Mick, or Keith determined to take it away. His anger was righteous, in that they were attempting to take the one thing, the only thing, in the world that mattered to him and that he had planned for so long.

His anger was also toward the music industry and how it treated its performers. The musicians and singers were treated like disposable meat that could be sold, transferred, or tossed aside at whim. He determined to never more let himself be treated as disposable meat—his early life had enough of that. When asked if the music the Stones were currently making wasn't really what he envisioned, he answered, "That's a tough question because our music making was an evolution, and it ultimately went in a direction that hadn't been in my mind at all. But in the band's early days, the music we recorded was what I had in mind.

"Plus the music industry, as it was, couldn't accept my level of creativity—since what the industry demanded all became schlock stuff being cranked out with no soul, and basically empty. The music became flat with a nothingness to it."

He genuinely believed that the Stones had it all wrong. The issue wasn't whether he fit in with them any longer. They were the ones who didn't fit in with his music and his concept of his band. He didn't need to fit in with them—they needed to fit in with him! That was how it got so confusing and weird, because the Rolling Stones was supposed to be his band and his music. And, whenever he did try to conform to their wishes, it all came apart.

When he realized he wasn't receiving any credit for his musical creations, he became angry. For a while it had been okay not to have the proper credit given to him, however, when he saw the respect that credit brought, he wanted it. Mick was taking all of Brian's credit for himself, and Brian was being disrespected and diminished. This was when he decided to lash out.

From the band's conception, everything he did was all about them and doing for them, but later on he had no idea what they wanted. They complained about everything he did or didn't do. "It was like being stripped naked over and over. They'd say either my timing wasn't right or my input was wrong…and perhaps I wasn't there for a few sessions, but when I was in charge everything used to run smoothly.

"At first I felt my relationship with the band was a great marriage; then it became a bad marriage. So I thought if I could 'fix' myself, then maybe the marriage would work, and I continued to blame myself for everything. Later on, you could say I became the original troublemaker when I realized I was being deposed as the band's leader. Then I fought like Hell; I was irritated and angry. I felt like the proverbial husband who was being disrespected.

"Afterwards, I tried to find a way to continue on and work with them, but I found myself going further and further down the tubes. Bad marriage? Yes, but I had four mates!"

Early on, when he found himself being shunned, he threatened to quit altogether and go on his own. "It was my power play for a while. Okay—so I was playing Mick the way I was being played. Yes, I was serious at times, though, about leaving. The band begged me to stay at first, but then they decided they'd be better off without me and should get rid of me. The gig was up after a time. And yes, Mick did feel badly originally when he thought I might leave, but that was only because he still needed me and hadn't finished feeding off me."

Bill Wyman suggested that Brian didn't fight hard enough to keep his band. To that Brian said, "I don't entirely disagree with Bill's assessment, but I was so tired. It was a deep blow to me emotionally to be so disregarded by my band after all I had done, and it hurt very deeply. But hurting deeply and having the fire to continue waging the battle are two different things. The way I was treated was demoralizing, and it weakened me. Mick and Keith started writing together, and I became less and less included in all aspects of decision-making."

Typical of the decisions that Brian was now excluded from making—and had always made as the band's leader—were choosing which album covers to go with and which publicity shots to have reproduced. When Oldham unilaterally decided Mick should take over, Mick ensured all photographs and covers showed him in the best light, minimizing the rest of the band.

In addition, the press was accustomed to contacting Brian for interviews, but once Easton was let go and Oldham took over, he told the press they had to talk to Mick from now on, and not Brian. "Andrew told them that I wasn't available or that I was too ill to speak, which naturally wasn't true. Then to me Andrew said, 'Let Mick handle this; he's the lead singer, Brian, and they need to hear his voice.' Mick was reluctant at first, but then he overcame his shyness, I guess. Andrew was doing all this, the plotting to make Mick the spokesman, to push him up front. The rest of the band didn't care that I was being shoved aside—they just wanted to play music and be stars!"

Perhaps the cruelest cut to Brian occurred when Oldham ordered him to step aside on stage and let the entire spotlight be placed on Mick. From the band's inception, Brian and Mick had pretty much shared the spotlight, with Brian singing back-up or playing harmonica and guitar directly in line with Mick's singing. That was the way Brian taught Mick to throw his voice—to match the music Brian played. Audiences loved their performances, which were vibrant and sexual.

After Oldham's direct order to step aside, Brian expected his band mates to speak up for him, as he had always done for them. But they either looked the other way or said, "Let's give Andrew's ideas a chance, Brian. Let's try it."

Once more, he felt isolated with no backup; but since he didn't want to seem the spoilsport, he put his true feelings aside and went along with their theory. As time passed, he was pushed more to the side and the back of the band's performances, until the cameras found it hard to even locate him on stage. They had to hunt him down in order to videotape him, as he played his assorted instruments.

In an attempt to joke the absurdity away, he said, "All I can say is—I didn't voluntarily move myself that far off center stage! Being moved further away wasn't my choice. Andrew told me it was the new choreography, as an excuse naturally, and Mick went along with it. Maybe some day I'll be able to laugh over it.

"There was a part of me that would come to life at times, and I would try to make things work—but those times became fewer."

At times he would fight back ferociously and when that didn't work, he'd attempt to kiss and make up. He was in shock and had no idea what else he could do. Sadly, he didn't realize the die had been cast, and nothing he could've done would ever make King Mick happy. Brian said his efforts to turn things around were made out of "part anger, part self-defeat, and part preening to get back in the band's good graces. I was bloody pissed off, and at times it looked as if I were behaving arrogantly—but that wasn't my intention.

"I knew I was good (at creating music) and I knew I had always been good, but at times my mind caused me to I forget who I really was. At times Mick and Keith said I was no good, and it all became very confusing. I became dead to myself for a while, and then I'd become angry if they said I wasn't any good. But I knew I had created remarkable things—and they couldn't take that from me.

"I felt like the old man losing his potency, but I was too young to lose it yet. Hell, I knew I was still good!"

When he thought back to the times Mick had ordered that the microphones be shut off on him during recording sessions—completely behind his back—he became enraged. "It was so intentional and so very cruel! That really hurt, but it took a while for me to recognize what was happening. Mick made it appear to the others as if it were only a gag—to exclude me. But it wasn't funny.

"What made me the most angry was being put down. I didn't like feeling put down or feeling excluded. I don't like put downs, and I don't like what they considered gags and jokes to discredit me, because ultimately my music was a very serious thing. Their games became a pattern that evolved over time, which started out as fun to put me down. Afterward, when I did drugs and behaved foolishly because I was so depressed, I gave them reason to laugh at me and put me down. It became a self-fulfilling prophecy.

"I always felt they should listen to my opinions and that my opinions were valid. Since the Rolling Stones was my band, I didn't feel especially democratic about hearing their opinions. I was the one to bring them on board and teach them what I knew, and for that I should still be in charge. But later on they stopped listening to me.

"At first, Charlie and Bill performed on a more mediocre level; then as they evolved as part of my group, their skills as musicians and their confidence as performers changed dramatically, as part of the Stones. That was due to my coaching, but they'll say we grew together—and that's true, too. Mick and Keith were diamonds in the rough and only really blasted off after learning from me.

"Hiring managers changed everything. I had intended to keep my input and never meant to turn it all over to them. Despite that, I knew the business was too big for one person to handle and certainly bigger than I wanted to deal with. But by the time I realized the shocking, cold, calculated sense of having no control over my own band, it had already gone too far. The 'machine' had to run things, but I never dreamed I wouldn't have a say any longer."

***

While the Stones were unceremoniously ousting Brian from the band and erasing his musical contributions to their hit songs, the rest of the music world continued to herald him as their king. He began to feel more comfortable, more accepted, and more appreciated among the hierarchy of the rock industry and its fans.

What professional musicians saw in Brian was the radiance that naturally surrounded him whenever he performed. Mick witnessed others drooling or fawning over Brian—whom he now considered his number one adversary. He turned bitter over Brian's connections, talent, and abilities.

Other musicians automatically gravitated towards him, even though he never could understand their personal feelings of respect for him. He never felt worthy enough to be so well liked and in many cases—especially among the newer up-and-coming entertainers—revered and idolized. He said, "When I allowed myself to feel that special, I acted arrogantly toward everyone. Inwardly, I tried to hide the fear that I was never special, or that I had once been special, but now it was no longer true. I was riddled with self-doubt."

His fear in not being special or relevant had nothing to do with his musical ability—he was always confidant about his music. His fear lay in not being liked or appreciated as a human being, feelings he could never shake.

From the beginning of the Stones association with the Beatles, the latter group showed open enthusiasm for Brian's musical ability and preferred being around him as a regular, fun guy when compared to Mick, Keith, or the others. Brian didn't push himself into the Beatles inner circle; they openly sought him. This infuriated Mick, and he determined to be king, no matter what the cost. Ironically—while Oldham could push Mick down the fans and media's throats—the entertainment world was free to choose whomever they wanted to be close to, and that was Brian Jones.

Among the Beatles, Brian considered John Lennon his closest friend, with George Harrison and Paul McCartney close behind. He never felt especially close to Ringo Starr. "I don't know why," he said. "It's like Ringo wasn't on the same planet, not that I'm disregarding him. We just didn't come together like that.

"Once the Stones and the Beatles met—and since both bands were frontliners—we had stayed close. I'd make time to get together with the Beatles, and we would play together. So, was it a real friendship? Yeah, I thought it was. There were very few people who were able to share that same level of celebrity, which we were all involved in at that time.

"John and I were like brothers, and I always admired his writing and his music. He was lucky, in a way, in that Yoko was his shield—so he could feel free to be in his own head, away from everything. To me, it seemed he had the best of all worlds because of that."

There was a rumor that John and Brian were lovers, to which Brian responded, "No. The chemistry thing wasn't there. He was too weird even for me! And, he wasn't pretty, was he?" he added both as a joke and with great admiration for his close friend.

Afterward he added sadly, "John's appearance changed, though, and I thought he was aging badly. His connection to Yoko seemed to have affected him somehow."

What hurt Brian a lot was the difference between the manner in which the Beatles treated John and the cruel way the Stones treated him. He described it this way, "John always had more latitude than I. He could screw up with his band and get away with it. They all thought he was being 'interesting'. He was doing his evolution thing, and no one could figure out if he was being spiritual or simply out of his mind. When I acted the same way and screwed up with the Stones, I became a 'low-life' to them.

"My musical expansion was called ruination, and Lennon's was called legend. You figure it out!"

Ironically, the same situation occurred between the way the Beatles' manager, Brian Epstein, and their producer, George Martin, counseled and guided George Harrison's writing ability, and the way Andrew Oldham and Allen Klein treated Brian's ability to write music. George was also very insecure about creating new, original pieces on his own and felt intimidated by the Lennon/McCartney combination. Nevertheless, with Epstein's and Martin's backup, together with Lennon and McCartney's encouragement, George eventually stood on his own and wrote many hit songs.

Why were things always different for Brian, and the way his band—his creation—discouraged and ridiculed any musical pieces he tried to show them? One answer can be found in the class distinction between the members of the two bands. Whereas Lennon and McCartney presented more refined, polished personas, the Jagger/Richards duo chose to maintain their scruffy, negligible characters.

Brian fit more comfortably with the former songwriters' traits and realized all too late the error in judgment he had made when originally putting his band together. When he first scouted musicians and singers, the older professionals, such as Ginger Baker and Alexis Korner, showed skepticism towards his choice of Mick and Keith. Brian felt he was his own man at that time, however, and felt secure in what he was doing.

The Beatles' mutual respect and friendship for Brian has been reflected in some of their comments. George said, "I always used to see Brian in the clubs, and I would hang out with him. He was a good mate, and I liked him."

George's birth date and Brian's were very close, and because of that he truly felt he and Brian had much in common as far as their more reserved temperaments. He invited Brian to his home at Kinfauns, and the two enjoyed each other's company. (Photo #845)

Paul McCartney said, "I liked Brian a lot. He was very shy and quite serious. A lot of people used to get a bit annoyed with him, but he was lovely…smashing."

Towards the end of Brian's life, John said some disparaging things about Brian, such as the fact he acted needy, paranoid, and would constantly phone him with his problems. To that, Brian said, "John and I were friends, but he was on smack and available to no one at that time."

***

Brian perhaps considered no other entertainer closer to him than Bob Dylan. The two were seen together socially countless times, especially in New York City. Brian said, "I have the greatest respect for Bobby. Bobby's a love, a real love." Again, he meant that as a brotherly love—family.

Soon enough, Mick became jealous of Brian's relationship with Dylan. According to Brian, Mick was furious that Dylan didn't recognize him as "the one". These feelings of vivid jealousy on the part of Mick towards Brian weren't imagined. Several others noticed this, too, among them Jerry Schatzberg, one of the band's personal photographers. Jerry said, "I'm sure there was that competition between Mick and Brian. And I think that when Brian and Dylan started hanging out, Mick may have felt put out."

An especially memorable time that Brian got to spend with Dylan occurred during New York's infamous citywide blackout during the fall of '65. Luckily, the two wound up together, along with a few other musicians, in the same hotel room and waited out the long hours of darkness, with no electricity. Regardless, he and Dylan took out their instruments and jammed the night away, even though they had no speakers and no recording devices. "That night was great fun!" Brian said enthusiastically.

Towards the latter part of the 1960's—when almost everyone in the music industry realized Brian wasn't going to be part of the Rolling Stones band very much longer—taking the last remnants of Brian's self-respect and shredding it to pieces became a sport among the classless few who called themselves professional entertainers.

One such classless individual was songwriter/entertainer Bob Neuwirth. Neuwirth was also close to Bob Dylan. One evening, during a gathering of friends and acquaintances, Neuwirth decided the time had come to openly poke fun at Brian, to the amusement of all those around. A couple of years, or even months, earlier no one would have attempted such a spectacle, since Brian had the respect and admiration of everyone in the rock world.

But now, with legendary stories of Brian's massive drug abuses and sexual escapades—together with the many derogatory rumors about his mental state passed around by the Stones band—he was fodder for every insult someone might care to throw. Additionally, the two Bob's—Dylan and Neuwirth—were known for humiliating any public figure they considered emotionally weak, with Andy Warhol having been their latest target. The two disparaged Andy's life and paintings and ultimately desecrated him.

On this particular night, Neuwirth verbally abused Brian. He claimed the Stones were a lousy band in general, but that Brian's voice was so weak and pathetic—as he was—it was no wonder his band planned to dump him. Brian broke down in tears in front of everyone, with no one coming to his defense. When he was asked what happened, he said, "Neuwirth did hit on every emotional insecurity that I had. As they say, I broke into tears—kind of a breakdown. In situations like that I never really did know what to do. I didn't have the quick comeback, and I didn't know how to deal with it.

"I don't know what brought on his attack. I think they hated the Stones and me for our success. People like Neuwirth wanted to be with us and around us on the one hand, and on the other, they wanted to put us down. That's a peculiar male kind of thing that my feminine side didn't know how to handle."

Sadly, the other Stones weren't there to take up for either Brian or the band as a whole. Brian went on to say, "When I was alone, they (people like Neuwirth) would take pot shots."

Bob Dylan was there that evening, together with Bob Neuwirth; however, Dylan wasn't the mouthy one. "Obviously Dylan felt some panic to have witnessed this and done nothing to take up on my behalf," Brian believed. "I didn't hold what happened against him. There was a crowd around, but afterwards when Bob and I were alone, he said something very simple like, 'Hey, Man, that was wicked,' about what they did to me.

"It's funny how all of the great song masters are very sparse on words that relate to their own feelings and their own emotions, especially when those feelings and emotions aren't related to their music making."

When Brian was pressed further to talk about how the humiliating events of that night impacted him, he said, "There's several things that came clear to me later on that weren't that night. For example, if we're going to discuss who can or cannot sing, do we need to discuss Dylan any further? Aside from that, the two attacked me just to be cruel and decided to attack and diminish me at a time when I was in a fragile place, and when I felt quite paranoid about life. It was the cruelty of the assault that I think really disarmed me, 'cause I always like to feel that—when I'm among other musicians—we could enjoy camaraderie and mutual respect.

"But Bob Neuwirth was on the outside of great success and looking in, since many don't even know who he is—nor would they care to, if they did!

"The entire situation was a personal affront to me, Brian, the person. And to say I was weak, a coward, shallow, and that I couldn't even sing was every assault he could pour into that one attack. It did unnerve me at the time, as I was in a weakened place and had a hard time dealing with what they said."

Brian's personal hurt was further made clear with these words, "If Dylan and I are such good friends, why did he not speak up for me? And, to carry over—why didn't lots of people take up for me? Or be on my side or try to help me when I was down? This all went back, for me in my mind, to my own family and then everything that happened afterward, along the way. Supposedly all these people in the world loved Brian Jones. But who were they? And what did it matter when no one was ultimately there for me?"

He tried to chalk up the unnecessary cruelty to the two Bob's being jealous of his instrumental talent—and especially his looks. "Just look at Dylan's face—neither of them were as blessed as I was, were they? I had it all, and the women—their women—threw themselves at me. Well—hey! Who can blame them?" he went on to joke, while flipping his long hair to the side.

He tried to laugh, but he was hurt because he couldn't understand why they turned on him, his friends, and why they didn't treat him well. He was always surprised when people attacked him in that manner, as it was so much against his true nature—that was, when he was straight and sober.

Brian knew he had a fantastic voice for folk-singing, as represented by the solo he sang in Jimi Hendrix's *Little One,* and in the pub scene during the movie, *A Degree of Murder,* in which he sang softly in the background. Even though he knew he had a good folk-singing voice, he still said, "Yes, but the Stones aren't a folk-singing band. We're rock stars."

Bob Dylan often advised Brian to leave the Stones once he, too, realized the band would never play the music Brian wanted. Since the band was still widely referred to during the early to mid-sixties as *Brian Jones & the Rolling Stones* among the press and public, Brian was asked why he didn't at that time take the band's name with him and start another new band? He answered, "I don't know. It seemed like so much work to start up again. Plus, it's like being in a bad marriage. You keep hoping things will straighten out and get better.

"The other thing is that we, the Stones, were moving forward so rapidly. We had gotten into a larger and larger place of recognition in the public eye and in sales. We were in a whirlwind, and I couldn't find a good spot to stop and change directions, even though I knew it was taking us into places I didn't intend to go. Yes, Dylan told me to leave them, but I still felt so much loyalty toward the Stones. They were my project, and I hated to abandon my own project.

"I thought I could still turn them around. I guess I was under that delusion for a while. Besides, it became easy to get caught up in the demands of what the band wants and expects you to do, and what they think the public wants versus doing the music you really feel you want to create inside yourself."

*\*\*\**

Bob Dylan wrote at least a couple of songs with Brian in mind. The most famous was *Like a Rolling Stone,* which was Dylan's tribute to the band that Brian built. The ideas behind many of the lyrics were based around Brian's basic philosophies, especially relating to the many chances he took originally to get his band noticed. One theme of Brian's that Dylan focused on was, *when you got nothing, you got nothing to lose...you're invisible now....*

With *Ballad of a Thin Man*, Bob reflected on the deep paranoia and troubled life Brian endured at the time. Brian said of these lyrics, "Isn't that a kick? To degrade me and say I'm frail and neurotic—while on the other hand to be jealous of my sexual prowess!"

He went on to say, "Historically men think any man who's getting more than they are sexually—they've got to bring him down in some way. Even friends. Even Mick—who should have been my good friend and who was my good friend at that time—Mick would dig at me, and then we'd dig at each other. That's how guys do it. But it hurts, and it exposed my weaknesses publicly, and that was very painful. I wanted to say to them, 'Oh, no! Don't tell them that!'—like the things about not being a good singer. Even though I knew I wasn't a good singer, I still didn't want to hear it."

Despite everything, Brian always considered Bob Dylan to be one of his closest friends. Whenever talking about Bob, he would automatically entwine his index and middle fingers to show the sign of togetherness.

As the years passed, Bob Dylan began to be especially afraid for Brian. He sensed that something was terribly wrong between Brian and the rest of the Stones, and he tried to help and advise him. Brian said, "Dylan was afraid for me. He sensed the danger. He's a very psychic guy, and he warned me more with his energy than by saying it. He wanted me to pull away from the Stones. Dylan thought it was better for me to be isolated, as he was. He preferred being his own man and hoped I would follow his example. We recognized a mutual genius in each other."

Additionally, when Dylan looked at Brian, he would see his own worst fears come to light. The fears were borne out of the extreme fame and notoriety both men realized, even though Dylan wasn't the kind of star—like Brian was—whose fans would rush to rip off his clothes. He wasn't a sexual idol by any means but still had his own level of paranoia of what could possibly happen to him.

Bob looked at Brian and saw how good fame could be and how scary it could become. He felt himself warned in ways, by observing Brian, his close friend. On the other hand, Bob did envy certain things about Brian, as in feeling Brian had such an easy time sexually. Brian said lightheartedly of Bob's envy, "Yes, I did have people after me for sex all the time, but that's not the same as good sexual experiences."

Then, as a joke he added, "But I have to say—Bobby Zimmerman—just look at that face you have! I *know* I'm the pretty one."

There was a true brotherly love between these two friends. As soon as Bobby Zimmerman—Bob Dylan—heard Brian had died, he bought the most expensive casket he could find and had it flown out on his private jet, in time for Brian's funeral.

*** 

Brian took a few moments to talk briefly about some of his other associations, or thoughts, on those he knew within the world of music:

He called Eric Clapton a "real prince!" Roy Orbison "was a good bloke, and I liked his singing."

Rod Stewart, Brian said, was a "cocky little bastard! It's not that I don't like him…I just don't care about him." The two men never performed on stage together but did attend the same parties.

The team of Peter & Gordon were fortunate to have worked with Brian. He helped produce an album of theirs, for which he was paid a nominal amount. He said, "It wasn't about the money. I tried to help other musicians and friends along the way. It was just a lot of fun doing it. There's so much talent, and you can really feel the energy that was coming forward at the time."

He personally enjoyed Simon & Garfunkel's music and liked the softness of their sound. "Let me say that their music struck a note or a chord with me that hadn't been struck that way before, and I liked that. We only met in passing." Then, as a joke, he added, "You know, they have problems getting along. So, imagine, if the two couldn't work things out—imagine me and the four Stones!"

Of Elton John, he said, "You gotta love him. But I'd rather if he were more about his music and not so much about his stage presence, which is brilliant in its own right. But his music seems somewhat lost now in the personification of his various stage routines."

Brian had a special fondness for the music of Sam Cooke, and especially liked his song *Bring It on Home to Me*. "Don't you just love those words?" he asked rhetorically and added, "Sam's got that Black/bluesy soul energy." Brian was asked why the Stones didn't do their own rendition of *Bring It on Home to Me*, to which he replied, "How can anyone top Sam Cooke!"

While thinking back to his time with the Drifters (Photo #808) he said, "That was a nice time. Although, the cynical part of me would say I had wished for more depth, but overall they were good chaps."

Of Neil Diamond, he said Neil was a "really good sport actually, but we never got to share a friendship." Of Tom Jones, he said mysteriously, "I remember him well from a birthday party given for me."

Bobby Goldsboro was "shallow". Eric Burden "made a few contributions for a short while but didn't have staying power. He tried to learn some things from us, and maybe he did. Most people can't make it for years or decades in the industry."

He really liked Glen Campbell. "I knew of him and had a high regard for what he did. We crossed paths and there was no animosity whatsoever between us. We acknowledged one another." As far as the Dave Clark V, all he could say was "cheerleaders, and I didn't take them too seriously."

About Elvis Presley, he said, "We thought the King had some pretty good moves until we started making some of our own. But he influenced us; he was influential in seeing what could be done on stage. We met Elvis and spoke briefly; he was a bit standoffish. He hated to see the British invasion and resented the British bands that he felt were taking over the world. He was insecure about that, even though we weren't trying to take over his territory, but wanted to develop it in a whole different way."

Brian used to imitate Elvis when he was a young boy. He would stick out his leg and foot, gyrate his hips like the King, and think it was cool. Later on, he realized those moves were just the beginning of what could be done on stage, and he took those initial steps and turned them into a more sexual and sensual presence.

As far as the other bands that were part of the British Invasion, such as the Kinks, Zombies, and many others, Brian said, "We (the Beatles and the Stones) really started something, didn't we? But there were few that lasted. It was a kick to see so many coming to America, from England. This was a really fun time, and we didn't have any animosity towards the other groups. We really wanted to see them also do well, because it had always been that music was a predominantly American phenomenon that the whole world listened to. And we wanted to make our place in it, too."

Of The Mamas & The Papas, he said, "Yes, cool! Really nice band." And of the Beach Boys—"Boy! What a class difference as far as music."

Brian had kind words when speaking of the American crooners from the previous generation. He said, "Ones like Frank Sinatra and Tony Bennett, I never met them face to face, but I knew who they were, and I presume they knew who I was. I have great respect for those who have quality and control over their singing voices, because I don't have it. That's something I really admire."

When the Rolling Stones appeared on Dean Martin's TV program, Dean went out of his way to put the band down and embarrass them in front of his audience. The Stones said nothing at the time, but later on Brian said of Dean, "What an asshole! He was disrespectful and treated us like children who were only a fad—as if we were laboratory frogs to be studied. He was demeaning. We took it then and thought of him and his show as something we just had to get through. At the time we still needed to be seen as much as possible. Clearly, we weren't his favorites. As far as why some of these veteran singers didn't appreciate us, I figure it's because we were breaking new territory and new ground. So that may justify why some of them didn't like us—particularly the older musicians who'd been at it for a while. Not many were as rude as Dean Martin though; it just depends on who we're talking about."

Brian was asked about the rumor that he and Gene Pitney didn't get along. The rumors stemmed from manager Andrew Oldham's brainstorm to have the two very different entertainers collaborate and write a song together. The brief union between Brian and Gene had disastrous results. When Brian was asked why Oldham thought the two might have worked well together, he answered, "God knows!" He went on to explain, "Gene Pitney and I were on different pages musically. My interpretation of what happened is that Gene had a more grounded, solid feel to what he was doing. And mine was more poetic, ethereal, and complex. I liked him personally, but we were just…well, I don't think he liked me personally. I think he thought of me as a spoiled brat, but I had to be me.

"Gene had a strong voice, which I didn't. Talk of mixing fire and water! I was more the fire, but I guess we took turns pouring water on each other's fire."

***

Brian had the top three rock stars in the world as close friends, John Lennon, Bob Dylan, and Jimi Hendrix. Not only did the three respect and admire him as a musician, but they were also proud to call him friend. They cared about him, but when he needed them the most something went horribly wrong, and they weren't there.

Brian tried to explain it this way, "Yes, I was close to all of them, but—you know—it's like you know you're friends and you're close, and everyone has his own world going. There's this mutual respect, but guys don't have the tendency to talk about those things—the feeling of closeness to one another. We feel it, but then we don't get together often enough. We don't say many words, but we express ourselves through our music. That's why we do it, the music. That's how we talk."

\*\*\*

Among the many bonuses of being a rockstar—in addition to meeting and interacting with other legendary musicians and entertainers—was the opportunity to travel widely and become familiar with different lands and cultures. Brian took a moment to talk about some of his views and experiences in foreign lands:

"The Fiji Islands are beautiful! Once I arrived there, I thought I had died and gone to Heaven. Their sunsets reminded me of an instant in photographic time that has to be captured before it disappears. The land was peaceful, which adds to the feeling of coziness. Being among such beauty made me feel safe and comfortable, especially since I wasn't mobbed there.

"Of course, Morocco was a blood-stirring experience and got the old juices going, while firing everything up.

"Naturally, I liked Germany, Sweden, Holland, and Amsterdam—oh, yeah! That was fun! The band and I got into a bit of trouble there but…hey…drugs and broads.

"Australia was a good, substantial place. I did have some depression there, but overall I liked it. Although, the people seem a little crass in ways, don't they? I noticed a class difference with the Aussies; they were rougher around the edges. I guess in ways that was liberating, but in other ways…I wasn't quite sure what the wild card might be.

"We had a few blokes we partied with, but not many. The band was well protected. It's an odd thing to have such a large country with so much freedom, and then wondering what that freedom might cost you—such as your life. Yes, we had the feeling of either being robbed or killed.

"Britain's prisoners were originally sent to populate Australia, you know, so it's more wild, with less laws, less structure, and with less of a feeling that there's a system in place that can handle things.

"New Zealand was different. I loved it! I didn't feel the danger there that I did in Australia. New Zealand felt more natural in a purer way; although, it's less modernized than Australia, but still felt more humane. Australia felt wilder, and wild can be a good thing—but I wasn't sure about it."

## CHAPTER EIGHTEEN
## From Bad Boys to Glamour Girls

*"Brian Jones was a fine man; he seemed very interested in what I was doing. You know, I've got the feeling that he wrote 'The Last Time' & 'Satisfaction'. I know these songs are credited to other people, but…"*

Don Van Vliet a/k/a Captain Beefheart, Artist & Musician

The evolution of the Rolling Stones wouldn't be complete without discussing the significance that sexuality played, as well as the strategy that Brian laid out for his band to depict. Once he presented his idea, Mick enthusiastically backed him all the way. One area the two men had in common was their sexuality. They were fond of the feeling of silk and lace against their bodies, "much nicer than traditional masculine clothing," Brian said. "If they gave it a chance, most men would prefer it—but they just don't know it."

He went on to explain the band's evolution, "We decided to take advantage of the experimental nature of everything we did, from drugs to sex. The next step was to bring us from personifying bad boys to glamour girls. We were crossing all boundaries that we could possibly find and thought doing so was really cool and outrageous. That was the thing we wanted—to be outrageous and notorious. With regard to all those hidden sexual compulsions and proclivities that humans lock away under the façade of what's proper in society, we were blowing the doors off all that."

Typical of the cross-dressing the band took part in was the promotional video and photo shoot for the release of their new single *Have You Seen Your Mother Baby, Standing in the Shadow?* The photograph the band selected for the record's cover was the infamous girlie shot, with each band member dressed and made-up from head to toe as a woman.

Brian appeared especially seductive pouting and blowing cigarette smoke while dressed as Jean Harlow; whereas Mick, dressed as a woman looked—as Brian put it—"especially froggy!" Brian was very comfortable dressed as Harlow and looked especially beautiful. He said, "I was always one of the girls even at home, and with Mick I was one of two sisters, while Keith was our brother."

During the photo shoot for *Have You Seen Your Mother Baby* the band went all out hiring professional make-up artists to enhance the Stones' appearance. Brian joked, "Trying to cover all of Mick's blemishes was a huge job!" When he was asked which of the two, he or Mick, was more girlie, he answered honestly, "To tell the truth, sweetie, it was a toss-up! But I was always more fun and effeminate, whereas Mick was very critical and judgmental of everything. He always acted like he had something up his ass, but when he's on stage jumping around like the frogman, he wants to pretend he's not.

"We loved taunting the regular establishment, especially when shocking our parents. We imagined all parents were the enemy. Mick and Keith thought my dressing up girlie was cool, and they began to copy me. The others thought this cross-gender dressing was hip at that time. Even Charlie and Bill went along with my theory, because every child's been hassled by their parents at some time. Maybe the two didn't appreciate the depth of what we were doing, but they knew that the impact of the current rebelliousness of youth—as it went against the establishment and parental control—was extremely strong. You see, it was considered very cool to be anti-parent and anti-world as it currently was, and we were creating the new freedom."

If truth were told, the impetus for the lyrics behind *Have You Seen Your Mother Baby* was especially cruel, as written by Mick and purposely directed at Brian's past. He explained, "The lyrics are disparaging against me. It's very deep, since Mick knew about mother and me dressing up, and her influence on me. It was like mum tried to turn me into her little drag queen.

"I had always thought I could use my early background at some point in our careers. One day during a train ride I said offhandedly to Mick, 'Yeah, my mother had lots of nice things to wear,' and probably something else. But Mick was so good at reading me that he took what I said—and knew what had happened to me—and so that gave him the idea for the lyrics. He wrote them partly to poke fun at me, with a major touch of cruelty."

While reflecting on the impact his parents later had on him, with regard to cross-dressing, Brian said, "A child always wants to be loved by his mother, and I always wanted my father's approval, but never got it." The way he got to retaliate was to let his parents see him dressed wearing women's clothing, as a personal dig, while part of the Rolling Stones band.

Brian was asked whether he believed he acquired any of his talents from his parents, to which he answered, "Can you see my father gyrating on stage as a Stone? But, I got the prim and proper seductress from my mother. Oh, yeah—what an inheritance!"

Needless to say, the change of the band's attire from being the bad boys of rock to the glamour girls of rock was highly successful. Soon other bands adopted the premise of appearing feminine on stage and felt free to perform wearing full-face makeup, wigs, and girlie dress. Brian's natural instinct proved correct once more, and he was recognized as being the first to take the initiative in leading the way for the continued Sixties' sexual revolution of the days' youth.

***

Brian's successes, while appreciated from afar, were continuously being minimized by the band for which he would give his blood, if asked. At times he felt so isolated that he took to phoning various friends and acquaintances on the outside during the middle of the night— begging for advice. He couldn't sleep because he was haunted by the ever-increasing reality that nothing he could do would ingratiate himself back into his band. Every effort seemed futile, and so he cried out to strangers for help. He searched vainly, wanting to know who he really was and what everyone expected of him. He truly was the lost child who couldn't find his way home.

To regain acceptance, he thought he had to act the wise-ass and be the baddest rockstar in the world. Since he felt so small, at least in his own eyes, he thought he had to act bigger than life. Typical of his willingness to do anything to please the Stones—even if it meant humiliating himself, if that's what they wanted—was the famous or infamous "masturbation video" he made at their request. This was done on the eve of the *Have You Seen Your Mother Baby* photo shoot, when all the guys were dressed as women.

The Stones, plus a few close associates, were locked away in their hotel rooms, when Mick brought in a movie camera and said what a fun idea it would be for Brian—who looked especially vampish—to hoist his skirt up, take out his cock, and masturbate for the camera. At first Brian teased back and said, "Sure, let's try it." He opened his legs and began to touch himself erotically while the camera rolled. Before he realized it, he had gotten himself hot and between the baiting and eager coaching from Mick and the others, he continued on with the sexual act until he completed, and came.

The video was supposed to be made all in fun and never meant to be shown to anyone outside the band's inner circle. As trusting as he always was Brian forgot about the tape, but Mick to this day continues to show the cruel video at parties, to the delight of his guests—forever continuing to demean Brian's memory.

***

Brian's true place in history, as far as his contributions to the Rolling Stones success, had always been openly acknowledged by each of his band members. Keith and Bill especially glowed over the integral part Brian played in turning even their most mediocre songs into major hits.

A year or so before his death, as rumors of his drug addiction and the falling out with his band took center stage, the band's producer, Allen Klein—who was now doing business as ABKCO Productions—together with Mick Jagger and Keith Richards, began their brutal campaign to re-write the history of the band. Whereas Brian's name had already been eliminated as having arranged and co-written the lyrics and melodies to a majority of their songs—and whereas Mick and Keith had already ensured that all compositions went through the industry as having been written entirely by the "Jagger/Richards" songwriting team—the public and press were easily duped into believing that Brian only had minimal input as far as musical contributions, even from the band's early days.

Nothing could be further from the truth, and true music aficionados ascribe how many of the band's top songs were directly the result of his instrumental input. (See Appendix)

According to Brian himself, he took an active part in the creation, arrangement, and ultimate success of the majority of the Rolling Stones hits. Following is only a partial list—continued and woven throughout the remainder of this chapter. Brian's comments appear in quotations:

*Andrew's Blues*—Brian co-wrote the hilarious lyrics. The song poked fun at Andrew Oldham. Brian said putting it together and recording it was "Fun! Fun! Fun! We certainly made Andrew the butt of the joke, didn't we? Each of us put in our little contribution to the lyrics—even though Mick was trying to take over everything as usual. We would just jump in with whatever we could think of. A lot of it was bantering back and forth, before we came up with the final idea to record it. It was just too good not to!"

*Satisfaction* and *The Last Time*—Brian co-wrote the famous guitar riffs with Keith (Photo/Letter 813)

*Paint It Black*—A musical collaboration between Brian and Keith. Brian said the idea for the melody was borrowed "by me from Ravel's Bolero. This classical composition was a favorite of mine since a youngster. It's my way of honoring Ravel. The final credit was thrown into Keith's lap, though, with even Bill taking more credit for it than he should have."

Brian's playing the sitar made this hit song the musical masterpiece that it ultimately became. (Photo #822)

*Honky-Tonk Women*—"This was an old song that I wanted to do my way. I did the guitar work initially and even sang the words. I presented my thoughts for the final arrangement. I found the song and brought it to the band early on—but they didn't want to do anything that I wanted to at the time. Finally, when I was at the end of my time with them, they decided to record it."

Ry Cooder was the musical originator for *Honky-Tonk Women* and came up with the storyline for the song. Mick and Keith heard Ry do it, as Brian already had. Brian was the first to offer the suggestion for the band to re-do the song his unique way, and he presented his guitar licks and chords for the way the song should ultimately go down. "The final version I came up with was different from Ry's. Mine was my personal bluesy way of working it, and when Mick heard it, he got a woody over the song.

"I put my three cents worth in with the steel guitar and drummed out the beat. Keith became more solid playing it as time passed. I thought I had taped the final version, and I should be on the recording."

Indeed, Brian's final memory of this song, which he dearly loved, was that he would be on the final recording. Still, his band chose to eliminate him and dubbed in their new guitarist, Mick Taylor. Could the Stones perhaps have planned ahead of time to eliminate Brian from the song and have Mick Taylor take his place, because they already knew Brian wouldn't be alive long enough to promote it together with them?

*She's a Rainbow*—Brian handled the orchestral arrangement and wrote the majority of lyrics. "I pushed my energy to get the lyrics and melody across. Then Mick took it and brought it forward under his name."

*Under My Thumb*—Lyrics were Mick's, but Brian showed him how to rework and embellish the phrases to make them work with the melody. Brian arranged the music and ensured the lyrics were in sync. His unforgettable marimba playing made this otherwise mediocre song the hit it became. (Photo #821) Brian explained, "Mick wrote those lyrics for me. That's where he wanted me—under his thumb! The rest of the Stones suspected that's what was going on. Mick and I communicated these thoughts with our eyes and not with our words."

*Play with Fire*—Brian said the piece's dramatic music was "fueled by my emotions, and once again, the lyrics were done by Mick for me as a warning." Once the listener understands the true meaning behind the sinister lyrics, they leave a lasting impression.

*Heart of Stone*—A collaboration. "Mick did much of the lyrics. He was the hard-hearted one, and everyone knew that. He always wanted to appear heartless." There was some controversy as to whether Brian or Jimmy Page played on *Heart of Stone*. Jimmy claimed to have played on the final recording, saying the piece was too difficult for Brian to handle. Brian disputed that claim, saying that while he was too ill to play during the song's rehearsals, he did indeed play on the final recording. He said, "It was a difficult piece, but I did it." Asked if he had ever encountered a piece of music he couldn't conquer, he answered, "Not that I know of."

*Mother's Little Helper*—Lyrics were Brian's. "Mick had a part in it, too, but it was my experience as a youngster, watching other mothers' lives. We reveal what they needed to make it through the day—namely, tranquilizers."

*Time Is on My Side*—"A collaboration, and we harmonized beautifully, don't you think? I sang backup, but Mick really did shine here. Let's give the devil his due. I wrote the basic melody and decided on how the harmony would go."

*I Am Waiting*—"Both the backup vocal and arrangement were my idea. Keith took it and imitated my feel for the song."

*Dandelion*—Brian came up with the melody. "I was the music man for this one."

*Prodigal Son*—Even though Brian played a great harmonica on this piece, unfortunately it can hardly be heard on the final recording. Mick purposely minimized the sound of Brian's harmonica playing, to make it appear inconsequential.

*\*\*\**

What Brian basically did with each of the Rolling Stones songs—and with very few exceptions up until the very end of his time with the band—was to "pretty up" all their melodies and lyrics. He arranged most of the compositions, especially the large orchestral ones.

His heart, soul, and essence were behind all of the band's music, and as time passed, Mick and Keith learned how to memorize his unique talent for creating and embellishing music, and tried to adapt them for their solo works.

Brian referred to all of his songs as his babies and nurtured and protected them as best he could. When asked which songs he preferred, he declined to answer, saying a creator should cherish all his works equally. When he discovered that his name had been erased from so many of his works, he said, "That really pissed me off!" His music was his soul connection and his gift to the world.

As to which musical instrument was his favorite, not counting the sitar, Brian claimed the keyboard or piano. He used the keyboard mainly to direct how the music should go and to compose. He said, "The keyboard held unmastered secrets for me, and I never had time to master them. To conquer, understand, and become the instrument is very important to me." He didn't feel as comfortable with the keyboard as he did with the other instruments. "There was a lot to master, and it never bored me."

*\*\*\**

Without ever realizing it, Brian was the inspiration for many wonderful things. He inspired countless lyrics, innumerable melodies, and various musicians in many genres, many of which he never had any idea. These musicians and singers admired and respected what he could do and the uniqueness of what he was, both in his personal life and his creative life.

Pete Townshend of The Who expressed his feelings for Brian in several ways. He once said simply that Brian's harmonica playing was intoxicating—much better than Mick Jagger's could ever be, as was Brian's guitar playing in the Stones song, *The Last Time*.

When Brian died, Pete wrote a poem for Brian called *A Friend of Mine*. Some of the ways Pete wished to remember his friend were to say how the girls in the audiences screamed more for Brian than for Mick. He went on to say affectionately that Brian was musical, almost a musicologist in nature, and that he always loved to talk about the subject. He later added that of all the Stones, Brian was the only one with whom he could have a serious conversation regarding music and its impact on the world, spiritually and religiously. In Pete's opinion, Mick was only willing to talk about his own charisma, Keith was completely indifferent, and the rest…he implied they were a waste of time to try and converse with, in general.

Pete thought back to a time when he and Brian sat in the audience together to watch Stevie Wonder's first show in the UK. When Stevie was informed the two were watching him, he actually fell off the stage! Pete went on to say Brian was always considerate and kind to him, and was very encouraging of his writing.

Some of the other bands and singers that Brian worked with and secretly recorded a bit with were the following:

The Byrds' Gene Clark openly claimed that Brian inspired their mega-hit *Eight Miles High*. Brian also played tambourine with them on one or more recordings but—as with any other bands' recordings that he participated in instrumentally or vocally—he could never have his name put on the recordings for credit. That was contractually unacceptable, since he was signed exclusively with ABKCO. Brian said the Byrds "used some of my ideas for songs, and I helped them with my tambourine work. I did it for fun, not for the credit. We'd just hang out and play, and it used to be fun back in those days."

Brian played saxophone on the '68 Mick McGear song *What Do We Really Know?* and played harmonica on a couple of songs in a Peter and Gordon's album. He also played guitar on Nico's single *I'm Not Saying*.

There were many others that he also took an active part in, but unfortunately Brian didn't keep a written record of all his contributions.

The Beatles were probably the band he played or recorded with the most, not counting the Stones. He played oboe on *Baby You're a Rich Man* and percussion on *What's the New Mary Jane?* When asked to fill in, he occasionally played bass guitar.

For the Beatles recording *All You Need Is Love*, he played tenor sax. Some thought he wasn't physically present for the final recording—which was true—because he was with Jimi Hendrix and Eric Burdon on the day the final version was cut. However, Brian explained that his playing actually was dubbed in and, therefore, was on the final recording since he had been present "to lay down all the tracks."

He took part in *Yellow Submarine* and *A Day in the Life*, also for the Beatles. He said he jammed on many of their songs and often their final creation would come out of those sessions, but again he couldn't have his name placed on any of these, for legal reasons.

A few months before his death, Brian and John Lennon put together a group they flippantly called "Balls". He said this was something they did privately and not for public consumption. "We played at making the album, and some recordings were done. We were always going to do more," he explained. Had they gone public, he and Lennon wouldn't have used their own names but—as "our little joke to the world," he claimed—they would only use the name Balls to see if anyone would get the humor behind the sexual moniker.

One of Brian's favorite Beatles songs was *Norwegian Wood*. He loved it, he said, "For many reasons, in particular the sitar playing." The other was *In My Life,* of which he said, "Those lyrics have a soft spot in my soul—that's a fine song!"

Another Beatles favorite, but of which Brian said he especially liked Joe Cocker's version, was *With a Little Help from My Friends.* All these tunes brought a special smile to his face.

However, nothing brought a smile to his face more than when he spoke of Jimi Hendrix and his music. Brian was very proud of the joint collaboration between Jimi and him for their song, *Little One*. Brian played sitar on the recording and also sang solo on the final version. Jimi wrote the lyrics that Brian sang, using his folksy-style singing voice. While speaking of the song's lyrics, he literally oozed, "Yeah, Jimi's got soul!"

Brian also harmonized on other Hendrix pieces, although none have been formally written down for posterity.

There was a rumor that Dave Mason may have played sitar on *Little One*; however Brian wasn't particularly fond of Dave and turned down Dave's offer to join in with the final recording.

***

Brian said he would have easily outgrown the style of music Mick Jagger and the rest of the Stones wanted to continue performing. He always respected classical composers and musicians and even hoped to some day write his own classical masterpiece, and hopefully, a classical piece of literature. He humbly thought that what he had created so far in his career hadn't been actually great, yet.

The Rolling Stones spread the unfounded rumor that Brian had no idea what direction his music would eventually take. Nothing could be further from the truth. He had a definite vision. He said he saw his band's music evolving into more electronic and classical compositions. "My theory is all about evolving the music and continuing to add new components of experimentation into creating something unique and different, which will include classical.

"This music will include the bare, basic roots of things; the pieces will include strokes, licks, and levels that we (the band) have previously heard and picked up, or that we may even have imagined. So, for me it has always been about wanting to take music into a higher, finer, and more expanded direction. For someone to say that classical works charm me is basically true, but not a box that I would want to be specifically stuck in. We'll use the parts that I want to use and then refine them in different ways that are more personal and unique to my specific style."

Will his music still appeal then only to the younger generation? "No, I don't think so. I think it will cross over and probably even go over many heads. That's a problem, you see. The pop music industry only wants to crank out things that will sell many records to screaming teenagers. But there has to be a time when we go beyond that and go into the discriminating quality of what's considered superior music. That will be the ultimate, major issue I'll have to conquer—being allowed by the music industry to create that superior music—if other things don't go badly with me, as far as drugs and my being ill so often."

What most people never realized was the fact Brian had a clear vision for creating world music. "My concept for music is global," he said. "I want all pieces, all instruments, incorporated as the musical sound of the entire world. I want to start with Eastern music—the Moroccan sound—and then progress into Russia's great musical history. I can envision myself as a middle-aged Russian Cossack in uniform," he went on to say with a grin, "and learning their dances and finding out about all their musical traditions firsthand. I want to travel more, especially to Russia. Their music feels very exotic, mysterious, and mature, somehow.

"I've tried talking to Mick and Keith about doing this, in bits and pieces, and in ways I thought they could comprehend. I've tried to play some chords and music for them as samples of what I foresee, using any and all instruments...depending upon what I was bringing in at the time. The sitar is very useful for anything Eastern, as is the flute or other reed-type instruments.

"But, when I presented my ideas to them, Mick looked completely unaware of what I was saying, even as I played for him. Keith listened, too, but remained oblivious to the possibilities. I believe what I'm proposing is so exotic that the band can't grasp its significance yet. They don't understand how to incorporate these foreign sounds using arcane instruments or what they can do with them. I'm really asking them to stretch their imaginations. Bill and Charlie listened and said they'll go along, but then they turned more wooden, more inflexible, on me.

"This idea of world music—to blend music borne out of native traditions—that concept, is my passion, my fire, but not theirs. The Beatles have experimented a bit in this way, but not that much." For Brian, this represented his ultimate dream for an all-inclusive, global feast of music that he wanted to consume, devour, and then spit out in a blaze of musical glory.

He went on to say, "All Allen (Klein) and the band want is for us to record for the purpose of money making and nothing more. They all say to me, 'Later, Brian, later...we'll do it later.' But for them, the time is never right."

Drugs played an important role in giving him the freedom to mentally expand his musical horizons, and he explained, "There's a certain freedom in having all these walls, these barriers, blown off (by the use of drugs) if you know what I mean. I tried to have a formal sit-down with the band, but it just isn't the direction they want to go. They want only mainstream, Americanized musical sales...the sure bet."

He presented his ideas to Bob Dylan also. "Yeah, Bobby understood, but what was he to say about what the Stones did? He was alone, too, in his adventure and felt limited by the restraints of what's expected and what's wanted. It's okay to be an individual, they say, but then they claim you can't sell any records if you wander too far off base.

"Although, no one has tried yet. Lennon is more interested, but again, his interest is fairly narrow compared to what I want to do—which is to bring all musical forms out and to become a part of the total creative process. I realize there's a lot of education that will be needed for me to understand and fully get what the sounds and notes of all lands are, and how they all came about. But, this is my passion and what fascinates me. I want to know what happened during the history of music that led to the development of the differences in the way sounds were made, and how the sounds were perceived in different cultures and climates.

"Then I'll have to apply these sounds to American music. Yes, this is very much a frontier. There are those such as Pete (Townshend) who think this concept is very cool and interesting, but yet very few who are willing to take up and work with me. I still have a lot of growth and learning in front of me, and I hope to one day feel free to do this."

Brian went on to explain how the initial process of writing a good lyric works. "A line is basically a line of lyrics. Sometimes a few lines of something very poetic, or a thought, a phrase, will come to me and be the seed that eventually germinates into something much larger. It always starts that way, you know, from something small. You have to match the lyric with a melody, and you never know how it's going to come in. That's part of the excitement and the awe of winding up with a terrific song, as in thinking, 'Oh! That's a great piece!'"

One peculiar theme stood out—relating to the fact that Brian was welcomed and often invited to join other bands in creating and recording their songs—which was, the Rolling Stones didn't usually reciprocate by inviting others to join them. He said, "Other musicians played much less with us. Somehow, we (the Stones) were much more guarded with our material. It seems odd, doesn't it? It's like going into another's camp somehow. But for me, it was great fun, hanging with the other bands."

Towards the end of this thought, his expression took on a more serious, reflective look—as he remembered how things had been when he was in the company of other musicians. "They treated me like a king!" he mused soulfully.

***

Bill Wyman wrote how hard it was for him and Brian to get Mick and Keith to listen to their ideas for new songs—and especially to get any form of credit for whatever they already had contributed to the band's music. A typical example has previously been mentioned in Chapter Seventeen, regarding Brian's original song *Sure I Do*.

Bill stated that he and Brian frequently contributed riffs and suggestions to songs, which ultimately wound up being vital to many recordings' final success. However, when the song or album was produced, their names were nowhere to be seen. He even claimed that it would take him and Brian hours and sometimes days to get Mick or Keith to even agree to hear their opinions. On the other hand, if Mick and Keith decided to do a certain song and—even if no one else in the band liked it—they would still do it. All these unsettling and inconceivable issues were occurring within the band that Brian named and created—and in which he was the one to have originally hired Mick and Keith.

Brian was the first to complain of this situation and said he and Bill even thought of going on their own, for a while. Bill spoke of a time right before the Beggars Banquet sessions, in which he and Brian wanted to introduce a couple of new songs to Mick. Bill said he had two new ideas for songs, and Brian had one.

Brian later explained what happened during that particular time. "Yes, there were many pieces of songs that would come to me. Some were just thoughts and some were very specific phrases. Marianne Faithful and I were always close, as friends. She was my bud. When she asked me whether I'd ever really leave the Stones, I always used this pat phrase to answer her, 'Wild horses couldn't drag me away.'

"The band was mine, and no matter what, I was duty bound to stay with them. Then as time passed, whenever things got tough, she and I would often say that phrase—wild horses—as a private signal to each other."

On a side note, a few years after Brian's death, Marianne became increasingly depressed and overdosed on drugs. She lapsed into a coma and passed away, ever so briefly. When she came to, she spoke with Mick, who had constantly been by her side while in hospital. She told Mick that she had dreamed she died and that she saw Brian's spirit waiting for her. She reached up with her hand to take his, and that was when she woke from her coma. Upon awakening, Mick told her how anxious he felt that she might have actually died, to which she instinctively answered, "Wild horses couldn't drag me away!"

Brian continued with his tale of trying to present his new song to Mick. "That time before Beggars Banquet, which Bill Wyman referred to, I tried presenting a new melody to Mick and even sang the lyrics to him. I called it *Wild Horses*; but Mick was in a nasty mood and didn't want to hear me. I even recommended playing dulcimer for the final piece, if they should record it. The sitar would also be used.

"Mick heard me play the original melody while I sang that day. He pretended to ignore me, but I know he listened. We all knew that Mick had developed this great talent for taking another's creations, especially mine, and making them his own—and then placing his and Keith's name on them."

Undeniably, Mick had a great memory for hearing sounds and later turning them into recordings for which he had no trouble claiming were actually his originals.

The big difference between Mick's and Brian's style for developing final pieces was that with Brian, he insisted on having instruments as the focal point of any song, with Mick's voice as a complement. On the flip side, Mick would take all Brian's ideas and make his voice, not the instruments, the primary focus—instead of the other way around. Brian chose to honor the music that instruments could create, whereas Mick chose to honor himself as King of his songs.

***

Brian had another idea for a melody for a soulful ballad, and presented it to Mick. Once more he played the licks or chords, and once more they were turned down by Mick, who said, "Not interested." Brian's idea was to do a play on words for both the lyrics and the title—a play off the word, angel. A few years after his death, the Stones recorded the ballad *Angie*, and we know that Brian called the woman who gave birth to his daughter, Angie.

Another beautiful ballad the Stones recorded was *As Tears Go By*. Brian originally told Marianne about his idea for the lyrics to that song and claimed the lyrics were his. To the press, Mick claimed that he was the one to have come up with the lyrics when he reflected on feeling old, or when he related to watching the older generation, as they engaged in their daily routines.

Mick was incapable of either serious reflection or the ability to relate to anyone but himself—let alone the older generation. Brian had once said that he honestly envied Mick, in that Mick was lucky enough to have never felt old. Whereas Brian claimed, throughout his life, he always felt as if he were the one born old, and he forever carried the aches and pains of someone one hundred years of age.

Does it not make sense, then, that Brian was telling the truth and that he was the composer who created the melancholy lyrics for *As Tears Go By?*

*Lady Jane* has Brian's imprint written on it. He came up with the original idea for the lyrics and melody, which relate back to King Henry VIII. As with *She's a Rainbow*, Brian said, "I pushed my energy to get the lyrics and melody across. Then Mick took it and brought it forward under his name."

The one song on which Mick and Keith came the closest to acknowledging Brian's input was *Ruby Tuesday*, because Marianne Faithful was there when Brian came up with the melody. Therefore, Mick couldn't arbitrarily claim it as his own.

Both Marianne and Keith describe in great detail the day Brian sat with his recorder in hand and began to work out the mellow tune, which they portray as a tender, delightful lullaby. He was determined to create a sound that would combine Elizabethan lute music together with the Delta blues.

A typical example of his meekness, in pushing his own works forward, was the way he reacted once he realized his playing held Marianne and Keith spellbound. He felt so self-conscious that he turned red and immediately went to put the recorder aside. They had to cajole him into continuing with the harmony.

If one compares the drastic difference between the caustic, bitter lyrics and true implications in songs that obviously were Mick Jagger's creations—such as *Heart of Stone, Under My Thumb,* and *Play with Fire*—and stands them side by side with the hauntingly beautiful, graceful ballads and lyrics that one can easily imagine Brian Jones creating—such as *Wild Horses, Angie, Lady Jane, Ruby Tuesday,* and *As Tears Go By*—the composer is obvious.

Perhaps one of the most artistic and imaginative songs the Stones ever recorded was *She's a Rainbow*. The band utilized a full orchestra, for which Brian did the majority of the arranging to ensure harmony between the Rolling Stones and the orchestra. The key lyrics also came from Brian's refined baroque or renaissance-inspired style of speech. The words glow with images of colors and grandeur—very much his essence and inspiration. He said that for him this song "wakes up parts of one's soul that are sleeping."

***

A psychological theory, which has not been disputed, states that if a person repeats a lie often enough, they eventually believe the lie as true. This hypothesis has proven true with major felons, including murderers, who repeat their fictitious testimony over and over. These felons can eventually take a lie detector test and pass it because they honestly believe their wild tales.

Since Brian Jones' premature death, Mick Jagger and Keith Richards, together with Andrew Loog Oldham, have regularly repeated the tale that Brian—with the possible exception of *Ruby Tuesday*—neither wrote nor contributed seriously to any of their hit recordings, nor did much in the way of musical arrangements.

Brian loved to take the sounds of older blues music and make them his. He placed his personal stamp—by implementing unique sounds and exotic instruments—on countless existing recordings, to make them his creations. After his untimely death, the Stones took credit for all his concepts and arrangements, which also included taking personal credit for new compositions that Brian had created, but for which he didn't have time before his death to formally record.

Over the years, his inspirations have continued to integrate themselves into the creative juices of each of the Stones. Every now and then, while putting together a new recording—and before they realize what they are saying—one of them will blurt, or at least think to himself, "Hey—this sounds like something Brian might say or create."

Then, one can imagine the cold shudder that must run through their bones.

Moreover, since Brian's death, every so often Keith would get brainstorms for what he believed was new material, but then in the back of his mind he would get a pang of guilt when he realized his brainstorm actually came from one of Brian's influences.

Two songs, which were released years after Brian's death, were *Start Me Up* and *Anybody Seen My Baby?* An anecdotal tale claims that, in the case of *Start Me Up*, Brian actually pounded the original beat for this song on his guitar. This was during one of the times his manic energy was working full throttle and sparks of creative genius, plus energy, flowed through him, and then—just as quickly—evaporated for him.

As luck would have it, the band went ahead and taped the hook for this song, which Brian had struck up during an earlier jam session.

According to Brian, the habit of taping the band's jam sessions was very important because that was how simple ideas or licks would later get turned into hit songs. Shortly before his death and when he was no longer a Stone, he said, "Taping was everything in those sessions, even if many hours or days would sometimes pass when we still didn't know if we actually had anything, and then later on something would click.

"I know Mick, and now Keith, deny most of my influence, but I know I was the inspiration, the heartbeat, maybe even the mother and father—if you will—of the group. Not to sound arrogant, but the truth is, I was also their teacher and guide. That was my role, and that was what I did for the Stones."

This same truth related to *Anybody Seen My Baby?* The original theme for this song came about by Brian beating out the sound on his tambourine. At the time he did so, no formal, full song was created; however, Mick and Keith remembered Brian's tempo as he strutted around the room, hammering out the basic rhythm.

When talking about the many sounds that Mick took from him and later put under his own name, Brian said, "Mick took all my good stuff. He wouldn't have wanted them if they weren't good. That was classic Mick and the classic power play by our producers. Working in that manner wasn't my game."

***

The melancholy ballad *No Expectations* from the Stones' Beggars Banquet album was Brian's swan song to Mick and to his band. Critics have agreed that Brian's hauntingly beautiful slide guitar playing on this piece was most likely his greatest work. Additionally, he wrote and arranged the song's ending piano solo, even though he didn't perform it.

He composed the majority of the lyrics to *No Expectations*, with some input from Mick. One only has to read the lyrics, and know the personal history between Mick and Brian, to realize the song had to have been Brian's farewell to his band. The song was written in five stanzas. All of them were Brian's thoughts and words except for the third. That stanza was Mick's farewell to the man he once loved. (See Chapter Twenty-One)

With a degree of certainty, musical pundits and aficionados have stated that, of the few hit recordings the Rolling Stones managed to produce after Brian's death, the vast majority carry his imprint. Two that they especially mention—and of which some have claimed to have heard Brian playing a few chords, for his own amusement—are *Miss You* and *Brown Sugar*. These tunes remind the pundits of the band's early hit songs—when he was the Stones leader and had a major say in how their recordings were arranged.

The only major hits the Rolling Stones had, which were said to have come after Brian's death, were *Honky-Tonk Women* (which we now know he played a vital role in re-creating, arranging, and playing guitar) *Brown Sugar, Angie, Miss You, Emotional Rescue,* and *Beast of Burden.* We also now know that Brian himself claimed to have written the original chords, licks, and riffs for all of those, with the only exceptions being *Beast of Burden* and *Emotional Rescue*. However, some evidence suggests that he originated the concept for *Emotional Rescue* at a taped jam session when Mick, Keith, and he shared their flat at Edith Grove.

Look at the facts—how long has it been since the Stones had a new hit record? And, how long has it been before that? As Brian often said, "They're content with rehashing and replaying the same old stuff over and over again."

Even though Brian was never given formal credit for all the melodies he created and all the lyrics he wrote for the Rolling Stones songs, it is clear to see the flavor of the man in many tunes, such as *She's a Rainbow*. These were always credited to Mick and Keith, but we know Brian's distinctive style and approach to creating music has been imitated over and over by the duo. Furthermore, once Brian was deceased, his name—as anything more than an add-on instrumentalist—was mysteriously and magically removed from all the band's recordings.

So, with how many of these records can we say that error or phenomenon occurred? We can only speculate on the answer, whenever we feel Brian's energy, soul, and sound in so many of the band's works. When we listen to the Stones music, can we then ask, was this Brian's writing? Was this his influence? In light of the fact that Brian's imprint—his aura, if you will—has been stamped on so many of the band's hits, as noted by musical historians everywhere, the human race is left to wonder.

# CHAPTER NINETEEN
## The Dark Side

*"Never let a lover get into your head."*

Mick Jagger

During the mid-sixties the power struggle for control of the Rolling Stones between Brian and Mick filtered through to the duo's every waking moment. At the same time the band continued to vigorously promote experimentation with sex and drugs.

At first, some band members expressed a reluctance to pursue the experimental nature of everything. However, in time Mick became strongly versed in how to use sex and mind control as forms of power and dominance. He had already given in to Brian sexually for both fun and love, but now he discovered that sex could also be used for the darker aspect of achieving power. And so, he began to use sex as a psychological tool instead of a pleasing, emotional sensation.

As has been mentioned, whenever Mick and Brian disagreed about how to create a piece of music, how a lick or two should sound, or the way Mick should throw his voice, Mick would withhold his affection until Brian gave in. (See Chapter Fourteen) As Brian explained, "Any little thing that I would be hell-bent on doing, Mick would get bitchy over, become bossy, and act unenthusiastic. At first I thought we were only engaging in petty bickering—acting bitchy, you know. We were both brats, and we were both petty. Little did I realize the game ultimately was for my own band." Mick even demanded Brian allow him to make all final decisions for the band.

Eventually, Brian pulled away from Mick permanently and said their personal relationship was over. However, he still tried working with Mick to get things done for the band and talked about using "mind fucks" with Mick. An example of what Brian called mind fucks was—instead of formally presenting his own, original ideas to Mick, which he knew Mick would automatically turn down without considering—he would go to Mick and pretend the ideas were Mick's originally.

He said with a grin, "It was fun to play tricks with Mick's mind. That was the best way to always get him—to make him crazy. The way I said things—I'd loop him back around and he would know I got him again. It made him furious! I'd sucker Mick into agreeing to do certain things, and that reminded him of who really was in charge!

"I'd say something similar to, 'That was a great idea you had, Mick, for us to (whatever). I'm glad you thought of it. It really worked out—so let's do it again.'"

He tried this a few times and got Mick to do his bidding. Eventually, though, Mick realized Brian was screwing with his mind, and then the game was over. With a big sigh, Brian said, "Well, it did work for a while!"

Originally he believed Charlie and Bill would come to his side and back him against Mick, since their philosophies on many issues were similar to Brian's. Alas, that wasn't the case, and he explained, "I don't know why they didn't take up for me. I guess they didn't care so much where the chess moves came from to get the band ahead. All they cared about was how it would flow better for them, personally, in the future. So, I became the dispensable Stone, and that really hurt.

"Although, I have to admit that later on I gave the guys every opportunity to doubt that I still was what I used to be, and that I could still produce. Whether it be from not showing up, from being ill, or from the continued drug use. Even though my really heavy drug use didn't come until later, it became apparent almost from the beginning that I never could handle drugs as well as the others."

That last statement was more than true. During 1963 and most of '64 he wasn't heavily into drugs. He did cocaine and uppers mostly, to give him the stamina to continue touring. He used those drugs along with his other band mates, but he realized through some terrifying moments of trial and error that his constitution couldn't handle even a minimal amount of drug use.

Mick observed the effects drug taking had on Brian and decided two separate things. One was that he would never put himself in the position of taking too many drugs and have them adversely affect him, to where he might lose control of either himself or the band—as Brian had. The second was that he could use the power of drugs to control Brian both personally and professionally.

Brian said, "Mick could start and stop drugging and drinking with no problem, and that always blew me away. Initially he did the same drugs as the rest of us, but he had the power to turn it off and manage it, which I seemed to lack. With me, when drugs were available and I felt like doing them, I did." He admitted that the more he saw himself losing control over the direction the band's music was taking, the more he took part in drug experimentation. "By the excessive use of drugs, I made it easy for the band to ultimately disrespect me. They saw me as getting weaker and less reliable, and I fulfilled their determination to get rid of me."

He was asked how much being frequently ill and beset with so many physical pains added to his use of heavy drugs. "That's a great question! Yes, my illnesses interfered with everything. At the time I didn't think I was really letting myself go with drugs, and they did help me control my physical pain—which was so important.

"But, in terms of partying and using whatever was available regardless of the consequences, I never could handle drugs as well as the others."

***

While the band decided to carry on with their image as the bad boys of rock—as opposed to the bands they considered sanctimonious—they became intrigued with the theme of going over to the Dark Side. They didn't know how to go about achieving that and at first didn't focus much serious attention on the subject; but at the same time, they did hold a certain amount of curiosity towards black magic. They considered the subject matter intriguing. Brian said, "We all laughed at first thinking there were powers from the darkness that could elevate us. We'd say, 'Oh, yeah, we're selling our souls, but do we even have souls? Ha, ha!'

"We were emotionally immature, and it seemed the smart thing to do. As far as me personally taking it seriously and carrying it out to any conclusion—I felt I'd already been cursed at times and had bloody little to do with it!"

He went on to say, "The times were experimental, and the nature of who we were was experimental—even experimenting with our testosterone. We weren't trying to be choirboys, but I still didn't take seriously into my heart the concepts of evil. Plus, I never thought of what we were doing as evil. It was again simply intriguing from an intellectual perspective, at least for a while. Mick, though, he ate it up heart and soul, as you could say."

The band even consulted with professional warlocks, but again, that was supposed to have been purely in fun and to shock the public. Brian said, "The initial consultations with warlocks were about image and how to project that sort of implication to the world, to shock the rock world, and all that. It started as a new set of costumes for us to wear, and a new way of looking at things to project. But then, Mick got deeper and deeper into it—the same as with any drug addiction. As drug abuse became a more permanent part of my life—with Mick, it was all about him getting into the dark and manipulative aspects of black magic that seemed to take hold of him. (Photo #846)

"So, it's the kind of thing that looked better for Mick on the outside because he was creating something that looked successful. Most never knew Mick was actually doing it from the inside of darkness, hiding it; but for me, everything I did was all on the outside and available for the whole world to see. I never hid who I was."

Guitarist Jimmy Page had been fascinated with the occult for some time and was invited by Mick to introduce the band to the more intricate aspects of the Dark Side. Brian knew Jimmy from his days with Alexis Korner's band and felt no personal danger from the musician's presence. Andrew Oldham also invited Jimmy to act as house producer for Oldham's company, Immediate Records. The innocent introduction of Jimmy Page into the heart and soul of the Stones band could perhaps have been the one major deathblow to Brian's career.

When asked about the effect Jimmy had by bringing the occult into the group, Brian said, "He was like a drug dealer bringing bits and pieces to the table—for us to laugh about, talk about, and share. And to encourage us in using it. I'd listen to him, but I decided to turn away from it." Within Brian's few naïve words, the difference between him and Mick was disclosed. One turned away from the darkness—the other embraced it.

Brian added, "Jimmy Page drew Mick into his world; Jimmy's energy went straight into Mick, and Mick ran with it. At first I honestly thought the band was playing dress-up, pretending to be part of the Dark Side. Then I learned it wasn't merely pretend dress-up, and I said, 'You mean we're doing this for real? We're actually worshipping Lucifer?' You see, Mick thought he needed black magic to make him a good musician. I didn't need it—I knew I was a good musician!

"But Mick needed it to bring him money and fame. Especially fame. Mick desired it because he didn't feel adequate or talented enough. Me—I didn't need it to make me who I already was. I always knew I was the real article.

"Keith listened to everything going on with his big ears," Brian added with a laugh. "He was stunned and at the same time oblivious to the seriousness of black magic. But Keith tries not to have original thoughts, so he can go along with whatever Mick orders."

Mick wanted to cheat the system to achieve personal success and by using the Dark Side, it worked for him. Even though Brian spent so much time tutoring him, Mick simply didn't have the talent. Mick's actions in front of the cameras and the audiences started out as stiff and robotic. All the ease, comfort, and flow of his movements came later on. Conversely, at the beginning Brian's actions were animated in front of the cameras and the audiences; he had a natural rhythm and grace that couldn't be taught. His persona was of a man who was in control of what he was doing; whereas Mick's was of someone who would rather shrink into the background and give Brian the limelight.

As time passed Mick so much wanted to upstage Brian and decided to become vampirical in sucking out Brian's image—if that's what was needed. He determined to take Brian over, body, and soul. Brian held a kaleidoscope of talent and could look enticing in so many ways. He was referred to as the backbone and the texture of the Stones.

After Mick embraced the darkness and cast his spell on Brian's innocence, the cameras and the audiences suddenly saw Mick performing magically in the spotlight and saw Brian transferred off to the sidelines, with no animation left in his body. Brian seemed to have melted away, with no evidence of what happened to him. Video after video of the early, mid, and late 60's performances of the Stones attest to the mysterious metamorphosis of Mick Jagger into Brian Jones.

The answer to the mystery of the real Brian Jones' disappearance was clear. Brian never needed witchcraft to turn him into Brian Jones. But Mick needed the darkness to turn him into Brian Jones.

Brian always had the utmost confidence in his music and his ability to create and perform. At first he believed Mick's actions against him were strictly personal—since he had fallen out of love for Mick—and nothing to do with business. If Brian had not possessed the strong, inner confidence in his professional ability, he never would have had the strength to bring the Stones to super stardom. Certainly he never could have or would have imagined that the powers of black magic, when combined with his existing emotional and mental afflictions, were a strong enough mixture to destroy his creative genius.

His plethora of outfits and costumes were all part of his captivating chameleon-like appeal for audiences worldwide. (Photo #824) When those who were working against him beckoned the forces of the Dark Side into play, those forces helped to suppress and depress his vibrant spirit—an easy task since he had already been weakened by all life's hardships.

Because of Brian's basic naïveté in matters of deception, he didn't know enough to speak out and ask for help or guidance, once he realized the forces of evil were being used against him, to overpower him. "You see, I wasn't used to reaching out and getting help in my whole life growing up. And so, I felt that I had to figure things out for myself.

"When people did try talking to me, though, or try to understand why I was in a bad mood, I'd get mad and slam my hand down and yell and act obnoxious. My bi-polar disorder had much to do with my acting sweet and kind, I guess, and then lashing out and ordering everyone about. It's so complex. The more I felt everything was getting away from me, and the more angry or scared I felt, the more despicable I'd behave.

"Yes, Keith said I should try to go with the flow, since that would be much easier on me—I suppose that's true, but then again I wouldn't have been Brian Jones!" he tried joking away the insanity of his situation.

Nonetheless, by the time he realized what was occurring, what influences were working to destroy him, the deed had already been done. He said, "I became very frightened because I realized that the forces against me were total. Prayer seemed empty and hollow to me at the time. I thought back to my own parents going to church and how hypocritical that was. I didn't even know if there was a hell. But I was too enmeshed with the band to pull away and change directions. I couldn't even see what was happening to me objectively at the time. It was such a gradual pulling and taking away from me, inch by inch. Suddenly I was off the boat and in the water."

Mick developed a strong conjuring power and managed to convince the rest of the Stones that it was a good thing to abuse Brian. Mick learned to use his powers of mental concentration to get the band to do his bidding. He personally worked on Brian's mind and damaged his psyche in many ways. By his close association with Brian, he knew how to take advantage of the weakness of the latter. Using the Dark Side, Mick shot energy thoughts into Brian's mind that made Brian think he was really crazy and imagining all the horrible things he saw taking place. Eventually, Brian couldn't tell whether Mick's ranting incantations were nothing more than the result of his imagination and paranoia, and so he said, "I didn't want to believe Mick had the power to cast a spell—but in just saying it to me, he was casting a spell over my belief in my abilities to survive and fight back. Simply saying it to me was undermining me, and when I was paranoid Mick's 'spells' would loom up very large.

"At other times, I'd say to myself, 'Mick can't do that; he has no power over me. Besides, I'm the one who taught him everything he knows!' This was my way of fighting back and standing up to him. But then, I'd go deep into my insecurities as well, and then everything would just get very bizarre."

Mick even used mind control on himself, telling himself, "I'm going to take over! I'm smarter than Brian! I'm going to be in control!" He pledged and beseeched the Dark Side to give him those powers and used many books on the subject of darkness. Utilizing the name of Lucifer, Mick used historical conjuring techniques to achieve his sinister goals.

\*\*\*

While Brian and Mick still believed looking into the world of black magic was a game, they studied books that Jimmy Page brought for their reading pleasure. Brian said, "The main book was about magic, manipulation, and making things go your way. It also taught how to cast spells to get what one wants."

With his sardonic sense of humor, he went on to say, "The only so-called spell I could cast was on my audience, but that was a different thing, wasn't it? Although, I did wonder how certain people could cast such very high spells and elevate themselves to such a degree, and become so highly thought of in the field of darkness.

"I'd forget all of that during my performances because, for me, my performance would just flow naturally. So, who could think of spells or casting anything on anyone, when I didn't need them? But I did wonder about such things, how they worked, and I was quite intrigued by them for a while."

Was Brian intrigued with simply getting someone to do his bidding or more intrigued because that power came from the Dark Side? He answered honestly and with a touch of humor, "Having my will done was necessary as leader of the band. I didn't find my will was ever done during my early life, so whether it came from the Dark Side or from my very sharp mind and effervescent personality—I didn't believe or understand that contrast or that difference."

He was basically explaining that, no, he didn't feel he needed any super power or the ability to cast a super spell on any audience to achieve success—he was comfortable with his natural talent to create and entertain. He heard of a nasty rumor being spread that on his body there existed what was called a "witch's tit" or mole identifying him as a member of Satan's community, and he emphatically stated that was not true. His body was clear of any such imperfection, and the only blemishes on him were those of everyday beauty marks. "Naturally if one wanted to claim a particular mark on my body was from Satan, they could claim it to be so—but I can say all I ever had were assorted discolorations and such."

***

The story of how Mick learned to use his power—to manipulate the thoughts of others to do his bidding—was interesting. As a young boy and teenager, he didn't have much confidence in himself. To others he appeared cold, heartless, and even clumsy. Many even thought of him as a dullard with no personality. (Photo #826)

After he met Brian, he saw in Brian all the things he wasn't and probably never could be. Brian was deep and intellectual, and Mick desired to be that. Therefore, he decided to do whatever necessary to take away and imitate those qualities in Brian, and make them his own. Once he developed those qualities by using the force from the Dark Side, he did become deep. But his deepness was never borne out of kindness, as Brian's was; Mick's stolen deepness was borne out of cruelty.

The fame, power, and success Mick achieved only brought out the dark, brooding side in him. One could say, a little bit of fame brought out a lot of darkness. While he determined never to become addicted to drugs or drinking as Brian had, Mick developed his own even stronger addiction—he became addicted to fame. He main-lined fame, which proved worse than any form of chemical drug.

He understood that Brian—despite the fact he was the one to have left Mick—still carried feelings for him and probably always would. He also understood that Brian still thought of Keith as his soul-brother and would always stick by both men and the band he created. According to Mick's value system, Brian's major weaknesses were his sense of honor and loyalty, and he determined to use Brian's weaknesses to hurt him and destroy him.

Brian, too, understood that his sense of honor and loyalty towards his band was his weak spot, but he also understood he would never abandon his band. He felt he was fucked! Mick wanted to own him, possess him, and wanted to dominate every aspect of Brian's life. He could never forgive Brian for being the first to say, "Mick, we're through!"

For Mick, Brian was easy to love and he loved Brian for all his "faults". Unlike Mick, Brian wasn't cunning, deceitful, dishonest, cold, calculating, or manipulative. Brian was kind, gentle, patient, and capable of great love. Brian also was very beautiful, something Mick desperately wanted to be—beautiful to the audiences. But, he wasn't. Nevertheless, Mick discovered that if he studied hard and learned all of Lucifer's tricks, he could achieve that outward beauty. Mick wanted to take Brian's beauty and make it his own.

Whenever he wanted something from Brian, such as advice or guidance with a new song or even business agreement, he'd cozy up to Brian and whisper gently in his ear. He'd tell Brian that they could still work things out—for the band. That was Brian's weak spot—his band, and no matter what transpired between them, no matter how brutally Mick may treat Brian when it suited him—when Mick used those magic words "for the band"—Brian would give in and provide whatever assistance Mick asked.

That basically was what Mick's version of love was all about—even with his women. To Mick, love was comprised of caring for whoever suited him or gave him what he wanted at that particular time. The song for which Mick wrote the lyrics *Under My Thumb* was very personal, for that was exactly where he wanted Brian to be at all times—under his thumb.

Mick was also extremely, as Brian claimed, "pissed that the girls still didn't think of him as 'the one'." Mick wanted to show the world how small and inconsequential Brian was, and figured by turning Brian into the most demented, drug-addicted rock star anyone had ever seen, he would accomplish his goal.

Had management, especially Oldham and Klein, not taken such an active role in forcing Brian out as leader of the band, Brian would never have done all the drugs he eventually did. Brian explained, "The Dark Forces reached out to Mick from the beginning. Satan came in through the money handlers to recruit him. They knew what he wanted—money and power. For a long time it was apparent who was in charge of the band—I was. Mick couldn't put words together in a sentence, and I did all the talking for us. And, at the beginning Mick didn't care that I was in charge, but then the power structure changed drastically and was thrown into Mick's lap. Mick, then, changed drastically, and the problem was, I didn't see the power change coming. It seemed to sneak up on me. You know, some said I wasn't paying full attention or I would have seen it."

Brian further insisted that, if Mick hadn't joined management in callously pushing him out, he would never have gone overboard with drinking and drugging. "Right! I don't believe I would have. I know I was more responsible than that. Everything happened so fast, plus my intense sensitivity made it easy for me to lose control of who I was. When I realized I'd lost all power I acted mean, hard, and brash towards everyone. That was my pathetic, protective device to hide away from showing how hurt I really was. I used bad language, became derisive, mean, and acted out. I felt so hurt when I saw Mick taking everything away from me, which included taking all my inner strength that I had worked so hard to attain."

He never realized how quickly the forces of drinking and drugging could take over his weak system. "I was pissed off about a lot of things, and yet I imagined experimenting with all sorts of drugs as fun and a great ride. Then the addictions took over, and I couldn't function any longer. The spiraling downward took over. You see, I wanted so badly to fit in and really thought the drugs would help."

Mick became his stalker, in effect, and as Brian explained, "A regular stalker, though, wouldn't have available the methods Mick did. Mick played mind games from the beginning but when he learned how to gain power, he did them more strongly. The mind games started out as we, the band, pretended to be the anti-Christ, the Darkness, the bad boys. What was nothing more than a publicity stunt became more and more serious.

"Mick used what you could say was my hair and my blood to stir a concoction against me. Yes, he even came into my dreams. I could see Mick's face beside my head, whispering to me, warning me, telling me to do or not to do certain things."

Could this have simply been Brian's mind playing tricks on him, and not the Dark Side? "Probably a bit of both, but Mick cast the spell or curse out there, and it worked its way into my psyche. I couldn't tell what was real or what was paranoia. Although, Mick did instigate much of my paranoia and much of the degradation that I felt within myself."

Together with Keith, Brian witnessed Mick as he practiced and put into work—by means of incantations, rituals, ceremonies, and sacrifices—what he wanted to accomplish. The two witnessed Mick wearing the symbols of the Dark Side, black cloak and hood, while plotting in his mind to telepathically throw his thoughts into others—to get them to do his bidding. Brian could envision Mick sticking pins into voodoo dolls.

At first Mick pretended this was all a joke, not to be taken seriously. Later, Brian knew there was no more joking about what Mick wanted and what he was willing to do to accomplish his sinister goals. Occasionally, Mick would straddle up beside Brian and whisper, "You're weak, Bri. You're not up to the challenge. You're small, inconsequential, and you've got no cock."

Brian wanted so much to speak up for himself and say, "Really, Mick? I have no cock—then what is it you've been sucking on all along?" But, he was too taken aback and too shocked to answer. Mick's cruel words left him speechless. Brian explained, "Remember, I was quite shy in many ways. The stage persona was just that and not the real me."

Which again was why Brian normally used drugs before each performance—to give him the courage to get up on stage in front of the thousands who adored him. He could never adjust to having to live up to everyone's expectations. While the drugs took their magical effect, he'd study himself in the mirror, to ensure his well-thought-out ensemble—from his wide-brimmed hats to his bejeweled jackets—matched to perfection. Never again, would he be the dirty, downtrodden young man who couldn't bear living in his own skin. (Photo #834)

He reflected upon what he believed made Mick so bitter towards him. "Mick still wasn't getting as much attention as I was, and he wasn't being sought after by as many. He saw me as his natural competitor and sought to tear me down, shut me down, and take what I had and what I was. Mick wanted to consume all that I was and make it his own."

Mick could take the energy from anyone, once he learned to use the powers of Darkness, and suck it out of them. He was especially adept with those whom he bedded down, such as Brian—who would always be, in his own sweet way, innocent and naïve no matter what life threw at him.

Brian said the main reason he was so distressed over what had become of Mick was, "I could never forget the strong feelings we once had for one another. Mick was the most real connection to actual love that I ever had. All the same, we weren't trying to be the 'queers' out there. There was a lot of confusion between us, and so we felt safe by calling it experimental. I still thought of myself as heterosexual, as did Mick. But, I believe what Mick felt towards me scared the hell outta him, and he couldn't let go."

*** 

While Brian still thought pretending to walk on the Dark Side was fun and games, he wanted to do something extra special to impress Mick. Since he and Mick were accustomed to using one-upsmanship when the mood called for it, he decided to get a distinctive license plate for his most prized possession, his Rolls Royce. By whatever means necessary, which included the pay-off of a government employee, he managed to get the license plate that carried the devil's insignia—DD666. The symbol stood for the words, devil's disciple, plus the triple six, the mark of the Dark Side. Brian wanted to prove to Mick that he was "one of them" and thought a brash act such as this would once again win Mick over.

Unfortunately, his naïveté came back to haunt him because many among the media and public were shocked and horrified by his blatant action—when they saw him driving around proudly with the offensive license plate. He was content for the time, though, in that he did succeed in impressing Mick and Keith with his ballsy move. This brief success in entertaining Mick was short-lived, though, when their relationship spiraled further downward not long after, with the advent of a shocking incident.

***

The incident occurred among the three, which at last proved to Brian how far along Mick actually was in mind control. Each of the Stones dealt with the reality of what was taking place in their own way. Keith dissolved further and further into the world of hard drugs and heroin. Brian did the same, but also reinforced the art of disassociating himself from the reality of what he knew was occurring—including the ritualistic sacrifices and Black Masses in which Mick engaged.

Charlie Watts and Bill Wyman chose to remain blissfully oblivious to everything going on within the band with regard to the Dark Side. Since they were both married and didn't normally socialize with the three when the Stones weren't on the road, they could ignore the more personal goings-on of Mick, Keith, and Brian.

One evening while the three were heavily drugged, especially Brian and Keith, Mick decided to demonstrate his newly-learned mental powers by ordering Keith to have anal sex with Brian. At first the two thought Mick was joking and mimed the act, but the laughter ended when they realized Mick wasn't laughing.

Not only wasn't he laughing, but they could also see the fire emanating from his eyes, because they weren't taking his order seriously. Brian looked over at Keith, and a shudder ran through him. He hadn't been forcefully taken sexually since his days on the streets, some five years earlier. However, he recognized the insidious look, and Mick was clearly demonstrating the look of a man who was deadly serious about what he wanted done.

The shudder that ran threw Brian was also due to several strange experiences that had occurred, during the times he'd partied the night away in Mick's company. Because of his drug use and because of his untreated mental electrical shorts—a form of narcolepsy—that caused him to pass out wherever he may be, he was especially vulnerable to any predator who wanted to hurt him. Many a night Brian had passed out for either reason and had awakened the next morning with not much memory of what had taken place. All the same, he would realize he was hurting, even injured, around his anal area. He'd then look over at Mick as if to ask, "What happened?" but all Mick would do was grin back at him maliciously.

Brian knew Mick preferred anal sex—even with his women—and also knew that Mick often preferred rough, aggressive anal sex. The first few times the unexpected soreness to the lower regions of his body happened, Brian thought he was imagining it, but afterwards he began to realize it happened only when Mick was around. If he had merely passed out and perhaps fell on the floor—that wouldn't explain the soreness to his sex organs. Brian said of those times, "Yes, I do remember waking up sore and not being sure what went on. But, that's how Mick was. It was always about whatever Mick the King wanted at the moment. For him, anal sex was always a big part of it."

*** 

Keith and Brian were still very close, and Brian still thought of Keith as his big brother. An example of their closeness was again proven one day when someone tried to cajole the two into engaging in a fistfight. Brian said, "Did Keith and I ever get into a fistfight? Well…we'd bop each other upside the head from time to time. Yeah, that was kind of a fistfight, but it was more of a 'Come on, come on, let's see what you've got!' instead of anything. And then we'd both burst out laughing. Really—just look at me and look at Keith!" he chuckled. Obviously, he was referring to the big difference in their physiques and the fact the two couldn't even hold together the energy necessary to fight one another—they were too close.

Nonetheless, Brian might have noticed that when choices had to be made, Keith had begun to side with Mick. When Mick first decided he should sing solo without any further backup from Brian, he didn't want to appear selfish by making the suggestion himself, in front of Bill and Charlie. Instead he whispered to Keith to make the suggestion for him, to stab Brian in the back. Keith dutifully made the proposal when the band was grouped together that evening. He said "Why don't we see what Mick can do on his own, without Brian alongside him?"

Brian was stunned. He had choreographed the band's songs, and he had always sang and performed alongside Mick from the beginning. The audiences loved the duo's performances, and there seemed no reason for a change. However, Bill and Charlie said, yes, they'd go along with the change—since Keith thought it was a good idea. Mick pretended to be surprised by the proposal, but afterwards Brian learned the real truth behind Keith's suggestion. He said,

"Keith never was a leader or had an original idea! Plus, Mick always tried putting Keith and me down for our closeness. He doesn't say things out loud, but he uses his eyes, his energy, to talk. He was always trying to figure a way to climb to the top, and Keith just went along with everything.

"But, God, I don't know why Keith turned against me, especially since he'd spoken up for me for so long!" What Mick had done to convince Keith to go over to his side was lie to him and say that Brian was really screwing things up for the band. Brian went on to say, "In general, Keith knows that I put everything together for the band, and I feel I got very little back from them for that. Keith also knows that he's only riding on what I created—but at the same time I'm not saying he has no talent."

Time and again whenever Brian would get angry with his band and criticize them, he couldn't help but at the same time take up for them. Was Mick right in thinking that Brian's great weakness was his sense of loyalty and honor?

*** 

That night the most horrifying incident Brian ever experienced with Mick and Keith occurred, when both he and Keith were especially messed up in a haze of drug taking. Mick, as usual, hadn't done as many and remained in control of his faculties.

Brian was accustomed to enjoying group sex and didn't pay much attention to whether he was having sex with males, females, or all of the above. The use of heavy drugs erased normal sexual boundaries between the sexes, and there were no rules left as to what was right or wrong. However, Brian never thought of experiencing sex with Keith, and more importantly, never wanted to. Keith wasn't an outgoing sexual being. He was introverted and hardly ever had sex in front of anyone.

Mick, though, wanted total dominance and control of both Keith and Brian, and he wanted to debase both. If he could get them in a position of feeling humiliated and degraded, he believed he would forever have the upper hand in dominating them mentally. That night, he knew he had his band mates where he wanted them—Keith was too doped up to make a rational decision, even if he would ever have had the balls to openly defy Mick, and Brian was weakened by the drugs and no match against Keith's physical strength. Plus, Mick knew Brian still desperately wanted to stay on his good side, no matter what the cost.

In Mick's eyes, Brian was no more than a lovely doll to toy with and play with. In Mick's eyes, Keith was no more than a wooden puppet, whose strings he could pull and manipulate at will. Mick began his verbal barrage with Brian, "You know how you keep complaining that the band is nothing more than monkeys performing for the circus, Bri? Well, let's see how good a performance you can give tonight. We'll pretend I'm the ringmaster, and this is our little circus. Keith!" he pointed, "Keith, I want you to get on top and fuck him! He's only a bitch—take him!"

Again, the two laughed until they realized Mick wasn't laughing back. Mick ordered louder for Keith to mount Brian. "He's just a little bitch. He can't fight you off. Fuck him!"

Brian watched Keith unzip his pants and take out his cock. He thought his eyes would pop from his head because he couldn't believe what he was witnessing about to take place. He needed Keith as a brother—not for sex. Besides, to Brian, Keith wasn't in the slightest physically attractive. Keith wasn't remotely close to anyone he'd ever want to touch in a sexual way. In that regard, he considered Keith especially ugly.

But Mick was making it clear he wasn't going to back away from his orders.

Brian looked up at Keith and pleaded with his eyes not to approach him. He knew he was no match physically should he have to fight Keith off. His eyes continued to plead with Keith for compassion, as he watched the larger man teetering between action and complete immobilization. Mick walked right up to Keith and said, "Show him who's the man, Keith. Do it; do it! For me."

For Brian, shock or disassociation had always been his personal defense mechanism, all the times he'd been attacked and overpowered by bigger, stronger men. By now, Keith had gotten himself hard by using his own hand and walked up to Brian. Neither man had said a word to one another aloud, but each was speaking volumes with his eyes, especially Brian. He continued to hear Mick, as he screamed commands from the sidelines. He had become the ultimate, perverse ringmaster ordering his subjects about. If Mick could get Keith to do the deed—rape Brian—he'd have accomplished his greatest trick. The rape would be the leveler among the three, with Mick forever being in control of the dastardly secret.

The drugs had mercifully numbed Brian's senses, and so, he wasn't totally cognizant of what was about to happen. Besides, he felt there wasn't much he could do to protect himself, and he also knew the next step might be for one or both of his band mates to hold him down and take him forcefully. Consequently, he looked away and allowed Keith to push inside him. He let his mind go blank and pretended nothing unusual was taking place, as he felt Keith move back and forth.

When it was over, he curled up in a fetal position and closed his eyes, still pretending nothing had happened and completely disassociated from the horrible deed that had been executed upon his body. He later said, "Keith is a great hetero, you know, and he might have had sex with me, but no one enjoyed it, except for Mick. This was a great mind fuck for Mick to have had me as the girl. I actually thought it was all a game at first, but Mick manipulated everything. Mick would never let me go, and he had to get even because I wouldn't give into him any longer."

Brian believed Mick truly accomplished his goal that night. Nothing would be the same between the so-called brothers ever again. That's what hurt him the most—not the physical rape, but the mental rape of him and Keith.

Keith, too, was forever damaged mentally by what he felt he had no choice but to do. Brian said, "Keith felt wretched when it was over. He and I were now bonded, but not in a good way. Our relationship as brothers was forever gone. We continued to work together for the band, but what happened was the ultimate insult and betrayal."

Afterwards, Keith remained silent to the outside world as to the events of that night. Mick had him where he wanted him—Keith was forever afraid that Mick might out him some day and say what he had done to Brian. Nevertheless, even though Keith remained silent to the outside world, to Brian he felt he had to say something.

When Brian was asked if Keith ever apologized, he said, "Almost, but not quite. But I knew what he was trying to say. A couple of days later, he came into the room and said, 'Brian, about the other night....' Then he stopped talking and just looked at me, and I said, 'Yeah, Man, I know....'"

From that night forward, Keith became more and more withdrawn into himself and more and more dependent upon heroin to see him through life.

*** 

The recording of *Sympathy for the Devil* had perhaps the most far-reaching result for the Stones' quest to personify the Dark Side. The song became Mick's personal anthem and ultimate homage to Lucifer.

Mick initially got the idea for the song from one of the books Jimmy Page brought him. Brian said, "The book described Lucifer's presence in everything in the world from the beginning of time. His hand is everywhere, taking part in everything we as humans do. *Sympathy's* theme, heart, and core rest in that philosophy."

When Mick composed the piece, he made a pact with the Dark Side to forever perform the anthem at every concert and live performance the band played—a promise Mick has kept to this day. In return for the promise, Mick was provided with a long lifetime of money, fame, and success, which also included the future security of his family. The quid pro quo has worked incredibly well for both sides.

Brian went on to say, "Originally the concept for *Sympathy for the Devil* was for the band to be cool. The song was to project the vampire lust underneath all of us, and our fearless leader was to be the vampire image. The theory was to use the innocence of others to create strength for the people who support the darkness. This theory was widely supported among the higher segments of the British populace at the time, including royalty. Blood thirst was also very popular at the time *Sympathy* was created."

With the Stones' continued performance of the sometimes twenty-minute homage, their audiences have been shrewdly lulled into a false sense of security—to feel safe and secure with the theme of the Dark Side. Brian said, "This song gave favorable notoriety and familiarity with the Devil, as appearing to be 'not such a bad guy.' That's what Mick wanted."

At first, Brian did dabble a bit with the Dark Side and felt enticed to take part in it, but he ultimately chose to push himself away. When he told Mick and Keith that he didn't want to take part in their ceremonies any longer—he was told he didn't have a choice, as they had already signed him on!

He felt he had traded his soul, and he fought to get it back. However, Mick told him that he had acted on Brian's behalf, and for the entire band, to become instruments for a pact with the darkness. He actually had made the pact, which included Brian's name, using the term "we"—with Mick as the main enforcer.

When Brian felt pressured to take part in the final taping of *Sympathy for the Devil*, he dove deeper into the world of heavy drugs. He both dreaded and felt panicked about the recording sessions, which were videotaped for posterity by means of Jean Luc Godard's infamous video *One on One*. Among the female participants in the video were Marianne Faithful and German actress/model Anita Pallenberg.

Whether anyone else besides Brian, Mick, and Keith knew the actual purpose for the anthem wasn't divulged. Although, what was known was that Brian deeply feared being present during the taping. Unfortunately, he felt he had no choice but to be present, as he was contracted through Allen Klein and ABKCO to be part of any video or performance the band took part in—barring ill health. By drugging himself heavily, he desperately tried to not be present due to ill health.

The final taping took place over a two-day period. Brian appeared normal during the first day's taping, except for the fact he didn't appear animated but instead very subdued. By the end of the first day's long session, he was seen even more distracted and not openly interacting with the rest of the band. He even took time to lie on the floor while reading a book, in an attempt to block out the reality of what was taking place around him.

For the second, final day of taping, Brian absented himself completely, due to "not feeling well." And, as a result, his guitar playing was never on the Stones final homage to the Dark Side. Therefore, he knew he had won the ultimate battle of wills—even if it meant that, to the outside world, he appeared nothing more than a drugged-out addict.

By sheer strength of will, in an already-weakened body, Brian decided to not go down in history as part of the recording that would forever be Mick's worship of the devil. Brian said the song was, "Pure Mick, pure Satanism. Maybe my guardian angels saved me from the final result."

Brian believed some of his worst downtimes were actually his salvations, in that they kept him out of certain situations and places for which he wasn't meant to be present. He explained, "There were times when I was blissfully in my own cocoon of unawareness by a drug-induced stupor. The fact that I wouldn't or couldn't participate in the regular world at times kept me from certain assaults, which would only have served to take me down, further and faster.

"For example, there were times that Mick and Keith planned to treat me badly or humiliate me in front of others, but I spoiled their evil plans by never showing up because of drugs, or even my mental blackouts. Without knowing it at the time, I managed to save myself from further embarrassment at their hands."

He was asked if Bill or Charlie ever took part in those heartless sessions that only served to hurt him and mentally brutalize him. He answered, "No they never said anything bad, but—if someone does a cruel thing and you participate in the audience with your laughter—I think that is participating. It's like the onlookers who sit on the sidelines and don't do anything to help."

As far as the final taping for *Sympathy for the Devil*, Brian concluded, "I hated being there! My heart hurt, and I felt denigrated. The session started out fine, but then Mick started believing he was the devil. I wanted out of it! Mick, acting as the devil, turned on me. Then the band, my band, became nothing more than a prison run by Mick, the jailer."

# CHAPTER TWENTY
## International Brahim

*"Fighting was what turned Anita on sexually, but it didn't make for a good family life."*

Brian Jones

Brian had a restless spirit and constantly moved from place to place. Sometimes he would live at a hotel, other times he would rent an apartment or house—but nothing was ever considered home. The places he rented, however, were not average. By this time in his life, 1964-67, he had caught the eye of royalty and those considered the social hierarchy in the world of entertainment and the arts. Because of that, the many dwellings he lived in were owned or leased by members of high society.

He changed girlfriends as often as he changed dwellings, and soon his band mates and close friends took to teasing him over the fact he only dated women who looked just like him. Normally he didn't realize a new paramour was his carbon copy until someone pointed it out. Then he would joke, "Oops! I did it again!" His lighthearted explanation was he was trying to find his other half, and in his naiveté he believed if he found a woman who looked just like him, she'd have the same personality as he. He said, "I tended most often to go for blondes who were rather like me. I guess I can say that I was looking for the reflection of myself in my female counterpart."

He never lived alone, and he made sure he wouldn't have to face many nights of sleeping alone. During this time he was seeing his French girlfriend, ZouZou. When she wasn't with him, he frequently relied on his close friend Ronni Money to spend time with him. Ronni and he were only friends, because she was happily married to another musician. Ronni's story was unique in that she had connections that Brian used, to deliver prostitutes up to his apartments to stay with him when no one else was available. He said frankly, "I paid Ronni well for her introductions."

He didn't necessarily want sex with these paid escorts but simply human company. If sex were involved, it usually consisted of the girls' going down on him, just to relax him. He explained, "I was too afraid to be alone. Many of those times the paranoia took over. I felt the need for privacy and desired it but yet had the paranoia of being by myself. I was a mess!"

His regular drug supplier was Tony Sanchez, or Spanish Tony to his friends. Brian really enjoyed Tony's company, and he often asked him to stay over a day or so just to keep him company—and to ensure he had a steady supply of his favorite drugs. Brian didn't hide what he was and never pretended to be what he wasn't. He didn't pretend not to be friends with those whom others might think unsavory, such as Tony. He openly beamed, "I couldn't help but love Tony!"

More than anything, he loved to travel, and he made his first trip to what would become his favorite country, Morocco, in August '65. He traveled with Linda Lawrence, the mother of his son, Julian. He and Linda had always remained close, no matter who he dated or what escapades he took part in when she wasn't around to rein in his wild nature.

From the moment he saw Morocco and met its people, he felt captivated by the country's beauty. At this time, he and Linda once again discussed marrying, but once again he gave it serious thought and then declined. He had a deep aversion to feeling captured, controlled, and being taken over by another. He believed that if he totally committed to another as in marriage, he would lose control over who he was. He usually gave too much of himself in relationships, so he swore to stay away from them. He tried to explain his fear of commitment this way, "When I started to care for anyone I pulled away because it felt dangerous, so I found myself doing stupid things to screw it up. I was very big on having my freedom. That was the ultimate dilemma—wanting to be close to someone and adored, and wanting to be free. I longed for a relationship; I wanted it, but then again it scared the hell out of me."

He blamed part of that on the type of woman he normally met. "The whole world of who I met was a bizarre neon facsimile of what natural living should be. Everybody was out for what they could get, what they could do, and who they could do it to. The fame thing brought many people who seem to worship you and adore you. I always knew and always had the feeling that it was really all about fame for them, and not about me, the person. Who really knew me? Who knew my heart? Very few!"

Shortly after the Moroccan trip, he and Linda came to a financial settlement over the fact he had fathered Julian. He gave her approximately one thousand pounds British, with which she eventually bought a boutique.

***

In September '65 while the Stones performed in Munich, Germany, Brian met the woman who would forever leave the longest-lasting impression on him, Anita Pallenberg. Anita was into fashion and modeling, and hoped to become an actress. She was a strong woman, both mentally and physically, and was even a bit larger and stronger than Brian. (Photo #827)

What Brian didn't know at the time he met Anita was that she had a hidden desire to enmesh herself into the famous Rolling Stones band, and she didn't particularly care which of the men she trapped. As she studied each of the Stones that night, she couldn't help but be attracted to Brian first. His fantastic looks and well-spoken, charming manner caught her attention immediately, and she focused all her energy on him.

Fortunately or unfortunately for both, she met Brian at a time when he felt especially isolated within his own band and felt completely unloved and unwanted by life in general. Using her feminine charms, she made him feel safe and secure at a time when he needed someone very strong in his life, to give him direction and meaning. He went home with her the first night and spent much of the evening in her arms, letting her hold him tenderly while she stroked his hair. He cried and confided to her how he feared losing the only thing that mattered to him in the entire world—his band.

The two became a couple almost immediately, and Anita was able to do what his previous, steady girlfriends couldn't or wouldn't, which was to travel with him and be with him full-time. What Brian didn't see, until it was too late, was that all the love and attention she so-willingly showered upon him had a price. She expected to become Mrs. Brian Jones, or—in her mind—Mrs. Rolling Stones. "Anita didn't have her sense of loyalty in place," he tried to explain. "She always had her eyes roaming to capture one of the Stones. I didn't see it in the beginning, but then I came to see it. Her true intentions annoyed me, but I tried to roll with it, regardless."

Anita and he did have much in common as far as quick wit and sharp sense of humor. Both were shopoholics, or, as he often joked, "Being a professional shopper was my feminine side coming out."

Anita moved into his beautifully furnished house on Elm Park Lane in prestigious Chelsea. He had already developed a marvelous collection of art, especially anything antique. He loved the feel, smell, and touch of old-world bronzes, crystals, paintings, tapestries, and anything else considered valuable objects of beauty. He took refuge in the arts and believed that owning all these magnificent treasures from antiquity could obliterate the horrors he had tried to erase from his mind, from his days living among the filth and vermin of the streets.

He shopped throughout Europe with his newly-found friends from the inner circle of the art world. These people eagerly embraced his charismatic, golden persona as one of their own. They introduced him to the best spots from which to acquire fine art, a discriminating taste he had already developed on his own. He said, "I always loved shopping and always maintained a genuine interest in the smallest details."

His personal interests included not only clothes, appearance, make-up, and music, but also wide-ranging subjects such as literature and poetry. He enjoyed discovering what made things work from larger items such as motor cars, buses, trains, and planes, to the insect and plant worlds' tiniest members. He wanted to devour and absorb all that life had to offer, in as fast a time as possible. Although he wouldn't admit it, he had a feeling he had to experience everything in as short an amount of time as possible, since his gut instinct told him he wouldn't be a part of this world for all that very long.

Like many "professional shoppers" once Brian located and successfully purchased a unique or hard-to-find item—unless the item held a specific purpose or love for him—he would give it away as a gift or forget he had even bought it, and never look at it again. For him, the thrill was definitely most often in the hunt. More telling was the fact that, as he observed the truly ugly sides to life, he purchased even grander and more magnificent objects d'art in an attempt to hide the real unpleasantness of his existence.

Despite that, the objects d'art that he did keep close, he treasured. This was one area where he and Anita had a major difference of opinion. Whereas he had an affinity for those items that originated from as far back as renaissance or medieval times, she only valued avant-garde art or fake, plastic-looking objects.

The couple also acquired furnishings of every sort during their travels abroad, and he explained, "We acquired belongings while setting up temporary quarters in hotels and various other establishments, as we traveled. Anita had her own wild ideas of what art was good, and I had mine. We both decorated, but the beautiful tapestries, paintings, rugs, and crystals came more from my taste than hers."

He loved the classical and baroque appeal in merchandise that demonstrated opulence and grandiosity. Anita was much more modernistic. "To me, she was into the phony appearance of what was art," he explained. "I like the old, thick-to-the-touch quality of fine materials. Those were the things I felt comfortable with. Anita never was a queen in the real sense of royalty."

Once the couple moved to their even more prestigious home on Courtfield Road, South Kensington, Anita felt so secure with her place in Brian's life that she took it upon herself to get rid of his most treasured pieces of art—without consulting him. With a heavy heart he said, "I'm not sure what happened to so many of my things because of Anita's temperament at different times. She'd get angry or aggressive and decide to get rid of my things. They'd suddenly be gone, and she would replace them with her plastic material. She said, 'It's better, Darling. It's all the rage—you'll see. Your things were just old junk.' She said that about my beautiful from-the-castle antiques!"

He was a very strong man when it came to knowing who he was and what he wanted, and because of that it was surprising he allowed someone like Anita to browbeat him. He wanted to find true love so badly that he was willing to do almost anything for the feeling and said, "My greatest desire always was to have a mind-blowing sexual experience with a female, which would create a feeling of love and bonding, and take me to heights I had never known. But, sexual experiences so often carried so much baggage and expectation—that they seemed inadequate to fulfill in real life. I don't suppose I ever really learned how to please a woman or a man, but only myself. And, even that became harder and harder to do.

"I couldn't really bond or connect with anyone, and I missed out on knowing what the experience of love could really be. Either I was too uptight or they were too demanding, or we were too wild or too crazed. Or we were trying to get only the pure physical sensation out of it, and it never occurred to me that there was a deeper soul I could connect to.

"Either the women tried to be my mother, or they tried to be the sex queens, and it didn't really match up to what felt comfortable for me. The arms I ultimately rested in could have been anyone's—as long as they held me gently and let me rest. I so much wanted to feel safe and comforted, and not have them expect anything of me.

"The problem was—if you were a rock star, you were supposed to be a stud man. I tried…I really tried."

***

Anita's tactics in getting Brian to fall so quickly for her were ingenious. She managed to get him to confide stories that he never told anyone about the abuse he suffered at the hands of his mother. He never went into great detail—since he couldn't face the reality of what had happened, even to himself. Nonetheless, he told her enough to enable her to complete the picture in her own mind.

By the time they met, Anita already was an accomplished manipulator and more advanced than Mick in the Dark Arts. She used her powers of mind control to make Brian feel completely dependent upon her. Once he realized what she was doing, he fought hard to regain control. He said, "I enjoyed Anita's antics until I realized our battle for control was for real. It didn't take very long to figure her out—about three months."

She deliberately fought the battle of wills with him. Everything had to be on her terms, and she took no prisoners. Brian said, "She was very much into the Dark Arts, and I wasn't. I thought it was fun for awhile, but I didn't realize what I was doing. Plus, I didn't know how mean she could be! Mean to me, mean to everybody. It had to be her way, or she would shriek and carry on. She'd fight about what food we ate…when to go to bed. Everything."

He claimed she wasn't the true love of his life, despite what so many thought. He said he never found that person. "No, I didn't say she was my true love, did I? Although, it did hurt to lose her ultimately. I can't believe the mind games, manipulations, and weird energy she had me wrapped up in. I didn't know if I was coming or going with her. The sickness of having her or not having her was painful. She was like an addiction—even if you know it's bad for you, it was still better to have someone familiar around. Better than being alone.

"Anita was more the sadist. Her big thing was control. Even if she acted submissive, her thing was to control me into becoming more dominant than I wanted. Weird! I was just trying to keep up with her…it was quite a ride. We never had 'regular' sex. It was a very abusive relationship that catches you up and spits you out. It was very painful.

"What kept us together for so long was the intensity, the love/hate over-the-edge kind of thing that keeps things exciting, riled up, and keeps you coming back for more.

"One big, sore spot was that she wanted to marry into the Rolling Stones tribe, and I wouldn't marry her. She wanted both the white dress and also total domination. So I just put off talking about marriage; to me, forever is a very long time. I couldn't let myself think about it.

"She told me she was pregnant with our baby. Then she told me she lost the preemie baby, but I never knew how—whether it was an abortion or a miscarriage. I never saw the baby. She told me it was a boy, about four months along. She said she buried him herself. She was evil!

"Had she given birth that would have been one more way for her to get her hands on me. Yes, for a while she did have me by the balls…and if that's what love is…well, it lasted for a time." (Photo #828)

Brian and Anita's convoluted affair had as many highs as lows. Everyone who came in contact with the couple complained how vicious they were to others. No one was spared from their mind games. Brian had fallen prey to Anita's will. She led him to treat friends and associates in a way he never would have on his own. The two manipulated people and situations to irritate and embarrass anyone who crossed their path.

Kathy Etchingham, musician Jimi Hendrix's girlfriend, was a victim of Anita and Brian's trickery. Supposedly, he sent Kathy into a darkened room to get something, knowing she'd trip and injure her leg. Later on he said, "I didn't mean to hurt anyone. At the time it seemed like good fun. Anita was actually the wicked one—she taught me a lot. We were definitely using drugs—everything we could get our hands on. Our jokes seemed funny then, but I was out of my head!

"I'm sure Anita was hallucinating. The LSD made us act freakier. For us to understand the consequences of taking the acid—plus all the speed, the pot, and the downers—would have required mature, rational thought, wouldn't it?" he attempted to joke.

On the flip side, one area in which Brian would never change was his interaction with certain supporters with whom he felt a special affinity. No matter how the drugs, or Anita, may have altered his personality at times and made him appear a non-feeling monster, on days when he was straight and sober he maintained his basic, down-to-earth, humble nature. Typical of this duality in his personality were a series of letters he wrote during these times to a fan named "Shandie" or Shandy—a name for a popular UK drink that combined one half English beer, not lager, and one half lemonade, which was then served in pint glasses. (Letters/Photos #811-820)

On his own, Brian was a juvenile prankster who set up little jokes to humor others. When Anita joined him, those harmless jokes turned cruel. He gave one example of a mind game she played on the Stones, when they needed him to be at rehearsals. However, she had decided she wanted him to take off for a couple of weeks with her instead, and so she told the band that a close family member of hers had unexpectedly died, and she had to leave the country to attend the funeral. They all believed her, and off she went with Brian by her side. In reality, no family death or emergency had occurred, but she and Brian enjoyed the free time away from the band for a short vacation.

He frankly admitted that when the band did things like that to him, he got upset and cried for being treated unfairly. He said, "With us (the band) it was always tit for tat. But I enjoyed Anita's antics, for I felt that she had a much more wicked brain and could think of things that I hadn't thought of. It became a little battle thing we had against the others—as in 'us against them.' We were always on each other's side, against the others, until she decided she wasn't on my side after all."

He wound up having more than one battle of wills to fight against Anita. She unilaterally decided to use her superior powers of darkness to help and assist him in keeping his power over the Stones. However, he didn't want her help. He was very much his own man and especially didn't want her using the Dark Side to assist him. "Her offer had everything to do with her control, and that meant very little to me. She and I cat fought. I maintained my desire to be in control of things myself—even if that control meant giving away control, due to my drug use or other things. It still was my control and me doing it! I had a very, very strong wall against anyone manipulating me and telling me what to do.

"Anita wanted to control me and use her powers of persuasion. Sometimes I felt they worked, but I still resisted her and was annoyed with her. And so, we fought. Even though she said, 'Let me help you, Brian,' I still got so mad, exploded, and just blew up. Who was she to think what was right for me? She wasn't a Stone. She wasn't leader of anything! Who was she to tell me what to do with my band and my life?"

Whereas that may sound like back to front thinking, he chose to remain true to himself. Keith once referred to Brian as "the little Welsh bull," since he was of Welsh ancestry, and since he was that stubborn. No matter how much he might have needed help—because he'd been so accustomed to never having anyone around to help him—he felt as if he had to fight like hell to maintain his individualism.

***

When Brian refused to allow Anita to help him keep the band and then also put off marrying her, she turned on him and showed her viciousness. She ran to Mick and offered to conspire against Brian, and told Mick that the two should combine their powers. She and Mick were both predisposed to the Dark Side, and to them, Brian represented the Light—and the Light represented danger. They knew he basically was an innocent in matters of outright cruelty and malevolence. His light had to be extinguished.

Once she solidified her plans with Mick, Anita went to Brian and told him he was doomed—that she and Mick, together, would destroy him. Brian explained, "She both scorned me and laughed at me for letting the band do to me what they were doing. She called me weak and pathetic because I wouldn't fight back the way she wanted. She and Mick used their powers to make my physical pains even worse, and I felt powerless to stop it. When I felt them working against me, I'd double over with stomach pains. They were excruciating! There was always the chance it was my paranoia dreaming this up, but I did feel weaker and even worse about myself and lost confidence in my ability to continue."

Mick thought he had to use the powers of darkness as a survival tool with which to beat Brian. Mick knew that if he only used his natural talents, he could never achieve supremacy of the band. One example of his and Anita's successful collaboration to destroy Brian was when the two coaxed Brian into wearing the infamous Nazi S.S. uniform for a series of photographs taken by the press. Naturally, posing in such a hated uniform—so close to the end of World War II—brought loud cries of anti-Semitism against Brian. The act even alienated the police force against him, and they refused to protect him.

Once more, his simplistic way of looking at situations backfired on him. He trusted both Anita and Mick when they told him it would be a lark and a great joke to dress as a Nazi. He just wanted to please everyone and never realized how those innocent maneuvers and misjudgments would be held against him.

Take note of the beautiful, but at the same time prophetic, mural (Photo #825) that Brian painted on a wall in the Courtfield Road apartment he shared with Anita. He painted a black cloud hanging over a tombstone on top of a gravesite—meant to represent his life—and yet stood with an almost angelic smile on his face while posing for the photograph. He felt he forever had a black cloud surrounding him, expected bad things to happen to him, and in a way felt he deserved those bad things. He never realized how much his clinical depression added to those feelings of hopelessness and helplessness.

***

Even though Mick and Anita succeeded in using the Dark Side to terrorize and intimidate Brian, in many ways he was his own worst enemy. Back in September '64, actor Dennis Hopper introduced him to art dealer Robert Fraser, while they all were in Paris. Fraser in turn introduced him to the art world's inner circle of high society. The rest of the Stones weren't invited, only Brian.

While his relationship with his band continued to deteriorate, and he let the heavy use of drugs overtake his better judgment, he began to think these people were truly his friends. There's an old saying, "Keep your friends close and your enemies closer." Brian hadn't heard of that saying. He thought of the band as his worst enemies and continued to push them away. He thought those artsy folks—who were his real worst enemies—as friends, and eagerly embraced them, putting all his trust in their callous hands.

He said, "These great artists magnetized me into their group. I'd always been fascinated by many art forms and expressions. I let them suck me into their web of drugs and group sex. At first I felt great prestige in being invited into what I imagined was a higher thought group. I didn't see the danger from the drug addictions that came along with that life."

He wanted to fit in so badly with people he thought truly treasured him that he let himself be further dragged into a world of perversion. He entered the art scene bright and beautiful, but once there he felt dirty and bedraggled—everything had been an illusion. He said, "I wanted to live life my own way and be happy, but my self-esteem was always so low. I needed praise and adoration, and desired people to think I was good and to tell me I was good. Sometimes I believed it, and sometimes I didn't. I knew my music was good—but me, personally—I'd been taught that I wasn't worth anything.

"I didn't understand how I could have a gift, such as music, that could be meaningful and important, and still be such a loser as a person. Once I joined the artsy group, it felt good to have all these people sucking up for a change. Then there were times when their praise and adoration just annoyed me because I knew it was fake, and they were only doing it because they wanted things from me. It all got weird after that. When they started to parrot one another and become nothing more than 'yes' men, it all lost its sincerity."

Group sex, or orgies, held a special fascination for him. He explained, "Trying everything that was presented without questioning its wisdom was done under the guise of freedom—including free love among all the bands. That was the rage. We weren't seen as gay, or even bi-sexual, but as really cool, experimental, and not afraid to try new things. It was more of a philosophy we were espousing and not deviant sexual acts."

He said he wasn't sure himself what were good sexual acts or not, or whether it was or wasn't good to be a fag. He believed "it was good to be unafraid, fearless, and experimental in everything. Although, I wasn't a nudist and as much as I flaunted my 'shaker'—I kept it under wraps," he said with a sly grin.

He lost himself in the world of drugs and orgies, and his system rapidly deteriorated. Additionally, his drug or alcohol-induced blackouts continued and possibly increased. During these times of intense partying, he would frequently wake up to realize that once more his body had been abused. Because of his intense beauty, sexuality, and international fame, the professional partiers got off by using and abusing him, and he'd wake up never knowing what had gone on around him. The feelings were the same as the times he would wake up while with Mick and know something unclean had happened to him.

He never could understand why others could do the same drugs and drink as much as he did, and yet weren't affected to the same degree. Since he didn't understand how the drugs impacted him, he didn't know enough to discontinue using. He'd take both uppers and downers at the same time, by the handfuls. He said, "Quite a rush! One never knows what the effect will be. I'm not saying it was a smart thing, but it was quite popular for a while. We were all doing the same things. It was fun."

He continued this self-destructive lifestyle for approximately three years, while he saw himself slowly being eliminated from the band he created and loved. Subconsciously, he was self-destructing and engaging in masochism of the worst form, since he felt so unloved and unwanted by anyone or anything that mattered. Eventually, he stopped sexing and drugging among the larger groups and larger parties, and sought out more intimate surroundings in which he only wanted drugs, without the human contact.

He thought his money could buy him anything, and he sought the best and most exotic drugs available. After awhile everything got old for him and lost its magic. Looking back, he said, "There were times I used stronger and harder drugs and knew I may be killing myself. But I continued regardless, even though I really didn't want to die."

There were times when the Stones needed him for recording sessions and performances, but he was nowhere to be found. He didn't do that purposely to spite them, but life had lost all meaning for him. Life only had meaning when he was creating music, but both the Stones and ABKCO wouldn't listen to or acknowledge anything he attempted to create. He didn't know whether he was trying to purposely hurt himself by taking so many drugs or trying to spite the people who wanted to see him destroyed. There was probably a bit of both, and he succeeded in drugging and drinking himself into oblivion. He said, "I knew things had gotten bad for me when I forgot which day it was. The days turned into nights…I lost track of time."

He was asked if Mick and Keith came to get him and bring him back. He answered, "Who knows? I don't remember." What he actually meant but didn't say was—if he couldn't create the music his heart ached to create—why show up simply to play the same old stuff that meant nothing, over and over?

He often said that the sex and drugs started out as a diversion from his reality—the reality he desperately needed to escape. He got lost, however, in the world of sex and drugs. And, once he found out he was lost, he couldn't and didn't know how to find his way back.

Ironically, Mick eventually adopted the persona of the art lover and the classical literature lover, and pretended to be the one seeking out higher thought through the world of art. But once again, he was only copying and following Brian's initiative. Brian explained, "Mick dabbled with drugs the same as I, but it was never his thing. However, he took my association with artists and pretended it was his own original idea. It was just one more piece of me that he adopted. He'd never say that, of course. Mick was fortunate, though, in that he had a gift for taking the best of something without the pitfalls that often showed up on the other side. His ego always demanded that he carry himself upright."

***

On the bright side, Brian's years as part of the international art world's inner circle and his years with Anita Pallenberg were crowned with two major, individual achievements. These did not include the Stones many hit recordings in which he played a major role creating. These individual achievements consisted of two original soundtracks that he composed and put together almost entirely on his own.

One was an album he created in honor of Morocco's Master Musicians of Joujouka, and the second, the soundtrack for the movie *A Degree of Murder*.

After his initial trip to Morocco with Linda Lawrence, he made repeated trips to the country. Some of those trips included Mick, Marianne Faithful, Keith, their driver Tom Keylock, and art dealer Robert Fraser. In talking about the country, Brian said, "Morocco was a blood-stirring experience. It gets the old juices going and fires everything up. I felt a soul connection and loved everything about the place, from the intense heat, the passionate rhythm, the slow pace, and especially the ganja! The pace is easy, smooth, and rhythmic. I like the simplicity of the people—to me that's what the real world is about, with no pretense."

During one particular trip to that part of the world, Anita and Marianne joined him on an excursion to the Rock of Gibraltar. The three were especially high on acid, and each has a different version of what occurred that day. Anita—who loved to spread horrible tales once she and Brian broke up—swore that Brian brought a tape recorder containing original music he had composed, up the Rock with him and played it for the tribe of monkeys who lived there. She said that the monkeys ran away from his music, screaming in horror, and as a result Brian broke down and cried while he cursed the animals.

He told a different version. He said the monkeys chirped excitedly while they enjoyed his taped music, and added that, "Yes, the monkeys ran away in fear but not from my music, but from Anita! I did get angry that day over something—but don't remember over what. I was fooling around and acting like a monkey myself, but I certainly didn't need monkeys to appreciate my music! Remember, we were all on acid, and the monkeys seemed like they were too," he said with a laugh.

In a way Morocco was responsible for his and Anita's final breakup. One night, he ordered up two prostitutes to the house where he and Anita were staying. He wanted the ladies of the evening to be a surprise for her. She was out shopping and would soon return. Anita loved threesomes or even foursomes, especially with other women, and Brian wanted to please her. Instead, when she returned and saw the women, she flew into a rage and threw them out.

Then she took her rage out on a hapless Brian, who had no idea what went wrong. He said, "I have no idea why she had that fit. I had the prostitutes there as a gift for her, to please her, and I thought having them as a surprise was a fun idea. I didn't want them necessarily for myself, but it was hard to interpret what would make Anita happy and not happy. She hit me hard first, and I grabbed her arms to stop her, but she was strong. I hate to say she was stronger than me! I couldn't hold her back any longer.

"She could have been really happy about my present. I didn't do it deliberately to make her angry. I really wanted to make her happy," he repeated over and over.

He struck back at her hard that day, but this was only one of many fierce battles they had. "Anita punched me many times. The fighting was part of what seemed to turn her on—not the making for a good family life," he said.

On one occasion, he stopped himself from striking her back—after she again attacked him—and he punched a windowsill instead, breaking his wrist. This was a major injury for both him and the band. It was the hand he needed to play. As a result, he missed many sessions with the band and his music had to be dubbed in, until the wrist healed enough for him to resume playing.

After their bitter battle over the prostitutes—and Brian retaliating just to get her off him—Anita ran to Keith and told him she needed his protection. At first Brian laughed at her assertion, saying, "Anita ran off to bed Keith not because she was a shy flower in need of his protection. I can assure you of that. She became unmanageable that day, and I also turned obnoxious against her. She brought out my surly side. She went to Keith to annoy me, and it worked. The two of them—they needed the comfort and dependency of one another and they enjoyed the same drugs…."

He thought that, even though he and Anita had fought and she had run to Keith, they were still a couple. It wasn't until they abandoned him in Morocco and took off without him that he realized the relationship was finally over. The way the group conspired was especially cruel. Anita took off with Keith and the band's driver, Tom Keylock, who helped them leave the country. From sheer vindictiveness, they also took all of Brian's money, credit cards, and even his personal identification.

For a man—who feared isolation and abandonment more than anything in the world—this cruelty was unpardonable. He called out to his friend, Brion Gysin, to come for him and help get him home. By the time he managed to return, what clothing he had left on his body was torn to shreds and hanging, as he had been left with absolutely nothing. His hair was in disarray, as were his mental and emotional states. The man he still called brother, Keith Richards, had once again played the ultimate betrayal upon him.

Brian said, "Causing the rift between Keith and me excited Anita. What she did in a way seemed like a set-up—like I was purposely being set up to be the bad guy, so she could run and do her will with the others. It could've been Mick or Keith that she ran to. But, you know, Keith was the easier one for her to run to.

"For a time, I actually thought she was the one for me, and so I was devastated to lose her—despite the fact she was that wicked and horrible a person. For a time she and I discussed buying a house together. She wanted Southern France, the Riviera. But, it just didn't materialize and turned out to be more wishful thinking, as things turned out.

"Also, it was understood among the band that you didn't mess with another's girl. There were many times when the other Stones' women came on to me, but I turned them down. The girls did it all the time, like a game. I flirted back with them, but that's all, and even that made me feel a little uncomfortable."

Again, everything was a matter of honor and decency for Brian, but he never was treated reciprocally. At one time, he and one of Keith's girlfriends, Linda Keith, did have sex with each other—however, her relationship with Keith wasn't serious. As Brian explained, "Linda Keith was only a small fling…a momentary sexual encounter. She came onto me, and I don't know what motivated it. We had sex, and that was it.

"When we (the band members) knew another bloke's feelings were real, we stayed away from each other's girlfriends. You see, there was so much group sexual activity that it got borderless in a way. But with Linda, Keith had no problem. They weren't serious."

Over the years both Mick and Keith were known to have beaten many of their women—to them this was a feeling of entitlement as a Rolling Stone. "Everyone was throwing blows at one another," Brian said. "Mick beat up Marianne Faithful, and eventually Keith beat Anita."

At that time, Brian only beat Anita because he couldn't get her off him, and she was attacking him—a completely different scenario from the one she presented to Keith. Brian went on to say, "I feel like such a fool to have fallen for her games. After they abandoned me in Morocco, with no money—nothing—I thought I would lose my mind. I was always being abandoned…my family had abandoned me…my band was abandoning me, and now my woman and my best friend abandoned me. This was something that played out throughout my life.

"The experience in Morocco nearly killed me. I felt humiliated, knowing they were all back at home laughing at me. Their action at stealing everything from me was criminal! Anita planned the entire thing, and Keith didn't have the balls to say 'No!'

"Afterwards, she approached me and tried to coax me back into bed with her, but I turned her away. I figured she was playing me again. As big a mess as I may have been…I didn't want to sleep with her any longer. She was vicious, and I'm happy I fought her back. Still, she acted differently with Keith. He was her security—but not that she really wanted him, personally. As long as he plays along with her, she'll act okay. You see, when I got in her face because I wouldn't allow her to own me and control me—she became angry."

***

Years later, Keith and Anita married but that didn't make her faithful. She openly had sex with Mick, while the two acted in a low-rated movie called *Performance*. She succeeded in marrying into the Rolling Stones, just as she planned. She may not have married the Stone she really wanted, but she did marry. Her career wasn't as successful as she would have liked, and because of that, she fixed her eyes on capturing a Stone. As Brian said, "Anita worked off and on. She tried to pull deals off. She tried hard, but nothing of significance ever came her way. She definitely wanted to be an actress."

Anita could control Keith, and he went along with whatever she wanted. He was quiet, complacent, and non-confrontational. Brian always had to be his own man.

Brian's relationship with Anita lasted approximately one and a half years. He was still only twenty-five years old but felt he'd already lived a hundred. Years later, Anita found it in her heart to say some very nice things about him—after his death. She said that he was the one to have gotten the Rolling Stones all their music deals and taught them everything they knew about the business. She also said that Mick and Keith had to play at being sexy on stage, whereas Brian was the real deal when it came to sexuality. He was the one to have hustled to get the band noticed and arranged all their play dates.

She added, Brian had a natural charisma and had to teach Mick and Keith everything. For whatever reason, Brian started out the sophisticate, while Mick was the child. By the end of Brian's life their roles had reversed, with Mick turning into the sophisticate and Brian becoming almost childlike in his dependency. What she failed to mention was that she had assisted Mick in increasing his manipulative powers and energy, which enabled him to take over Brian's energy. Together, they sucked out Brian's life force. Mick acquired even stronger powers of Black Magic than he already had, from Anita.

***

Anita acquired the starring role for the murder mystery *A Degree of Murder* in 1966-7 and brought Brian in to create the musical score. He was hesitant at first to take on this huge project alone, since so far he had only composed one song at a time, together with his band. This would be his first solo project of such magnitude.

Even though the storyline for the film wasn't love, but murder, he incorporated many of his feeling of love for Anita, which he truly felt at the time. He read the script and chose which scenes he thought required musical accompaniment. The majority of the music was fast-paced to match the action, and the rest were dramatic pieces to complement the presence of murder and the resulting cover-up.

The script had no love scene in it; nevertheless, Brian wanted to create a composition based on his and her emotional attachment. The resulting love song has no words but is a beautiful piano solo that he masterfully incorporated into a scene with a car traveling along a highway—in which Anita rode. He said, "She was the star of the film, and she pulled me into it. I was more than happy to go along. I was inspired by her to do most of the score. My emotions were running at different heights, and I was rapt with her."

The majority of the music reminds the audience of children skipping happily along, like at an amusement park or riding a carousel. The tunes are extremely upbeat and full of energy. Brian said of his compositions, "I wrote them based on how love was supposed to feel—how I wanted it to feel—how I hoped it would feel." He admitted that the lovely piano solo was inspired by classical music, and it brought much-needed softness to the movie where there had been none.

He appeared in two scenes. In one, a pub scene, you cannot see him, but his soft voice can be heard singing in the background. This song was also his original, in which he sings a moving folk tune. In the second scene, you can see him but aren't supposed to know it's actually him in it. This was his comedic side coming out, in which he dressed as Anita and performed a stunt. Unless the viewer specifically looks for Brian, he cannot be spotted—especially since he and she purposely wore their long, blond hair identically.

He was proud to say that he did a bit of directing for the film, which was filmed in Germany, to ensure the music was properly incorporated into the various scenes. He also said he helped direct Anita. "I made suggestions to her about how to do certain things. She took it well at times, depending upon her mood."

When he was asked if Anita interacted well with all her male co-stars, or if she flirted with them, he answered, "She more stared them down and took over!"

For the film, Brian himself played harmonica, organ, sitar, and harpsichord. Among the other instruments used by various musicians were guitar, piano, and drums.

The director of *A Degree of Murder*, Volker Schlondorff, said of Brian's extraordinary musical contribution to his film, "It wasn't just that his music was special. It was that the score was so spontaneous and vital. Only Brian could have done it. He had a tremendous feeling for the lyrical parts and knew perfectly the recording and mixing techniques to achieve the best sound."

Brian's other crowning achievement in his too-short life was producing the moving ethnic album entitled *Brian Jones Presents the Pipes of Pan at Joujouka*.

He visited the village of Joujouka in the Rif mountains of Morocco during the summer of 1968. His friend, Brion Gysin, took him along to hear the villagers' magical music performed. Outsiders weren't normally invited into these private ceremonies, but Gysin was looked upon as a special friend, for introducing this local music to a restaurant he owned in Tangiers.

As soon as the villagers and their leader—Hadj Abdesalam Attar—met Brian, they took him in as one of their own. He wore long, elegant, colorful robes to complement their style of dress. His flowing blonde hair glistened brightly, which made an imposing contrast to the villagers' usual dark hair. What they liked most about him was the honest respect he showed for their culture and their native music. There was nothing pretentious about his radiant smile.

The instruments the Joujoukan musicians played were the same as from ancient times and not common to Western musicians. Within a few minutes, however, Brian was able to take their instruments in hand and play along with them. He was honored as a special guest and invited to take part in their ceremonial dinner.

During the evening, he danced along with the men and even wore their ritualistic dark make-up—that showed he wanted to be one of them. The Master Musicians were so flattered by his genuine interest in their ancient ceremonial music that they allowed him to tape hours upon hours of the music played that evening.

To further honor his presence, the village children sang a song composed especially for him, which they called *Brahim*—his name in their native Arabic tongue.

Once home, Brian played back the hours of tape he had recorded, and from that he produced the only album ever done from that part of the world. This was his first attempt to introduce and integrate global music into his band's repertoire. At the time, however, neither the rest of the Rolling Stones nor ABKCO thought Brian's attempt to bring a different culture's music to the rest of the world as notable, and they ignored his continued attempts to market his album.

Sadly, after his death, in 1971 ABKCO posthumously released *Brian Jones Presents the Pipes of Pan at Joujouka*. Additionally in 1989 the Stones released their *Steel Wheels* album, in which they presented for the first time the music of the Joujoukan musicians.

Brian never got to see one of the crowning achievements of his musical career recognized by either his band or the world.

825

826

827

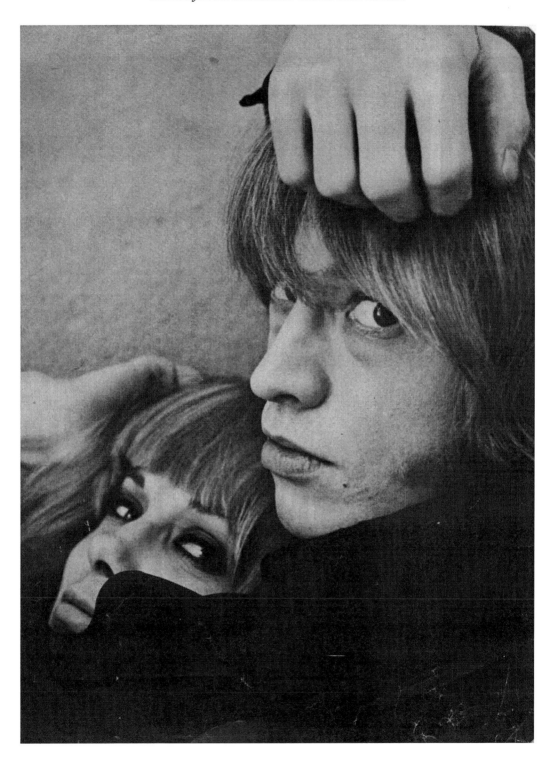

828

# GLORIA SHEPHERD

829

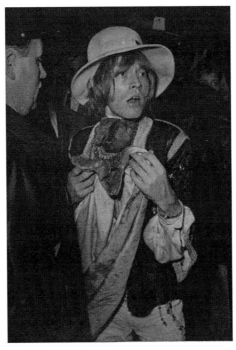

830

831

832

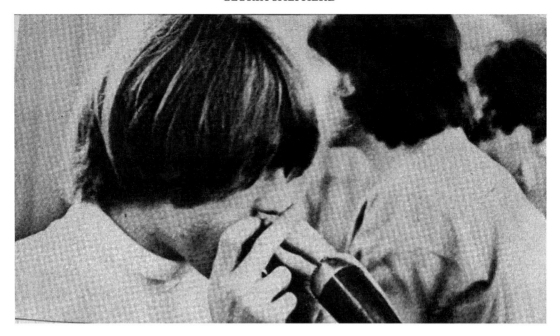

833

834

835

836

837

838

840

841

842

843

844

845

846

847

848

# GLORIA SHEPHERD

849

850

852

853

854

855

856

857

858

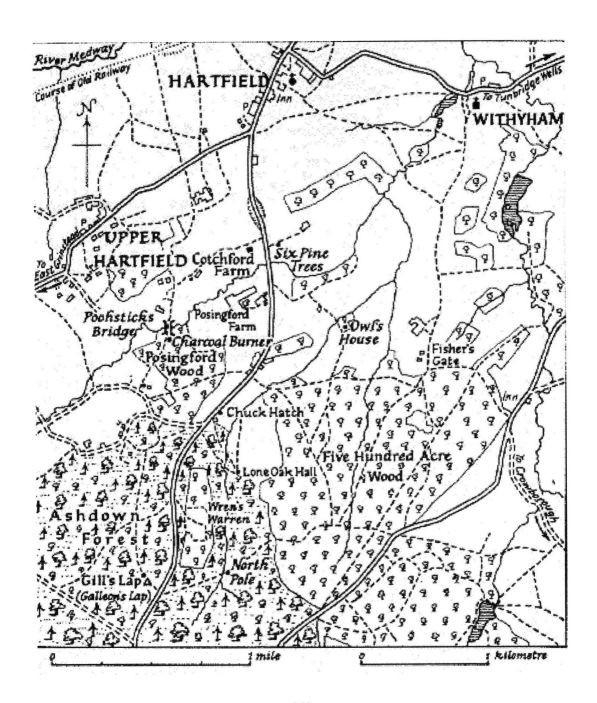

# CHAPTER TWENTY-ONE
## The Land of Oz

*"The band's use of drugs started out as partying and the fruits of our labors. Drugs were free flowing & everyone was doing it. But for me, I did them to self-medicate—to mask my depression & anxiety—and to hide the fear of wondering whether I could keep measuring up."*

Brian Jones

Brian described the years 1967-68 as living in the Land of Oz. Nothing was as it should be or how it appeared. The Rolling Stones were still promoting free love, free sex, all the drinking and drugging one could engage in, plus dressing and behaving as one felt free—with absolutely no consequences. In the band's mind, the legend of Oz promoted the philosophy that true joy and happiness could only be realized from external devices and external actions.

What Brian and the others appeared to have forgotten was that the tale of Oz included the lesson that true joy and happiness can only be realized by looking inside one's heart and soul, and looking to one's home and family. Naturally for Brian, this was impossible since he had no family and no true love to call his own. Additionally, the other love he normally counted on to see him through the day—the freedom to compose and perform his own music—continued to be stripped away from him with each day that passed.

Drugs had now become his main source of enjoyment, especially since the double loss of Anita and Keith. Besides having no love to come home to, Brian also felt he had no true friend to talk to or rely upon, and so he relied on drugs. "They were available everywhere," he said. "We all thought it was fun; Mick even encouraged my use, but I had no strength and no sheer will to not let it overtake me, as he did. I was susceptible from the very beginning, but it sure seemed like fun for a while. Unfortunately, I never realized how it would affect the business end of what I did.

"I didn't fear drugs at first because by the time the Stones became known, I thought I had felt all the pain in life there was to feel, so I did them just to feel better. Everybody was doing it, whether they told you they were doing it or not—whether they got their photos taken or not, as I did." He was always honest and upfront about his drinking and drugging, unlike the majority who pretended to be sanctimonious about their lifestyles.

He further explained, "The paranoia and insecurity that came with drugging made me more pliable. I may have participated, but I was also set up. The weaker I got the more it was used against me, and the more I drank and the more I did drugs—the worse I became. I was an addict but didn't think so at the time. I thought I could stop whenever I wanted, and I partied. Then I got so confused, I didn't know who I was any longer...."

During this time Spanish Tony Sanchez became even more indispensable to the band to keep them supplied with whatever quality drugs they desired. Tony became an unwitting pawn in Mick's private chess game to keep Brian sedated—only to be awakened from his drug-induced slumbers when Mick needed him to compose music.

Mick would pay Tony from his own money to deliver any drugs Brian wanted, day and night. Since Tony was also an occasional lover, Brian had no reason to distrust him. Not until much later, after he left the band—and when he was finally weaning himself off drugs—did Brian finally realized the cruel maneuver Mick had devised to keep him from functioning as a human being.

Even Allen Klein encouraged Brian to do more and more drugs whenever Brian was in America. "Yes, I wanted the drugs, and Allen thought I should get them," he explained honestly. "He knew it was my own demise, and I didn't realize what was happening. It was like giving poison to someone, when the person handing it out knows how bad the poison will be to the one receiving it. When I was in New York, Allen made sure to have drugs sent to my room."

Allen never encouraged drug use among the rest of the Stones—only Brian. He both encouraged Brian to experiment as much as he wanted, and also made it seem as if he were doing Brian a big favor by keeping him steadily supplied. "I had no idea of Allen's dark intentions," he added. "The drugs hampered my ability to reconnect to my band. The ability to make lucid decisions, such as the good or bad sides to taking heavy drugs, was way beyond my ability."

He had a double jeopardy working against him, with Allen Klein in the States and his close, personal friend, Mick Jagger, back home in England. Mick stood by and watched Tony bring his instruments of slow death to Brian, and when he thought Brian's mind was pliable enough to get him to compose and arrange whatever new music he needed—he would go to Brian and prompt him to perform. Brian said, "Tony was my drug pimp, but Mick treated me like his trained dog. In my haze, he prodded me to compose music as it suited him. He'd then snap it from my hands and put his name on it."

He admitted doing everything available, coke, speed, PCP, Quaaludes, and heroin. Sometimes he'd party with Marianne and Keith from three to six days at a time. "But not Mick," he always said. "I'd go into blackouts but never realized it at the time. I'd wake up disgusting—smelling bad from not washing. We all did, but I hated waking up smelling my own armpits and not have the fresh, clean face everyone was used to seeing."

He didn't have many track marks from the heroin use; instead, he often smoked it. As a form of defense, he explained that during times of yore pharmacists provided heroin to treat various ailments. "I felt so blissed out when taking it," he waxed poetic.

While he dated Anita, drugs had played an important role in their relationship. She also encouraged him to use heavily, to achieve her own goals. He said, "PCP really fucked my brain! But that bitch (Anita) could do anything. She'd lead you to water to drink, if you will, and would pretend to take the drugs, but then she stepped back and let me do it, alone."

Getting off drugs became harder and the blackouts more frequent, and soon he suffered bouts of DT's, chills, and quaking, while his body spasmed when he tried coming down. He would then use more downers to help steady his nervous system.

As a whole, the Stones openly encouraged the use of heroin among their peers and insisted on being at the forefront of the drug movement. They wanted the reputation of being the biggest, baddest, and the most over-the-edge of any outrageous experimentation. Brian said, "If we were the leaders of this drug revolution, weren't we supposed to be the ones to first do them, and in the know? How would it look if everyone else knew what those experiences were first, and we had no clue because we were afraid and playing it safe? Besides, we thought of it more as being experimental and pushing boundaries, expanding the consciousness, and all those things we said at the time. LSD was cool! Sure it was scary, but my whole life had scary experiences, with or without the LSD. Yes, it was very dangerous, but we always seemed to bounce back. I had that invincible feeling of youth."

Reality struck home hard in the beginning of 1967, however, when in February the British authorities raided Keith's home at Redlands and confiscated heroin and cannabis from Mick, Keith, and art dealer Robert Fraser. In May, the three were formally charged with drug possession and allowing Redlands to be used for purposes of drug taking.

At the same time, Brian's Courtfield Road apartment was raided in May and searched for drugs. Prince Stash was staying over with Brian during this time, and he was charged along with Brian for possession of cocaine and hashish. In June, the two elected to have a trial by jury.

Whereas Mick and Keith were emotionally strong enough to depend upon their attorneys to get them through the horrible experience of possibly spending much time in prison, Brian completely fell apart. His worst nightmare once more seemed to be coming true—being locked away in isolation, or locked away with human predators who could overpower him and assault him. He suffered flashbacks to his days of living on the streets, a time of his life he could never forget.

*** 

Just as the drug busts were taking place, the Rolling Stones had initiated an entire new concept for putting together an experimental record album—experimental in that the songs would be comprised of new sounds utilizing instruments that heretofore hadn't been used by the band. The album was Mick's baby and his plan to compete with the success of the Beatles' *Sergeant Pepper's Lonely Hearts Club Band*.

Brian and Bill Wyman were opposed to Mick's harebrained scheme to knock the Beatles out of the number one position in this manner. However, the only ones whose opinions seemed to count any longer—Mick, Keith, Oldham, and Allen Klein—outvoted them. Mick's wish was to have the music entirely psychedelic.

Nevertheless, Mick and Keith realized that they were incapable of putting together an album with that quality of ingenuity and uniqueness. They needed Brian for that. He was the only one who possessed the knowledge to gather these sounds, had the strong musical background required, and had the far-reaching imagination to see the project through.

Notwithstanding the heavy drugs with which he was abusing his mind and body, his musical genius appeared to be reaching new heights. His ability to master countless instruments boggled everyone, and he became conscious of a renewed energy and confidence from within.

The album's development, which would eventually be called—at Mick's insistence—*Their Satanic Majesties Request* enjoyed a wild and bumpy ride. The band disagreed on almost everything, including the strange title. Brian wanted to give it a more blissful name, perhaps including the word *Christmas*. Mick, being the strong manipulator he'd now become, won out and decided to give respect to his god instead. Additionally, Mick won out as to how the band should appear while promoting the album. On the cover, Mick sits prominently center garbed in black, depicting his dedication to the Dark Side. The remaining band members, while dressed more colorfully, are equally costumed to give the appearance of denizens of the netherworld.

Even Allen Klein went to Brian, telling him how much the band needed his backing and direction in order to get the album off the ground. Brian said, "Eventually, *Satanic Majesties* did contain most of my sounds. They used me for that. They pumped up my ego and made me feel exalted once again, so I'd help with the music. They decided to use up whatever energy and creativity I seemed to have left. You see, they would never miss out on the chance to make a buck—even if it meant making me feel important again."

The band complained, though, that he wasn't taking the project seriously. In reality, he couldn't. He saw the weakness in the project but still gave producing the music his best shot. He said, "I tried smiling through it all, but they took it so damn seriously! I wanted to say, 'Relax, it's only an album.' It was hysterically funny in a way, and they wondered why I was acting out. To them, they were the normal ones who thought they were the genius behind the project."

*Their Satanic Majesties Request* took 'til the end of 1967 to complete, since the drug busts and subsequent trials disrupted the band's lives. Despite all the up's and down's they went through, Brian was really proud of his final product, in that the music was comprised of all instruments with no synthesizers. Despite the fact he suffered ongoing bouts of feeling incapacitated and unable to perform, his genius, and what he saw as the future of music, flowed brightly. The music played on the album, which incorporated several exotic instruments—such as mellotron, harpsichord, tamboura, and sitar together with a backing orchestra—was made with his essence that played purely with real instruments and man-made sounds.

He never wanted to see synthetic music—now used widely since his death—take over. Countless bands have unsuccessfully tried to mimic the sounds he achieved without synthesizers but have found they need to use them in order to get the same effect.

In spite of his drug taking, with *Their Satanic Majesties Request* Brian still managed to contribute greatly to the musical history of the world. Two of his personal songs in particular receive continuous acclaim and wide recognition. They are *She's a Rainbow* and *2000 Light Years from Home*—both turned into single recordings.

Of the meaning behind the latter song, Brian said, "You have to remember that our entire lives have been affected lately by social/political influences. I believe in changes in our values and attitudes. *Satanic Majesties* is a personal thing and songs like *2000 Light Years* are prophetic, not at all introvert. They are the things we believe to be happening and will happen."

What was amazing was, despite the fact that he was accused of living the debauched life of a wasted druggie—who would frequently be found passed out wherever he'd happen to fall—whenever he was asked a serious question about his music, he had no trouble expressing himself in the most clear and lucid manner. He was entirely coherent and believable.

***

Even though 1967 appeared to outwardly bring renewed vigor to Brian's musical genius, and the band once again openly asserted their need for his talents, inwardly he realized things were going horribly wrong for him. He finally admitted that he had suffered periods of blackout due to stress and alcoholism since '63. This admission to his severe alcoholism—during an early time when he was the band's leader and extremely happy with the nature of their success—was surprising. He explained his situation, "I still had my emotional roller coaster to deal with, back in '63, and I realized I had this problem since I was six or seven years of age."

How, then, could he believe he ever had the wherewithal to lead and tour with a band? "My chemistry was my chemistry quite early on," he answered. "As I evolved, I learned how to cope with it—or thought I did." Regrettably, because he was left relatively untreated by the medical community, his condition quickly worsened.

***

The drug busts by British law enforcement brought a new reality to Mick, Keith, and Brian. The authorities had long planned to teach the rogue band a lesson in respecting civil order, and in '67 they finally acted with full force to quash the band's blatant rebelliousness.

As a result of possibly facing much time in jail, Brian tried to get help for his mental and emotional afflictions. He placed himself under psychiatric care several times during the year in various hospitals, or clinics, and rehab centers. The prognosis was usually the same in that he suffered from chronic depression, fatigue, stress, and paranoia. However, pharmacological companies hadn't progressed much during the sixties to where any significant medical prescriptions or treatments were available.

The fear that he couldn't keep up with the rest of the band scared him to a great degree. Music was his entire world. Yet, he had to face the reality that he couldn't cope with all the stresses brought by fame and success—not to mention the unremitting physical pains that racked his body.

He spoke frankly of his sad experiences with the medical community. "There were times when I spoke to doctors about my physical pains, but they thought I was making it up—same as the Stones did. Very interesting, eh? They thought I was just spoiled and looking to shirk responsibility, unless I were lying in bed or hospital, unable to move. There were times I was clearly very ill, even to them, and they knew it. However, I found it wasn't very helpful to go on and on about my pains, and frequently I'd have the feeling of wanting to say, 'Just give me the medication, don't ask me any questions, and leave me alone!' because it seemed the most they could possibly do was to provide medication. Pain killers were very high on my list, and then there were the uppers that would give me the energy to function, when I didn't have any."

Were any of the medications he took illegal? "Either way. They were both prescribed and also the ones outside the law. Then I would need something else, so I could come down and rest after all the highs, too. Well—you get the picture! Better living through chemistry, eh?" he said contemptuously.

Besides the chronic depression and mood swings, there were other reasons he placed himself in clinics, to try and figure out why his brain seemed to stall out at times. "I felt my brain traveling to different dimensions. There were periods where I couldn't talk, walk, and couldn't play music. I had to pull back from the world. But, no one understood me or what I was going through."

During those times of being unable to communicate, he naturally felt embarrassed and humbled. He desperately wanted to cry out for help—to scream that something was going horribly wrong with his mind and his body. No one, including the professionals, however, seemed able to or interested enough in hearing his plight to help him.

Even vacationing became a chore, as his system would shut down at the most unexpected or inopportune times. He could be in France or any other country trying to enjoy a respite with friends and lovers, and he'd find himself collapsed and going to hospital. During those times, his system would suffer a form of toxic shock that had built up from the use of drugs, plus improper nutrition. His body was continually being weakened, and his digestive system, pancreas, heart, kidneys, and liver all showed signs of disease or extreme inflammation.

His sinuses also were usually inflamed and infected. Low-grade fevers would haunt him, as they flared up and down. Viral infections were common, and his young body both looked and felt as if it were aging very quickly—a situation that had started from childhood.

The medical doctors that he constantly sought out for help didn't believe his afflictions a big thing and thought that, since he was a drug addict and alcoholic, he should just stop imbibing. It was all thrust back on him to save himself. The theory of caring for the patient's entire body—physical, mental, and emotional—was sorely unheard of during his lifetime. Any medications prescribed were just pills and more pills.

The pathetic irony in Brian's situation was, despite the fact the doctors thought of him as a lost cause, they continued to see him for his money.

The doctors viewed him clinically almost as an aberration, to be studied from afar, but never with compassion or caring. The practitioners didn't think of him as a feeling, thinking human being. Instead, they were repulsed by him as a punk kid, as if, "Who does he think he is?" In their minds, he was nothing more than a druggie who was strung out and extremely pompous.

In reality, he was far from pompous but instead a very humble and insecure young man. Because of his naturally regal demeanor and his way of presenting himself, the good doctors misunderstood him. He had a way of speaking with confidence and was also accustomed to accurately explaining what was wrong with him. All he wanted in return was an explanation as to how he could be helped.

What saddened him was, he was thought of as an arrogant prince who always whined about some ailment and ordered others about. The physicians didn't like being treated as paid servants, but nevertheless they had no trouble billing him an exorbitant amount of money for whatever meaningless assistance they provided.

***

Between worrying over the drug arrests and trying to complete the *Satanic Majesties* album, the band was divided and felt harassed and anxious.

June '67 was the trial date for Mick, Keith, and Robert Fraser. Mick was found guilty of the drug charges, but the case was quashed. Keith's guilty ruling was overturned.

Art dealer Robert Fraser became somewhat of a scapegoat. He was the only one to actually serve his prison sentence of six months. Rumors flew that ABKCO paid a large sum of money to get Mick and Keith off with serving no jail time, except for a day or two.

Of the two, Keith took his time in jail as good-naturedly as possible, since his temperament always had been to take life one-step at a time. Mick, on the other hand, wept during his stay behind bars. He didn't prove as brave or stoic as he would have liked the world to believe.

In June, Brian took his time off from finishing *Satanic Majesties* by attending the well-known Monterey Pop Festival in California. He considered this short vacation a personal party he gave to himself, after all the hard work he put into the album. "You didn't know I understood that concept, did you?" he asked with a gleam in his eye—meaning most people didn't believe that party animal Brian Jones comprehended the difference between work and play.

He flew out in a jet provided personally to him by The Mamas & The Papas. Weirdly, Andrew Loog Oldham—his arch nemesis—accompanied him on the trip. The two men's relationship was a convoluted one. On the one hand, Andrew despised Brian and wished to eliminate him as part of the band. On the other hand, he continued to maintain a social relationship with Brian and accompanied him to assorted debaucheries, including wild drug and group sex orgies.

While Andrew looked down his nose at his fair-haired rival's lifestyle, he more than willingly jumped headfirst into that lifestyle. One humorous anecdote was the fact that Brian knew a popular medical doctor, whose office was located in Manhattan. This doctor enjoyed the pseudonym of "Doctor Feel-Good" to which Brian affectionately referred to the man. Dr. Feel-Good would provide private appointments at any time of the day or night to celebrities who could afford his services.

Brian went to him for unique prescriptions that the average medical doctor wouldn't provide. During his and Oldham's days of partying, Andrew realized he had contracted a sexually transmitted disease and implored Brian to set up a time for Dr. Feel-Good to treat his unwelcome ailment. True to his trustworthy self, Brian graciously complied and delivered Andrew to the good doctor's office sometime during the wee, small hours of the morning.

While the two flew to the Monterey Pop Festival, everyone, including Brian, was aware that Oldham's time with the Stones was about up. He had begun to argue with decisions that Mick and ABKCO made, and they felt the need for his services had passed its prime. The occasion of Oldham's upcoming dismissal should have been a great opening for Brian to take retaliatory pot shots, since the former was the main reason for his unmerciful ousting as the band's leader. For whatever reason, Brian didn't act upon it. He said, "I consider that one of my personal victories—that I didn't throw it up in his face. I was glad I didn't and that I took the high road. Regardless, Oldham acted his usual snarly self. He felt pushed out by us. We talked a bit about his upcoming dismissal, but we still had all that bad blood between us. He was upset that his money deal with the band was going away. Yes, he was pitiful!"

Brian was asked how he and Oldham even wound up traveling together to Monterey. "You can say it was a rite of passage. He wanted to come along and was also keeping an eye on me I think, at Allen's request. Nevertheless, he was flying high during the entire trip."

Did he believe Oldham was as high as he during the festival? "Hardly anyone was!" he answered and laughed. "But, he had a good time. We were all ecstatic and felt on top of the world. The rest of the band didn't show up due to scheduling conflicts," he tried to explain. "You know how Mick is—if he can't be on the front of the stage, he doesn't want to go!"

Even in this case, Brian took the high road and chose not to overtly put Mick and the rest of the band down for not making an appearance at what was considered the biggest event of the season.

Monterey was akin to a Woodstock in that the promoters presented it as a love fest with free sex, free music, and all the drugs anyone might fancy. Of all the celebrities and musicians present, no one was more photographed, followed, admired, and quoted than Brian. Dubbed the King of the Festival, he enjoyed being surrounded by his peers and fans during the several-day event.

He wore an outfit for which he has always been remembered, with bells, furs, brocades, jewels and every imaginable color material and fine silk adorning his body and setting off his platinum blonde hair. (Photo #847) He bragged to admirers that he was solely responsible for selecting and putting together the costume he wore and explained it was made from old European and British attire.

During this time away from all the trials and troubles of his life, he truly was maybe the happiest he had been or would ever be in his short life. He was loved and adored by all and enjoyed a peaceful time. Perhaps all the drugs he took played a part in the bliss he felt, but regardless, he was at peace with both himself and the rest of the world that he all-too-often imagined conspired against him.

As to whether he was called the King of the Festival because of his music or his personal fame wasn't clear to him. He said, "I hope to think they're one and the same. Although, I thought they loved me mainly for my music."

The fact they may have actually loved him purely for himself was beyond his greatest wish. When that very real possibility was presented to him, he became teary-eyed and maudlin. He couldn't let himself believe anyone could love him for anything other than his music.

To say he was seen at that time almost God-like and capable of walking on water, during the Pop Festival, would not be an overstatement. Among the observations he made was that he felt safe for the first time in years walking freely amongst the crowd. He said, "Yesterday I was walking through and joining rings of kids and fans. You know, I've never had a chance to do that much before. People are very nice here. From what I've seen so far they are acting as a community. They have the community spirit, the community feeling. I haven't seen signs of any trouble or any enmity. It's very nice and very beautiful. I'm glad I came.

"It's nice to let people know that the Stones are still functioning (despite the drug arrests) and still on the scene, doing all we can. I'm going to be here for a very few days. Just a little break from recording and everything."

The press asked Brian about the course of the band's future music and their plans to tour. He answered, "We feel at the moment that our important work is to be done in the studio, rather than in baseball halls and stadiums around the country. There's a lot to be gained by letting the fans share our evolution because we are progressing musically very fast."

Once again, despite the fact he may have been high with an assortment of hard drugs, he was still more than capable of being the Rolling Stones' spokesperson, and sounding clear and lucid.

Blonde beauty and singer, Nico, was Brian's constant companion at Monterey and photographed with him over the entire course of the festival. The pair strolled throughout the celebration enjoying everyone's open admiration. Brian loved being called King—if only for that brief period of time.

On the other hand, what few knew was that Nico was—and eventually openly admitted to being—an avowed sexual masochist. Unfortunately for both Brian and her, the couple took a quantity of LSD and other hallucinogens, which had disastrous results for their lovemaking. As he has claimed, while under the influence of certain drugs, he would go into deep blackout and become someone who in real life he would never want to be. He basically was a gentle soul, who'd never want to hurt anyone physically or sexually. This fact was easy to understand since he knew all too well the pain that could be associated with sex, especially forced sex.

However, he was also meek enough to allow a partner to coax him into performing acts that he would never initiate on his own. With the combination of hallucinogens and the desire to please Nico sexually, he wound up hurting her, even causing her to bleed. For that, he was labeled a sexual sadist who took advantage of his lovers.

He was truly ashamed for what occurred between Nico and him. He cared for her and thought her extremely beautiful. "I feel horrible about that relationship and don't like the feeling of what I did, and how others now look at me about what I did to her sexually," he said with his eyes lowered. "I'm not clean with that experience and don't like hurting anyone—that's not what I want. That memory hurts me. Nico and I are considered the 'pretty people', who look good on the outside but not who we are necessarily on the inside.

"Nico wanted what she got, though. She kept saying, 'Harder, harder, Brian! More, more!' She wanted blood and she got it, but no, I'm not proud of what I did. But, why does she now tell everyone I'm a complete bastard?

"From my point of view I'm not a womanizer but only someone who had much sex while on the road, and not otherwise. Contrary to some of my later extravagance and decadence, at that time I thought I was just having fun. But when I realized the bad that was happening to me, I wanted to take my soul back."

*\*\*\**

For Brian, the main legacy of the Monterey Pop Festival was the opportunity to get together with and become as one with Jimi Hendrix. Their mutual attraction was instantaneous—but it must be noted definitely not sexual. Their attraction was purely of one musical genius for another. Each saw the strengths and weaknesses that no one else saw or appreciated in the other. Brian said, "I felt the similarity of our lives. Take a look into Jimi's eyes—he's got a deep appeal. To me, he's a gentle soul with nothing mean or cunning about him."

His eyes lit up whenever Jimi's name was mentioned. "We had fun. We had hope," he said. "We thought we were really cool together, Jimi and I, and the quintessential odd couple. Yeah, I like Blacks!" he added with great exuberance. "Jimi is the real King. Sure we snorted coke—it was way cool. Quite a ride."

He was asked how Jimi felt when he learned Brian had purposely treated his girlfriend, Kathy Etchingham, badly. He had gone so far as to tell Jimi that Kathy was treating him like a bitch. He said, "When I told Jimi my opinion of her, he said to me, 'No, Man, she's cool. Everything's cool.' But she was a bitch and always sullen. Jimi was 'whipped'."

He saw a profound similarity between the offensive way Jimi's fans ultimately started to treat him and the way he was being treated by his own fans. Brian described what happened when both tried to play music that was more advanced and not the usual, mundane sounds the fans were accustomed to hearing. "The fans booed Jimi, too, when he didn't play the traditional. The fans can really hurt you; their attitude hurts you when they only want to hear and see what they want and not anything that we, as musicians, want to do. Like a love gone wrong between fans and performers."

Similar to Brian—in that ABKCO wanted to keep him steadily supplied with drugs—Jimi's management also kept him supplied with all the drugs he wanted. This was done in order to "keep Jimi in a state of mind to be more compliant and easy to bend to their will," Brian explained.

He was also asked whether he or Jimi were scared about taking heroin. "No, I really wasn't worried about drugs taking me out. I don't know why. Jimi said that he, too, could handle it. Although, in his case I could see in his eyes that he couldn't. No, I never tried to talk him out of doing heroin. You see, we were in the same boat in feeling that the more drugs we used, the more we wouldn't have to think about all the hurt. Sometimes, though, Jimi would give me a look that said, 'What the hell are we doing, Man?' but then he'd do it anyway. Jimi was the only one to get as high as I did.

"Our managers and producers used drugs to ensure their control over us—over our drug addiction. We were like a science project to them, weren't we?" he said upon reflection.

He went on to explain that the music industry's dirty little secret has always been keeping control over their musicians through drugs. "The younger the musician, the more control they eventually get by hooking them early on into heavy drugs. They think of their performers like little pieces of meat…disposable meat that can be replaced at any time. Total compliance is what the industry demands—nothing less, and I refused to be part of it."

He worried about Jimi more than he worried about himself, and said, "The business of music is hard on Jimi. He also has emotional weaknesses and heart problems, but he'll not admit to it. I love the guy, though. Sometimes I feel that Jimi is getting ready to leave this world, as if our friendship isn't meant to be. Jimi's imprint on the music world is very big, but I also fear it may be very short.

"We share feelings of bitterness, too, towards our fans who are fickle." When Brian made that statement, he made a face—sticking out his tongue—at the imaginary audience.

*\*\**

Immediately following the festival, Brian returned to England and the reality of life. "I don't like reality much, do you?" he asked rhetorically. "But I had to go back home—responsibilities, you know. I couldn't just stay in America and party forever, could I? Although, I damned well tried at times!"

England appeared dreary after all the color and excitement of Monterey. It was a pivotal time in his life, because he decided to take the road that would be for him cold, dark, and painful. "As if going back into the forest," he explained. "Stash and I were never the same after the drug bust. When Stash and I were first arrested, he cried openly; as for myself, I was horrified. We were separated, and we spent time in separate cells. Previously, I'd been able to say that much of my paranoia was due to drug-taking but after the arrest and being constantly watched by the authorities, I realized all my paranoia was real."

While at the California festival he hadn't been fearful of doing drugs, but once he returned home all the horrors returned. He was actually afraid for his life—afraid of jail, afraid of his own government, the police, and now finally afraid of drugs. He also feared having handcuffs slapped on him once again.

Additionally, returning home meant he had to get off the drug parade at once. This hurried action brought severe withdrawals to his frail body. He said, "I'd always tried to take things to slowly level myself off or pull myself back up as I withdrew from heavy drugs. I used medications provided by the pharmacist and prescriptions from doctors. That was so I didn't actually go cold turkey, but still the hallucinations were extreme. I tried to stay awake and keep my eyes open, and that was hard. I was exhausted. I'd do anything, take anything, to knock myself out and have all my fears go away."

In October '67 he and Stash appeared for their trials. Brian decided to do the honorable thing and plead guilty—against the advice of counsel. He was still naïve enough to believe that, in matters such as this, doing the honorable thing would be the most beneficial. Regretfully, this decision would come back to haunt him a few months later when he was arrested a second time.

Mick and Keith had done the opposite. Even though they were as guilty as Brian with their drug possessions, they pled not guilty and let their attorneys plead them out. This was a hard lesson learned by Brian and too late to save his reputation. With his guilty plea, he was sentenced to twelve months in jail and immediately herded off to his cell.

As a result of this final hearing, Prince Stanislaus Klossowski de Rola's case was formally dropped, since he claimed he was nothing more than Brian's guest and not responsible for any drugs housed there. Brian was pleased that his close friend didn't suffer any consequences for what he accepted as his own actions. The two would forever remain close friends and spend much time together, including vacations.

Stash continued to worry about the impact the court proceedings had on his friend's already fragile psyche and openly claimed that Brian was never the same person afterwards. Stash further said that he couldn't see how anyone, especially someone as gentle as Brian, could possibly continue to perform and create music while under the constant threat of impending doom brought on by a hostile police force.

Brian's time in jail was horrific. The guards took full advantage of what they observed as his naturally pretty appearance and effeminate manner. Plus, they were extremely jealous of the strong attraction the female sex had for him. The police couldn't equivocate Brian's feminine appearance and refined style of speech with the fact he was also a heartthrob to thousands, if not millions, of women worldwide. They determined to teach him a lesson and used whatever means possible to humiliate, embarrass, and terrorize him.

While taking him to his cell, they purposely paraded him slowly in front of the hardened criminals—who enjoyed whistling and calling out to him, telling him the depraved things they would do to his body once he was alone in their midst. He had no way of knowing if this would all come true and relived in his mind once again all the horrors he'd previously suffered.

Additionally, one of the guards hit him and elbowed him in the face. Brian said, "This was a very scary, dark time. Very frightening. It was on par with the utter paranoia that would come over me in crowds, when they'd rip at my hair and tear at my clothes—like I was being devoured.

"The police couldn't really beat me up, however. You see, I was a rock star! But, the one who did hit me that one time—he was a loose cannon. The guards threatened to cut off or shave all my hair. I was called faggot. I didn't answer them, maybe because in the back of my mind I thought I actually might be. They were simply bullies."

Luckily the next day, October 31, he was released on bail, (Photo #857) pending an appeal. In December he appeared in court, with Mick attending to show support. Brian's physicians provided much medical and psychiatric testimony that showed their client extremely suicidal and stated he would never do drugs again. They further added justice would not be served by having him actually serve time in prison.

The courts agreed with the doctors and placed Brian on three years probation. He left court and celebrated his newfound freedom with Mick and other friends, including his current paramour, Suki Potier.

Like Brian, Suki also was a gentle soul. The blonde model had been engaged to marry Guinness heir, Tara Browne. Sadly, Tara was killed in a horrific car accident the previous year. Brian and he had been very close, and Tara's death had taken place at an unfortunate time for Brian, because—during this pivotal time of his life—he needed all the true friends with whom he could surround himself.

Originally, he had taken it upon himself to console Suki over her personal loss. The two leaned on one another and eventually became lovers. She wasn't judgmental or egotistical, as the majority of women he was used to meeting. In her, he found the peace and solace he so much longed for.

Unfortunately, she hadn't been with him long enough to completely provide him with the internal fortitude he so badly needed. Between the time he first heard the twelve-month sentence imposed upon him and the two-month interval in December to hear whether he'd have to actually serve that time in jail, a hundred years could have passed. Each day, he pictured himself imprisoned and unable to protect himself from his human predators. Therefore, even though he celebrated with others the fact his sentence had been reduced to mere probation, his mental state had by now deteriorated to the lowest level of his life.

Shortly thereafter, he was found unconscious in his apartment and immediately rushed to hospital. The doctors determined severe mental stress and fatigue were the cause of his collapse, and suggested he spend the night. However, he couldn't bear the thought of confinement, even in hospital, and signed himself out. He subsequently flew to Ceylon and spent Christmas with Prince Stash and others.

This example of how easily his mental and emotional state could deteriorate confirmed the doctors' testimonies at his trial and sentencing. One psychiatrist in particular, Walter Neustatter, played a major role in diagnosing part of Brian's problems. He stated what no one had said before, including Brian—that Brian had an abnormal fear of phallic objects being used against him and a fear of close sexual intimacy with women in general. He went on to say that Brian's natural passivity fueled his fear of sexual attack and sadism.

His patient, he said, alternated mass confusion between being childlike when it came to what's considered normal heterosexual activity and then having to live up to his image of a pop idol and sexual stud.

Had the prospect of spending months in jail not been so dire for him, Brian would never have allowed Dr. Neustatter's testimony to be given publicly. This was very humiliating for him, naturally, but he needed as strong testimony as possible to free him from imprisonment. Then again, the doctor's assessment confirmed the secret that Brian had tried to hide his entire life—that as a child, his mum and others had assaulted him and at times used objects to hurt him. No wonder he had never successfully maintained a relationship with a woman.

On the one hand, being with a "regular, normal" female such as Linda Lawrence only served to make him feel guilty and dirty about his sordid past—despite the fact his past was never of his own choosing. Because he felt dirty about his own body, he couldn't very well maintain a love with someone like Linda, who—in his childlike mind—would only be soiled by having him touch her.

Opposite that was the fact that the year and a half relationship he had with Anita Pallenberg lasted as long as it did because she reminded him so much of his mother. She, too, caused physical pain and degradation to his manhood. Often the only way Brian was able to feel comfortable with a female was to feel physical pain and agony during sex, together with a degree of humiliation and bondage. That type of relationship made him feel close to the female hurting him and brought feelings of once again having a mother figure in his life.

Another tragedy of the drug busts was that they further alienated him from Mick and Keith. Under both counsels' advice, the three were told to stay apart as much as possible, except when having to record. Perhaps at no other time of his life did Brian need the strong support of his fellow band mates, especially Keith. Even that had been taken away from him by the callousness of fate.

***

The Rolling Stones' Land of Oz continued into 1968. In the spring, the band began what many consider one of their finest albums, *Beggars Banquet.* The band members were still reeling from the very real possibility of further drug arrests, and all of the five were being subjected to vindictive, unwarranted, and embarrassing strip searches whenever they traveled abroad. Here, too, the authorities who conducted the body searches relished making them last as long, and sometimes as publicly, as possible.

One reality that all the Stones agreed upon was the sad fact that of all of them no one was more followed, more questioned, and more harassed by the establishment than Brian. Keith spoke often about the cruel tactics used to hound Brian into permanent distraction. Once again, Stash feared greatly for his close friend's safety and well-being.

No longer did Brian allow himself the luxury of a permanent residence. He knew the law was following him wherever he went, and because of that he moved every few days from hotel to hotel or borrowed house and apartment. In spite of that, the Stones undertook putting together what they hoped would be their biggest and brightest album—to counteract the debacle many considered that was Mick's personal baby, *Satanic Majesties*.

Brian said honestly that composing music for the band was ne'er impossible during this time. While speaking of the band's struggle to create their new album, he said, "Everything had gotten too big for us to handle—the parties and especially our fame. The fame alone interfered with our artistry and creativity. Naturally, the drug busts were hard on the creativity as well. For me, the hardest thing to deal with was the public humiliation and scorn resulting from these busts. The dread I felt of re-arrest was constant, and I felt everyone was looking at me and laughing at me."

Life, which had always been hard on him, became an agonizing comedy—however, a comedy with hardly any laughter. He had kept his word that since his drug arrest he managed to detach himself for the first time in many years from either doing illegal drugs, having drugs around him, or allowing people around him whom he knew might have drugs in their possession. "The fear of re-arrest was deeply disturbing and humiliating," he said. "I was fearful for what could happen to me, and that was horrifying. Nothing could get me passed the fear of that intimidation, and so I thought it best to play it clean and keep drugs away."

Regardless, *Beggars Banquet* had to be made, but contradictions within the band continued to surface. In one case, Mick was making it clear he wanted Brian permanently out of the band and continued to spread tales—with ABKCO's direct approval and support—that Brian was delusional and hopeless to work with. Contrastingly, once he realized he needed Brian's help with the music, he ran directly to him.

Mick and Keith tracked Brian to an apartment at which he was temporarily staying while living with Suki, and they asked that he work with them on putting together their ideas for *Beggars Banquet*. As always, he welcomed the duo, since he longed for the days of yore when the three had been inseparable. He liked to believe the two also had fond memories of what life had once been like. During these times of coming together, they'd get along as if nothing had ever interrupted the brotherhood. The music would pour freely, and Brian's creativity would reach even newer and brighter heights.

Even if he wasn't at that time enthused about putting a new album together—especially one in which he'd still have minimal input as to which direction the music would go—*Beggars Banquet* offered him that special time to spend with his mates. He said, "I don't exactly know what first led to them coming to me (for help). For whatever reason, they felt more comfortable coming to me once again, and I was very open to having those times with them. Their reasoning was hard to explain, but everything out there was so crazy for all of us. Besides, it was really nice to have the simple, basic core of what we once were show up again.

"The drug busts did bring the three of us together, but at first I didn't remember actually thinking that. Understand that it was one thing to be seen as wild, reckless, and free, but it was another to be thrown in jail. That was going over the line into what was comfortable and what was truly frightening."

He described how Mick and Keith would often come to him for musical direction. "Off and on we would come together all during our relationship. Sometimes there'd be six or eight months where we wouldn't have these special times, but then they would show up again. At the time, I'd feel or hope that maybe everything could be all right again. Then, I'd come to realize these were only temporary times, and as I looked back on it, I came to realize they were with me just to pick my brain. Yes, it felt really comfortable during the times we were together, but now that I look at it, I can see—it's like they were only looking for new inspiration from me or to see if I had any thoughts I hadn't yet shared with them. All they wanted was to get more out of me.

"It's like someone once said to me—I took their visits at face value but later had to think, 'Was I that stupid? How could I think things would be all right again?' But, I enjoyed their company and always liked it when we had those times."

His childlike innocence had never tarnished, and he still kept the faith that his band mates would reconsider and welcome him back into the fold. He so much wanted to pretend everything that had passed between them—all the bad blood, back-stabbings, Mick's going over to the Dark Side—all that could magically disappear. He truly prayed life could go back to the band's early days of friendship and camaraderie—days of all for one and one for all. (Photos #842 & 843)

He had to face the bitter reality, however, that they had only used his talents once more, for when he'd later phone them to get together, Mick and Keith were never available. He said, "They'd say they were too busy to get together again. You see, it was all based on when they wanted to get together—not when I wanted to. In the beginning everything was based on my saying it was time for us to do this…it's time to practice…it's time to come together. But the time I'm talking about now, it only had to do with what Mick and Keith wanted and what they made time for.

"You have to realize that if they were making time for me, they had to think it was going to be of value and benefit them in some way." He also had to face the bitter truth that no one in his own band really showed compassion or caring for him throughout all his feelings of isolation, illness, and tribulation. They all thought he should simply pick himself up and dust himself off.

When he first began to miss concerts due to his illnesses, the Stones would dub his music into the halls from their recordings, which gave the audience the impression Brian's sound was still there. Despite the fact that worked well, he said, "Later, they stopped including my instrumental sound in order to prove the band didn't need me. Oldham first told Mick they didn't need me except as a ghostwriter to arrange and create, and what they should do was always keep my physical presence in the background. Out of sight, out of mind."

Oldham was gone by now, but the practice remained the same. What hurt Brian inwardly was knowing that he was not the only member of a band who couldn't tour consistently. Other bands also had performers with various infirmities, but they found ways to work around their problems and continued to honor what those band members originally contributed. Two examples were the Beach Boys' Brian Wilson, who could no longer tour due to severe stress problems. In place of touring, Wilson continued to write and produce the Beach Boys' hit recordings, earning them the title of "America's Band".

Another example was Pink Floyd's co-founder, Syd Barrett—who had written many of the band's early hit songs. Syd left his group in 1968, since he suffered from years of mental instability brought on by both natural causes and the use of hard drugs. Nevertheless, his former band mates spoke well of him and ensured he continued to receive all royalties due him from his work with Pink Floyd.

Therefore the Stones—if for no other reason than honor alone—could have and should have worked around Brian's absences. If only they would continue to respect him for what he could do—what he could bring as far as original sounds and ideas—his absences wouldn't have been such a big deal. His unique instrumental sounds, which were what set the Rolling Stones above the rest, could have continued to be dubbed in during the times he couldn't appear. However, Allen Klein and Mick decided Brian was pretty much extraneous, and the band could get buy by cranking out the same kinds of sound over and over.

Brian said, "To perhaps the untrained ear some of their songs may seem different or original, but I could tell it was just cranking out some kind of machinery, cookie-cutter music. I got bored with it, and our audiences deserved better. Once ABKCO decided Mick was their golden child, they threatened the rest of us to tow the line or be replaced. Mick was their bankable star, their golden goose. They couldn't get rid of both of us (if Mick should start creating problems, too) so they decided to get rid of me. That way, Mick could be number one exclusively."

Without realizing he had done so, Brian stated one of the main reasons ABKCO wanted him out of the way. Allen Klein had decided the Rolling Stones couldn't have two leaders. Since Brian was the "rogue element", as management had taken to calling him, and not reliable to show up for tours, he was the expendable one.

Mick purposely shut Brian out of many practice sessions for *Beggars Banquet*, telling everyone and even telling Brian personally that he was too ill or too disabled to take part. This wasn't true since Brian wasn't doing illegal drugs, except for taking some alcohol or other prescribed medications. However, he had no way of knowing that the combination of alcohol with prescribed tranquilizers and sleeping pills could be just as disastrous for him.

As far as his ability to create, arrange, or perform, he knew—or at least hoped—he was still as good as ever. He would take chances and create music that could only be described as magical. Many of those creations, ironically, were due to the effects the drugs had on his psyche, which enhanced his ability to create and take risks he normally wouldn't have.

Because Mick told him he wasn't as good as he once was and because of the ever-present paranoia that engulfed him, he believed what Mick said. "I felt I was both dead and alive," he tried to explain. "The earth was shifting under my feet, and I didn't even know where I was at times, much less where I'd wind up."

What no one knew, including Brian, was that some of the doctor's prescriptions were harming him rather than helping him. Whereas sleep aids or tranquilizers helped the average patient, because Brian had the triple problem of clinical depression, bi-polar disorder, and extreme paranoia, the effects of his medications only clouded his mind and further disabled him. "During *Beggars Banquet* I tried to play but often felt out of sync on the album, due to the medications. I just couldn't get in sync with what the rest of the band wanted. I was in my own world and playing my own tunes. Although, I thought the album sucked and many times purposely acted out of sorts, to be spiteful. My multiple personalities would show up, I guess. Sometimes I'd be hopeful about my future with the band, but other times....

"I didn't like the way the album was going, and the band wasn't happy with what I was trying to do. What they started out with was boring—more of the same. Besides, they didn't really want me anyway, or so I felt. Mick acted like he had something up his ass. He wanted the album all his way and didn't want new sounds.

"Mick and Keith convinced me I couldn't create or perform music any longer, and I bought into it. Mick had to put me down—humiliate me—to raise himself up, and Keith was the puppet following behind. Charlie and Bill remained mute as always. From an outside perspective it looked bad, as if they were publicly judging me to turn my life into a ridiculous storyline. They acted like they didn't want to get dirtied by me. Mick didn't want the Brian Jones energy to sully him, and so he symbolically brushed off his shiny top coat, ridding himself of me!"

His bitterness further showed in this statement, "Charlie and Bill pretended to not be responsible for anything Mick and Keith did. Sheep is what they were, but you couldn't tell any of them that. After all, they were the Rolling Stones!"

Brian felt the "new" sound of the Stones was nothing more than their regurgitating the same old stuff, and he wanted to advance and create new, far-reaching sounds to further the band's musical career. He wanted to implement his dream of creating global music by incorporating the sounds from many foreign lands, including the Near, Middle, and Far East. (See Chapter Eighteen) He also wanted to study how different sounds affect people spiritually and religiously, and then use these sounds to enhance the world's ambiance.

However, his band would have none of it, same as ABKCO refused to hear him. They wanted to play if safe and continue doing what had worked for them all along. They believed their audiences didn't deserve any better and weren't sharp or bright enough to realize what they were doing. He said, "They didn't want to be fresh, revitalized, or creative. Their process to undo me as a major player in the band was to slowly edge me out, and I cooperated by not fighting back."

Oddly enough, many—among them Bill Wyman—wondered why Brian wasn't openly fighting back, so as to not be edged out by the rowdy duo of Mick and Keith. In response, Brian attempted to explain his convoluted thought processes. "My parents threw me out too, didn't they? So, I felt I deserved what I got. Then the drugs played a large part in further weakening my already weak body and enhancing my disassociate disorder. The more arrogant I became, the lower my self-esteem became—these worked together to undo me. And of course, with Mick subtly encouraging my drug use all along, that helped my final collapse."

Mick relished taunting and embarrassing Brian in front of the band, even when he did show up fully ready to work and produce. Typical of Mick's self-indulgence in putting Brian down was a time when Brian, rejuvenated with new hope and energy, showed up with guitar in hand and simply asked, "Can I play?"

Mick's retort was, "That is a good question, Brian. *Can* you play?"

The rest of the band burst out laughing at Brian's expense. Pathetically, since his self-esteem was so low, he truly believed Mick's brutal assertion and stepped aside, weeping.

Still, whenever Mick or Keith needed inspiration during *Beggars Banquet*, they had no problem resurrecting Brian from his self-induced slumber and asking for assistance. He said, "Doesn't anyone find it odd that I was in the band…that I wasn't in the band…that I was gone…that I was welcomed…that I couldn't function…?"

Had anyone, including Brian, been totally coherent, functional, and sane, they still would have succumbed to the mind games continually being played. As a result, he hated taking part in this album, despite the fact professional reviewers consistently claim the end results for many songs on *Beggars Banquet* were Brian's crowning achievements. Over the years, the majority of his original works were continually referred to as his crowning achievements, which only proved that his genius for music would only have grown with each year that passed. Unfortunately for him and the world of music, everyone has been deprived of his future musical contributions because of his premature death.

Brian said that he absolutely "hated the Stones trying to exert dominance or power over me, by forcing me to work on the album." He stuck to being the music purist by believing—if he couldn't grow and enhance the world of music by being allowed to freely express—he didn't want to take part in a substandard album, just to take the money. "There was so much crap going on during those rehearsals, and I couldn't stand it. Mick wanted to do and redo, even though we already had the sounds laid down. I wanted to say, 'It's just a song, Mick—not life and death!'

"I also couldn't get excited over this album because I felt dismissed for what I had brought to the band originally. So I felt, why should I participate or honor what they were doing when they didn't honor what I had done for them? I wasn't present for much of the recording of *Beggars Banquet* due to despair over what I believed was its lack of quality music. That belief led to my overdoing prescription drugs, which led to further drug-induced episodes."

Among the drug-induced episodes he referred to were days when he'd show up and immediately go to sleep on the floor, many times with musical instrument still in hand. Mick would order the guys to pick up their apparently comatose band mate, deliver him to an isolated room, and lock the door behind him. When he woke up, instant panic set in because he didn't know where he was or what was expected of him. They continued to tell him he was out of the band, but then they repeatedly went to him and asked him to play during their recording sessions. He attempted to describe his frustration. "You can see my confusion, can't you? If I was out of the band, what was I doing there? I felt like I was out of the band…they told me I was out of the band…so, why was I there?"

Even the rest of the Stones didn't know whether he was part of the band any longer. "It was confusing for all of us but most of all for me," Brian said. "Mick considered me out of the band, and so it was just a matter of kicking me out. The scenario was set up to look like it was all about my weaknesses and my own pathetic demise that they were witnessing, rather than the truth. The truth was Mick helping me out the door. Yes, I needed help—but not help out the door. I needed medical and mental help, but everything else was damaging to me as well."

In reality, any help would have been too late. Brian was going down fast, and there was no one who could help him. Anyone who might have helped or who had wanted to help was now separated both geographically and professionally from him. A mass hypnosis of the music world seemed to have taken place, in which the rumor mill had won out. The words, "Brian is weak; Brian is pathetic, and Brian is a drug addict with no redeeming qualities," had taken hold. The term, politically correct, was not yet known; however, if it had existed during those times, the phrase would have applied to his situation. Among the world's musicians, for one to openly be on Brian Jones side would be a politically incorrect move that could sabotage friendships and business deals with the powerful Stones organization. Mass intimidation was the norm, which included threats of being removed and ostracized from the Stones inner circle, if anyone dared to take up for him.

Things had gone too far, and Brian was alone in the world with no one to throw him a safety net.

***

Since Brian had been asked to create or improve many of the sounds on *Beggars Banquet*, he took advantage by incorporating some of the music he had heard in Joujouka the year before. He said, "Yes! That was the big difference, at least to me psychologically, between *Beggars Banquet* and *Satanic Majesties*. *Satanic* was experimental in so many ways, and we ultimately felt we didn't want to pursue that direction any longer. *Beggars* was more of a return for the band, in a way, but there was very flat energy to all of it. There was kind of a numb feeling about the album. As far as *Satanic Majesties*, in its experimental phase, we felt good releasing new creativity—even if I didn't particularly like the album.

"With this new album it seemed like we were back in the fray, as it were. Although, it still seemed off somehow…lacking in essence. The only thing I was crazy about was that I got to do the album and not been entirely shut out.

"There's a tendency to look at these periods of time as 'good for Brian, bad for Brian,' and all that. But I can honestly say that with every bit of excitement and pleasure we had with the band—since its creation and ultimate recognition—we had good stuff going on. It was always like that. Even when I was a drug addict and depressed, I still had fantastic moments of lucidity and fantastic times of clarity and hope.

"There even was a bright smile inside me at times—even though I may have seemed out of it and depressed to everyone else. I just want to state that it was the good and the bad weaving in together before so much darkness took over. It was really never just one way."

The band's producer at the time, Jimmy Miller, tried hard to get to know Brian and understand him, so they could work together. He showed Brian respect and appreciated his raw talent. Miller said, "When we started working, Brian really got into it and started to get excited. He is very insecure and has to have people around him all the time, but when he's doing something that really interests him, he's almost a different character." His viewpoint of

Brian confirmed some of what the psychiatrists who had testified at the drug trials said—that Brian has a childlike personality and needs constant reassurance that he does well, when he's doing what's expected of him. He required praise and affirmation constantly to offset his natural lack of assurance.

Jimmy was patient with Brian during this time, even though Brian had no patience for himself. The dream he once had of being able to continually lead and direct his band to new directions and new heights had by now been forever stripped away. With no self-respect remaining and no dream to look forward to, each day seemed harder to get through. Jimmy claimed that they never knew when Brian would show up for rehearsals or final recordings, and when he did, he would often attempt to play an instrument that wasn't needed on that particular day. Mick would tell Jimmy to just kick Brian out on his ass and tell him to get the hell away. That was the way Mick treated and spoke about the man he owed his entire career to.

Fortunately, Jimmy never did that, and he placated Brian by putting him in a separate booth, apart from the band, and just let him play his instruments there. Often enough, Brian didn't realize that he wasn't actually taking part in the band's session.

Despite that, by the time the album was completed general agreement was—with the songs Brian did take an active role in creating, arranging, and performing—the final result of those songs were works of great passion and extraordinary genius. Among those songs were *No Expectations, Parachute Woman, Jig-Saw Puzzle,* and *Street Fighting Man.*

The sometime producer and engineer for *Beggars Banquet,* Glyn Johns (See Chapter Twelve)—who had known Brian since the band's creation—by this time of their relationship had bad feelings toward him. Glyn, along with other members of the crew, had no way of understanding Brian's many emotional problems and because of that interpreted his lack of grace or tolerance as purposeful acts of intimidation.

Not until much later did Brian realize that at times that was the impression he gave many—including his own band mates. He said. "I didn't realize I treated Glyn like dirt, but evidently I did. A lot of it was due to me being whacked out and not caring who was around. He and I had a long history, and because of that he was there during some of my worst moods and worst places with drugs and depression. I was glad Glyn was around, though, and I'm sorry I took him for granted. I suppose Glyn had it with me for believing myself to be the band's leader, always wanting things my way, and having everything go how I said it should go. Yes, I might have been tyrannical, as they say. I didn't see it exactly that way, but I know I always needed to be right."

Without even realizing he was doing so, Brian could act a bitch. He'd use foul language—however, if the guys didn't cross him by going against his wishes, he would act all right. But then, if he felt provoked, he would go on the attack. These were symptoms of the bi-polar disorder taking hold. He had a fear of being second-guessed or blindsided by those who wished him harm—a fear that eventually came true.

The band complained that most days they didn't know "which Brian would show up for rehearsals," and they shuddered when he entered the room. They didn't know whether the mean, tyrannical dictator or the sweet, fun-loving guy would appear. Brian said forlornly, "I guess it was all part of my illness, but I didn't know how to handle it. You know, it was very hard on me too—just being me!"

***

Brian's life in the Land of Oz became even more convoluted in May '68—during the creation of *Beggars Banquet*—when he was arrested a second time for possession of cannabis. He went into immediate shock, because he knew there were no drugs in the apartment he was renting. He had only lived there a short amount of time, since he continued to move from location to location. Therefore, the tiny amount of drug found had to have been planted.

He vociferously protested this charge and even phoned his father to plead his innocence. Keith and Mick backed him up, and Keith claimed he believed there was an insider, a mole, among the band who was conspiring to further tear them apart.

After this unwarranted second arrest, Brian refused to live in his own place any longer. Once again, his paranoia—which everyone had ridiculed him over—proved accurate. He needed to recover from this new shock and agreed to temporarily move into Keith's home, Redlands. Keith was away, and Anita was off leading her own life at the time. As a result, Brian had the huge house to himself, except for the first of many "minders"—men that ABKCO paid to keep an eye on him.

Despite all the bad blood that had passed between Brian and Keith, Keith still was the closest thing Brian could find to a brother figure, and so he settled for that. He said with a laugh, "Getting along with Keith at that time was the damndest thing, because I felt that I needed him more than ever, while at the same time I also felt that he deserved getting stuck with Anita! I think he was extending his hospitality at Redlands because he felt guilty for taking her and having her. Keith and I got along okay, just not a lot of talking between us."

He admitted to feeling like a little boy lost in a dark castle while at Redlands but still imagined it the best place for him at the time. Even though he was still seeing Suki, she didn't stay at Redlands with him, and the only human companion he had for a while was the hired minder.

In June, he appeared in court and elected to have a jury trial. This time he pled not guilty. Afterward, he flew to Spain with Suki for a brief respite.

He had always maintained a disdain for authority figures believing that, just because they were in charge, they weren't necessarily smarter or wiser than anyone else. He didn't feel they should be in charge of his life, especially at this point in his life. He said, "After all, I was Brian Jones!"

With his fame and notoriety, he believed he had grown above authority, and that was one reason the continued drug busts were so painful for him to deal with. He had thought that, by being famous enough and wealthy enough, he'd built an invincible barrier around himself, which no one could get through.

He said, "After the second arrest I felt the full weight of the authorities on top of me. They were bent on destroying me, but I thought I might destroy myself first. If they didn't succeed in getting me, I would do it to myself. I couldn't shake the feeling of doom all around me. I never thought it would come to that—jail…prison. I might have left England if I could have, but I felt chained up, unable to get away. Yet, my life was England, in spite of how frightening it had become. England was home and still felt safer than being in other countries, as strange as that may sound. I guess I'm just a simple boy at heart!"

Stash witnessed Brian getting much worse psychologically after this trauma, which he said led to Brian's taking additional sleeping pills and drinking even more alcohol, just to feel numb.

The only other person who stayed close to him during this very dark time was Suki. Her softness helped soothe him. However, because he was so traumatized and didn't know when he might be taken away in handcuffs, permanently—due to perhaps other trumped-up charges over which he realized he'd have no control—his terror-stricken rants and hot temper took over.

The couple's fights escalated to the point where blows were exchanged. Despite this, Suki stayed by his side and hoped for better days. She remembered that he had seen her through her own hard times after the death of Tara Browne, and now Brian needed her, and she determined to stick by him. She went so far as to tell him she expected him to marry her, in exchange for her devotion.

That was always the wrong thing for women to tell Brian—that he owed them something in exchange for their time and devotion. This only proved to him that they never did care about him personally but always expected something in return, which they believed he could provide due to his fame. He said, "I felt Suki didn't know who I really was, and that bothered me. I was trying to get clean and stay clean, but everything was moving so fast that I couldn't see any permanence in my life."

While he lived with her, he continued to pass out from the stress and narcolepsy that frequently haunted him. Here again, when he woke up, he started to find parts of his body bruised, with black 'n blue marks. He didn't know exactly what had happened, especially since she also told him—as so many others had—that he'd fallen over and passed out, and that's how he got hurt. However, he wasn't stupid and realized the bruises couldn't have come from merely falling over but had to have come from actual battering. Sadly, Suki must have resented him more than he ever imagined, for not agreeing to make the permanent commitment she demanded.

Once more, a promising relationship with a woman seemed doomed to fall apart, mainly because of all his afflictions—some major, some minor—over which he had no control.

***

Even with the renewed possibility of spending much time in jail due to the false drug charges, Brian managed to play a major role in composing, arranging, and performing in what many say was the greatest slide guitar presentation of his entire career. The song to which they referred was *No Expectations* from *Beggars Banquet*.

Perhaps this musical masterpiece came to be since great inner pain does help create great outer glory. For the very last time, Mick and Brian teamed up to make sounds as one, with the combination of Brian's slide guitar that offset Mick's rugged voice. The uniqueness of the piece was the melding of guitar sound with human sound, creating the perfect mixture.

Brian put the music together first—music that many called haunting, echoing. The lyrics that followed were entirely prophetic. This was Brian's true swan song to his band, but maybe even more meaningful, his farewell to the love that he and Mick once had shared. (See Chapter Eighteen) The majority of the lyrics were Brian's, as he bid farewell to a love for which he had no expectation to ever revisit. For his part, Mick claimed—in the song—that Brian's pending departure would impact his peace of mind.

The peace of mind that Mick was so fearful of losing was the realization that—once he succeeded in throwing Brian out of his own band—Brian would be free to create another new band. What Mick knew all too well was, with Brian's extreme genius, this new band could and would easily overshadow the band left behind.

For this brief period of time, while composing *No Expectations*, Mick allowed his true feelings for Brian to come forward, and he turned into the poet he could at times be. Brian admitted that Mick was a true poet from time to time and had sparks of light that would flare up. He said, "Mick has a well-developed pattern of turning phrases that he hears into great lyrics. Many of the phrases he turns into song originally came from things I would say to him—but Mick will never admit it."

Keith worked with the pair on putting the music for *No Expectations* together, and Brian said, "Keith follows well where the sound goes. He never leads, but only follows."

After the album was released, Brian was once again disheartened to see that Mick had completely erased his name as creator of the song that was to be their farewell to one another. However, reviewers claim the song captured Brian's final, awe-inspiring contribution to the band. "His beautiful slide playing adds tremendous texture to a wonderful gem of a song," one critic said. "His playing becomes a true part of the song and as important as the lyrics." Another claimed Brian's part in putting together *Beggars Banquet* was, sadly, his last meaningful work.

A fact that cannot be overstated was, with all of Brian's personal problems, his musical talent never diminished. Bill Wyman once said, "Brian was the most progressive musician of the five of us, but he was never encouraged to tilt his talents in a more commercial way." Bill went on to say that one of Brian's more personal dilemmas stemmed from the internal pressure he felt because he believed the Rolling Stones had sold out from the original blues band they once were. The sell-out referred to was the band exchanging their musical integrity for fame and wealth. Brian believed he hadn't done enough, while he still was strong, to have preserved that integrity and had even allowed himself to wallow in the pleasures of the flesh.

Bill also added that Brian's other problems, naturally, stemmed from his poor health and ultimately losing all control over his own band. He then repeated the sad but true fact that, whenever Brian tried to present his own songs to Mick and Keith for consideration, he was dismissed out of hand. What's remarkable about the first statement was that Bill openly admitted the Rolling Stones band was originally Brian's, but now the pathetic truth was—as Brian himself had stated—the earth had shifted.

Brian was now relegated to pleading with the men he had originally hired, Mick and Keith, for permission to have his songs recorded.

***

As a result of Brian's feeling so minimized by his band mates, tensions between him and Mick finally exploded on a day when several friends had gathered together at Keith's home, Redlands. Whatever brief magic had resurfaced, during the creation and taping of *No Expectations*, evaporated.

Mick was back to taking swipes at Brian's musical abilities, and manhood in general. Once again, he was turning Brian into a joke in front of the band and their closest friends. This was typical of Mick's method of fighting Brian for ultimate control. He wasn't a physical fighter but instead used his overgrown mouth to fight.

Brian, though, was a brazen fighter despite his smaller size, and he'd often confront Mick to engage in physical combat. Brian would take a punch or two at Mick, hoping the latter would finally retaliate and thus give Brian the opportunity to beat him. He had learned solid street-fighting techniques while living off the streets, and he knew his strengths well. He said, "There were so many times I wanted to kill Mick's ass, but then restrained myself. Mick would never fight back, though. Instead, he used his voice, eyes, and mouth."

The two men constantly used the one-upsmanship style of combat, each capable of undoing the other on any given day. On this day at Redlands, however, Brian was feeling especially down as the drug trial loomed ominously over him. Mick said something disparagingly and this time, instead of taking a punch at Mick as he normally would have, Brian ran for and jumped into a moat that surrounded part of the Redlands property.

Mick saw Brian disappear under the water and not come back up. He panicked and ran into the moat himself, hoping to rescue Brian from drowning. What Mick didn't know was that this moat was no more than four feet deep, and Brian—being the prankster he could be—purposely held his breath under water, waiting to see what Mick would do.

When Mick lifted Brian's head up and out of the water, and realized the joke had been played on him—he went into frenzy and tried to hold Brian's head under, for real. Everyone broke into laughter at the end, except Mick. He had worn a new, expensive pair of slacks that day, and they were now ruined.

Brian said, "I really got Mick going there for a while, didn't I? I suspect the symbolism of Mick diving in to save my life as a perfect example of our love/hate relationship. In a way, I really did feel like I wanted to kill myself because I felt so worthless—as Mick constantly assured me I was. But yet, our love/hate edge was always there and had been for a long time. It was bad timing for me to act so poorly that day, with Mick saying he would drown me.

"Mick puffed so much anger over the moat incident that the energy of what occurred impacted his brain. He started to see how easily my own suicide could occur, and everyone saw 'how upset Mick was' over my drowning in the moat. Therefore, no one would ever believe he eventually might try to kill me." Once more Brian's paranoia proved extremely prophetic.

He referred to the moat incident as "the day when I pretended to be dead." However, another bizarre incident occurred between him and Mick shortly thereafter at Redlands. The two got into another scuffle, and once again Brian wanted to bring their altercation to a physical fight. With much bravado, he pulled what he called "just a little pocket knife" on Mick and pretended to try and stab him.

With a mischievous twinkle in his eye, he said, "Mick pissed me off, and I wanted to teach him a lesson. It was all a joke, in a way. We pushed each other around a bit, and then we just started to laugh at the absurdity of it all."

He went on to describe the situation between Mick and him for ultimate victory as "a territorial battle as in ancient days of armies and knights facing off on their fiery steeds. We shared an instinctual manner of retaliating against one another."

*\*\*\**

Now that Keith and Anita were back home, Brian left Redlands and moved temporarily into a small flat with Suki. He was waiting for the estate he had recently bought in Sussex to be made ready.

He said the reason he hadn't brought Suki to live with him while at Redlands was because Anita might possibly be there, too. Anita was extremely vicious towards any female she perceived a possible rival, even if she and Brian were no longer a couple. He didn't want Anita to attack Suki, and so he sacrificed himself by staying alone. "And, I was so alone," he lamented afterwards. "But I didn't need the problem of the two women confronting one another."

As far as seeing Anita in her new dwelling with Keith, while many thought that would really sadden Brian, nothing was further from the truth. By that time he had come to see the vicious witch for what she truly was—a cruel sadist. He explained, "I was in a completely different frame of mind at this time. I felt as if I had come through a battle, and survived. I felt lighter but also felt a different sense of doom—as if, 'What the Hell! What else could happen to me?'"

He admitted, though, to temporarily giving up the constant one-upsmanship with Mick—and would even allow Mick to take the band over—if that meant he could finally have peace of mind. If the rest of the band didn't want him, what could he do? "I don't know exactly when this change came over me," he said honestly. "I became very depressed over all that was going on in my life. Especially with the arrests. You don't think well when you're so depressed. Because I was, I did some drugs, and those drugs made me even more depressed, so I drugged even more hoping to get out of it. Drugs—a vicious cycle!"

*\*\*\**

The last half of 1968 might well have been a hundred years for Brian. He still wasn't sure whether he was or wasn't a Rolling Stone—or even if he cared. If he couldn't get the band to improve and grow with the quality of music they performed and recorded, he really didn't care to participate in what he considered a sham and a farce.

Amid recording *Beggars Banquet*, he took time to travel with Brion Gysin and sound engineer George Chkiantz to Marrakesh, and recorded the music that he eventually turned into *Brian Jones Presents the Pipes of Pan at Joujouka*. Suki Potier accompanied him, but because women weren't allowed in the enclave where the ceremony was conducted, she patiently waited for him in their hotel room.

The month of September saw him appear for his official trial for possession of drugs. Surprisingly, Mick and Keith were in the audience to show support for their band mate. Naturally, Suki was present, along with several close friends.

The jury deliberated less than an hour before finding him guilty. He very nearly collapsed when he heard the verdict for a crime for which he was framed. Just as he had lost all hope for any type of life—knowing he would never survive any time in confinement—the court's chairman, or judge, decided not to give him any jail time. Instead, he reinstated the probation originally given Brian, plus imposing a fine. He emphatically warned Brian, though, that if he ever were re-arrested and found guilty, he would serve years in prison.

When Mick and Keith first heard the guilty verdict they also were near collapse, but like everyone else present, cheered as soon as Brian was given no jail time.

When they all gathered outside the court, Brian, Suki, Mick, and others did a little dance for joy. Afterwards, Brian was asked what he thought of Mick showing support for him, and he answered, "It wasn't so much support but intimidation for me. Mick wanted to make sure I didn't spill the beans over our drug dealings. It's funny how he pretended to look so happy when I was released. Mick's position was that he wasn't a user or had an addictive personality—as I had—even though he had his own guilty verdict. Mick claimed no, he wasn't a drug user, but simply a person who 'has various experiences in life.' The rest of us are drug addicts and weak. In his mind, Mick is above all of us weaker mortals."

Mick's sympathetic attitude about Brian's drug problems changed almost as soon as he was freed, sadly. Mick and Allen Klein—under the umbrella of ABKCO Productions—began their official campaign to disgrace Brian in the public eye. Because he had made the horrible, naïve misjudgment of declaring he was guilty of the first drug charge and was now found guilty of the second, trumped-up charge—whereas Mick and Keith pled not guilty, despite the fact all three had committed the same offense—ABKCO spread the rumor that Brian could no longer be a viable member of the Rolling Stones since he would never be able to get a Visa to travel abroad and perform.

Mick and Allen viciously smeared Brian's name to the public and the press. No mention was made of the fact that ABKCO had paid large sums of money to get Mick and Keith's verdicts overturned or quashed, which left them with no criminal record. Because Brian had done the honorable thing and admitted his crime, fate punished him by now making him a *persona non grata* in foreign lands. If he couldn't travel with the band, that would be disastrous. Coming to America was as important to them as traveling throughout Great Britain.

However, he didn't live long enough to see if his conviction would be annulled, to where he could travel in the future.

On the other hand, if ABKCO and Mick actually wanted to circumvent the rules, Allen had enough money to get Brian a Visa. But, he wouldn't. Brian explained, "Of course, ABKCO could have gotten me a Visa. Allen and I talked about it, and he said, 'There's nothing we can do for you, Brian.' You see, he was already done with me, so he wouldn't help. But if he wanted to help—absolutely—he could've gotten it done!"

Mick made a public announcement that he had personally contacted the US Ambassador in an attempt to obtain a Visa for his band mate. As Brian described the situation, "Mick said he did that for me, but I don't technically know if he did. You know how these things go, don't you? If you have the money…and Allen did…and you want a Visa, you get the Visa. If nothing else, it was a good photo op for Mick to say that to the press, about helping me.

"And, yes, I believed him at first, but now it feels like he didn't try. You might ask how I could still be innocent and naive after all that had happened between him and me…but I still wanted to believe."

For Brian, his most important roles were arranging, composing, and adding the musical flourishes the band had become known for. However, the Stones organization continued to claim that he was useless to them and needed to be replaced. What was equally sad for him was the fact that—just as he actually was off hard drugs and trying to lead a clean life—he was now punished for things he had both done and not done over the years.

In actuality, he never hurt anyone except for himself with all his drug taking, but he was portrayed as an ogre and incapable of redemption.

***

Contrarily, just as Brian had claimed that life with the Rolling Stones wasn't black or white or good or bad for him, but varying shades of gray, he experienced two of the happiest times of his life during the *Beggars Banquet* party and photo shoot.

The band was attired in medieval costumes, and the banquet—or party—was held in a grand Elizabethan-style room. The scene was staged to look medieval, where the band members could enjoy every form of debauchery and wickedness available. Every imaginable, extravagant food and drink, complete with suckling pig—placed on long banquet-style dining tables—were provided. The furnishings were antique, resplendent with brocade drapes and heavy linens. The costumes were equally as extravagant as were their surroundings.

For the day, each of the Stones set their differences aside and played like happy-go-lucky boys who had never known a care in the world. No party would be complete without a pie throw, and that was exactly how the ceremony ended—with cream pies being thrown at everyone. Brian took relish in cramming Mick in the face with a cream pie, to which Mick reciprocated with his own meringue pie—but neither minded—and a great time was had by all.

The album's official photo shoot was held in December, out in the British countryside. The band enjoyed the most lovely of pastoral scenes as a herd of cows kept them company. (Photo #841) The mood was serene, and Brian described his feelings, "I actually was very pleased with life that day. And, in spite of what the Organization was saying about me, I knew my part in the band from the beginning. I knew my role in the band's success, regardless of whether anyone else admitted it or didn't. I spent the day smiling both outwardly and inwardly—smiling at my own feelings of peacefulness.

"There was a crowd of photographers present that day, some were invited and some were simply the news or press showing up. Many of the photos were posed for at the direction of our manager, but in others we were just being us." Art dealer Robert Fraser was also present, as his time in jail from the previous year had already been served. (Photo #837)

Brian dressed in brilliant colors, while Mick chose his usual solemn black and white costume, with a top hat so high it added approximately one foot to his already tall frame. Brian said, "Mick could never be tall enough or big enough. He loved that stove-pipe hat because it represented the circus atmosphere that he preferred."

Brian's hair had a wonderful curl to it that day, and he explained that his hairdresser blew it dry to look that way. Some commented that he looked like a little boy, which affirmed his feelings of joy and tranquility. He wore a large, antique rose quartz ring he had bought for himself and admitted to acting as if he were seven years old again. For once in a long time, he felt very free and comfortable with himself. "I was feeling good…feeling really good! I had new energy with thoughts of hope for a new life. I think that bothered Mick to a degree, as he worried about how to handle me once I got out of his grasp. I began to feel a new surge of energy and revitalization, since I moved to my new home at Cotchford."

Suki was at the photo shoot, keeping him company. She was a terrific, supportive companion at a time when he most needed her presence. (Photo #838)

Photo #840 depicts Mick cowering, since he was extraordinarily afraid of any heights—something he normally tried not to show. Mick hated to admit he had any human weaknesses, having to always be King, but that day his fear of heights couldn't be masked. Brian claimed he purposely coaxed Mick up there on the ledge just so he could kick back and grin at Mick's awkwardness. As for himself, Brian showed the grace of a gazelle while perched on the high ledge. Keith, being true to his laid-back nature, took everything in stride and showed no emotion either way. (Photo #839)

Years later, as some looked more closely at the many photos for the *Beggars Banquet* shoot, they noted Mick and Keith came across more like the "Gloomy Twins" rather than the "Glimmer Twins" that they eventually took to calling themselves.

Brian waxed poetic when speaking of his feelings on that day, "I did my best to have fun, but so much of my fun eventually turned into darkness. Although, I must admit, hitting Mick in the face with that cream pie was fun! And that is why, it's strange that everything is made to look so black and white—Brian is good…Brian is bad…Brian is a drug addict…or he's this, or he's that.

"We were everything that we ever were all of the time, we were complex, and we were spontaneous. I thought that was the point of what we were doing—being free and uninhibited—living big and living large. We were to be an example for all those things, instead of exemplifying the historical repression of the Brits and—as God only knows—the repression of the entire human race.

"We were experimenting with new ways of being, thinking, expressing, and playing. Some of it went well, and much of it did not. That was my history, but it seemed to later turn into crap."

He was the leader of the revolution to feel free to experiment—the sexual experimentation, the fashion experimentation, and the drug experimentation—but especially—the musical experimentation. His death was a loss to everyone. He was the beautiful golden boy, and he was the wilted beautiful flower. His life was as much an exposé of the times, as much as he was the individual at the head of the Sixties' parade. (Photo #835)

Any revolutionary leader has always been misunderstood, and for us to think that because Brian did drugs—to think that fact should take away from everything else that he did—would be an extreme injustice. In his mind, Brian was the experiment. He agreed to it, and that ultimately cost him his life.

*\*\*\**

The end of 1968 brought with it the last days of Brian's time in the Land of Oz. Mick developed another bizarre brainchild, the filming of *Rock 'n Roll Circus*. The Rolling Stones, together with numerous celebrities, were to be the focal point of a make-believe circus.

Actual circus performers, some with trained animals, added to the colorful, rowdy atmosphere. The videotaping was held on a sound stage made to look like an enormous tent, and Mick appeared as the official ringmaster with the rest of the band attired in assorted circus-style costumes. (Photo #851)

Brian shuddered and declared, "My God! Mick's finally turned my blues band into freaking circus performers!" He refused to take part in the farce at first; however, ABKCO still held all the cards and held all his money. He had to perform. Even though the Organization and the rest of the band knew his days with the Stones were numbered, they still demanded he show up and perform one last time. He did and outwardly looked magnificent, despite his inner angst. (Photos #850 & #853)

Appearances were all that mattered to Mick & Company, and to hell with Brian if he were too physically and emotionally ill to take part. What they never could understand was how important Brian's music was to him and how seriously he took his musical career. Maintaining dignity was paramount to his self-image. "Although, I imagine they'd have a good laugh at hearing me say how important dignity was to me, after some of my more memorable drug and alcohol-induced episodes," he said honestly.

But the truth still was that—up until the time he first realized he was being ousted from the band he had created and by the men he'd personally hired and trained—maintaining dignity and respect for great music was the core of his existence. Once he understood, all that he had worked so hard for and dreamed so long for were being stripped away from him, appearances no longer mattered. His life as he knew it no longer mattered. Because of that, he had allowed himself to follow the debauched life of sexual perversion and drug addition.

Now that he tried going clean, however, and his brain was once again turning lucid, he couldn't bear to participate in turning his beloved band into a sideshow.

For Brian, creating and performing wonderful music and entertaining all his fans with that music were all that he cared about. For Mick, elevating his position in life and giving the impression he was the most heralded rock performer and money-earner of all time were all that he cared about.

Brian tried to explain the complete horror he felt, taking part in what he considered a major debacle for the band. "The idea for *Rock 'n Roll Circus* was embarrassing and humiliating. We were babbling monkeys in a circus—that's how I felt. The rest of the band didn't see it that way, but they didn't have the self-awareness that I had to be embarrassed. I felt people were laughing at them and at me, and—let's face it—how serious a performer did I appear to be at that time?" he asked rhetorically.

Despite his reservations, critics agreed Brian gave a great musical performance, even if ABKCO ultimately cut most of his guitar sounds from the final recording—to further minimize his role within the band. (Photo #852) Nonetheless, when speaking of the critical acclaim he received for playing in *Rock 'n Roll Circus* he said, "It just goes to show, you can still perform even if you're not happy at all in what you're doing. But, I really did think the other musicians were laughing at me. I felt ridiculous and believed Mick had this uncanny control over my mind."

\*\*\*

That last comment might sound a bit silly, especially coming from someone as bright as Brian. However, the medical community has since come to agree that when a person—and more often than not a person with a high IQ—suffers from manic depression, their brain becomes susceptible to purposeful suggestions planted within it.

For example, in many societies the foundation for practicing voodoo has been premised upon the results their witch doctors—or other religious hierarchy—achieve through the power of suggestion. Mick and Anita both knew all too well Brian's weaknesses due to his paranoia and from all his years of drug abuse. They also knew exactly how to use those weaknesses against him, to make him believe he had mentally deteriorated to the point of utter worthlessness, and incapable of performing musically any longer.

***

Regardless of what Brian thought of *Rock 'n Roll Circus,* many of his and the band's closest friends within the world of music either performed in or attended, as part of the audience, the official videotaping. Among the notables were John Lennon and Yoko Ono, Eric Clapton, Keith Moon, Pete Townshend, Taj Mahal, and Jethro Tull.

At the start of the taping, Brian was seen attired in a gorgeous outfit of gold lamé trousers and burgundy jacket that offset his golden hair. He sat with and enjoyed the company of close friends such as John Lennon, Roger Daltrey, Keith Moon, and Pete Townshend. (Photo #849) These friends, too, were happy to see him ready to perform and looking better than he had in a long time—especially since they had also bought into Mick's and ABKCO's public statements that Brian was too ill and too drugged to talk to anyone.

Tragically, fate played against him that day, in that Mick's and ABKCO's statements were proven true when everyone present saw the gradual meltdown and complete humiliation of Brian, by the time the taping ended. While he started the day lucid and sober, when the reality of taking part in something he considered an aberration overwhelmed him, he succumbed to imbibing in large quantities of alcohol and strong drugs, including heroin. He had to mask the terror he felt, of performing live with the band for the first time in a very long time, and also of having to listen to Mick's constant public and private jabs at his musical ability, in general.

He explained both his and the Stones' outlook on that day, "My mind was fogged, and I had no energy. I wasn't eating well, only occasionally. You see, I still wasn't quite sure whether I was part of the band or not. They demanded my presence, but they also didn't want me. Mick, especially, made that clear.

"The rest of the band were wasted. A feeling of bitterness lay underneath everything and with everyone. They were empathetic. We were a sad bunch! Mick had ass acne, and so I wasn't the only one depressed. Being famous didn't make you feel great. We weren't really happy. It was insane—all of it—being ripped to shreds, having to look good, act right, be brilliant!"

Mick had developed a habit of not smiling, which has lasted to this day. He took everything much too seriously and took his orders much too seriously. Whereas Brian was at first deemed a dictator by the rest of the band, Mick now actually lived and breathed the part.

Brian was still reeling from his recent drug arrest and trial. What wasn't publicly known—but known among the band and ABKCO's offices—was that a certain London constable, who was an active member of drug enforcement, had decided to turn Brian into his personal bank. He demanded Brian hand him an exorbitant amount of hush money every month or he'd plant drugs on Brian—ensuring he would certainly be sent to prison for a long, long time.

Brian's paranoia once again proved true—he had said for awhile that he didn't feel safe anywhere and felt the world coming down on him—although he didn't know why. To ensure his freedom, he made those monthly payments to the fine constable. This severely hurt him financially because all the Stones were still being treated as children by ABKCO and not receiving monies due them for all their hard work.

The band continued to turn all their expenses over to ABKCO, who in turn was to pay their bills. However, the guys weren't allowed much money of their own, except for little pocket change. "I had around ten to twenty pounds on me at any time, and nothing more," Brian lamented.

Not only did the constable's blackmail further terrorize Brian, but this also contributed to the embarrassment he felt in the band's presence. "The hardest things I had to deal with," he said, "were the public humiliation and scorn over the drug busts, and my feeling of worthlessness in front of the Stones. So, I started doing drugs again—including heroin. I believed, 'What difference does it make any longer?' I was screwed whether I took them or not."

As the day for taping *Rock 'n Roll Circus* progressed, Brian's speech began to slur, and his walk became unsteady. His eyes were clearly glazed, and, as he tried to joke, "My blue-green eyes were offset by the redness, making a unique rainbow of color!"

Even though he later tried to laugh off that horrible day, he realized he had allowed Mick to defeat him and make him appear ineffective as a performer. In a subtle, subconscious manner Brian willingly handed his band over to Mick by drowning his senses in alcohol and numbing his mind with heroin, as the circus rolled on that day. He said, "I felt so diminished by Mick's opinion of me and the band pulling away from me. I felt I wasn't a part of anything anymore. I allowed Mick's putting me down to conquer me…I lost it! This time I couldn't snap back, even though Mick screamed for me to straighten out and get down to business.

"The drugs altered my performance, and I couldn't get my act together to present well in front of others. I didn't answer Mick, since I could feel his and the band's disgust with me. Hell, I disgusted myself!

"Mick said demeaning things about my drug use, but still he always managed to fire it up for me and provide it to me. I was so nervous going into that day (the day of *Rock 'n Roll Circus*). Mick was on me…on everything I did. He got on me about little things…play it that way…stand this way…look over there. I was fucking everything up, he said. He kept reminding me that he was the Ringmaster, after all, and he had to be listened to! A pattern of abuse, if you will. He made me feel the outcast—shouting orders at me, and it affected me. That, plus the public humiliation I felt every time I went outside—I didn't feel okay or up to par."

While Brian admitted he desperately needed emotional support from his band mates, and could have especially used Mick's encouragement, none was forthcoming. Mick apparently had completely forgotten the day, not that long ago, when Brian jumped up on stage with him and worked with him—as Ginger Baker and cohorts purposely poked fun and intimidated a novice Mick Jagger, when he tried to demonstrate his singing ability to these professionals. (See Chapter Seven)

None of the guests knew what was going on behind the scenes between Mick and Brian, unfortunately. All they saw was Brian's slide downhill, and in their eyes there was no explanation for it, except maybe the fact that what Mick and ABKCO had been trumpeting for so long was true—that Brian was beyond redemption and had lost all self-respect and control over himself. He'd become a disgrace to himself and the band.

An example of how harshly Brian was being judged that day were the comments made about how soiled and unkempt his outfit and appearance, from earlier in the day, had become. Yes, he admitted, his suit and tie were soiled and spilled on, "But, it was a very long day of taping and—from all the jostling of the party and people bumping into me—we all spilled over ourselves and onto each other. I wasn't alone drinking and drugging that day…all the others were acting, too, not unlike a circus or a carnival," he said. Nevertheless, he had became the popular one to poke fun at and criticize.

He went on to say, indignantly, "Keith was a mess at the end of the day, too, but no one makes that same comparison."

The press had also become indoctrinated into believing all the gossip ABKCO spread about Brian. The press knew him well from his days as leader of the Rolling Stones, and so they were as confused about his apparent loss of dignity as anyone. He was bitter when asked about the press' change of attitude towards him. "Yes, the bad press bothered me. You see, no one could ever tell me I wasn't doing well at that time because I knew it ahead of anyone. But—what about when I did really great? Did anyone say anything about that—how fantastic a job I'd done for so long? No! It was always expected…I was always expected…to perform, no matter what occurred."

He was also asked whether, at that time, he ever reminded Mick that he was the one who had taught Mick everything he knew. "No, and this was part of the reversal of power and psychological battering for me. It was a mind fuck! I did get into Mick's face at times, though. He'd simply blow steam out of his ass and walk out. He wanted to re-write history and change all the facts, over who I was and what I had done for all of them."

Brian's drastic change in demeanor and performance on that day was radical to everyone who saw him. What no one knew was the further shifting of Mick's personality into who Brian had once been. Brian could see it taking place, but he didn't know how to deal with what was happening, or how to make anyone believe what was happening. "Mick took so much from me. He even wanted to take my life from me," he tried to explain.

During the entire time the Stones performed their routine, Brian played with his back turned to Mick and the rest of his band. He performed with his eyes closed and his jaw set. His body language expressed what ABKCO wouldn't allow him to say aloud—that he disagreed with the entire charade being played out in front of an oblivious audience, and that the way the music was being interpreted was not of his choosing. What he could never forget, or let go of, was the simple fact that the entire band, including its name, was his creation and his baby. He was the baby's father, who was now forced to watch the baby slowly being stripped from his body.

Perhaps what stunned him more than anything, and finally threw his psyche over the edge, during *Rock 'n Roll Circus* was the all-too-real performance Mick gave as he turned himself into a woman while singing *Sympathy for the Devil*. Mick wore bright lipstick and dark eyeliner—very much over the edge from the usual make-up worn during regular live performances. His hair was longer than normal and had a clear curl to it, which also wasn't his norm.

The persona that Lucifer embodies takes many forms, we've been told. And, the image of woman as seductress has always been prevalent, especially as woman being the androgynous one—who mates with all and everyone. The Stones image, which they had purposely embraced for a few years, was that of androgyny.

During the taping of *Sympathy*, Mick intentionally showed himself as a man and as a woman. His transformation, visible on the videotape—which took place during the song's twenty-plus minute re-creation—was planned. If the viewer, or audience member, chose to see the act take place, the transformation was clear.

At first Brian wasn't entirely certain whether he actually saw what his mind told him he was seeing. He didn't always have a handle on whether he was hallucinating, whether the drugs were creating the vision, or whether something actually was taking place. As he watched Mick transform into the She-Devil during *Sympathy*, the fright he already felt was enhanced one hundred per cent. In his mind, he was so scared that he hoped taking even more drugs might make the fright go away, or at least numb it. He said, "Yes, afterward, some picked up that Mick had looked like a woman. They mostly thought it was all an illusion they were witnessing and couldn't explain it."

What Brian and others did witness, but couldn't quite understand, was the fact Mick's transition had become part of the deal he had cut with the Dark Side, to forever honor that philosophy of life, in exchange for never-ending fame and wealth.

At the end of the day, Brian's will and self-esteem were totally destroyed. He left the building alone and in tears. His humiliation was complete. (Photos #854-856)

He believed there was no future for him with his band. The explanation given for those bitter tears was, "It was so obvious I was being suppressed, put on the sidelines, ridiculed, and demeaned. Mick did this, but the rest followed along with him energetically. To them, I was the dancing monkey!

"They wanted me there to perform, but they didn't really want me there. It was all for show to prove the Rolling Stones were still together, but with Mick as the frontman and Keith as his personal prop. The act was ridiculous! It was insane, and it had nothing to do with my music."

Prophetically, Brian ended his thoughts for that day, "I felt like I was dying."

# CHAPTER TWENTY-TWO
## I'm So Lonesome I Could Cry

*"Cotchford Farm! My Home...My Palace!"*

Brian Jones

Famed *Winnie-the-Pooh* author, A.A. Milne and his wife, purchased Cotchford Farm in 1924. The original farmhouse was built during the sixteenth century and shares a common border with the Ashdown Forest.

Brian Jones, who had never enjoyed a fairytale childhood but instead suffered every form of childhood abuse known to man, fittingly chose Winnie the Pooh's home as his own personal fairyland. He said, "Mick and Keith, both younger than me, had already bought homes of their own. I guess I was the last to become an adult, but I thought the concept of Cotchford really neat, and I love Winnie!"

Brian had been living at the lavishly landscaped acreage known as Cotchford Farm approximately one month by the time the debacle of *Rock 'n Roll Circus* played out. As he left the taping in tears on that fateful December day, he hoped to find the healing, serenity, and solace he longed for at his home by the edge of the forest.

Brian especially liked the country folks who lived in the small country town, Hartfield, of which Cotchford is a part, in Sussex County. Even though the majority of the populace was comprised of older folks, he enjoyed living among them and was soon considered one of them. "My neighbors appeared to care for me," he said with a proud smile. "These people weren't authority figures or in charge of me in any way, but they do have a long history of knowing about things. I find them very interesting and smart.

"I didn't buy Cotchford to party...that wasn't a part of who I was at the time. I was looking for inner peace, since there was an emptiness and loneliness that had always stayed with me. What I needed there to make everything perfect would have been someone to love, especially since my restless spirit was forever with me, driving me. I needed to relax."

He talked about the move to Cotchford as a place to purge or rid himself of the darkness of the past, and to try to find balance and peace within himself. Even though he had not yet fully embraced spiritualism, he had hopes of finding a life of brightness, light, and stability. More than anything, he wanted to heal his body. "What a joke that may sound," he openly admitted. "The rock 'n roll star wanting to be the peaceful seventy-year old man. But, I rather felt old and beaten up and said to whoever might hear, 'God! Pray for some wisdom for me.'"

He was reminded of a concept the Rolling Stones were known to have embraced—that anyone over thirty should be killed—so why was he now seeking the company of older folk? He answered, "As braggart rockers we may have said that...but not me personally. Although,

I must admit that I had gone along with whatever sounded cool at the time; at the same time I must also admit that I never really believed that about older people. In fact, I've always had a respect and high regard for those who have lived long enough to really know something. I felt they should have good points of view by that age."

Brian especially loved the bright blue outdoor swimming pool, off to one side of his farmhouse. He had always been an avid swimmer and capable diver. Besides being fun, the warm water felt a source of healing for his aching body. For personal reasons, he hated to see the pool empty at any time. To him a full, clean pool represented a full, clean life, whereas an empty pool represented barrenness and a return to an empty life.

The corrupt police officer, who had blackmailed him by demanding an exorbitant amount of money each month—in exchange for not further planting drugs on Brian—was still a painful part of his life. Some months Brian would make the pay-offs himself; other months he'd ask Tony Sanchez or others to handle the tawdry deed for him. "This was bleeding me dry," he said. "When I moved to Cotchford, my 'minders' were supposed to protect me and handle these things. On the other hand, do you notice my lack of freedom—either I faced imprisonment in a real jail, or I felt imprisoned by the minders who kept a watchful eye on every thing I did. My entire life had become a series of imprisonments."

The minders or "keepers" he referred to were the phony workmen that ABKCO paid to supposedly restore Cotchford Farm, since the building wasn't in great shape when Brian had purchased it. The reason he had acquired the property for a lesser amount than what was asked was because he agreed to assume the task of modernizing or rebuilding whatever was needed. However, what he didn't realize until it was too late was the fact these workmen were nothing more than ex-felons and street thugs, who were paid to purposely hold him prisoner in his own home.

Mick, Keith, and Allen Klein knew exactly who these men were, especially since Keith had already fired one or more of them from Redlands. The leader of the minders, or builders, was a huge, hulking man named Frank Thorogood. Among his assistants were two younger men named Mo and Johnny.

Tom Keylock was now Brian's official chauffeur and the only one at Cotchford with whom Brian felt at all comfortable or friendly. Aside from these men, Brian was completely alone in his new palace, save for a matronly housekeeper named Mary Hallett and her husband. His time of healing and serenity was made more difficult because he had no family and no true love with whom to share his palace.

Humans, unfortunately, are herd animals who require the company of others, and Brian was no different. If anything, he was the least type of young man who could survive on his own, without someone to share his feelings and thoughts.

Overnight, he had gone from one of the music world's top stars and sexual icons to basically living the life of a monk in a monastery. One of the cruelest acts Frank Thorogood played upon Brian was to scare away—and literally harass to the point where they refused to return to Cotchford—anyone who wanted to maintain a relationship with him. Brian didn't notice this happening until his isolation was complete, which was exactly what Mick and Allen Klein wanted.

The two wanted, and paid Frank and the other minders/builders, to preserve Brian's isolation from the rest of the world. They also fueled rumors that he wasn't seeing anyone or accepting any visitors because he was too ill, too drunk, or too incapable of dealing with human contact.

To further throw his psyche off balance, Frank & Company were sharp at coming up with assorted, cruel tricks to play on him. Typical of the hoaxes played on an ongoing basis were shutting off his phone, so he couldn't place outside calls or receive inside calls. If a caller did manage to get through, the workmen would go to the phone's base and turn it off—and then tell Brian the phone was working fine, and it was only his imagination that he couldn't finish a conversation or place a call.

Brian consistently ordered and charged quantities of fine food, liquors and wines from the town's grocers, including the most expensive steaks. As soon as his refrigerator was full, he'd wake up the next morning and find it empty once more. When he asked his minders where the food was, they told him he'd eaten it all or that he'd not ordered any and needed to go to town and place an order. ABKCO's offices in London were paying Brian's expenses, and his charges went through them. However, only small amounts of money filtered in for groceries, house bills, and such—through Klein's offices—and the keepers were abusing these credit lines.

At the end of the day, Brian had to depend upon the "kindness of strangers" that was the management company Mick originally hired—ABKCO—in order to put food in his mouth.

He had purchased a scooter so he could make quick trips around the countryside or into town. Frank and the others would often move his scooter off to the outer reaches of the property, so he couldn't find it. When he asked where his scooter was, they told him he had taken it out for a drive and come back without it.

The roof of Cotchford Farm's main dwelling—Brian's home—desperately needed repairing, but Frank refused to fix it correctly. Instead, when it rained and water drained into the house, Frank would locate which shingles were in disrepair and reluctantly fix the situation by moving shingles from another part of the roof. He did this in place of buying new shingles and completely redoing the roof, as Brian had ordered. When it rained again, those parts of the roof that had their tiles stripped began to leak. When Brian complained about the leaking roof, the men told him he was imagining it—that they had repaired it, and any new leaks weren't their problem.

Since he possessed a fear of much larger men, especially a group of larger men, the minders at Cotchford were very much his worst nightmare come true. Frank was the largest of the men and towered over Brian. Most likely, Mick and/or Keith had told Frank of Brian's hidden fear of sexual assault, and Frank took full advantage of the younger man's weakness. He relished terrorizing Brian by staring him down and calling him a poof, right to his face.

Despite his inner fears, Brian did argue with Frank over all the inconsistencies taking place at Cotchford. Frank's response was to growl back at him, while standing as tall as possible to further intimidate his smaller employer. Brian would back away, shocked by Frank's arrogance, to the amusement of the other workmen. The only way Brian found to deal with the increasing terror he felt, while living in his own home, was by drinking alcohol to excess and popping his prescription tranquilizers. Even as he stayed true to no longer doing illegal drugs, he naively did as much damage to his mind and body by over-imbibing these legal drugs.

After living at Cotchford Farm for only a couple of months, he began to think of himself as a beautiful, but injured, bird held captive in its gilded cage. He prayed for someone to come and open the door to his cage and free him, soon, for if no one came he realized he would go completely mad from the isolation and loneliness.

He said somberly, "Cotchford felt almost like a burial ground at times. To suddenly not have any fans surrounding me made me feel dead inside. I felt unimportant and wondered if my talent had all been an illusion. Where were the people now who were supposed to care about me...about me—Brian? Who? In my isolation I felt no one cared. It's very depressing to feel set apart, all alone, and not in charge of your own money. Like a child, actually."

As had always been true with the entire band, their money continued to be siphoned off and doled out in meager amounts to each of the members, as if they were nothing more than school children, incapable of handling their own funds. Mick, Keith, Charlie, and Bill—in addition to Brian—were forever phoning or wiring ABKCO's offices, demanding that sums of money be handed over to them—money for which they had worked long and hard. ABKCO dismissed their pleas out of hand, saying business and traveling expenses were very large, and they were doing the best they could.

Since Brian had originally handled all the band's money, he knew when funds were being diverted surreptitiously, and he refused to be treated like a puppet or doll being manipulated when it came to his own money. He began to keep records of where he thought the Stones' money was actually going and determined to hold Allen Klein accountable as soon as he had enough proof.

He realized Klein had so far broken every promise made, and he said bitterly, "I took it really personally—I took everything personally. But, this had to do with my money, the band's money, mishandled percentages, and not having any idea what money came in or what money went out. I demanded to know how we lost all control and why we couldn't access our money, except by submitting and working through ludicrous procedures. And, God—yes, ABKCO claimed rights to all our music, including what I considered my original works!"

He continued to claim, "Everything in the rock industry is about drugs and sex. The industry controls its 'little stars' with these things. By controlling our money, they control all our lives. Drugs and sex are used as tools to tap into the stars' core, and we're treated as nothing more than monkeys in a cage—ready to be trained the way our owners wish us trained. However, when we don't perform they way we're expected, we become dispensable. That's the way the business is. That's the real story—the story of the dispensable, expendable creatures who are called stars. Funny when you think of it, eh?

"Although, most musicians don't understand that they're captured by the industry, but they are. They become products of the money machine, and when I understood what was taking place, I refused to be part of it.

"In the beginning, I had to ride that train of success. God, it was exciting! We couldn't believe it was happening, but that image faded fast. At first, management could have marched all of us right into our own cages—and we wouldn't have noticed. I noticed though! But the others didn't, or they didn't care. I can't tolerate anyone making decisions for me but sadly realized how few decisions I ultimately got to make for myself."

The more he thought about the reality of being a rock star, how all rock stars were treated, and how his life now appeared destroyed by that reality, the more he shook his head in disbelief. Being alone at Cotchford, he had a lot of time to contemplate his life and how it came to be at the point it was. He attempted to explain his situation, "In truth, I don't know how I can endure these feelings of isolation and loneliness for many more months.

"On top of that, I've tried hard to have visions for a new life. I've tried hard to have hope for a future with a new band and for the new music I would create with them. Still, I have this niggling feeling that maybe I've lost my edge…or maybe lost it all! Of course, they told me I already did lose it…the band has told me, management has told me. Even the news headlines report what a fuck up I could be.

"I thought I knew all the contributions to music I've made over the years, but I've become confused. The band has taken away all my contributions to our music. I know my contributions were valid and real, and I know I created the band known as the Rolling Stones. My problem has become…how can I deal with all the bad press?

"Even though many tell me how great I had been—and everything had been fun for a time—I finally tipped over. I became self-conscious and made to feel a fool. Yes, I was an outcast and am an outcast, or so it seems. I'm not part of my own band any longer. I feel split apart by a knife cutting me and separating me.

"Suki was to be here with me, but she customarily isn't. My life has become surreal. Of course I would feel better if someone were here for me. Isn't that the truth!"

He did enjoy the company of friends from time to time, though. Well-known Blues musician and bandleader, John Mayall, and his wife Pamela came to visit. Brian and he had been friends from the early days of Brian's career. Of the couple's visit, he said, "Yeah, that was a really nice time! Their visit made me feel more like a human being—as if I still had something normal in my life. Luckily, Frank (Thorogood) wasn't around when they were here, and so they were left alone."

Brian's other longtime friend, Alexis Korner, often came to see him at Cotchford, and he was grateful for that friendship. Being on his own so much only added to his depression, not to mention the constant, numbing worry of what would become of him financially, if ABKCO didn't settle monetarily with him for his share of the band's proceeds. He also worried over what would become of him if he didn't start a new band.

Sadly, he wasn't able to feel the sense of peace that was necessary to truly enjoy the freedom that being alone could bring. He had so hoped all the solitude would give him peace, but with the thugs surrounding him and with no friendly company to surround him, making peace with himself was ne'er impossible.

He also felt physically drained. "I felt half-dead at this time and full of anger, confusion, and depression. I had this dread of everything being taken away from me that I had worked for. I didn't even feel that I owned Cotchford and felt more like a boarder on my own property. I couldn't believe this was really my home. I couldn't think clearly or make any plans for my future.

"I thought, perhaps in the future, I might bring my sons to live with me, but I wasn't yet straight enough to act on it. I thought having family around would help protect me, but I didn't seem to have the strength to make definite plans."

***

Part of Brian's feeling so alone stemmed from the fact that the woman he thought would continue to share his life at Cotchford—Suki Potier—wasn't playing as important a role in his life as he had imagined. Once again, she wanted to play a permanent part in his life through marriage, but he'd have none of that.

He wasn't trying to be selfish, but he also knew his own frailties at the time and realized he was in no position to consider the permanence of marriage. Infuriated, Suki argued with him and claimed he owed her for all she'd done to help him. Her action was déjà vu for him, as so many women over the years had played the same marriage game. As a result, he asked her to move out of the house and only return to see him for an occasional visit. No matter how much he might want a steady girlfriend, he refused to accept a relationship that wasn't real to him.

He explained, "I wanted to stay at home and not go out just so I could be seen in public, and so, if a woman had her own agenda to be seen in public with me—to foster her own goals—that was a problem. You see, to them I was always expected to be 'Brian Jones, Superstar' in public, to show them off or have them be on my arm for their photo opportunity. However, I'd mostly be in the mood to relax at home and just be the real me—whoever that may have been at the time—so that was also a problem.

"Generally, I'd send them all packing if they weren't happy to simply be around me, alone. I don't compromise very well, I guess." As naïve as he could be, he still knew when someone wanted to use him only for his fame.

Jimi Hendrix did come to Cotchford to visit his close friend. For Brian, the blues musician's personal visit was priceless. In reminiscing about their too-short-time together, he waxed poetic. "Jimi could only stay a couple of hours; he just came by. But looking back, it meant so much to me. The visit was so brief, and he didn't have a lot of time. We were just hanging, and I didn't have a chance to show him around Cotchford's grounds.

"You know, it wasn't a 'garden tour' day!" he said with a laugh. Then he added prophetically, "It's a shame he couldn't stay longer. Can you imagine the powerful team we could make? On some level, Jimi is serious about teaming up, but I think he just feels neither of us has much time. It's hard to explain why you look in someone's eyes, and you just know...."

Jimi visited Brian mainly as a friend, and even though the two jammed a bit together, that time was merely playtime for them. Hence, no official recordings were ever made.

Brian did originate some new material on his own, though, and he said, "I made my own recordings at the house...lyrics, chords, words. My creative mind was beginning to return. I know it was."

He met another blonde woman, Swedish model Anna Wohlin, and brought her to Cotchford to live with him. He simply hated living alone and continued to bring houseguests in, even if he had no intention of making any permanent arrangement with them. Anna was fine for what he wanted—someone to be there with him, eat with him, sleep with him, and talk to him when he wanted someone to talk to.

He claimed Anna wasn't a girlfriend but only a bedmate; however, he treated her very well and both nurtured one another. "I was comfortable with her," he said. "My life as a whole wasn't comfortable, but having her around was nice. We weren't serious, but what we had worked for the time. We didn't talk all that much. Many times, Anna was out of her mind on her own drugs."

In talking about his ongoing battle with alcohol, Brian claimed he didn't think he was currently drinking all that much. However, he was taking a lot of prescribed medications, especially sleeping pills, and when those were combined with alcohol they had disastrous effects for his frail constitution. He drank primarily because of the confinement and the fear he felt with the guards around him. "I don't know how my home became my prison. But once I felt it was, it was too late to make the necessary changes. I had become imprisoned by management. I felt too tired to fight back and too beaten down, even though I know I wasn't using alcohol all that much. What is strange is that I really felt more in control of myself than I had been for a long time."

Among the few people who did come to visit him at Cotchford were his parents, but still, he had bittersweet memories of those occasions. He so much wanted them to finally admit they were proud of him, but they refused to give him that. He claimed their attitude was, "as if they wanted to say, 'Yes, Brian, Cotchford is nice but things would be so much better if only you'd....'"

Despite that, he continually gave his parents money from his meager income. They'd take it grudgingly, and yet they couldn't make themselves see any real good in him or even acknowledge him for his musicianship. His mum, he said, couldn't understand how his fans could possibly idolize him.

***

Two factors weighed heavily on Brian's mind during the few short months he lived in his palace. The first was the healing of his mind, body, and soul—which he actively pursued each day. The second was whether he had any future in the world of music, or even if he wanted any future.

Much has been written, diagnosed, and dissected about what was said or wasn't said during this period, but perhaps no one was more qualified to speak of what was really taking place other than Brian, himself.

First and foremost, he had to have a free rein as to what music he created and recorded. In his opinion, the industry couldn't and wouldn't accept a high level of creativity, since it believed the fans who bought the Stones albums weren't sophisticated or bright enough to appreciate a higher level of music. He disagreed and knew that his fans thirsted for bigger and better sounds, and he couldn't bear to live with the fact that he hadn't been allowed to give the audiences what they deserved.

"All the new, global music I planned to formally produce while at Cotchford was held mainly in my mind. Then, I'd play it and record it using my own equipment. This was my way to hold onto my sanity. I could never return to playing the old sounds—for me there was no going back. Yes, all my new music was up here," he repeated while pointing to his head.

He had only been free a short time from the stifling influences of Mick and ABKCO, plus his mind as yet hadn't had time to clear itself from all the years of drug abuse. Despite that, he tried doing the best he could. He used his guitar mainly to compose new material, but it still wasn't feeling right to him. "I had the need for deep soul expression, but parts of my soul were already gone," he lamented.

Had he more time to create, his plan was to take an entirely different path musically, which would have even more depth and beauty than his earlier works. His vision was to form a band with either or both John Lennon and Jimi Hendrix. Jimi was enthused about the possibility, and Lennon had already played along with Brian while putting together their fantasy band called *Balls*. (See Chapter Eighteen)

One of the rumors to be dispelled was that Brian was enthused about starting from scratch with new or upcoming musicians and singers. Nothing could be further from reality. He had already done all the starting from scratch with the Stones, and—even though his name alone would open doors to him not available to any other entertainer—that wasn't what he desired.

What would have inspired him to work with others was the need to create again and to have the freedom necessary to once again be a viable creative artist. He no longer cared about fame—he had enough of fame, especially all the excesses fame brought with it. All he cared about was music.

He became very defensive when he heard he was quoted as looking forward to engage a green band. Sure, he enjoyed jamming for fun with other musicians, but that had nothing to do with the desire to form a band with them. "At one time or another I might have told Jimmy Miller that I planned to start another band," Brian offered. "But that was all talk of the future and not part of my life at Cotchford at that time. My talk was all about 'gonna get a band together…' as in going to and not now. I didn't want any little unknowns to perform with—that was clear and accurate.

"Occasionally, other musicians would show up, and we talked. Talking is mostly what we did. You see, some unknowns would come around, but that could be very annoying and worrisome. Others showed up—whether they were known or unknown—who would think they could automatically become part of what the Stones were. This is all confusing, since I'm the one everyone in the industry knows, and for me to start anew with a bunch of unknowns would lead nowhere.

"Guys like Steve Marriott and such, that was all talk that we'd play together. Our talk was basically, 'We can do this,' 'We can do that,' or, 'Let's get together and jam.' Sure, Steve would be fun to jam with, but nothing was definite for me yet. We've only spoken by phone, and yeah, we're supposed to meet. Nevertheless, this has been a foggy period of time for me.

"And—not to sound arrogant—Steve Marriott is someone who I wouldn't have given the time of day to, in an earlier period of my life. Plus, I've felt so isolated the longer I've lived at Cotchford, and so we never played together. We almost played, that's all I can say.

"After the vicious attack on me by Paul (See Chapter Twenty-Three) I haven't jammed with anyone. But as far as Steve or some others—that's all been a dream during some of my better moments, in which I thought I might enjoy jamming with them. As to whether I personally liked any of these guys…Hell, I just wanted to feel as if I were still alive! You see, while I like playing by myself, I really prefer to have other guys to jam with."

Brian's rambling back and forth diatribe was typical of the ebb and flow of his mental processes during those confusing weeks and months at Cotchford. He felt like a man grasping at straws.

Sadly, but unbeknownst to Brian at the time, Steve Marriott was another musician who Frank Thorogood had warned off or threatened to not come by and visit—further ensuring Brian's complete isolation from any wholesome outside influences.

Brian candidly said, "No kidding I want Jimi and Lennon to work with! Realize, Lennon and I are and were very tight, regardless of what others might say. John's my bud! And, excuse me for sounding harsh—but I do believe I've attained a caliber well beyond playing with little garage musicians. I'd never be happy working with the ordinary performer."

He then added, "When Jimi came to visit, I was happy to see his eyes clean and clear—beautiful, soul-filled eyes. You see, Lennon's and Hendrix's music is real to me. We want to create new universes of music with our combined sounds. John has a grander scheme of things, while Jimi's soul pours a combination of brittle together with the smoothness. His music is combustible. And what I bring to the table—not to be the braggart—is poetry, lace, and harmony, together with huge musical loops that bring in the essence from many different frequencies.

"I am the magician who will do all the arranging, gathering, and orchestration. My lace is the symbol for finely-tuned music. While I'm the soft concordant and universal player, Hendrix is pure soul fire!"

Of all the musicians who did make time to visit Brian at Cotchford, Alexis Korner was the one with whom he spent the most quality time. Alexis had been his true friend from the beginning, and Brian very much appreciated and welcomed his company.

Some thought he wanted to be part of Alexis' band called *New Church*, but again that wasn't true. While he respected Alexis for what he played, Brian's vision was very different. He said, "I want to pursue the purer forms of rhythm 'n blues and the blues' core music—and then take these sounds to a whole new level. Despite what others say, I never want to perform the old stuff but do want to take it and give it a new twist. Alexis and I basically don't agree on how music should go. Besides, I felt like I was juggling so many things that nothing was ever solidified. Anyway," he added with a touch of humor, "I don't like the name of his band, *New Church*!"

He spoke of what hope he might have about starting up again. "I hope I still can; I want to but don't know if I still have the juice. One thing for sure—I would only go with guys I know. Everything is all in here," he once again pointed to his head. "You have to realize—to me, starting another band is like throwing a lifesaver to a drowning man who's sinking in the ocean. It's a way out, perhaps a way to start something new, but not real.

"My dream would always be to once again jam with Mick and Keith. And yet, if they were to come to me now and ask, I would refuse, knowing it was just another set-up. Although, if you ask, off the top of my head I'd have to say, yes, I've always kept the hope in me to jam with them, at least one more time.

"I realize that sounds pathetic, but you must realize the Stones defined me. Being a Stone was my definition. They're me, and I'm them. It's like being a ghost—I don't exist without them—and now, when I'm not a part of that world any longer, I feel completely empty and lost. I wanted, no actually I prayed, for them to realize their mistake in letting me go.

"Originally my vision was for the Stones to be free, and not the institution that would close the doors down on creative freedom, soul, and life—as they have become. My music is about heart, soul, and ethereal sounding—and no one but me can do it. I hope to be back again, and my music will be back again…all in time."

***

Cotchford Farm was a magical place, but Brian's life had spun out of control before he realized what was happening. In the beginning, he enjoyed leisurely strolls around the magnificent grounds, which sometimes took him across Pooh Bridge and then on to the Ashdown Forest. For a shorter walk, he'd visit the garden that was home to the nearly life-size statues of all Winnie the Pooh's main characters, including Winnie himself.

The country air that surrounded Brian was pristine, and the aroma from centuries old trees filled his lungs—lungs that had suffered from years of relentless asthma attacks and heavy tobacco smoke. His mind wandered freely, and he welcomed these restful moments, uninterrupted by outside noises and worries. He spoke affectionately about his dreamlike surroundings. "My land had three streams. There was a meeting place for two of them, with the third running beside. They seemed to all be separate streams, but they did meet. At times I'd see various waterfowl, and at times the streams got very full but mostly they were simply basic streams. I could hear the water running on most days from the statue garden.

"From time to time, I'd rest along a stream, and when I had the opportunity I'd take a book. You would think I had a lot of free time…but where does the time go? So often I'd be caught in my own mind's imaginings, tossing this idea or that. That's partly how I created and partly how I tried to make sense of what my life had all been about. I could simply lean against a tree and have my thoughts come rushing in—or even just walking about, thoughts would hound in on me. You know, sometimes I had difficulty keeping my thoughts straight…in a line as it were. But I was never at a loss for having thoughts. Actually, most of the time I had too many of them. (Photo #859)

"The water rushing by would give me a sense of calm, so my thoughts could take on that linear aspect that was the sound of water. I do love that sound. Looking at my property makes my heart feel very poignant, kind of achy and soft, sad and happy all at the same time. The area I felt especially attracted to was 500 Akre Wood." He would meditate there and contemplate the atmosphere. "There was something about the way the air felt at that spot. Something…I think you'd call it the frequency of the land.

"I heard there were many deer there, and from time to time I'd see a deer. Someone nearby housed goats. As I think back to it, it did feel like a Neverland."

***

Alas, life came crashing down around Brian once again—this time in the shape of Frank Thorogood & Company. The two men's disdain for one another was mutual, since Brian spoke to and thought of Frank as nothing more than a common street thug, while Frank spoke to and thought of Brian as nothing more than a spoiled, rich kid who was also a faggot. Frank thought it laughable that Brian had women throwing themselves at him, and he minimized Brian's sexual abilities to his face.

When Brian began to realize things were very wrong at Cotchford, he lashed out. "Was I crazy? But all of those things were happening! They (Frank & Company) were trying to convince me they weren't happening. But, I had no money! Where did all the money go that I paid for reconstruction of my home, for groceries, for petrol? I was watched; I was prevented from having visitors; I was prevented from making contact with the outside world—even though I did try to call out, but I'd often get busy signals, or things would go wrong with the line...."

ABKCO went so far as to hire a nurse to keep a watchful eye on Brian's every move. Janet Lawson, who wound up becoming Frank's ladyfriend, checked Brian's pulse and blood pressure. She, too, discouraged him from using the phone to communicate, at Allen Klein's direction. She told Brian staying alone was, "for your own good. You need your rest."

This was more calculated mind control, since even the healthiest of people, if told they're really ill, soon show sings of distress. Most likely, one reason Brian accepted Janet's presence was due to the fact that at first he actually was very ill as a result of all his drug-taking, during the taping of *Rock 'n Roll Circus*.

When he returned to Cotchford after that long, agonizing day of taping, he decided to get off heroin without any chemical help. After a day or so he took to his bed, sweating and shaking from withdrawals. Tom, Frank, and some of the other keepers held him down, to protect him from the rabid seizures that were taking over his body. He had forewarned the men to watch him, since he knew he stood a good chance of convulsing. The only medication he took was the prescribed sleeping pills.

These withdrawals further traumatized him, especially coming so soon after the debacle that he considered the *Circus* taping, and he felt as if he wanted to die. The cleansing process took several days, during which time he went in and out of consciousness. For now, Tom and Frank actually nurtured him. Brian remembered someone putting a piece of wood between his teeth, so he wouldn't chew on his own mouth during the convulsions. His stomach couldn't accept any food, but they brought him broth, regardless. He'd take a few sips here and there, while he lay with cold, wet compresses on his forehead. His body alternated between sweats and chills.

His housekeeper, Mary Hallett—whom he thought of as a surrogate mother—brought him homemade chicken soup, as soon as he felt well enough to eat a bit more. During this horrible time, he admitted to believing that he, Tom, and Frank had actually bonded, since the two showed such care for him. However, he also felt embarrassed that they had witnessed him at such a weak time in his life.

Sadly, the bonding period among the three was short-lived.

After his system returned to normal, he began to invite friends over to Cotchford for swimming parties. The rest of the Stones didn't attend, nevertheless, his parties were fun and well-received by many within the entertainment community. Some parties got so boisterous and noisy from the speakers placed around poolside, which blared rock music, that the authorities were called in by nearby neighbors due to sound infractions.

Instead of taking part in the wild playtime around his pool, Brian was usually content to sit back, relax, and watch everyone around him having a good time. His mind and body were still reeling from the events of the past several months, and he wasn't up to the rough and tumble of the rowdier rockers.

During the times he did feel up to joining in the fray, he let loose and partied like a kid. "We were like adolescent boys playing in water…tussling," he said. "Sure it got rough—hell, if someone comes up and starts pushing you, you push back. No one ever held me under though; it was just mutual pushing and playing. I never felt threatened. I felt like it was my home, my place, and I was in charge. I'd have the final say, and the people there were either my guests or my employees.

"They had to show me respect; that's what I thought was supposed to happen. At times the parties would go on and on, and I'd be too depressed to stay, so I would have a few drinks and then go to bed. They'd continue on without me.

"No, the Stones didn't come for my parties. Isn't that interesting? They did only come to dictate orders—I guess that says it all. They'd follow Mick to my home to support whatever he came to say. It was never a light and frivolous time with them."

He was saddened to hear that his dear friend, Marianne Faithful, was going through some troubling times herself, from both drugs and Mick Jagger. She had become a serious addict, and Mick became disgusted with her for her addiction. He had no patience for anyone else's weaknesses, and so he ordered her to stop taking drugs. When she didn't immediately comply with the "king's orders", he demonstrated anger and little tolerance for what he considered her gross insubordination.

Brian began to notice, during these early times living at Cotchford Farm, that Frank had started to take it upon himself to mix and mingle with his invited guests. When his employer wasn't around to hear, Frank would introduce himself as Brian's close associate. Shortly, Frank's self-induced importance grew to where he ordered food, drink, and whatever else he desired, from the town's shops and charged everything to Brian's account.

Brian explained what these days were like. "At times I felt as if I worked for them! I felt trapped, and the paranoia was at times intense. I couldn't really tell if they were charging things up on me and doing what I felt they were with my phone—or if I had totally lost my mind. They tried to convince me I was doing things to myself, such as losing my own motorcycle, but I swear I couldn't remember being on the damn bike!

"I was terrified, having the workmen constantly around me. Although, I hadn't yet figured out how to get rid of them. I thought of so many things, but I never could think of how to carry them out. I finally realized I was in actual exile! And yes, at times they stopped me from using my own telephone. They tried to make me think I was crazy. Cotchford Farm became my prison and on occasion the Stones would come by, as if on visiting days, but only to order me about.

"I was alone there much of the time, although, I'd occasionally have someone come sleep with me," he said casually. What he would never say aloud was—given a choice—he'd much have preferred the uninterrupted companionship of his male friends, to that of the females.

With men, he felt free, able to play and act out without pretending to be someone he wasn't. On one day, when he felt especially open to expressing his inner thoughts, he explained, "Would my goal have been to have my male acquaintances come out to Cotchford and spend more time with me? Oh, yes! Sure! Definitely! You see, no matter how dark my life had become, there's that kid in me. That kid inside my heart who's always there with me—who yearns to feel free to play shamelessly, even if it looks at times like he's been buried alive.

"Friends like Stash appreciated that part of me. It's like we were playmates together. But, one reason I didn't ask him to move in was because I believed everyone, including him, saw me as really needy at that time and not so much fun after all."

During the times Brian and Stash managed to get together throughout the years, their friendship strengthened to where each was very comfortable with who they were. "Stash's sense of humor was wry—sort of there—but he was never the jokester, per se," he explained. "Even so, he would appreciate another's really good joke. I tried to cheer him up and make jokes, and he would laugh. He had that kind of humor, even if he took himself very seriously."

Brian went on to add, with a mischievous twinkle in his eye, "Stash liked the prankster in me, and said, 'I find it darling'!"

He returned to the original subject of—then, why not ask Stash to move into Cotchford Farm with him? "Because his presence there full time would have been too open…too honest. In my weakened and demoralized state, after being so horribly trashed by the Stones, such feelings of intimacy were all too real to face."

He continued to fight against—and at the same time played out—the masculine/feminine duality of his nature. "Having a close male friend was just a dream or a thought, but as for why the relationship between Stash and me didn't progress…it just wasn't there. That's not how we related to each other. It was okay to kiss and fondle but not to deeply nurture and care."

What he referred to was, while it had always been all right for males to playact and cop a fast feel with one another—especially while engaging in sports activities—taking part in anything more real and permanent wasn't. What Brian needed more than anything, during his recuperative time at Cotchford, was a full-time nursemaid, and he would have preferred someone like Stash to play that role.

However, with the rough and tumble workmen surrounding him day and night, such a relationship with a male would've been entirely unacceptable. Frank Thorogood would have surely attacked and chased away any male figure that Brian might have brought in to help him during the healing process. A gal would always be welcomed but not a guy.

That, ultimately, was the main and most candid reason Brian didn't think to have Stash come stay with him. While he needed a man to have something real and whole in his life, he couldn't because of the times.

*** 

Just as Andrew Oldham had earlier stopped the press and media from interviewing Brian—saying he was too ill or too drunk or too whatever—Brian's minders were now preventing him from speaking to anyone on the outside world, claiming he was incapable of conversation. When he did try to pick up the phone's receiver to place a call or answer a call, the men would snap it from his hands. Frank would shout, "Leave it! That's my job!"

Tom Keylock also stopped him from using the phone, but he was much calmer with his approach. Brian said, "Frank was aggressive and intimidating, while Tom was still portraying himself as my friend. Silly me! When Frank grabbed the phone from me, it was bloody frightening! I don't know what was happening…the men were just all over me. This wasn't the peace I was seeking. I told them to leave numerous times, but they just laughed."

He couldn't even call the authorities to remove the men, mainly because he wasn't the one to have hired them. The ex-felons' contract was with the Stones organization, and only the Stones could fire them. "I thought ABKCO was paying these men," Brian said. "But, my later thoughts were that Mick was directly in charge. What was weird was, while the organization wasn't paying what was due me either, Frank would yell at me 'cause his money wasn't coming in for his work. Why he yelled at me, I have no idea; I guess it was convenience."

Whenever Frank yelled at Brian over lack of a paycheck, Brian screamed back, which only further disturbed his peace of mind. Frank had expensive tastes, and when combined with his delusions of grandeur, he thought he deserved the best of everything. Everything that Brian had worked so hard for, Frank thought he could simply walk in and take from him.

The more time Brian spent in isolation, the more his neurological disorder—which consisted of short brain misfirings—manifested itself. His mind waxed and waned, and thoughts raced through him. To try and settle his nerves, he often took walks through the flower gardens or took a jog around his property. When he returned, he would settle down with a couple of drinks. He tried everything and anything to calm his restless body. The loneliness he felt in having no one close to talk to, or have fun with, destroyed all hopes he had for a change to his life.

No one actually knew what life was like for him during these short months at Cotchford. People who claimed he was doing great had no idea what actually was taking place behind the property's gates. Suki Potier was mistaken in her belief that Brian had gotten his life together and was happy and laughing again. Even though he tried to laugh and be happy, those times were fleeting. His other close friend of many years, Ronni Money, also misinterpreted their phone conversations, when he supposedly showed sparks of excitement and acted all "fired up," as she claimed. She went so far as to say that Brian was now "back to his old self," but she was wrong.

Brian felt bitter about all these comments. "Suki and I weren't really speaking—only briefly by phone—so she had no idea how I felt. As for Ronni saying that I was back to my old self…now, which one of those would that be?" he said mockingly. "Also, my hounds weren't letting me answer my phone, so I didn't speak with her nearly as often as she claims!"

He was also bitter about two other comments made about his state of mind during the last few weeks he lived at Cotchford. His father, Lewis Senior, babbled that Brian was "bubbling with enthusiasm," and that the weekend they all spent together was "intensely happy…probably the happiest and closest weekend we'd spent since Brian was a child." Brian's candid reaction to his father's opinion was—"Don't even bother to ask!"

Keith Richards said Brian was enthused about putting a band together and sounded full of hope. Brian's reaction to that was, "Keith making himself not feel guilty about my imprisonment at Cotchford."

\*\*\*

Despite all the obstacles, Brian did try to be happy and to be himself—whoever that was, as he said—however, outside forces wouldn't allow that to happen. Typical of the mercenary people who only wanted to prosper by his notoriety was professional photographer, Ethan Russell.

Ethan went to Cotchford to photograph Brian in his new surroundings. At first he was thrilled to show Ethan around his new home, and he offered to pose serenely among the gardens and statues. Ethan wanted no part of a cool, peaceful Brian Jones, and demanded he act the obnoxious rock star for the camera shoot.

Brian felt devastated, realizing no one wanted to know the real him or remember him as a caring, composed human being. He felt forlorn and said, "Ethan insisted I act angry and rebellious. He wanted me to perform one more time, it seems, and I wanted to just be me. That is always a problem, isn't it? But you'd think he would want to see the new, fresh Brian and not the same, old crap! That was both a curse and a struggle—not being allowed to present the way I chose to be."

What he wanted to do ultimately was chase everyone from his home, but then, he said, "I was too afraid to be alone. While I felt the need for privacy, many times the paranoia of being by myself was too much to bear. I guess I was just a mess!"

Two people he did enjoy having over to visit were Les Perrin and his wife, Janie. Les was both the Rolling Stones public relations representative and a trusted friend. Brian also considered Janie a good friend, and over the course of time he had taken to phoning her during the times when he felt especially distressed. She was always kind to him and patient—attributes he found lacking in most people. After a while, sadly, he was prevented from enjoying the couple's continued company at Cotchford because Janie said she felt threatened by Frank Thorogood's hulking figure on the property.

Whatever money either Mick or Allen Klein used to pay Frank to keep Brian isolated was money well spent.

Perhaps no other worse act of cruelty was played on Brian's mind than the day his beloved housekeeper, Mary, was brutally gang raped by the workmen. The act took place one day in the main kitchen at Cotchford Farm. So heartless was this act upon the body of the elderly lady that the keepers afterwards callously bragged to independent workmen about their dastardly deed. A distressed and disheartened Brian said, "Mary's rape was an act of intimidation for me…a warning of what may happen to me, too. I didn't find out until later that it occurred, and I went crazy! I loved Mary. She was loyal and kind to me. I even gave her my Moroccan table—she loved it."

As a result, his heart was completely broken. He believed he wasn't even allowed to enjoy the company of this sweet, older woman, and that life was punishing him for trying to reach out for any form of human companionship.

Another close acquaintance, a seventeen-year old young lady, was very much welcome at Cotchford. Her name was Helen Spittle. Brian first met her outside the rehearsal studio in

London. She'd been patiently waiting to meet him for weeks but wasn't aware that he hardly showed up for rehearsals any longer, since he didn't consider himself part of the band.

Originally, Mick spotted the pretty girl waiting patiently for Brian day after day and tried to make her personal acquaintance for himself. Helen wasn't interested and continued to wait for the day when Brian would hopefully show up. He did, and the two made fast friends with absolutely nothing sexual between them. Brian thought of her as a younger sister.

He explained, "I was very nice to her. Her innocence was refreshing—it wasn't the 'rock star taking the groupie' type of sordid affair. I saw in Helen a different time of my life and a different kind of person from what I had been meeting. She trusted me, and I wouldn't let her trust down. You see, I felt badly since the types of women I normally met weren't so innocent—and those types made me feel unclean about myself."

Helen was the last person at Cotchford to take photographs of Brian, and she most likely was the last true friend he had there before his death. He posed shyly for her around his gardens. At the time she snapped his picture, he so much wanted to reconnect to the innocence he once had inside him—an innocence tragically taken from him at an early age. When around Helen, he tried to relate to another period of time, when he'd still been young and carefree.

During all his years as a Rolling Stone, he had always been the most professionally photographed and had always taken great pride in his appearance. Now, his current circumstances had drastically altered his looks. Because Frank and the minders either ate everything in or emptied his well-stocked refrigerator as soon as he filled it, there was usually nothing left for him to eat. Consequently, over the last few weeks he hadn't been eating much but only drinking gallons of whole milk to fill his hungry stomach.

As in times of yore, when he couldn't eat well due to a lack of funds, his life had once again done a complete turn, and he went from riches to rags as far as sustenance for his body. After weeks of living off nothing more than milk and booze, his slim body had taken on a bloated, paunchy appearance, his skin's tone looked dull, and the bags under his eyes swelled to double their normal size. Additionally, the usual aches and pains he suffered—together with severe stomach cramping due to stress—had also taken their toll, and an air of general unhealthiness had taken over.

Just at the time when Brian's appearance was—at least for him—so deplorable, Helen had come around to take his picture. He wanted to hide when he saw the young lady appear, and he explained his thoughts this way, "Showing Helen around my property made me feel extremely uncomfortable with myself, in that I didn't feel especially clean. Although, I could see that she didn't see that in me. To her, I was still fresh and beautiful to look at, so I felt a bit safer with her after that. In a way, I felt her belief in my worthiness was something I didn't deserve."

If truth were told—during the last couple months of Brian's life, he had nothing and no close friendships to feel good about.

***

As the end of spring 1969 drew to a close, Brian still hadn't come closer to a decision as to where his future lay. Officially he still was a Rolling Stone, and until someone within the organization told him he wasn't, that was what he referred to himself as. Of course, he knew that was all a farce—both Allen Klein and Mick had made it clear over and over that he wasn't welcome.

ABKCO's offices in London and New York had long ago stopped accepting his phone calls. Brian had called Klein one too many times demanding an accounting of his band's money. Of course, the other four Stones were also coming up short each month as far as monies received that were owed them—but none was making the direct implications, as Brian was, that money was actually being siphoned from the band.

A couple of times when he had phoned New York directly, he heard the secretaries say to one another, "Oh! Oh! It's 'the rogue' calling for Mr. Klein again." Then his calls would mysteriously be disconnected or the secretary would come back on the line and say that Mr. Klein was busy and couldn't take his call. Time after time his calls were rejected, and he stopped phoning.

ABKCO's London office was a short drive away, however, so he took to showing up unannounced, hoping to catch someone in authority at hand. Once again, the receptionist up front had been forewarned that if Brian Jones came calling, to say no one was available. As time passed, he realized that even his chauffeur, Tom Keylock, had been ordered not to drive him into the city. Brian said, "ABKCO didn't want me showing up, knocking on doors, and making a scene in their offices. They didn't want me in the city, where I could get free to do what I thought necessary. They surmised I'd get legal help to extract monies owed me, or to regain some of my rights, which were being taken away from me."

By May '69 he realized he needed to take further aggressive action to get his legal rights honored. He had managed to put together whatever money he could out of his meager income and planned a covert trip to New York City to retain legal counsel. "That was my money squirreled away for the trip, but after I paid for the journey, my money was at an end," he said. "I asked Tom—who was still acting as my friend—to assist with making plans. I knew ABKCO wouldn't let me off my leash to travel, so I had to enter New York unannounced and wearing a disguise. I thought I had been so shrewd in laying out all my plans. Spanish Tony even played a role in getting me a false passport and Visa. He was always in the middle of my connections, and for him, doing something like this was no big deal.

"But I had no idea, until much later, that Tom was actually a plant and informing Allen of all my moves."

Staying unrecognized was paramount to Brian's plans, and so he flew first-class wearing a brown wig, phony moustache, large dark glasses, and hat. No one seemed to notice, since no one suspected a Rolling Stone would fly anywhere alone and unaccompanied by either his mates or guards. Once in New York, he hoped fans didn't recognize him, and he lucked out in the few short days necessary to make the trek, in that no one called out his name.

He had no idea Allen Klein had been tipped off and that his every move was being watched. He kept his disguise on as much as possible, except for the couple of fun outings he allowed himself—such as quick trips to a couple of New York's parks—where he dressed as himself. He did dress down, however, in simple jeans and a sweatshirt—but still wore the large, dark sunglasses. No one noticed, or if someone had, his presence remained unannounced.

With a sly grin, he said, "I wasn't wearing my stage clothes or frilly blouses. I stayed alone, even at my hotel. It was the oddest thing—it was like I was a ghost, moving in and out. All the time I tried to pull a trick, not letting anyone know."

He chose a particular attorney to retain, whose offices were located in mid-town Manhattan not far from ABKCO's headquarters. "Rumor had it that this attorney was the man to see for what I needed. His secretary knew I was coming, and he and I met. I guess this was my personal 'Magical Mystery Tour'!" he said and laughed.

Even though he tried to joke away the purpose for this clandestine journey, the ramifications were of major importance. With the attorney, he left detailed information as to his ownership of the Rolling Stones name, his personal contracts and agreements made with Allen Klein—which weren't being honored—and also data concerning the band's monies that he was certain were being mismanaged.

What Brian didn't know was that Tom had betrayed both his friendship and his trust, and had sold him out. Shortly after Brian's death his New York attorney, whom he had entrusted with all his legal affairs, was approached by henchmen representing ABKCO. After making vicious threats, the hapless gentleman felt he had no choice but to turn over Brian's paperwork. Since Brian's death, neither a will of any kind has surfaced, nor the information that he painstakingly gathered to prove that the Rolling Stones money was being illegally siphoned off.

*** 

Not long after Brian's trip to New York, Mick, Keith, and Charlie made a trip to Cotchford Farm at the beginning of June. The purpose for their visit wasn't social. They came to tell Brian that he was officially out of his own band and that his services were no longer needed. Mick acted as spokesman, naturally, with Keith as his prop or crutch—the only position with which he was comfortable. Charlie acted as the mute bystander, waiting to act as witness to the inevitable train wreck.

For his part, Brian didn't care to remain a part of this Rolling Stones band any longer. The only questions still opened for him were: when he would start his second Rolling Stones band—using the name he registered not that long ago—and how much money ABKCO would offer to buy him out, thus ending his contract as a member of the band.

The subject of buyout had come up previously, but to date nothing had been agreed upon or satisfied. As Brian described the negotiations, "I talked with Mick; I talked with Allen about monies I was owed, and he indicated…not directly…well, Allen was great at indicating something you're supposed to assume that you know, but you're not exactly sure what he's saying. What he said had something to do with—yeah, I'd get my money that was coming 'when it was all decided'—as if I were to know what that meant!"

Had Brian wanted to play along, agree, and act compliant with everything Mick and ABKCO demanded, he could have remained with the band. However, he knew that to continue performing within the situation he was currently placed in the Stones band—as second or third in line to Mick—was akin to death for him. Not being able to create and play his kind of music would kill him quicker than any drug. He was terribly conflicted—he felt damned if he stayed and damned if he left.

As soon as he realized the trio of Charlie, Keith, and Mick had come to officially disown him, he felt nauseous and actually broke out in a sweat. "Bill didn't come because he felt embarrassed to be a part of the confrontation. He didn't choose to follow and tried to be more human through it all," Brian said proudly of the man whom he had chosen as his bass guitarist.

Even though he knew the end was inevitable, he had hoped to have the timing of the event put off a while longer. "They just showed up," he explained. "I mean, I knew they'd be coming at some point. I knew we had to talk it out." He had this talk with Mick many times before—just the two of them—and he knew there was no reasoning with Mick.

He tried to brace himself for the bitter battle, but with all the bullying and intimidation he'd suffered during the past few months at the hands of the minders, his will to do further battle with anyone was destroyed. He believed this battle was no different from the battle he had fought to get from out of the bottom when he first attempted to get the Stones recognized—when they were still nobodies.

He explained his feelings on that fateful day—a day that has become known as "The Confrontation at Cotchford". He said, "Yes, I was back to having no money, just as when I tried to get the Stones first noticed. Things might look on the outside like they had changed for me, as far as my not having to fight my way back up from the bottom again, but inside things never changed for me. I was back at the bottom again.

"Mick showed up at my door as a God rising up out of the mountain—at least in his own mind! To him, I was the crumbled up old news, the dirty piece of paper with every bad thing said about me. And, in his mind, Mick was the shining wonder boy coming up to save the band from my degradation. He was the chosen one to save them all for eons to come. I knew that wasn't the case. I knew Mick was only that which I had given him and taught him, and what he had managed to become on his own—or had stolen from others.

"However, I never had the vision or foresight to see that he would actually do what I thought could've been done…what I planned to do but wasn't given the chance. The difference was, whereas I could have done it all on my own as I'd done everything else, Mick could never have done it on his own—not without the business monster of the organization creating it, and the business deals that were made through Allen.

"By now everything between us had gotten so distorted—all the physical and emotional dynamics, especially between Mick and me, and Keith. All the brotherhood, sisterhood, the love, the companionship, and then on the flip side—I imagined us as the warrior knights waiting to charge at one another. I was on my white horse being overtaken by Mick's dark horse.

"Plus, the dynamics of our leadership and control, and all of the more feminine characteristics of the emotional bond he and I shared—even though he always was much more feminine than me—were now sucked up by all the betrayals and competitiveness. I became caught in this spider web.

"For me, the battle was no different from past wars over philosophy, power, and land. I pictured myself putting on a cowboy hat and carrying my six-shooter."

Brian went on to describe the scene that day. "My heart skipped a beat…actually several beats, when I saw Mick go into his routine. He screamed, pointed, gesticulated—like a regular stage performance that he had choreographed in his mind. He demanded all the music that he knew I had created on my own, plus the Stones name. He wanted it all. I knew there was no going back for us. There was no going forward; there was no agreement possible. Mick made threats, intimidations…he threatened to ruin me.

"I knew at this time there was no 'out' for me. As far as the name of the band—I told him it was mine! I'd rather die than give it to them.

"Keith was very uncomfortable with the situation. He fiddled around with his hands and wished he was anywhere but here. He was a dog, you know—Mick's dog. Charlie huffed and puffed, ready to act, but never did. Mick was the talker. Then Charlie got upset 'cause I wouldn't give in…he expected me to give in just to get it over with.

"I didn't answer. I could feel everything shriveling up and being taken away from me. Although, they'd already taken everything away from me, and now they were pretending to offer me my life. Mick said it was my choice, whether I wanted to walk away with my life—but they'd already taken it. Mick pretended I had someplace to go…to get away. No, he didn't outright say, 'I'm going to kill you.' Not this time. But, everyone knew how Mick was in private, when he had to have his way.

"Mick screamed, 'Damn you!' as in damnation. I still wouldn't back down. It was my escape to choose death, if that's what it would come do. I was tired of the life."

He stood firm against Mick's barrage. "At first he tried the reasonableness tack with me, but it didn't wash. Mick said, 'We'll buy you out, Bri.' He offered to buy the Stones name from me. He didn't dare say cooperate, or 'I'll take your name off the music'—not to my face! On the other hand, he feared I'd form my own band. That was a big part of the arguing. He said he'd have no part of my going to another band."

As far as how Brian came to settle on the buyout figure presented to him, he said, "The one hundred thousand pounds upfront plus the twenty thousand pounds per year was offered by Mick. He just said, 'This is what it will be,' as directed by Klein. That was it—I wasn't asked whether I would accept the money. I was told I was accepting it! Mick hoped the money would smooth everything over, as if money would make it all okay. They wanted the buyout to include the Rolling Stones name, but I stood firm. I said, 'Oh, no! No!'"

Mick also asked Brian where all his original tapes were, but Brian shrugged him off, pretending he didn't know what Mick was talking about. "Mick wanted it all, demanding my tapes. Keith didn't threaten me with words. Keith never said anything," Brian went on to say, "but the way he looked, it was almost comical had it not been so evil.

"While Mick acted as a rooster strutting and clucking around the room, Keith would make a similar move or motion, copying Mick. Keith…as always in Mick's shadow…copying him! Keith…always walking around like a puppet, behind Mick…just doing whatever Mick does. Like the shadow person. Then there was Charlie, who continued to make faces as a monkey squirming…not knowing what else to do.

"Mick had convinced them that all this was the absolute best for the band—even best for me. Ha! Mick had convinced the others that I would be better off in psychiatric treatment, rather than my having to deal with the struggle of showing up for performances."

Brian was asked exactly what type of psychiatric problems they claimed he needed treatment for—and that the band as a whole should be concerned about. He laughed sarcastically. "That is funny! Actually I didn't need any illegal drugs, since the pot and prescription drugs were already doing plenty for me. Although, I'm sorry to say that on many occasions in the past, I had demonstrated or validated Mick's position about my not being responsible. Nevertheless—I knew how to act 'together' when I chose to," he concluded.

The confrontation ended with nothing being settled. "Mick just said, 'This is the way it's going to be, Brian. We're going on without you.'"

\*\*\*

During the time he was still active with the band, Brian had made from time to time his own, private, musical tapes. He planned to have them as his safety net, should he ever find it necessary to leave the band. To his horror, Mick somehow discovered he had this secret stash of music, and he threatened to destroy Brian, if Brian didn't turn the tapes over.

Brian didn't know for sure how Mick discovered his secret, but he surmised he must have spoken out involuntarily during one of his blackouts. He said, "I'd never give my stash up, not to anyone! I told Mick, 'You're not getting any more of my heart and my soul. It's all mine from now on!'

"But Mick yelled back just as loud, 'Your loyalty and dedication is either with us or not with us! Which is it?' The more Mick yelled at me, the more I hid what I created. I figured this would be my proof someday that I was the creative juice behind the band, and no one else."

He had a definite vision for the future of his music. He wanted his creative ability to reach its highest possible form. Deep inside, he had a feeling that his creative energy was special, but it had all become convoluted and distorted when the industry's machine wanted to take him over. His goal was to preserve the purity of his music, but he neither desired nor anticipated all the notoriety his actions would bring.

"I knew that I had not yet seen the clearest vision of all that I could be," he said. "I believed my creativity had been stunted within the Stones organization, and it had been changed into what they wanted…not what I wanted. The truth is—my original, creative expression is the basis, soul, and imprint of all the Stones' music, and into their future. I needed the freedom of musical expression, which would unleash my musical genius. But everything I did create was edited, criticized, and picked apart. I needed to soar free in order to create and not have my talent downsized by mediocre minds."

He had more than one motivation not to give into Mick's wishes. The truth was he wasn't feeling at all well at the time. He said, "Off and on my whole life I didn't feel well. Physical pain played a part, but it was more of what was happening to my mind at this time, rather than my body. Although, even if my mind hadn't been somewhat off, my sore body alone would've been enough to halt my future performances."

What hurt Brian the most mentally was being edged out of his own band and gradually stripped of his rank as leader. The words that came to mind for him over and over were the band's mutiny, and his personal feelings of being deposed and exiled. In a way, all the drugging he had done was a way to "out" himself from the band. He said, "They may have fired me, but I took the actions to precipitate it. They might as well have drained the blood from my veins. I felt robbed and tossed aside like so much trash. What had me fired up for a time was the thought of striking out with my own band, calling it *Brian Jones & the Rolling Stones*, and then moving forward and conquering the 'old' Rolling Stones with it."

He determined to take the Rolling Stones name with him, with or without their permission. He vowed to fight ABKCO all the way by whatever means possible, using any legal recourse available. He had purposely pushed that final, bitter argument over the Stones name into Mick's, Keith's, and Charlie's faces that day. "It was always my name. Right is right," he swore. "Letting them know that was the vengeance I needed at that time."

His rage wasn't simply at being thrown out of the Stones but at having his life threatened. "You don't joke about that! You don't constantly threaten someone with their life!" he blurted.

He would have loved for Keith to leave the band and go with him, but he was a realist and knew that wasn't possible. "Keith didn't have the balls to leave Mick," he said. "He was always Mick's lap dog. They should be married, you know. Mick could either be Keith's husband—or the bitchy wife who's in control. Ugly kids, they'd have!"

\*\*\*

Allen Klein didn't personally fire Brian. "Officially it wasn't Allen; it was Mick," he said. "Mick spoke for the band…for anyone who had any say in the matter. At least that's the impression he had given me. But, hell, no! I didn't want to hear it from Allen! I didn't want to hear it, period.

"It's not that I thought Mick's saying it meant it didn't count, since it was only Mick saying it. I knew they had all decided together. Officially, though, I quit."

After the debacle of the confrontation, ABKCO and the Stones announced that they and Brian had come to an amicable settlement, and that he had agreed to leave the band for a sum of money. He went along with the announcement, but privately said, "That was all bullshit! You see, I couldn't say what actually was going on. Besides, no one would believe it; it was all too deep; it was too personal. It was me, and it was them—and I knew I was dying inside. Although, they were the ones killing me. I felt nothing but despair.

"I never gave the press a formal interview because I didn't know what to say. I was too hurt by the whole thing, in addition to being so very angry and fearful. Not to mention, I was humiliated by what they were saying about me."

He was right in that no one knew how deep and how personal the battle waged between him and the Stones organization actually had become. The use of the Rolling Stones name alone was huge, but even without the name Brian could easily have overtaken the sight and sounds of the Stones.

The organization would never allow that to happen. They would never allow him to form another band and go on his own. Brian admitted, "There was a web of conceit and deceit, plus the emotional battering of me within the incestuous brotherhood, which was the Rolling Stones that no one else saw."

Many wonder exactly how angry Brian had gotten over Mick's threatening him in such a vile manner. Did Brian think of murdering him first, when Mick threatened to kill him if he didn't comply with all of Mick's demands? "Not really. I was more trying to maintain my own body and mind than I was thinking about how to 'off' other people," he answered honestly.

That statement was very true because, as Mick badgered him relentlessly during the confrontation, Brian responded by not responding. At times he sat, covering his face and head with his arms like a hurt little boy, who was trying to hide from the world. "I didn't actually feel rage at what was being done to me," he said. "I had rage towards myself mostly. I kept thinking, how could I have been so stupid as to let them do all this to me? I knew I was smarter, brighter, than any of them could ever be, and that was also why I got so angry with myself for giving them the chance to knock me down and push me out.

"What it comes down to, I guess, was the simple fact that I'm not as conniving and treacherous as they are. Sitting around and plotting another's demise is more Mick's deal than mine."

## CHAPTER TWENTY-THREE
## The Right-hand Man

*"My participation in my own demise made everything easier for them to strip me of my leadership. I lost my 'edginess' and up-frontmanship to drugs, paranoia, depression, and my own insecurities. I was the spark, the fire, the flame that ignited the creation of what was the Rolling Stones, but I got tired really fast. My constitution was weaker than the others and more fragile, and I felt bad all the time. Mick diminished me, as opposed to helping me get over being ill. He told me I was worthless, and in my weakened condition, I bought into it. The wolf dog showed up, and I let him take advantage. I didn't mean to give up my leadership, but I did give them the opportunity to take it from me."*

Brian Jones

Reality finally sank in for Brian. He was officially out of the band. He had tried so hard over the past several months to tell himself that it wasn't over, that he could somehow regain at least a semblance of leadership in the world-famous band that was his creation, and his alone.

He sat alone in his music room at Cotchford Farm and tried to think of where it had gone so wrong. He had meant for nothing less than the best to come out of the beautiful music he had helped to compose over the last eight years, most of which he'd arranged completely on his own. All he had asked for in return was nothing more than recognition for his creations. Aside from the musical score that he had composed, arranged, and in which he had played many instruments, *A Degree of Murder*, his name had been stripped bare from any and all final Rolling Stones recordings—as far as his contributions to any of their creations.

A cold shudder ran through him. He realized how completely helpless he was to help himself or to protect his rights to that music. Both literally and figuratively, his blood, sweat, and tears—not to mention his physical body—had been selflessly sacrificed to get the Rolling Stones to where they were, the most famous and widely-recognized band in the world, second maybe to the Beatles. However, the Beatles themselves had broken apart, and there was room for the Stones, his Stones, to overtake them.

He rose from the comfortable sofa, threw a wool sweater over his shoulders, and began to walk the magnificent grounds at Cotchford. He always enjoyed these solitary walks, as they helped to clear his mind and enabled him to re-focus.

He had sworn to Mick and the rest of the Stones, not to mention ABKCO itself, that he would never simply disappear into nothingness and let them continue to use the name of his band—the name he had conceived and legally registered. He would always remain the "little Welsh bull" to the end and not cave into their threats.

He had some hope that some day he, Lennon, and Hendrix would come to a formal meeting of the minds and start fresh with a band of their own. He might even talk them into using the name *Brian Jones' Rolling Stones* for this band. "Won't that be a kick in the teeth to those bastards!" he said to himself with a grin, thinking how Mick & Company would react once they saw that name in lights.

But, would they allow this to actually happen? Would the organization ever allow Lennon, Hendrix, and Jones to become a working band? He could easily imagine the repercussions that would follow. He knew—or at least prayed—that the magnetism, charisma, and raw talent he still had would quickly recapture the hearts and souls of the world.

Mick & Company wouldn't stand a snowball's chance in hell competing against his new band. The word "hell" brought him out of his reverie with a jolt. He had temporarily forgotten the deal with the devil that Mick had made, which had worked so well for him over the past few years. Would the Dark Side let Brian create his band and see it to fruition? Another cold chill ran down his spine at the thought.

He took a long swig from his flask and rested against the century-old tree in the main garden. He looked up at the Heavens and prayed that once more his gut instincts would see him through the treachery that seemed to forever loom before him.

As he started to pace the grounds once more, he began to rethink his "why's?" and "what if's?" What if he hadn't given in so easily to all the drug taking? On the other hand, Keith took even more drugs than he did, and he never lost it as Brian had. Mick had taken many combinations of drugs, too, but he was always able to pull away and stop any time he chose.

Why couldn't he? Why was his constitution so weak that he fell prey to the vultures, once they saw his debilitated condition? Most significantly, why had the medical community, into which he'd poured so much money searching and begging for answers, never grasped the seriousness of his condition and cured him?

He had always prayed, since day one, that whatever mental and emotional conditions he suffered from would be diagnosed by now, and a miracle cure or drug found to save him from himself. No miracle had ever come, and now he feared it was too late. Why was it that, whatever mental and emotional diseases that had so badly crippled him, hadn't attacked Mick, Keith, or the others?

Additionally, why had no one ever been there to support him and help him long-term? That was the one question that had haunted him since childhood. Why was no one ever there to understand the suffering he was going through, to bolster him, and to stay with him, at least long enough for him to someday get better and be whole?

The other big question in his life was, why did no one ever love him enough to want to see him through all his trials and tribulations? He thought back to all those who claimed to have loved him, both women and men. However, all they ever loved was the Brian Jones they wanted to see—the rock star. No one had ever taken the time to unconditionally get to know and love Brian Jones, the small, lost, injured boy who never stood a chance of growing up a strong, self-sufficient adult male.

Tears rolled down his face—the face that, no matter what cruelties life threw in its direction—continued to emanate beauty, grace, and innocence.

\*\*\*

By the time he returned to his house, Brian felt strong once more and had come to a new resolution. He'd been held hostage in his own home far too long, and he refused to any longer take a subservient role in how his life played out. Even though he knew he had stepped over the line when it came to his dealings with Allen Klein, he determined to regain control over his destiny.

He could no longer contact Allen personally. However, Allen was the only one with the power to return to Brian the recognition he deserved and that belonged to him. He didn't feel any particular anger or hatred towards Allen or anyone, any longer. His rage and anger had come earlier, and it hadn't made him feel any better. Whenever possible, his soul was that of pacifier, conciliator, and focused on non-violence.

What he was feeling was continued surprise, shock, and disbelief at what had happened to him, and what his life had ultimately come down to. He felt horribly overshadowed and used.

His life had been one long struggle for survival and recognition. Upon reflection, he realized the only real happiness he had occurred within a brief, three-year time span, between the time he formed the Rolling Stones and the time Andrew Oldham and Mick first conspired and then successfully stripped him of his position as the band's leader. Three short years out of twenty-seven—that was all the true happiness he could ever remember.

While these concerns ran through his mind, he picked up the phone and asked to talk to Paul, Allen Klein's right-hand-man in England. British by birth, Paul was a promoter, dealing in media hype and public relations.

At least to the outside world that was Paul's profession. In reality, what his line of business actually was, was to be the "go to" man if you needed something extraordinary accomplished. In Brian's case, what he desperately needed accomplished was to be given a second chance to get back in Allen's good graces.

He knew he wasn't the best at making nice, especially with someone who was a bastard—as Allen most definitely was—but he felt he had no choice.

He felt as if he were about to walk the plank while a school of sharks that smelled his blood swarmed beneath—ready to rip him to shreds should he take one misstep or make one misjudgment. He imagined his hands tied behind him, and it was only a matter of time before the bell delivering his death knell rang.

Nevertheless, he forced himself to shake off this feeling of impending doom and placed his call. "Paul, can we meet up for a pint?" he asked.

"Sure, where would you like to meet?" Paul answered.

Brian mentioned the name of a pub not too close to Cotchford Farm but not too far away either. He wanted to meet Paul at a place he knew offered complete privacy to those needing to conduct personal business. He gave Paul directions to a darkly-lit pub within a half-hour's drive from his home.

Before leaving the house, he took the time to freshen up so he would look as good as possible. He'd done this many times in the past when he had gotten ready for a "date".

He studied his appearance in the floor-length mirror and grimaced. He had not taken care of himself the past several weeks. His chronic depression had worn away his will to keep his body in its normally meticulous shape. His waistline was paunchy due to the fact he wasn't eating good, wholesome food but instead snacking on high-calorie junk and drinking gallons of the pure, fatty milk he liked so much. The volumes of milk alone would have given him a paunchy look, but the sweets and straight alcohol upon which he continued to imbibe only added to his poor diet.

As he applied the makeup base that matched his peaches 'n cream complexion, he noticed that the bags under his eyes were once again prominent. He tried to mask them with concealer, but they still protruded to a degree. Even his hair didn't have the high luster it customarily did, but he told himself it wasn't all that bad. He squirted his body with his favorite cologne, took one last look in the mirror, and decided he was ready to leave.

He couldn't remember the last time he had felt so compelled to offer himself up as a delicious piece of raw meat to a, hopefully, hungry target. He wasn't sure if he could even bring himself to do the deed—should it come to that. Preferably it wouldn't, and Paul would give him what he wanted based on a promise…the unspoken promise of lust to be satisfied at a later, unspecified date.

He didn't want Tom Keylock to know what he was up to and quietly called for a taxi to pick him up and deliver him. He wasn't exactly sure what he would say to Paul once they met up, but he would depend upon his gut instincts to guide him, as he always had.

He would also use that special instinct he had of knowing whether a man was either bisexual or gay. He doubted Paul was gay but figured him for someone whose sexual interest he could pique, if he played the game right.

Paul was waiting for him at the bar that night—actually early evening. Even though the pub's interior was kept rather dark, when he walked up to Paul he was temporarily taken aback by the man's size. He'd never before paid attention to how huge the man actually was, both in height and overall muscle, since there never was a reason for him to have noticed. Although, Paul's imposing presence was one of the things that made him the successful right-hand-man he was known to be.

For a split second, Brian's survival instincts jumped into high gear, and he nearly turned and ran from the building. However, he knew he couldn't. If there was anything left to salvage from his career as a Rolling Stone, he had this one, last shot at coming to a meeting of the minds with ABKCO.

He put on his most disarming smile and held out his hand. "How are you this evening, Paul?" he asked brightly.

"Not bad. You?" the older man answered.

"Doing well. Why don't we sit over to the back, so we can enjoy some privacy?" While pointing toward the back of the pub, Brian made it clear he wasn't asking but in his own quiet way, ordering.

The two sat in what was one of the pub's more private booths, separated from the others by high wooden dividers. There, they began to drink a series of rounds of Brian's favorite scotch. He acted as host and paid, which suited Paul fine.

When he believed Paul relaxed and open to approach for the favor he wanted, he sat a bit closer and gently put his hand on Paul's. This wasn't done in a sexual manner but as a sign of closeness between friends.

He needed a friend, desperately. No one knew better than he how alone in the world he actually was. He had always tried to pretend that he was fine, in control of both himself and his life, and that he was self-sufficient and needed no one. Naturally, nothing was further from the truth, and this night he was at his most vulnerable. Not surprisingly, because of this vulnerability he wasn't thinking as clearly as he normally would have, when attempting to play a man as powerful as his guest.

The phrase Brian had thought of earlier in the day suddenly came to his mind, "He felt as if he were about to walk the plank, while a school of sharks that smelled his blood swarmed beneath—ready to rip him to shreds—should he take one misstep or make one misjudgment," and he felt his mouth go dry.

Nevertheless, he felt he had no other choice and had to dance with one of the devil's flock—at least for this one night.

For now, Paul allowed Brian's hand to rest on his, and he gave his young host his full attention.

For Brian, the ability to play off another man's lust still appeared to be second nature, and he felt renewed confidence in that he had his routine down perfectly. "I know Allen will listen to you, Paul," he spoke with his soft lisp, "and I need you to speak with him on my behalf. I'm sure we can work things out. What I need to know…" he continued as calmly and offhandedly as possible. "What I need to know is what will make Allen reconsider his position. You both should know I'm willing to do whatever it takes to prove I'm still one hundred per cent behind the Stones. Their goals are my goals."

As he finished his plea, he purposely leaned forward in his seat facing Paul and let his lips get within inches of the larger man's mouth. He said the words that had worked for him so many times in the past—when he needed to get the attention of the media and production companies—the words that had always worked magic for him, that he would "do whatever it took" to achieve his goals.

As he continued to smile graciously, he made sure there was no mistaking what he was offering—his body, if that's what it would take to get the job done.

Paul smiled back and took full hold of his hand. "Why don't we discuss this someplace more private, Brian? My car is parked in the lot. We can continue this out there."

"Sure," he agreed with forced enthusiasm. As he followed Paul to the dimly-lit parking area, he began to let his mind go blank. Paul repulsed him, and the thought of having to perhaps give the man oral sex, or anything else he might want, made him want to puke. The only way he could get through this, he knew, was to make sure his mind went blank and he could disassociate and pretend he wasn't really there, but someplace else.

He continued to concentrate on nothing else except letting his mind go far away, and he continued to innocently follow Paul around to the side of the building. Before he could react, Paul wheeled around, grabbed both his forearms, and slammed him back against the stone building. The back of his head hit hard, and he immediately became too stunned by the blow to try to retaliate or defend himself.

Paul began to administer what would be a series of direct punches to his head, ribcage, and stomach area. Brian lost his breath from the rapid blows and fought for air. He raised his arms to protect his invaluable face—the gorgeous face that was his most prized possession and had always been there to get him through the worst situations. Now that face was getting battered, and he had to protect it.

"Stop, Paul, please stop!" he barely managed to sputter.

But the unrelenting blows continued, one harder than the next.

"You dumb, pathetic fag!" Paul growled in a rage. "Did you really think I'd fall for your bullshit? Do you think I'm that stupid?"

"No, I just wanted to talk, Paul. That's all. Stop!" he begged. He was scared worse than he could ever imagine and strongly feared Paul would beat him to death. He could think of nothing to stop the ferocious attack, other than to not further enrage the brute by fighting back.

Any attempt to try to fight Paul off would be useless. In the milliseconds he had to think, he decided the best way for him to live through this assault was to remain as calm and non-threatening as possible. At last, Paul stopped battering him. He could feel Paul holding him under his arms, as he was dragged away, toward his attacker's car.

When they got to the car, Paul's driver automatically opened the back door. "Get your ass in there, you damn bugger!" Paul continued to give orders, while he flung Brian headfirst across the back seat.

The driver slammed the door shut, and Brian realized he was locked in with two maniacs. He also finally realized that he hadn't been the one playing Paul, but that Paul had all along been playing him. His gut instinct had let him down at the worst of times. His intuition had been so beaten down by the events of the past several months that his calculations were way off their mark. He was now helpless to protect himself, and he prayed God would somehow see him through this.

With the car's doors and windows locked, he couldn't call out for help. However, within the darkness and isolation of the parking lot, he doubted anyone would notice his plight, regardless.

"You want to get fucked, Brian? Well, you're gonna get fucked!" Paul bellowed. He pounded Brian on top of his head, as Brian lay on his stomach across the back seat, still trying to protect his face.

He knew Paul was going to rape him, and there was nothing he could do to stop it from happening. He'd been raped so many times in his life and had thought that was all a thing of the past. He had truly believed that once he became one of the most famous rock stars and musical icons of his time, he would automatically be protected from this type of sordid deed happening to him. When the pathetic reality hit—the reality that his frail body was once again going to be used and abused in the foulest manner possible—he felt himself begin to cry.

Paul noticed his tears, and this only further angered him. He grabbed Brian by the back of his hair and yanked, hard. "Listen, you little bugger, you cry, and I'll make sure it hurts worse than it already is. Hear me!" he screamed into his ear.

As he had from a small child, who was forbidden to cry aloud by his dad, Brian forced his tears away and said nothing. He couldn't push Paul's massive body off him and knew any attempt to fight back would only further enrage his attacker, and so he submitted, and let the act happen.

While Paul pulled Brian's slacks down and mounted him, Brian tried as best he could to let his mind go blank. He let his mind wander off to another place and another time, and pretended this was all a scene from a bad movie. He pretended that the body being brutalized in such a callous and cruel fashion wasn't his, but some other victim's.

He let his mind drift away into his world of music, and in the depths of his soul, he hummed a melody that only he could hear.

When Paul was done, he ordered the driver to head for a specific address. No one spoke while the car traveled down a country rode and pulled up to a secluded inn. The inn was family owned and operated—the type that didn't have much commercial traffic passing by. Once there, the driver got out and opened the car door.

"Get out!" Paul told Brian. "Did you learn your lesson, faggot? Make sure you keep this between us and no one else, or…." He finished those words with another punch.

The driver took Brian by his left arm and led him into the inn. He asked the keeper for a room, explaining that his "friend" wasn't feeling well and needed a quiet place to recuperate. He took out a large roll of bills and offered much of it to the innkeeper. The man pretended nothing looked amiss, asked no questions, and accepted the roll of money offered. The driver made it obvious he was not one to be messed with.

Brian was utterly humiliated by what he was being put through and never looked the innkeeper in the face. What's more, he didn't want to be recognized. He felt absolutely wretched and could barely walk, as Paul's "lesson" had ripped open his anal passage. There had been nothing kind or gentle about the assault. The act was meant to hurt and maim him, and Paul, as was his norm, had gotten the job done.

The driver took the key provided and led Brian to an upstairs room. The walk up the stairs caused even more excruciating pain to his insides, but he continued to force himself not to cry out. He welcomed the deep shock into which he felt his body retreating.

The man shoved him into the room and closed the door behind him. Brian curled up into a fetal position on the bed, with his eyes open, but seeing nothing.

***

Brian didn't remember much about the next couple of days. He couldn't even remember how long he stayed curled up in that fetal position. His entire body was racked with pain from the excessive blows to his head and the pounding his rib cage and body had absorbed.

His rectum was another matter, and so he tried not to move about all that much. He called down to the innkeeper to bring him a couple of bottles of booze and was grateful he had extra cash on his person. He couldn't fathom the thought of any food, but he desperately needed to numb the pain he felt. He drank straight from the first bottle and vomited up some of it. But, whatever he could keep down, he did. He savored the warm rush the liquid delivered, as soon as it took hold of his nervous system. Since his stomach was empty from not having eaten for so long, the alcohol took immediate effect.

Once his inhibitions were numbed—he cried. He cried and cried as he had never cried before. All the years of having to survive alone, using only his God-given wits, came crashing down upon him. He asked himself the question he'd asked so often during his short twenty-seven years on the planet—what had he done to anyone to deserve being treated like this? And, as usual there was no answer.

He cried himself to sleep and awoke to what he thought may have been the third day of his personal confinement. Because he was completely alone, he had no one to call out to for help. There never was anyone there for him during his times of need, and this time was no different.

Because he had no family waiting for him at Cotchford Farm, there was no one to know anything was amiss. Mary Hallett was the only one who cared, but she was used to seeing him take a few days off at a time, without telling anyone where he was going, and so she wouldn't be worried that he had been gone these many days.

He soaked in the room's tub for a long, long time and cried all over again, as his aching body struggled to relax in the hot, soothing water. When he got out, he continued to walk gingerly from both the blows to his body and from the assault. He studied how well he could make himself stand erect, so as not to embarrass himself upon his return home. Surely, he wanted no one to know he had been attacked in such a brutal manner.

He was tired of being isolated in the tiny room and needed to return to his own home. He phoned Tom Keylock, definitely not his first choice, but he also knew Tom would come and not ask any questions. He was not about to answer questions as to why or how he looked so bruised and battered.

When Tom arrived, Brian once again put his head down and quietly left the building. He didn't know if anyone there had recognized him, and he prayed he wouldn't see his name printed in the local newspapers.

As expected, Tom drove him home without asking questions. He had to have noticed Brian's injuries, but neither man chose to say anything to the other.

*** 

During the drive home, Brian seriously wondered whether his dad, Mick, and some others had been right all along—was he so fucked-up, so dumb, that he couldn't even correctly judge a low life, son-of-a-bitch like Paul? How could he have been so blind as to so horribly misread Paul's true intentions?

Any confidence he may have had in his gut instinct, his reasoning, and his personal belief system disappeared.

Worst of all—he tearfully realized that now he truly had no one to depend upon for ultimate survival, not even himself.

# CHAPTER TWENTY-FOUR
## The Murder, Part II-The Death of an Angel

*"They really don't want me to have ever existed."*

Brian Jones

The month of June, 1969, was drawing to a close, and ten days had passed since Paul's brutal attack. Brian was still mentally reeling and still physically feeling the repercussions from the vicious assault. The constant ache in his rib area made breathing even more of a chore than the ever-present asthma. He still wasn't eating much since the burning in his stomach made holding down solid food ne'er impossible, not to mention the nagging nausea that swept over him from time to time.

To help mask all his ills he took additional prescribed tranquilizers and sleeping pills, and he made sure he had a constant supply of alcoholic beverages and marijuana by his side. He still hadn't made the all-important connection that the combination of the two—prescription medication together with alcohol and pot—had at least triple their normal effect on him, which caused blurred thinking and even blackouts. "I did try to completely quit all drugs but wasn't very successful," he admitted. "I was forever in my own world and playing my own tunes."

Among all the thoughts that continued to race through his mind during the last several days of almost complete isolation were the horrific things ABKCO and the Stones continued to say about him, publicly. "No one dared say anything derogatory about Mick," he mused. "But I was the one ABKCO said it was okay to defame, demean, and lay blame on personally, for any of the band's woes. I'm the drugged-out weirdo. How convenient!"

For whatever reason, stories continued to fly about his so-called sex crazed orgies—none of which were taking place, especially since he had no stomach for such excesses any longer. Plus his minders wouldn't allow any socializing on the property, even if he had wanted to party. "Yes, I did some humping in my time, but I would've had to be from three to six men to have fucked everybody I'm said to have fucked," he said scornfully.

He also felt bitter about the unfair way his own band mates continued to treat him, when compared to how decent, kind, and generous the Beatles treated one another. He explained, "The Beatles don't really have the fire, intensity, vendettas, and the darkness to plan to 'off' one another, nor do they have the obvious greed as the bad boys of rock—the Stones. Can you imagine Ringo creating a fight, or Paul? The Beatles live and play by the rules of decency and honor—attributes not part of the Stones' vocabulary."

What Brian had to admit was the hard fact that he originally sowed the seeds of the Rolling Stones philosophy, never imagining that philosophy of not caring and screw-the-world would apply to him. He understood any personal happiness at Cotchford Farm was being stolen from him. Worst of all, he had to face the reality that the very people he believed he could trust—his brothers in the band—had thoroughly betrayed his gentle, loving, and generous soul.

He was happy, nonetheless, that he had managed to take part in the last song he would create with his band, *Honky-Tonk Women*. The recording sessions, held at Olympic Studios, had taken place during most of the month of May. He had made appearances on and off, working with the Stones on their version of the Ry Cooder song. Keith had taken Ry's original guitar riff, but Brian had performed the magic only he could for the song—by twisting and enhancing the guitar sounds to make them sound fresh and brand new.

He was pleased with the way the song had come along and had looked forward to getting the final version down. In light of that, his confusion continued to rain. Mick had already told him he was no longer part of the band, but yet somehow, he expected to complete this last song.

However, recently the gnawing feeling that he had a date with destiny returned, along with the fear of death. Since a child he had fought the feeling, deep in his soul, that he would die young and unexpectedly. He was relieved that his New York attorney had all his legal papers in hand.

He had no way of knowing whether Paul ever told Allen Klein about the debacle into which their so-called business meeting had turned, or if Paul would even admit to Allen about the assault. Regardless, there was nothing he could do but try to pretend the incident never occurred.

His strong intuitive nature seemed to again be working overtime, along with his paranoia. Since Paul's attack, there had been no one for him at Cotchford—no friends, no lovers. Anna Wohlin was merely coming and going, and besides, he had pretty much lost interest in her. Hence, there was no one. He was totally alone.

"It was eerie as hell," he said candidly. He noticed that all those still around him, such as his housekeeper and the so-called workmen, kept avoiding his eyes or moved quickly in and out of the house self-consciously, once they spotted him. He imagined Mary was looking away because she didn't want to ask about the obvious beating he recently had.

The workmen were another matter. Brian imagined they looked away because of further sinister deeds they had in mind. He decided he couldn't stay alone in the huge house any longer. Although, he couldn't drive himself either. His rib cage was too sore for him to concentrate on the road, and he felt his eyes blurred and swollen from the constant worry and lack of sleep. Between the physical and emotional pains, he was back to feeling undone again and not in control of either himself or his fate.

He had tried to reach out to many people during the past ten days, even though he felt betrayed by everyone. He had even phoned one or two of his male lovers, but they weren't in or weren't returning his calls. Sometimes, of course, his own phone wouldn't work, so he really had no way of knowing if anyone was trying to get back to him. "The phone was my lifeline, but there were times when it wasn't available to me," he said sadly. His mind was telling him that perhaps none of this was real, and he was imagining it all.

This belief of being close to the end of his life terrified him. "I felt I was being buried alive, alone in my house," he admitted. He believed he had to escape from his prison and phoned a fellow musician friend from the early days, Graham Bond. He asked Graham to come by and take him to a hotel, where he could hide away for a while. He didn't want anyone, including Tom Keylock, to know where he was going. If they were coming to do him in, he needed to hide out until he could make plans for his future. He wasn't quite sure who the "they" would be, but he knew for sure they were coming, and soon.

A few hours later, he felt secure that he had managed to get away from Cotchford unnoticed and breathed a sigh of relief. He walked through the hotel's main lobby and checked in under a fictitious name. Graham had dropped him off alone but said he planned to come back shortly.

When Graham did return, he arrived with a ladyfriend, Dianne Stewart. Brian explained, "Yes, I called out for help. I called Graham. You see, I had stayed friends with those who I didn't necessarily get to see all that often. Actually, it was a pretty short period of time between all the years—at least to me. I had tried getting through to Alexis at first to come take me, but he wasn't in. I felt I needed a witness in case of another attack but was too fearful to trust the authorities."

He knew he was in no condition to keep Graham or Dianne company, unfortunately. Even so, he did tell the couple briefly about his feelings of most likely being killed at any moment. Graham seemed to grasp the significance of his friend's condition and tried to make friendly conversation, while Brian lay on his bed curled up in what had become his normal fetal position. He felt incapable of speech but tried to communicate with Graham with his eyes.

Once more, he found himself staring straight ahead, but seeing nothing. All he felt was despair and the darkness that surrounded him, and he took to sucking on his finger for comfort. He knew this wasn't merely paranoia he was feeling, not this time. He believed this was the result of a series of events he had created originally, which were now irrevocable. That series of events went back to the first days in which he vociferously fought Allen Klein and what had now become the all-powerful Stones organization. Mick had warned him all along that he had the choice to compromise and give them whatever they wanted or....

Brian had chosen the latter option, and now knew he had to pay for his decision. His attitude in fighting the demons had always been, "Come and get me!" And now, reality hit him hard, which resulted in his current fetal position. He felt wrapped in a drugged-out state, even though he hadn't taken any drugs. His mind was playing games and flashing him back to the days of heavy drug taking and moral degradation.

On the second day of his self-imposed exile, he heard the phone in his hotel room ring. He couldn't move to answer. He had no desire to answer either, since he believed he knew who could be on the other end. As the phone continued to ring, he pictured the walls closing in on him, suffocating him.

The phone stopped ringing for a time but then started all over again. He wondered who had turned him in to his tormentors. He trusted Graham, but didn't know all that much about Dianne.

This time Graham answered the phone's incessant ringing and said, "Hello?" Everyone in the room could hear a male voice screaming at the other end. Graham cupped the receiver with his hand and whispered to Brian, "It's Mick."

"Fuck! How does he know I'm here?" he answered, now struck with even more terror.

Graham didn't speak much to Mick, who continued to spew a barrage of curses in Brian's direction. One phrase Mick did say very clearly, however, was—"Tell Brian he's dead! Tell him I'm gonna kill him!" Then he hung up.

Brian had thought his terror level was already high, but now his fear rose doubly. "I was afraid to be at home; I was afraid to be alone. But where I had gone to hide out—so I could have my private nervous breakdown—was no longer a secret. Now I knew there was no place for me to hide. I was a mess," he lamented.

Graham and Dianne stayed with him, talking to him, trying to get him to settle down. After awhile, they mistook his slumped, shocked condition for tranquility, and so they tucked him into his bed and quietly left the room. Brian explained, "They did try to calm me down, and I did go numb after a while. Yes, I drank a good deal. I wanted to forget everything. I wanted to forget I was alive."

On the third day of his flight from reality—still too numb to either think or move—he decided to return home and face whatever demons awaited him. He called Tom to come bring him back to Cotchford Farm, believing there was no use in fighting any longer. Without consciously doing so, he relinquished his control to the powers that be. He felt resigned to his fate.

As they drove home, Tom reassured Brian that everything was all right and told him Allen Klein had phoned to say Brian's buyout money for leaving the Rolling Stones would be delivered to Cotchford Farm the next day, July 2. He continued to trust Tom to a degree, believing the chauffeur had been there for him many times in the past. For whatever reason, he'd completely blocked out the memory of Tom being the one who had assisted Keith and Anita in leaving him behind with no money and no identification, while they were all in Morocco two years earlier.

"Tom was supposed to love me (as a friend)," Brian explained. "At least I had hoped so."

***

When he arrived back at Cotchford, Brian went up to his room to try and revisit what actions had brought him to the state he was now in. During the previous weeks he'd tried reaching out by phone to everyone he could think of whom he considered a trusted friend. John Lennon had been among those, but he didn't respond. "John was still on smack," Brian explained, "and even though I was afraid for my safety, he was available to no one. I needed to talk to someone but also realized I could only tolerate being alone."

Mick's earlier phone call to the hotel was still affecting him, and he had a feeling of dread. "Hell! Mick threatened to kill me!" he exclaimed. "He and Allen didn't just want me fired…they wanted me gone. Mick wanted to scare me to death, and wouldn't that have been easy? He turned into a mean fuck, saying, 'I'm going to make sure you're done in, Brian,' but of course I knew he would send others to do it. Mick would never have the courage to do it himself. He wanted to pay me back for not giving in to him…all of it went so badly wrong.

"I believed I had sold my musician's artistic integrity in exchange for money, for a time, and I was angry with myself for having done so. I needed to turn things around and make them right again."

He stared out his bedroom window at the beautiful grounds that had once been the home to Winnie the Pooh. "Cotchford Farm must have been a happy place back then," he said to no one in particular. He felt he didn't belong there, but then he imagined the outside world also looked foreign to him, while he attempted to fight off the intense anguish of feeling completely broken and shattered.

He continued to talk to himself. "I knew I had fucked up so many times in my life. How strong-willed I'd been in deciding things and how I treated people. I let go of control of the band, when I could've maintained control—if only I could have controlled myself by not making all my illnesses and weaknesses worse, with the heavy use of drugs and alcohol. Everything I've done was to set in motion a downward spiral for myself. I tried to look at how I could have done it all differently…but now it was too late.

"I was concerned with how I had damaged myself, my reputation, and my relationships. I would continue to take another drink and another drug just to make myself feel better, but before I knew it, it had gotten away from me, and then it was in charge of me. I lost much by not being more aware, and I've been mean and cruel to people through my arrogance and by not respecting them. Although, I didn't mean any of it. I meant no harm to anyone."

***

Brian thought he would never be able to sleep through the night of July 1, 1969, but he blissfully surprised himself by sleeping the night away more peacefully than he had for a long time. Later that morning, perhaps for the last time, he turned on his recorder and began to speak. "Looking at it, it's as if my perspective let go of the fear in order to let me sleep peacefully. I think my soul knows it's the last time that I will sleep in my home. I didn't even feel the need to drink or take any sleeping pills.

"However, this morning I felt as if I'd been beaten up. My body felt bruised and battered. I ached all over and turned on my side, crunched up, as I tried to ease the pain. I'm emotionally wrung out, with feelings of dread and anticipation. As has become the norm, I couldn't eat. My abdominal area felt very raw, burning. So I drank a lot of milk. Mary came in and offered me breakfast. She made some toast, but I just picked at it.

"I gazed out the window and spotted the workmen. I tried to call my attorney but couldn't get him in. I'm trembling and feel a nervous wreck. I tried reaching out for help, if there ever was any, but yet again found none."

He no longer knew who Mick was, and believed Mick felt the same about him. Their contentious power struggle now felt a lifetime ago. "I know they're going to kill me. No, I didn't think of hiring my own guards to protect me—isn't that something! I feel overpowered, as if my own family has once again kicked me out and deserted me. So, what's the point? Besides, how could I hire my own guards when they control all the money I'd need to pay the guards?"

He believed he had to have been a horrible person if his second family also was tossing him out like so much rubbish. He paced around his empty rooms, walked to his living room, and stared out at the new day. He chewed on his own fingers like a scared little boy and talked to himself again. "I don't belong anywhere; I don't fit in anywhere. My life has gone so far beyond anything I could have imagined. I'm embarrassed at my state and not fit to be around anyone."

He spent the remainder of the day sitting on the floor of his music room listening to Creedence Clearwater Revival's *Bad Moon Rising*. He played the one song over and over, listening to the prophetic lines that told him this night would take his life. This only confirmed his strong feelings that for him the end was coming soon, truly amidst the voices of rage and ruin. "I loved that song and thought it the most appropriate for the day of my death," he prophesized.

As early evening approached Mary Hallett told him she'd be retiring for the night but also wanted him to know she had prepared him a light meal. As had become customary, he sat alone at his kitchen table and picked and pushed at his food—more moving it around the plate than actually putting any of it to his mouth.

He got up from the table and walked towards the front door, but once he saw Frank and some of the other men milling around, he retreated back to the safety of the house. He was certain death was approaching, and soon, but didn't know how to fight back, since he didn't know where the danger lay.

Tom had assured Brian that his payoff money was coming, and he needed it desperately. He rummaged through his pants pocket but only came up with some loose change. He so much wished there was someone for him to talk to—to hear the sound of a friendly, loving voice—but there was none.

Anna Wohlin was around someplace, but she really had nothing to offer in the way of genuine conversation or support. She still only carried the dream of what Brian could do for her career. He sighed and wondered what the world wanted from him. As night began to fall, he got the queasy feeling that another of ABKCO's promises would be broken, and he'd never see any of his money. He went up to his room and walked to the window.

Dave Gibson, the independent carpet layer whom he hired, was getting ready to leave for the evening. He looked up at Brian's bedroom window and spotted him staring back at him, sullenly. Dave waved good-night, just as Brian called down to him. "Dave, would you mind staying around for a bit? I'm not feeling really safe or well this evening."

Dave was a retired member of England's prestigious Royal Military Police and an honorable fellow. Brian felt comfortable having him around. Dave wasn't like the others. However, the carpet layer explained that his wife expected him home, and besides, he'd be back by seven the next morning. So, he told Brian, why not try to get some rest during the next few hours, and then the two could finish the conversation of whatever was bothering Brian at that time?

Brian lowered his eyes, understanding any attempt at human contact was again being denied him. "Sure, Dave, see you in the morning!" he called out. In the back of his mind, he knew he would not see another morning.

Within minutes of Dave's leaving the grounds, Tom hollered up to Brian from the music room, to come on down and share a drink with him and the guys. Tom affirmed the fact that a courier would be arriving shortly, with the one hundred thousand pounds expected. Brian thought the invitation over and figured—why not have a drink and some conversation with Tom—it was better than being alone. And so, he returned to the music room.

Frank was there as well, along with a couple of the other men, Johnny and Mo. Tom handed Brian a drink, which he described as being, "strangely soothing." The men were acting jovial, as if no bitter words had ever been shared, and were nearly in a party mood. Although, Frank did ask for his pay, to which Brian once again explained there was no money to pay out…at least until his own money arrived.

Brian sat in his favorite chair and relaxed with a second drink that Tom had prepared. This one's soothing effect was welcomed even more, since his agitated state continued to fluctuate up and down. To his surprise, he looked up and saw Allen Klein walking in the room straight towards him, with briefcase in hand. He definitely had not expected Allen there personally that night but instead expected a courier. He was aware the plump, balding producer was in country; however, the two hadn't spoken for a while.

Allen walked in with a plastic smile and tossed his briefcase on the desk, in front of Brian. Brian felt a cold shiver run through him, for despite Allen's well-rehearsed smile behind it lurked a sinister glare. "Allen reached his hand out to me. I too reached out, but the look in his eye told me he was going to nail me right then and there. I wanted to say, 'Allen, just give me the money and leave,' because seeing him was a bit more than I'd bargained for…something wasn't right."

Brian smiled back but knew his own smile had a forced, plastic grin. And, for whatever reason, the couple of drinks he had were making him feel exceptionally loose and relaxed—not a feeling he should be experiencing while in Allen's presence. He said, "I halfway heard Allen talking, while my lids began to close over my eyes. I tried to listen, but his words only came in fragments. I heard him say, 'Be reasonable, Brian. Do what's in your best interest, Brian. We can't let you continue to do this, Brian. It's for your own good, Brian.'

"Allen went into a speech about—how all that was important was the Rolling Stones name, and that I couldn't just take it with me and use it to start my own band. Tom even took a turn, saying, 'We've all been friends a long time, and things don't have to go this way, Brian.' Then Allen opened the briefcase showing me all this cash. He said, 'See this, you weak, pathetic loser—this could have been yours but now you'll never get it. You want to hang tough with me…you…pervert!'

"I couldn't believe he called me that—a pervert. I'd done nothing that Mick hadn't personally done and was still doing. Besides, the money was mine! The Stones name was mine, and they couldn't have it. I again told Allen that.

"But, by this time I was nothing more than a little fly to them…a pest…something they could swat away. I thought there definitely would be monies coming to me for all of my participation in the band—but the Rolling Stones name was mine, and it wasn't for sale!"

Even though he felt groggy, he tried getting up from his chair to further confront Allen, but he couldn't move. Tom was now holding his arms behind his back. Tom's grip was stronger than Brian could have imagined, and he was twisting and holding Brian's arms up and behind him. He tried to fight Tom off, but instead fell back…too weakened by the alcohol, he imagined. But then, he realized he'd only had a couple of drinks, not enough to so immobilize him.

He noticed that the workmen's demeanor had done a complete reversal, and they now stood with their arms folded, looking extremely tense, while they listened to Allen's diatribe. They were looking at one another, he believed, as if waiting for a signal to tell them it was time to leap into action. He could hear his dogs barking loudly in the background, but aside from that the house was eerily still.

Allen shouted a final, "There's no reason it had to lead to this, Brian!" while he snapped the briefcase shut, with all Brian's money still in it.

He still felt too weak to get up and at last realized he'd been drugged, most likely with his own sleeping pills, which must have been crushed into his drinks. He now knew his time had finally come, and he was about to die. Nonetheless, he fought to keep a semblance of consciousness with which to show Klein. He fought hard to speak, but the pills had successfully closed his mouth, and his eyes began to lose their focus.

He felt Tom's strong grip on his arms hurting him, but each time he tried to loosen the grip the bespeckled man only yanked him around more roughly. He was stunned, since Tom had never shown any type of aggression towards him before. "But now I knew whose side he actually was on," Brian lamented. "Tom probably figured my death was inevitable, so why not take their money and be part of the winning side?"

With a farewell scowl, Allen grabbed his briefcase and left the music room. Brian lost track of time, but imagined only a minute or so had passed when next, he couldn't believe who he perceived walking into the room. He knew the Stones were rehearsing at Olympic Studios in London that night—not more than an hour or so drive away from Cotchford Farm, if someone were to drive a fast car.

"No one will ever believe me, and it will basically be my word against his," Brian said, "but there standing in front of me was The Mick! He'd never come to Cotchford just to pop in and visit me…so, I just knew…my time had surely come."

The nightmarish dream he'd had several times during the past few weeks was now in reality being played out before him. "I saw Mick, the man, coming towards me but then I swear his shape actually changed into a one-eyed, seething pterodactyl—something you might see in a horror flick. It reminded me of a Bela Lugosi movie where a bat swoops down into the victim's room, ready to drink his blood. Mick walked up to me and pointed with his long, sinewy finger, right into my face. 'Bastard!' he screamed. 'I warned you, Brian! I told you I'd get you! You're dead!'

"I tried to answer, but nothing came as my eyes were quickly shutting closed on me. My jaws wouldn't work, and Tom still held me down. I couldn't elucidate. I couldn't move. I imagined Mick arrived to make sure the deed was getting done. He has to be in charge of everything, you know, even my demise."

Tom and Frank looked stunned to see Mick there in person, but neither man dared say anything. They knew who was in charge, and who was paying their way.

As Brian attempted to glare back at Mick, he sensed utter disbelief at what was occurring. Bouts of dazed fear and pure terror ebbed and flowed throughout his body, even though his consciousness was fading fast. The disbelief he felt was due to the fact that Mick—his brother, his band mate, his one-time lover—wanted the definitive pleasure of witnessing his death. No act of betrayal could be as cruel as this one, final act of heartlessness. With that final thought, his head fell to the side.

Once Mick realized his victim had lost consciousness, he went up to Brian's room to gather his swimming trunks. At the same time, Frank took out a syringe that had been provided him, with which to inject Brian. The syringe contained a high dose of insulin which—when given to someone who doesn't require it, and who has already been drugged—will bring on a massive heart attack. Tom injected Brian with the insulin and stood back to watch its effect.

Brian fell forward, and his head hit the side of his desk, hard. The force of the impact caused immediate bleeding to his temple area. The men panicked and tried to wipe the blood away. This was definitely not part of their plan.

Mick returned with Brian's swimming trunks and handed them over to his fellow collaborators. He then left as quietly and quickly as he had arrived.

Tom, Frank, and the remaining men stripped an unconscious Brian of all his clothing and slid his swimming trunks on. They dragged his near-lifeless body out to his beloved pool and tossed him in. Frank stepped into the water himself, desiring to personally have the pleasure of holding Brian under, until his spirit left his body. He wanted to ensure that whatever life Brian may have had left was taken away.

Brian's spirit knew his physical body was dead even before his heart took its last beat. He alternated periods of severe angst over what was being done to him, together with a great relief. His painful struggle to fit into a world he never felt a part of was at its end.

The last thing he remembered seeing in this lifetime was the twisted, distorted image of the man—whom he had once entrusted with his band, his music, and his most privately kept secrets—pointing and shouting epithets at him, telling him how worthless a human being he was and how he no longer deserved to even be called a Rolling Stone.

***

Shortly before his death, Brian spoke aloud about the very real possibility that people had been hired to kill him, since he refused to give into ABKCO's demands. He prophesized, "My death would be a sad little end to a miserable little life. I feel like a rat in a cage, even if others think of my life as gloriously being played out on the world stage.

"While that part may once have been true, at the end it all came down to a very small world...."

# EPILOGUE

*"Mick robbed me. He robbed me of so many things—
even my life."*

Brian Jones

The men who plotted Brian's demise made great effort to set an imaginary scene that a rousing party had taken place at his home on the night of his death. While he was losing consciousness, the workmen who weren't actively holding him down turned on the outside floodlights surrounding the pool. They also turned the outside speakers up full blast that played the rock music neighbors were accustomed to hearing during the times Brian had given parties.

One or two friends called the house late that night and remembered hearing music and noise in the background, which gave them the false impression that a party was taking place.

However, when the local authorities were called in to investigate Brian's death, only four people were actually at the house. One such person was Anna Wohlin, who was too drugged to give a coherent statement about what she saw or heard that night. Tom and Frank had also mixed her drinks with Brian's sleeping pills, ensuring she'd not be a witness to what had taken place. As a result, she had spent the last few hours of Brian's life asleep in her room and was only roused shortly after his actual drowning.

The second witness was Janet Lawson, Brian's assigned nurse and some-time girlfriend to either or both Tom and Frank. She was present when the inspectors arrived and parroted a well-rehearsed scenario that Brian had drowned after taking too many pills and drinking too much alcohol.

Tom and Frank also gave their well-rehearsed speeches that a party had taken place during the night of July 2, and that Brian had drowned after taking too many pills and drinking too much alcohol.

One oddity of the ensuing investigation by law enforcement into Brian's death was the fact that two junior investigators were called out to the scene. Under any situation, when a British celebrity dies either suddenly or suspiciously, senior, seasoned inspectors are immediately sent out.

However, even the two junior detectives assigned to the case—Robert Marshall and Peter Hunter—said they knew at once that the death scene was fabricated and that the witness statements were rehearsed, and even though rehearsed, not consistent with one another.

What further disturbed Marshall was the state of the interior of Brian's home. Everything was in complete disarray and not in the condition of a home supposedly remodeled. He was shocked to see doorways and other molding inside the house ripped and torn. Additionally, he noticed paving slabs, which were only used for outdoor street paving, placed in Brian's kitchen instead of regular floor tiles.

Both inspectors observed Frank Thorogood's overbearing personality and commented that he considered himself the one who had been in charge of Cotchford Farm, and not his recently-deceased employer.

Another oddity was the fact that the retired Royal Military Police officer and present-day carpet layer, Dave Gibson—who'd promised Brian he would return at 7 a.m. the next morning and visit with him over his concerns—was telephoned at his flat in the early morning hours of July 3. A male voice, which he didn't recognize, advised him there was no need for him to return to Cotchford Farm and complete his work there. He was also told he would receive full payment for his work, in the mail. At first Gibson thought nothing amiss until he received his check days later, which included an enormous bonus for him and his co-worker. The note also contained the mysterious message, "Take a holiday."

The bonus was so large that Gibson was able to take a Mediterranean cruise, while his co-worker used his share of the money to purchase a bungalow along the bay.

Since that time Gibson has completely rethought what had to have occurred at Cotchford Farm and decided that a murder had taken place. He has attempted to tell his story as to why he knew the party scene at Cotchford had been staged the night of July 2, and why Brian had been so frightened on the night of his death that he even asked Gibson to stay with him. However, each time Gibson has been put off or ignored by the authorities, and even anonymously threatened to forget what he knows.

A local taxi driver, Joan Fitzsimmons, was on duty the night of Brian's death. During one of her trips along the roads leading to Cotchford Farm that night, she happened to glance out her taxi's window and saw Mick Jagger driving away from Cotchford at a rapid rate of speed. Just as she glanced at him, Mick happened to look over at her.

At first Ms. Fitzsimmons thought nothing of seeing Mick leave Cotchford, until she read in the newspapers about Brian's drowning around the same time. She told friends of what she saw and mentioned she planned to go to the police and recount her story. Before she had a chance to do so, however, an unknown assailant threw acid in her face, and she was blinded. She has never spoken further about that night and has since disappeared.

Shortly after Brian's body was removed from Cotchford Farm, and during the early morning hours of July 3, a mysterious but large bonfire erupted on the grounds. Most of his personal clothing, tapes, and belongings, including his beloved sitar and Bible, were tossed haphazardly into the inferno.

Providentially, Mick Martin, the groundskeeper, bravely reached into the fire and retrieved Brian's Bible, which he has kept in memory of his employer. Inspector Hunter tried to talk to Martin about the strange events, but the man had been so traumatized by what he saw that horrible day, he was hard to understand.

Despite all these inconsistencies, both police inspectors were advised by their superiors to close the investigation into Brian Jones' death and move onto other cases. A short inquest was held within a few days—much too soon for any inquiry into a mysterious death that should have been taken seriously—and the coroner's office determined Brian's demise was something referred to as "death by misadventure".

Among all the strange occurrences that took place during the sham investigation was the fact that the coroner never explained why he bleached Brian's prized platinum blond hair white, at the time his body was released for burial. Those who know believe the bleach was added to mask any signs of blood that had soaked through Brian's hair during the time he fell forward and hit his head, after being injected with the insulin.

Despite the many witnesses and countless evidence that has shown Brian's death was not an accident but a calculated murder, Scotland Yard has steadfastly refused, and continues to refuse at the time of this writing, to re-open the investigation into his suspicious death.

Brian had said that Scotland Yard held him in disdain because of his earlier drug convictions and the rumors spread about his lifestyle by ABKCO and the Rolling Stones. That was why, when he truly felt his life was in danger during the last months of his life, he never attempted to phone the Yard and ask for protection.

The cover-up of how Brian died has been very widespread. Ralph Waldo Emerson wrote *Money Often Costs Too Much*, referring to the value of a human life. That saying pertains to one of the main reasons for Brian's death. ABKCO knew that Brian was actively "following the money trail," as he liked to call it, and that he was determined to prove the band's money was being mishandled.

The Rolling Stones empire is now worth billions of dollars, and shrewd businessmen, with all the necessary power, believe financial futures have to be protected. Additionally, Scotland Yard doesn't wish its reputation tarnished, should they ever feel compelled to admit that so many of their paid officials took hush money and chose to look the other way when evidence was presented.

Within a day or two of Brian's passing, large vans pulled up to his home. Reminiscent of Genghis Khan and his horde of rapists, plunderers, and thieves, heartless men descended upon Cotchford Farm. One can imagine Winnie the Pooh looking on helplessly as his and Brian's beloved home was callously ransacked of all its possessions.

The vans were quickly filled with any valuables not consumed in the earlier bonfire. Those valuables included all Brian's jewelry, artwork, tapestries, rugs, and crystals, plus his musical instruments. From time to time a piece or two from his collection shows up in auction houses. One such piece, which recently has been sold at auction in New York City, was a watch that Brian personally treasured. The watch was a gift given to him by his close friend, Alexis Korner, and inscribed from Alexis to him as a sign of their eternal friendship.

It has been reported that Tom Keylock made off with several of Brian's gold records, and some of those have shown up either in auctions or are currently hanging on the walls of various restaurants and clubs. Brian had taken great pride in his collection of the gold records he had earned, for all his work on behalf of the Rolling Stones.

Since Brian's death, Mick has collected a large and impressive art collection. He once claimed that one of his favorite oil paintings, which hangs in his home, depicts a long-haired man floating dead in a swimming pool. (See Artist Interpretation #858)

The people who ransacked and hoarded Brian's personal property thought of and treated their booty as mere trophies to do with as they pleased. His parents, Lewis and Louise Jones, managed to acquire several of his costumes that he enjoyed wearing, including his favorite bells, buckles, and other finery.

Interestingly, while no one has ever inherited the money Brian was to have received as a lifetime buyout from ABKCO and the band, his parents were allowed to keep a large insurance policy taken out in his name. Unusual, since a key stipulation of the policy stated that no monies would be paid out if the deceased were shown to have drugs in his/her system. The preplanned coroner's report clearly states Brian's body contained a high amount of assorted drugs. Perhaps the insurance company was told by "higher powers" to pay on the life insurance policy, in order to ward off the Jones family from demanding a closer look into their son's death.

Additionally, shortly after Brian's death, Mick took the senior Lewis aside and convinced him to sign off all rights to his son's music, including his name, in exchange for an undisclosed sum of money. Mick treated Lewis the same as he treated everyone else—as a puppet in his hands. He badgered and manipulated the older man into signing away Brian's name, telling him it was what his son would have wanted.

***

Brian would be happy to know that all the private tapes he had made of his music were destroyed, most likely by accident during the bonfire. He planned to have those tapes as his safety net when he left the band, and they were the ones he adamantly refused to hand over to Mick during the wicked confrontation between them. He chose death rather than hand his tapes over at that time, and fate saw to it that his wish was granted.

He would never want those tapes to have been found and later turned into mega hits by the rest of the Stones, and have the writing team of Jagger/Richards claim credit to his music.

The saddest thing about Brian's death was the fact the heinous act never had to have taken place. Mick and ABKCO mistakenly thought, if he were allowed to live and start a new band—perhaps with Jimi Hendrix and John Lennon—that super group would easily overtake what was left of the original Stones.

Also, they believed, if Brian were allowed to live and take the Rolling Stones name, any new band he might start would quickly overtake what was left of the original Stones.

What they didn't realize was the fact they had already won. Brian was so beaten down mentally and emotionally, after being tossed aside by his second family, that he had no will to continue the battle. Outwardly, he may have continued to boast that he was starting anew, but nothing was further from the truth. As he said, the Stones defined him. He was them and they were him. He had already created the world's most famous band. His body ached and his soul hurt more than they would ever know at the loss he felt by no longer being welcomed as one of them.

Chances were very good that he might never recover his musical genius; but Mick believed he had no guarantees, and so he decided to agree to plot Brian's premature death. Mick didn't have the courage, or the talent, to compete with a rejuvenated Brian Jones.

Brian lived and died by the code of honor he believed in, in spite of what others might say. He never made false promises or beguiled others to do what he wanted. He fought to keep most people off him and no longer wanted the seduction of fame. However, the people whom he loved and trusted most betrayed him. He once said that if "they" followed through with their threats to kill him, it was because, "Allen, Mick, and the others will do what they believe they have to do."

# CONCLUSION

Singer/composer Jim Morrison was a good friend of Brian's and wrote an ode in remembrance of his friend, which in part reads—

*Come back, brave warrior…*
*I hope you went out*
*Smiling*
*Like a child*
*Into the cool remnant*
*of a dream*

Similarly, a few days after Brian's death, Mick attempted to pay homage during a concert held at Hyde Park. His attempt to show sincere shock and grief at the unexpected loss of his band mate was at best embarrassing.

He chose to wear a white outfit that he hoped would portray his innocence and virtue. However, the frilly white mini-dress he wore—along with his hair that was so long the ends curled under in a pageboy effect—made a mockery of any sincere bereavement. Many commented that he looked not unlike a raven-haired Goldilocks. His make-up was stark, with false eyelashes and dark eyeliner, and his lips were full and round and highlighted by rich, red lipstick. Just as when he performed *Sympathy for the Devil* during the videotaping of *Rock 'n Roll Circus*, at the Hyde Park concert he looked very much a grotesque woman. Numerous audience members took a second look at the lead singer on stage, to ascertain whether the person performing was Mick or a female.

He read a tearful eulogy in Brian's memory, and for those who didn't know the true story of the men's relationship, he gave a wonderful performance worthy of an award. His portrayal of experiencing deep sorrow was purposeful, since he did his best to show himself as the true victim of Brian's final narcissistic act. The subliminal message Mick wanted to deliver was that Brian had managed to drown himself just as the Rolling Stones were attempting to rejuvenate their act with the debut of Mick Taylor—the new guitarist previously hired to take Brian's place within the band.

Needless to say, Mick Jagger used Brian's death, and any sympathy the audience may have felt for Brian's passing, to promote himself and make himself even more popular as the Stones leader. But, once again Mick found himself in Brian's shadow.

In 1972, Mick made another attempt to use Brian's death as a platform to garner sympathy, attention, and record sales from the fans. He and Keith wrote a song called *Shine a Light*, which is a lyrical attempt to depict one lover mourning the passing of the other. The lover is referred to as "my sweet honey love" that represents Brian's hair color, for which Mick had much affinity. Also, the lover is described as wearing Berber jewelry that jangles as he walks down the street. Brian was the only Stone to have a wonderful collection of Berber jewelry, which he proudly wore.

Among the other phrases contained in the song are prayers to the Lord to shine a favorable light on the departed, who is depicted as a dirty, discarded human laying in an alley, with swarms of flies gathering on his body. Mick was the only Stone to whom Brian had confided his horrible early days living on the streets of Europe and at times having flies and other insects around him, when he couldn't bathe or wash his clothes as often as needed.

Mick pleads in the song that he cannot brush all the flies away that are on his "baby", but yet continues to beseech the Angels to smile down and deliver up the pathetic soul, for whom he cries aloud.

***

To almost everyone who knew him or saw him, Brian Jones was a beautiful person—he was the epitome of a beautiful person. Fans, male and female, fawned over him and heaped lavish praise and adulation upon him. This adulation stirred enormous jealousy in the hearts of the other Stones, especially in Mick Jagger. With the male ego being what it is, and with Mick's ego being what it was, what had been Brian's ever-rising star could no longer be tolerated. In the beginning Brian received all the love, sex, and praise from the press and public. In Mick's mind, Brian was in the way of his receiving the praise and adulation that he believed he deserved.

Mick determined to be the Alpha male among the group. The lead singer of any band has and always will be the most desirable male sex symbol to fans everywhere. Therefore, in Mick's mind he deserved that status as the Alpha male and couldn't accept the fact that wherever the Stones appeared, it was Brian who received the majority of the lavish attention and sexual offers thrown in the band's direction. This was a slap in the face Mick couldn't handle. He decided something had to be done to diminish Brian. Maybe complete annihilation, if that's what it would take.

Additionally, Mick was the more physically powerful of the two. Mick was the tallest member of the band—Brian the smallest. Mick was determined to keep Brian under his thumb, in a subservient position. Mick's ultimate power trip was to continually dominate his more vulnerable band mate and permanently solidify his Alpha male domination over the one band member he considered (but would never admit aloud) more intelligent, more sexual, and in many ways more talented.

Extreme male and sexual dominance wasn't Mick's only goal—he needed to humiliate Brian. Totally. Completely. And, Mick was very good at humiliating him. This scenario began in early 1963 and continued until Brian's death, sadly. Sadly in many ways because these were the only years that were finally paying off financially, professionally, and socially for the group, and especially for Brian. Since Brian was the band, its very existence and ultimate success lay with him. To the other band members, their success was a result of their simply getting out to perform. To Brian, their success was a result of his life's work, his dream, and his personal fight against enormous odds.

The Stones' ultimate success as a band was in Brian Jones, same as Brian Jones' ultimate success was in the Stones. The two identities were interchangeable—a fact none of the band members disagreed with at that time. However, again sadly, after Brian's death, Mick and Keith did and continue to do everything in their power to eliminate and erase Brian's talent and memory, and the fact that he even was a Rolling Stone.

Whereas any band today, whether it's the Beatles or INXS—or any band who has lost a member—goes out of its way at concerts or interviews to acknowledge and respect the memory and contribution of a deceased member, Mick Jagger and Keith Richards (the Glimmer Twins) do everything to erase and ridicule the memory of the Rolling Stones founder, Brian Jones.

And yet Brian, being the devoted, honorable band member that he was, would never want the name or music of the band he loved more than life to ever be disparaged, especially the way his memory has been disparaged. Brian would never get down and dirty when it came to minimizing the Stones contribution to the world's music, as both Mick and Keith continually do to him.

Sometimes it is hard to separate the human animals from the rest of the animal kingdom, especially when the human animals act so ruthlessly and callously when compared to those innocents who truly are the noble ones.

A rock band is a brotherhood like any other brotherhood, whether it is formed from police officers, baseball or football players, or a military unit. And, whether the brothers are blood relatives or brothers in spirit, they do not kill one another. Many believe that a brother in spirit is actually a stronger bond than a brother by blood. One cannot choose one's blood brother, however, one definitely gets to choose one's soul or spirit mate/brother.

Brian Jones chose Mick and Keith, and Mick—together with Keith's assent by keeping a blind eye to what he knew would eventually occur—performed the act of ultimate betrayal upon Brian Jones, their brother.

# BRIAN JONES' FINAL WORDS

Before his death, Brian had a chance to reflect on his life, his music, and the world in general. Following are some of his thoughts:

"Regarding my life, I'd say that my good times were high and extremely good, monumental, and amazing. The high's were so high, and the only wrong thing with that was the fact I would ultimately come down to a crash landing. To this day, I would say that my life was filled with more spectacular times than hardships, for that is the memory I choose to have.

"I enjoyed great times, even if I often felt sadly inept with regard to my ability to function normally. The beginning of my days with the band were really incredible. But even without a band, simply playing, strumming, and being in my own world as I played was what made life worthwhile. (Photo #810)

"In the early days, the Rolling Stones were on the threshold of a new beginning of everything that was different in this world, which musically had not previously been heard or known. We were going higher and higher, but that was taken away by the money machine of the music industry. We had the choice to continue creating and broadening the vehicle of music, or going for the money. The band chose the money.

"The albums that I consider our greatest occurred early in our career. After that it all came down to cookie-cutter music, except for the brief times when I was still allowed a free rein for my creativity. I would say the life got sucked out of me during the first two to three years, as our videotapes show. The band began to feel bored pretty quickly, once we started to crank out the same old stuff. It was like a slow death, and as you know, I acted like a damn ass many times just to make the time pass.

"The road was deadly to me, and I couldn't live with that pressure for very long. As we traveled together as a band, the experiences were terrifying and exciting, yet empty. I felt such a sense of loneliness, even among my band mates. I was separate and apart from them. Of course, when we were turned into a circus act it was very humiliating, as if we were the go-go dancers in cages—not what I had in mind for our musical exploration.

"There were so many things I wanted to do, but I never managed the time to realize them. I wanted to develop a surreal film on the subject of love but never officially started. I have a photographic mind that can freeze frame scenes, and so I planned to create my own movies. I've always had a comedic streak and enjoyed dressing up in various costumes representing different time periods. The Actors Guild intrigued me, and if I hadn't become a Stone, I would have become an actor. I also planned to write my own storylines and direct, which was why I so much enjoyed working on *A Degree of Murder*.

"I could never have stayed only being a Rolling Stone and nothing more—I would have to break out into other areas. For that matter, staying in any group for long would've killed my creativity. Being a Stone alone would stifle me, and in ways it should have been a stepping stone for greater works yet to come.

"As a Stone, I fought not just for my personal control over our music, but for the dream we once had that I thought was all our dream. But, once the band hit the money wall, they wouldn't stop reaching for more money and fame. I wanted to raise a generation of young people who could feel free through music and not be stifled by the old stereotypes. I imagined our music would bring about that feeling of freedom.

"At least, this was all a passing part of my forming philosophy. My original vision was about my music exploding over the whole world. Then I toned down a bit and got into how free love might impact the population and knock the 'old ones' off their high horses, so we could be real and bathe in the sunshine. I must have been on drugs when I thought that—but it seemed so clear then! I hated bloody rules," he said with a laugh.

He thought back to the high esteem, approaching reverence, with which many in the industry viewed his musical abilities. "Yes, I felt it, I knew it, and I was delighted. If only in my dark times I could have remembered my worth, my value, and that some who I thought were the moon and the stars appreciated me. But, I couldn't manage to recall those feelings of worth during the times I most needed to.

"Yes, Dylan, Lennon, and Jimi all thought I was worth living, but it would have been so helpful to actually hear the words—even once or twice. Guys don't go around saying to each other, 'You're wonderful! You're marvelous!'"

Brian referred back to his feelings toward the music industry or the "soul robbers" as he liked to call them. "The bigger story about what happened to me, and what is important for people to understand about the entertainment industry, is that musicians—whom the fans praise, go to see, and buy their records—have little control over their own work. The profession has become so much about the industry's objective to hypnotize people into believing their only option is to sit back and enjoy the music offered, and not about the audience's right to demand or expect a superior product.

"The goal of the money machine is to get fans to spend money on the mediocre product that is being sold, rather than to allow the musical genius of the artist to surface. Even so, that was what I was really trying to do and what those of my time were all about. We (all the various bands) had the feeling of a tight-knit family, where we freely worked together and helped one another.

"We were about freedom of expression, the creative process, and coming up with new ways of seeing, being, and sharing with the audience. That's all dead now. The artists are completely owned by the contract makers, and that was the part of my life that was so very difficult for me to live with.

"Could I have been one of the last of a dying breed?" he mused.

"I want to get the message through to other young musicians to be wary of the industry. I want people to understand that even with the musical genius I possessed, learning to live with and understand the other frailties a body can have was very difficult. Because of my emotional ailments, I couldn't handle the overwhelming conditions of being so well recognized and then having to live up to the world's expectations of what a rock star should be.

"If possible, I would want to protect those musicians who are similar to me and have the same musical gifts, and be able to share with them the problems associated with the music industry, so it doesn't lead to their downfall and their demise. Many young musicians think they have to be connected to the wheel of the industry in order to be known and recognized, but that sheer recognition is what deflates their extraordinary talent and the creative juices in them. Then, they just try to cookie cut the music in order to conform.

"The musical poets feel betrayed by the lack of love inherent in everyday life. Our songs ask for love, and we point to the shallowness of love in the way it's expressed. We come into the world and sing about love, so as to help others get in touch with their feelings, but we rarely find love ourselves. We cry out about what hurts us, and so many of us cry out from the depths of the sad, lost inner child who has already been wounded.

"I'd like to be thought of as a dedicated journalist who wants to give insight as to what the music industry is all about. I felt captured by what my band had become, and I felt a loss of identity, like a corpse. However, I want Keith to know that I've always thought of him as my brother, and I know he has little interest in the band. Mick can barely keep him in the group any longer," Brian concluded.

Over the years, Keith has told Mick that he resents him for what happened to Brian, but Mick tells him he's crazy, and that he had nothing to do with Brian's death or even encouraged it to happen.

Keith, along with some others, have tried to block out a lot of what happened that night—July 2, 1969—in order to keep their own souls and sanity intact. If you notice, Keith has killed himself with heroin over and over since Brian's death, but they keep returning him to life. He has a deep conscience and keeps everything inside him, even though he personally did nothing to harm Brian. Unfortunately, he feels guilty over the fact he didn't stop from happening that which he knew was going to happen.

That is why Keith keeps making statements about how he wishes the murder investigation would be re-opened and cleared up. He can't help himself, because he prays that he will no longer feel responsible—if only the investigators can prove that the people he knows were behind Brian's death, actually weren't.

Keith keeps making certain hateful statements about Brian because, deep in his soul, if he can destroy the goodness that he knows was in Brian and continues to disparage his memory, he will feel better about the end result.

Charlie Watts knew Brian's passing had to happen, accepted it, and didn't fight it. He was a man with no heart and no conscience.

On the flip side, Bill Wyman has tried to somehow right the horrible wrong through his books, and in that case Brian never realized the friend Bill truly was.

After Brian's death, Mick and Keith pledged loyalty to one another to see the Stones through any crisis that may arise. Mick is the one who insists on keeping the band going, whereas the others would have retired long ago.

A man, who has been Mick Jagger's bodyguard for more than fifteen years, has claimed that—while in the presence of the Rolling Stones—to mention Brian Jones name aloud, or to even attempt to bring up the subject of his existence, is considered taboo. Others have verified this information and have added that Mick walks and lives as a paranoid, marked man, who constantly looks over his shoulder. Mick, they claim, imagines an unnamed man is walking close behind, trying to overtake him. This is a description of someone with an unclean conscience, who desperately wants to protect a deadly secret.

Brian went on to say, "Even though they've tried to erase my entire life and experience from the band, so they could re-write their own history, I know that my musical influence will always continue. And yet, you can safely say that the musical heritage I left the world occurred within the time period prior to the Summer of 1969. From the beginning, I was the maestro of the music, and Mick and Keith were more the wordsmiths.

"To wrap up my story, I want to repeat that the music industry is a dirty business. They will use you, trade you, and sell you. They are a vile, consumptive machine that disregards life, talent, the heart, and humanity.

"Sex, drugs, and rock 'n roll—where do you think the name comes from?"

Brian Jones

# APPENDIX

<u>Note:</u> *Since Brian Jones' name has either been erased from or incorrectly chronicled on many Rolling Stones recordings, following is the most accurate listing available for the various instruments on which he performed*

**England's Newest Hitmakers (1964)**

Not Fade Away . . . . . . . . . . . . . . . . . . . . . . . . . . . . . . . . . . . . . . . . harmonica
Route 66 . . . . . . . . . . . . . . . . . . . . . . . . . . . . . . . . . . . . . rhythm electric guitar
I Just Want To Make Love To You . . . . . . . . . . . . . . . . . . guitar, harmonica
Honest I Do . . . . . . . . . . . . . . . . . . . . . . . . . . . . . . . . . . . lead electric guitar
Now I've Got A Witness . . . . . . . . . . . . . . . . . . . . . . . . . . . . . . harmonica
Little By Little . . . . . . . . . . . . . . . . . . . . . . . . . . . . . . . . . . . . . . electric guitar
I'm A King Bee . . . . . . . . . . . . . . . . . . . . . . . . . . . . . . . . . electric slide guitar
Carol . . . . . . . . . . . . . . . . . . . . . . . . . . . . . . . . . . . . . . rhythm electric guitar
Tell Me . . . . . . . . . . . . . . . . . . . . electric guitar, tambourine, backing vocals
Can I Get A Witness . . . . . . . . . . . . . . . . . . . . . . tambourine, backing vocals
You Can Make It If You Try . . . . . electric guitar, tambourine, backing vocals
Walking The Dog . . . . . . . . . . vocal harmony, rhythm electric guitar, whistle

12x5 (1964)

Around and Around . . . . . . . . . . . . . . . . . . . . . . . . . . . . rhythm electric guitar
Confessin' The Blues . . . . . . . . . . . . . . . . . . . . . . . . . . . . . lead electric guitar
Empty Heart . . . . . . . . . . . . . . . . . . . . . . . . . . . . . . . . . . . . . . . . . harmonica
Time Is On My Side . . . . . . . . . . . . . . . . . . . . . . electric guitar, backing vocals
Good Times, Bad Times . . . . . . . . . . . . . . . . . . . . . . . . . . . . . . . harmonica
It's All Over Now . . . . . . . . . . . . . . . . . . . . . . . . . . . . . rhythm electric guitar
2120 South Michigan Avenue . . . . . . . . . . . . . . . . . . . . . . . . . . . harmonica
Under The Boardwalk . . . . . . . . . . . . . . . . . . . . . . acoustic guitar, percussion
Congratulations . . . . . . . . . . . . . . . . . . . . . . . . . . . . . . . . . . . . . electric guitar
Grown Up Wrong . . . . . . . . . . . . . . . . . . . . electric slide guitar, harmonica
If You Need Me . . . . . . . . . . . . . . . . . . . . . . . . . . . . . . . . organ, tambourine
Suzie Q . . . . . . . . . . . . . . . . . . . . . . . . . . . . . . . . . . . . . . . . . . . electric guitar

## The Rolling Stones Now! (1965)

| | |
|---|---|
| Everybody Needs Somebody To Love | electric guitar |
| Down Home Girl | electric slide guitar |
| You Can't Catch Me | rhythm electric guitar |
| Heart Of Stone | electric guitar, tambourine |
| What A Shame | lead guitar, slide guitar |
| Mona (I Need You Baby) | electric guitar |
| Down The Road A Piece | rhythm electric guitar |
| Off The Hook | electric guitar |
| Pain In My Heart | rhythm electric guitar, piano |
| Oh Baby (We Got A Good Thing Goin') | electric guitar, piano |
| Little Red Rooster | electric slide guitar, harmonica |
| Surprise Surprise | rhythm electric guitar |

## Out Of Our Heads (1965)

| | |
|---|---|
| Mercy Mercy | lead electric guitar |
| Hitch Hike | electric guitar |
| The Last Time | lead electric guitar |
| That's How Strong My Love Is | guitar |
| Good Times | acoustic guitar |
| I'm All Right (Live) | lead electric guitar |
| (I Can't Get No) Satisfaction | acoustic guitar |
| Cry To Me | electric guitar |
| The Under Assistant West Coast Promotion Man | harmonica |
| The Spider And The Fly | electric guitar |
| One More Try | electric guitar, harmonica |

## December's Children (1965)

| | |
|---|---|
| She Said Yeah | electric guitar, backing vocals |
| Talkin' About You | rhythm electric guitar |
| You Better Move On | acoustic guitar, backing vocals |

## December's Children (1965) (cont...)

Look What You've Done . . . . . . . . . . . . . . . . . . . . . . . . . . . . . . . . . harmonica
The Singer Not The Song. . . . . . . . . . . . . . . . . . electric guitar, acoustic guitar
Route 66 (Live) . . . . . . . . . . . . . . . . . . . . . . . . . . . . . . . . . . . electric guitar
Get Off Of My Cloud . . . . . . . . . . . . . . . . . . . . . . . . . . . . lead electric guitar
I'm Free. . . . . . . . . . . . . . . . . . . . . . . . . . . . . . . . . . electric guitar, organ
Gotta Get Away. . . . . . . . . . . . . . . . . . . . . . . . . . . . . . . . . . . acoustic guitar
Blue Turns To Grey . . . . . . . . . . . . . . . . . . . . . . . . . . . . lead electric guitar
I'm Moving On (Live). . . . . . . . . . . . . . . . . . . . . . . . . . electric slide guitar

## Misc Songs (1963-1965)

Come On. . . . . . . . . . . . . . . . . . . . . . . . . . . . . . . harmonica, backing vocals
I Want To Be Loved. . . . . . . . . . . . . . . . . . . . . . . . . . . . . . . . . . . harmonica
I Wanna Be Your Man. . . . . . . . . . . . . . . electric slide guitar, backing vocals
Stoned. . . . . . . . . . . . . . . . . . . . . . . . . . . . . . . . . . . . . . . . . . . . . harmonica
Bye Bye Johnny . . . . . . . . . . . . . . . . . . . rhythm electric guitar, backing vocals
Money. . . . . . . . . . . . . . . . . . . . . . . . harmonica, electric guitar, backing vocals
Poison Ivy . . . . . . . . . . . . . . . . . . . . . . . . . . . . . electric guitar, backing vocals
Fortune Teller . . . . . . . . . . . guitar, backing vocals, tambourine, vocal harmony
Don't Lie To Me. . . . . . . . . . . . . . . . . . . . . . . . . . . . . . . . . . electric guitar
I Can't Be Satisfied. . . . . . . . . . . . . . . . . . . . . . . . . . . . . electric slide guitar
My Girl. . . . . . . . . . . . . . . . . . . . . . . . . . . . . . . . . . . . . . . . . electric guitar
I've Been Loving You Too Long . . . . . . . . . . . . . . . . . . . . . . . . acoustic guitar
19th Nervous Breakdown. . . . . . . . . . . . . . . . . . . . . . . . . . . . . electric guitar
Sad Day. . . . . . . . . . . . . . . . . . . . . . . . . . . . . . . . . . . . . . . . . . . . . . . organ
Ride On Baby . . . . . . . . . . . . . . . . . . . . . . . . . . . . harpsichord, marimbas
Sittin' On A Fence . . . . . . . . . . . . . . . . . . . . . lead acoustic guitar, harpsichord

## Aftermath (1966)

Mother's Little Helper ............................................. sitar
Paint It Black .............................................. sitar, acoustic guitar
Stupid Girl ..................................................... acoustic guitar
Lady Jane. ................................................. dulcimer, harpsichord
Under My Thumb ............................... marimbas, piano, guitar
Doncha Bother Me. ............................... electric slide guitar
Think ................................................................. electric guitar
Flight 505 ....................................... rhythm electric guitar
High And Dry. ............................................. harmonica
It's Not Easy .................................... electric guitar, organ
I Am Waiting ............................................. dulcimer
Going Home. ............................................. harmonica
Out Of Time. ..................... marimbas, piano, backing vocals
Take It Or Leave It. ................. harpsichord, koto, percussion
What To Do ................................... acoustic guitar, piano

## Between The Buttons (1967)

Let's Spend The Night Together ............... organ, backing vocals
Yesterday's Papers. .................... marimbas, harpsichord, bells
Ruby Tuesday ........................................... recorder, piano
Connection ............................................... electric guitar
She Smiled Sweetly ............................................. organ
Cool Calm & Collected .............. sitar, banjo, kazoo, harmonica
All Sold Out ............................ recorder, electric slide guitar
My Obsession. .......................................... electric guitar
Who's Been Sleeping Here ............................. harmonica
Complicated ........................................................ organ
Miss Amanda Jones ............................... electric guitar
Something Happened
To Me Yesterday .............. saxophone, trumpet, trombone, other brass
Backstreet Girl ................................... organ, accordion
Please Go Home ............................... electric guitar, theremin

## Their Satanic Majesties Request (1967)

Sing This All Together . . . . . . mellotron, flute, trumpet, other brass, percussion
Citadel . . . . . . . . . . . . . . . . . . . . . . . mellotron, harpsichord, brass, saxophone
In Another Land . . . . . . . . . . . . . . . . . . . . . . . . . . . . . . . . . . . . . mellotron
2000 Man . . . . . . . . . . . . . . . . . . . . . . . . . . . . . . . . . . organ, acoustic guitar
She's A Rainbow . . . . . . . . . . . . . . . . . . . . . . . . . . . . mellotron, tambourine
The Lantern . . . . . . . . . . . . . . . . . . . . . . . . . . . . . . . . . . . mellotron, brass
Gomper . . . . . . . . . . . . . . tabla, other percussion, sitar, tamboura, flute, organ
2000 Light Years From Home . . . . . . . . . . . . . . . mellotron, piano, percussion
On With The Show . . . . . . . . . . . . . . . . . . . . mellotron, brass, percussion, harp

## Beggars Banquet (1968)

Sympathy For The Devil . . . . . . . . . . . . . . . . . . . . . . . . . . . . . backing vocals
No Expectations . . . . . . . . . . . . . . . . . . . . . . . . . . . . . . acoustic slide guitar
Dear Doctor . . . . . . . . . . . . . . . . . . . . . . . . . . . . . . . . . . . . . . . . harmonica
Parachute Woman . . . . . . . . . . . . . . . . . . . . . electric slide guitar, harmonica
Jigsaw Puzzle . . . . . . . . . . . . . . . . . . . . . . . . . . electric slide guitar, recorder
Street Fighting Man . . . . . . . . . . . . . . . . . . . . . . . . . . . . . . . sitar, tamboura
Prodigal Son . . . . . . . . . . . . . . . . . . . . . . . . . . . . . . . . . . . . . . . harmonica
Stray Cat Blues . . . . . . . . . . . . . . . . . . . . . . . . . . . . . mellotron, slide guitar

## Let It Bleed (1969)

Midnight Rambler . . . . . . . . . . . . . . . . . . . . . . . . . . . . . . . . . . . . percussion
You Got The Silver . . . . . . . . . . . . . . . . . . . . . . . . . . . . . . . . . . . . . autoharp

## Misc Songs (1966-1969)

Long Long While . . . . . . . . . . . . . . . . . . . . . . . electric guitar, acoustic guitar
Who's Driving Your Plane? . . . . . . . . . . . . . . . . . . . . . . . . . . . . . harmonica
Have You Seen Your Mother, Baby,
Standing In The Shadow? . . . . . . . . . . . . . . . . . . . . . . . . . . . . electric guitar
Dandelion . . . . . . . . . . . . . . . . . . . . . . . . . . harpsichord, soprano saxophone
If You Let Me . . . . . . . . . . . . . . . . . . . . . . . . . . . . . acoustic guitar, dulcimer
We Love You . . . . . . . . . . . . . . . . . . . . . . . . . . . . . . . . . . . . . . . mellotron
Child Of The Moon . . . . . . . . . . . . . . . . . . . . . . . . . . . . soprano saxophone
Jumping Jack Flash . . . . . . . . . . . . . . . . . . . . . . . . . . . . . . . . electric guitar